Lecture Notes of the Institute for Computer Sciences, Social Informatics and Telecommunications Engineering   343

More information about this series at http://www.springer.com/series/8197

Phan Cong Vinh · Abdur Rakib (Eds.)

Context-Aware Systems and Applications, and Nature of Computation and Communication

9th EAI International Conference, ICCASA 2020
and 6th EAI International Conference, ICTCC 2020
Thai Nguyen, Vietnam, November 26–27, 2020
Proceedings

 Springer

Editors
Phan Cong Vinh ⓘ
Nguyen Tat Thanh University
Ho Chi Minh City, Vietnam

Abdur Rakib ⓘ
The University of the West of England
Bristol, UK

ISSN 1867-8211   ISSN 1867-822X (electronic)
Lecture Notes of the Institute for Computer Sciences, Social Informatics
and Telecommunications Engineering
ISBN 978-3-030-67100-6   ISBN 978-3-030-67101-3 (eBook)
https://doi.org/10.1007/978-3-030-67101-3

This Springer imprint is published by the registered company Springer Nature Switzerland AG
The registered company address is: Gewerbestrasse 11, 6330 Cham, Switzerland

Preface

ICCASA 2020 (9th EAI International Conference on Context-Aware Systems and Applications) and ICTCC 2020 (6th EAI International Conference on Nature of Computation and Communication), the international scientific events for research in the field of smart computing and communication, were held during November 26–27, 2020 in cyberspace, due to the travel restrictions caused by the worldwide COVID-19 pandemic. The aim of the conferences is to provide an internationally respected forum for scientific research in the technologies and applications of smart computing and communication. These conferences provide an excellent opportunity for researchers to discuss modern approaches and techniques for smart computing systems and their applications. The proceedings of ICCASA and ICTCC 2020 are published by Springer in the series *Lecture Notes of the Institute for Computer Sciences, Social Informatics and Telecommunications Engineering* (LNICST; indexed by DBLP, EI, Google Scholar, Scopus, and Thomson ISI).

For this nineth edition of ICCASA and sixth edition of ICTCC, repeating the success of the previous year, the Program Committee received submissions from 8 countries and each paper was reviewed by at least three expert reviewers. We chose 27 papers after intensive discussions held among the Program Committee members. We really appreciate the excellent reviews and lively discussions of the Program Committee members and external reviewers in the review process. This year we had three prominent invited speakers, Prof. Herwig Unger from FernUniversität in Hagen in Germany, Prof. Phayung Meesad from King Mongkut's University of Technology North Bangkok (KMUTNB) in Thailand, and Prof. Waralak V. Siricharoen from Silpakorn University in Thailand. Moreover, we also had two short talks presented by the General Chair, Prof. Phan Cong Vinh.

ICCASA and ICTCC 2020 were jointly organized by the European Alliance for Innovation (EAI), Thai Nguyen University of Technology (TNUT), and Nguyễn Tất Thành University (NTTU). These conferences could not have been organized without the strong support of the staff members of the three organizations. We would especially like to thank Prof. Imrich Chlamtac (University of Trento), Aleksandra Śledziejowska (EAI), and Martin Karbovanec (EAI) for their great help in organizing the conferences. We also appreciate the gentle guidance and help of Prof. Nguyen Manh Hung, Chairman and Rector of NTTU, and Prof. Nguyen Duy Cuong, Rector of TNUT.

November 2020

Phan Cong Vinh
Abdur Rakib

Conference Committees for ICCASA and ICTCC 2020

Steering Committee

Imrich Chlamtac (Chair)	University of Trento, Italy
Phan Cong Vinh	Nguyen Tat Thanh University, Vietnam

Organizing Committee

Honorary General Chairs

Nguyen Duy Cuong	Thai Nguyen University of Technology, Vietnam
Nguyen Manh Hung	Nguyen Tat Thanh University, Vietnam

General Chair

Phan Cong Vinh	Nguyen Tat Thanh University, Vietnam

Program Chair

Abdur Rakib	The University of the West of England, UK

Workshop Chair

Waralak V. Siricharoen	Silpakorn University, Thailand

Publicity Chair

Vu Ngoc Pi	Thai Nguyen University of Technology, Vietnam

Publication Chair

Phan Cong Vinh	Nguyen Tat Thanh University, Vietnam

Sponsorship and Exhibits Chairs

Bach Long Giang	Nguyen Tat Thanh University, Vietnam
Nguyen Kim Quoc	Nguyen Tat Thanh University, Vietnam

Local Arrangement Chair

Pham Thanh Long	Thai Nguyen University of Technology, Vietnam

Web Chairs

Do Nguyen Anh Thu	Nguyen Tat Thanh University, Vietnam
Nguyen Van Han	Hue University, Vietnam

Technical Program Committee

Ashish Khare	University of Allahabad, India
Bui Cong Giao	Saigon University, Vietnam
Chernyi Sergei	Admiral Makarov State University of Maritime and Inland Shipping, Russia
Chien-Chih Yu	National ChengChi University, Taiwan
Cindy Lopez	National Polytechnic School, Ecuador
David Sundaram	The University of Auckland, New Zealand
François Siewe	De Montfort University, UK
Gabrielle Peko	The University of Auckland, New Zealand
Giacomo Cabri	University of Modena and Reggio Emilia, Italy
Hafiz Mahfooz Ul Haque	University of Lahore, Pakistan
Hamid Ali Abed AL-Asadi	Iraq University College, Iraq
Huynh Xuan Hiep	Can Tho University, Vietnam
Ijaz Uddin	The University of Nottingham, UK
Issam Damaj	The American University of Kuwait, Kuwait
Krishna Asawa	Jaypee Institute of Information Technology, India
Kurt Geihs	University of Kassel, Germany
Le Hong Anh	University of Mining and Geology, Vietnam
Le Nguyen Quoc Khanh	Nanyang Technological University, Singapore
Luu Gia Thien	Posts and Telecommunications Institute of Technology, Vietnam
Muhammad Athar Javed Sethi	University of Engineering and Technology (UET) Peshawar, Pakistan
Nguyen Duc Cuong	Ho Chi Minh City University of Foreign Languages – Information Technology, Vietnam
Nguyen Ha Huy Cuong	Da Nang University, Vietnam
Nguyen Hoang Thuan	RMIT University, Vietnam
Nguyen Huu Nhan	Nguyen Tat Thanh University, Vietnam
Nguyen Manh Duc	University of Ulsan, South Korea
Nguyen Thanh Binh	Ho Chi Minh City University of Technology, Vietnam
Manisha Chawla	Google, India
Ondrej Krejcar	University of Hradec Kralove, Czech Republic
Pham Quoc Cuong	Ho Chi Minh City University of Technology, Vietnam
Prashant Vats	Fairfield Institute of Management & Technology in Delhi, India
Shahzad Aahraf	Hohai University, China
Tossapon Boongoen	Mae Fah Luang University, Thailand
Tran Huu Tam	University of Kassel, Germany
Tran Vinh Phuoc	Ho Chi Minh City Open University, Vietnam
Vijayakumar Ponnusamy	SRM IST, India
Waralak V. Siricharoen	Silpakorn University, Thailand
Zhu Huibiao	East China Normal University, China

Contents

Context Aware Systems and Applications

Formal Verification of Multi-agent Plans for Vehicle Platooning 3
  Thao Nguyen Van and Kurt Geihs

Contextual Defeasible Reasoning Framework for Heterogeneous Systems . . . 16
  Salwa Muhammad Akhtar and Hafiz Mahfooz Ul Haque

Abnormality Bone Detection in X-Ray Images Using Convolutional
Neural Network 31
  *Hiep Xuan Huynh, Hang Bich Thi Nguyen, Cang Anh Phan,
  and Hai Thanh Nguyen*

Statistical Properties and Modelling of DDoS Attacks 44
  Pheeha Machaka and Antoine Bagula

Estimating Land Surface Temperature from Landsat-8 Images Based
on a Cloud-Based Automated Processing Service 55
  Phan Hien Vu, Tan-Long Le, and Cuong Pham-Quoc

A Comparison Between Stacked Auto-Encoder and Deep Belief Network
in River Run-Off Prediction 65
  Bui Tan Kinh, Duong Tuan Anh, and Duong Ngoc Hieu

Developing Data Model Managing Residents by Space and Time
in Three-Dimensional Geographic Space 82
  Dang Van Pham

Trigger2B: A Tool Generating Event-B Models from Database Triggers 103
  Hong Anh Le

Predicting the Level of Hypertension Using Machine Learning 113
  Pham Thu Thuy, Nguyen Thanh Tung, and Chu Duc Hoang

Can Blockchain Fly the Silver Fern?: Exploringthe Opportunity
in New Zealand's Primary Industries 123
  Mahmudul Hasan and Johnny Chan

Design and Implementation of a Real-Time Web Service for Monitoring
Soil Moisture and Landslide in Lai Chau Province, Viet Nam 131
  Hong Anh Le, Bao Ngoc Dinh, and Dung Nguyen

Optimizing the Operational Time of IoT Devices in Cloud-Fog Systems   141
    Nguyen Thanh Tung

Proposing Spatial - Temporal - Semantic Data Model Managing Genealogy
and Space Evolution History of Objects in 3D Geographical Space   148
    Dang Van Pham

Modelling Situation-Aware Formalism Using BDI Reasoning Agents   169
    Kiran Saleem and Hafiz Mahfooz Ul Haque

Using Empathy Mapping in Design Thinking Process
for Personas Discovering   182
    Waralak Vongdoiwang Siricharoen

Taiwanese Stock Market Forecasting with a Shallow Long Short-Term
Memory Architecture.   192
    Phuong Ha Dang Bui, Toan Bao Tran, and Hai Thanh Nguyen

A Convolutional Neural Network on X-Ray Images
for Pneumonia Diagnosis   203
    Hiep Xuan Huynh, Son Hai Dang, Cang Anh Phan,
    and Hai Thanh Nguyen

Counterbalancing Asymmetric Information: A Process Driven Systems
Thinking Approach to Information Sharing of Decentralized Databases   216
    Mark Hoksbergen, Johnny Chan, Gabrielle Peko, and David Sundaram

Nature of Computation and Communication

Towards Service Co-evolution in SOA Environments: A Survey.   233
    Huu Tam Tran, Van Thao Nguyen, and Cong Vinh Phan

Analysis of a HIPS Solution Use in Power Systems   255
    Tomas Svoboda, Josef Horalek, and Vladimir Sobeslav

Behavioral Analysis of SIEM Solutions for Energy Technology Systems   265
    Tomas Svoboda, Josef Horalek, and Vladimir Sobeslav

Threads Efficiency Analysis of Selected Operating Systems   277
    Josef Horalek and Vladimir Sobeslav

An Architecture for Intelligent e-Learning Platform for Student's
Lab Deployment   288
    Peter Mikulecky, Vladimir Sobeslav, Matej Drdla, and Hana Svecova

Improved Packet Delivery for Wireless Sensor Networks Using Local
Automate Based Autonomic Network Architecture
in a ZigBee Environment... 300
     K. N. Sanjay, K. Shaila, and K. R. Venugopal

Hybrid Domain Steganography for Embedding DES Encrypted QR Code
Using Random Bit Binary Search 310
     B. S. Shashikiran, K. Shaila, and K. R. Venugopal

Design and Testing a Single-Passenger Eco-Vehicle 323
     *Tri Nhut Do, Quang Minh Pham, Hoa Binh Le-Nguyen, Cao Tri Nguyen,
     and Hai Minh Nguyen-Tran*

A Study on the Methology of Increasing Safety for Cometto
MSPE System 330
     *Hai Minh Nguyen Tran, Quang Minh Pham, Hoa Binh Le Nguyen,
     Cao Tri Nguyen, and Tri Nhut Do*

Author Index 339

Context Aware Systems
and Applications

Formal Verification of Multi-agent Plans for Vehicle Platooning

Thao Nguyen Van and Kurt Geihs$^{(\boxtimes)}$

Distributed Systems Research Group, University of Kassel, Wilhelmshöher Allee 73,
34121 Kassel, Germany
{vtn,geihs}@vs.uni-kassel.de

Abstract. The collaboration and coordination of autonomous vehicles into convoys or platoons have been used on our highways. However, before deploying such vehicles on the real road, their autonomous behaviors must be certified to act safely. The vehicle platooning can be considered as a multi-agent system where each agent can make its own autonomous decisions. In order to ensure that these decision-making agents in the platoon never violate safety properties, we use the Uppaal model checker to verify them. Furthermore, to facilitate the checking process and create a consistent translation process, we have developed an automated translation program that can map our multi-agent plans to the Uppaal model checker format.

Keywords: Verification · ALICA · Model checking · Multi-agent plans

1 Introduction

The "driverless vehicles" will be critical elements of the future of transportation systems. Within these systems, vehicles perform as individual systems, and at the same time, they interact with each other as well as with the environment, i.e., pedestrians, roads, and signs to achieve common goals. Because of the legal constraints, there must always be a driver in the vehicle. However, even though having full autonomous vehicles on the road is still in the future, the automotive industry is using already "car convoys", "platoons" or "road trains". Here, a platoon consists of a leading vehicle being driven manually and one or more following vehicles automatically driving and following the leader one after another.

The platooning concept was introduced by the COMPANION project with the aim of improving the safety and efficiency of vehicles on the congested road [1]. In cooperative autonomous driving platoons, each vehicle obviously must be able to communicate with the others, at least with the leader and cars immediately in front and behind in order to share their intentions, for example, adjust the speed and the distance according to the other vehicles information. Also, the platoon leader is responsible for managing the overall platoon formation by accepting new vehicles or responding to vehicles leaving.

© ICST Institute for Computer Sciences, Social Informatics and Telecommunications Engineering 2021
Published by Springer Nature Switzerland AG 2021. All Rights Reserved
P. C. Vinh and A. Rakib (Eds.): ICCASA 2020/ICTCC 2020, LNICST 343, pp. 3–15, 2021.
https://doi.org/10.1007/978-3-030-67101-3_1

In this paper, we propose and verify ALICA (A Language for Interactive Cooperative Agents) as a formal description language for a specific scenario, i.e., car convoys where an unplanned platooning temporarily creates or joins in an ensemble to share part of their journey. Originally, the language was developed for robotic football in which the opponents (environment) are dynamic. They change frequently and unpredictably. Therefore, we also applied ALICA for other domains like Cooperative and Extraterrestrial Robotic Exploration Missions[1] and Cooperative Autonomous Driving Scenarios [16]. Platooning is one of the promising concepts towards autonomous vehicles in order to deal with traffic jams and, at the same time, increase the overall safety and fuel efficiency.

The ALICA plans for this work focus on a platoon scenario where the different vehicles' behaviors are organized in various modes [17]. A mode is a concept for structuring the system's overall behavior in different behaviors, and each of them is activated at a specific time. The behavior of each mode is then represented in terms of a state machine that captures the behavior of the system in a species modality, e.g., during the selection of a leader of the platoon, leaving a platoon, etc. Transitions among states can be triggered by timing constraints or external events and can lead the system to a different state or mode. Figure 1s shows a vehicle platooning scenario that involves different heterogeneous vehicles. Each vehicle is in a certain mode according to its behavior; we will describe the modes in more detail later. The communication among the vehicles is presented with dotted lines.

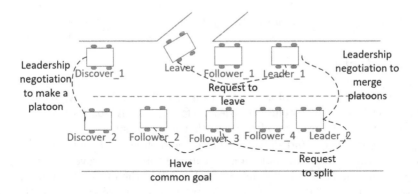

Fig. 1. Overall platoon system

As part of safety verification, we need to verify the agent's decisions, particularly when it collaborates with the other vehicles. An autonomous agent controlled by the ALICA program makes decisions based on not only its beliefs or goals but also the other agents. Our approach is to use model-checking to demonstrate that the agent always behaves according to the platoon requirements and never chooses options that end up in an unsafe situation. We verify

---

[1] https://www.uni-kassel.de/eecs/fachgebiete/vs/research/previous/impera.html.

the properties of the plan using the Uppaal model checker [4]. Unfortunately, designing multi-agents plans that control the agents to behave as expected is labor-intensive and time-consuming work. Moreover, the process of converting those plans into a model checking syntax to verify their properties while retaining the original characteristics of the plan is not only difficult but also requires consistency of designers. For example, a transition X that is used in plan A and plan B, when it is transferred to Uppaal, must be translated in the same way though it can be translated by different designers. Therefore, we have developed the A2U translator to solve that problem.

This paper is structured as follows: Sect. 2 presents a literature review on the verification of multi-agent systems and vehicle platooning. Section 3 describes all the modes in the ALICA plan for a platooning scenario and its requirements. The formal description of the ALICA program is presented in Sect. 4. In Sect. 5, we present the Uppaal model of vehicle platooning and properties that we checked on this model. Finally, conclusions are reported in Sect. 6.

2   Related Work

The verification for vehicle platooning is proposed in [8,9] in which the properties of the system are taken into account. Kamali et al. [8] evaluate individual autonomous decisions using the Agent Java PathFinder (AJPF) model checker and use Uppaal to verify timing behavior and the system. Similar to our approach, [9] verifies on-the-fly vehicle platooning abstracted in a unique genetic Uppaal model. However, our approach not only addresses verification of the collaboration and coordination for ALICA plans but also develops the A2U tool to map the ALICA plan into Uppaal syntax.

Answer set programming(ASP) has been used in [14] to verify abstract state machines with bounded model checking techniques. The purpose in [14] is to translate abstract state machines and linear time logic expressions to ASP and search for examples that violate the system properties that have to be validated. However, their focus is on validation, while we are focusing on verification. In [10], the authors use ASP to verify the ALICA program, but no property requirements have been carried out. Therefore, the unsafe plan can still be created. The approach in this paper addresses the verification of the platoon for different situations.

J. Campbell et al. [5] have presented a framework based on π-calculus for formal modeling of high-level decision making of platooning. In this work, the authors use hybrid automata to model closed-loop control systems. Similar to our ALICA program, the discrete and continuous aspects of the system are separated, though the verification properties are not considered in [5] to ensure the correctness of the high-level decision-making component.

The model for platooning driverless cars using an integrated formalism combining CSP and B is introduced in [6], where the system behavior is specified via the CSP and B formal methods. The vehicle behavior is modeled as a B machine, based on its stepwise refinement feature, and the communication models as a CSP controller. The focus, in [6] is on representing a correct model of a real physical vehicle for platooning while our approach aims to verify the cooperation between vehicles in the automotive platoon. Similarly, El-Zaher et al. [7] present a compositional verification method for vehicle platooning, where feedback controllers and agent decision-making are mixed.

3   Multi-mode System

We modeled the ALICA plan for autonomous vehicles platooning, as shown in Fig. 2. The general purpose of partitioning a system in multiple modes, each of which describes a specific behavior of the system, leads to various advantages, such as reducing the software complexity and easing the addition of new features [15]. This plan can be considered multi-mode systems; if the environment changes, it switches to a corresponding model for adapting to the new conditions.

In the top-level plan, we have created the following modes:

- *Searching*: this is the first mode of the plan, where the vehicles want to search other vehicles that have the same goals to make a platoon or join an existing platoon;
- *Forming*: the two vehicles that want to form a platoon enter in this mode. To do that they decide which one will be the leader or follower of the platoon;
- *Leading*: the leader is the vehicle having the highest safety index in the platoon. Each vehicle shares its safety attributes with the other vehicles. Once the vehicle is a leader, it can steer the following vehicles, propagate information, keep track of the list of the followers, and accept new vehicles that want to join and manage the followers' leaving;
- *Following*: all the vehicles inhabiting in this mode drive in automated mode and follow the leader. A follower can receive information from the leader or transmit information to the other members of the platoon;
- *Splitting*: a platoon with at least four members and two of them have the common goal can split into smaller platoons. The new leader will be chosen from follower vehicles, which share the same goal. If the old leader no longer has any members after dividing the platoon, it will move to *dissolving* mode. Otherwise, it continues to lead the platoon with the remaining members.
- *Joining*: if the leader of an available platoon has found a *free* vehicle that wants to join, it sends a joining request to the "free" vehicle. This non-member needs to be accepted within a certain time interval;
- *Leaving*: all vehicles can request to leave platoon at any time, for example, when they have reached their goal. If a member of the platoon leaves, it must send a leaving request to the leader and leave only when it receives an authorization from the leader. When the leader leaves, the platoon will dissolve if there is only one member left and if the remaining members are greater than or equal to two and have the same common goal, they will choose the member with the highest safety index among them to be the new leader;
- *Dissolving*: a vehicle moves into the dissolving mode when (i) is a follower and it does not have a leader anymore or (ii) is a leader and it does not have followers anymore. From this it can either leave or go back to the *searching* mode and start a new platoon toward their goal;

– *Negotiation*: when a non-member vehicle wants to join an existing platoon, it has to negotiate the leadership with the current leader, either it becomes a follower or a new leader. The one with the highest safety attributes will always be the leader. The leaders of two or more platoons that want to merge also can trigger the leadership negotiation.

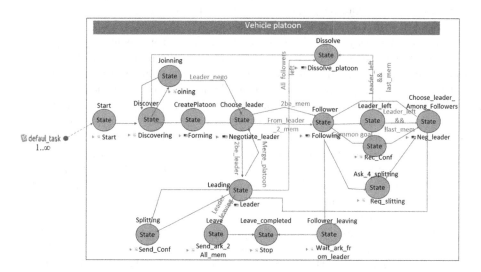

Fig. 2. ALICA plan for an autonomous platoon

4   A Language for Cooperative InteractiveAgents

ALICA is a far-reaching language to describe a sequence of actions of multi-agent systems. Its design is based on three principles, including domain independence, locality, and autonomy. Through calculating redundancy, ALICA can address the unreliable communication problem, which means all agents decide autonomously to solve mutual problems. With the necessary and available information, such as communication or action recognition, ALICA can recognize and tackle inconsistency in making the multi-agent systems' decision process. Thus, according to [13], ALICA may even work in unstable network conditions. These abilities are a crucial requirement in the domain of autonomous car driving.

All regarding agents' states are joined as a global state to execute an ALICA program. The ALICA program's hierarchical structure application allows it to overcome struggles when solving problems in a group. For any problems happening, solutions are planned and assigned to members. Besides, ALICA uses subplans to deal with sub-problems locally.

4.1 ALICA Syntax

An ALICA program includes multi-classed plans in which each plan consists of several finite state machines. $\mathcal{P}$ and $\mathcal{Z}$ represent the set of plans and states in a program, respectively. $\mathcal{L}$ is the language describing the belief base of each agent logically. The logic in $\mathcal{L}$ is not fixed, but we assume that its expression is comparable to the first-order language like C++, C#, or Java. Therefore, all conditions, for example, guards for transitions, are elements of L, and each element of $\mathcal{Z} \times \mathcal{Z} \times \mathcal{L}$ contains a transition τ.

There are two ways that ALICA uses to abstract from agents, by *tasks* and *roles*. An agent's role depends on its capability, and this assignment for each agent only changes when there is a change in team composition or its capabilities change. For example, due to being damaged, the current leader cannot continuously stay in a platoon. Hence, ALICA immediately chooses the members having the highest safety index in a platoon to become the new leader. That means ALICA changed the roles of a member from a follower to be a leader.

Tasks are used to annotate finite state machines of plans and restricted by the minimum and the maximum number of cardinalities of the assigned agents to ensure that they are capable of executing this task. For example,the finite state machine that is annotated with the task *Mer_Pla* in Fig. 3, only can be executed by two agents.

The appropriateness of a plan in a specific circumstance is estimated in two different ways. Initially, each plan ρ must satisfy a precondition Prep$(\rho) \in \mathcal{L}$, which must hold when the agents begin to execute a plan, and a run time condition Run$(\rho) \in \mathcal{L}$, which must hold during execution of a plan.

4.2 ALICA Semantics

ALICA uses a transition system [11] for its operational semantic. This transition system describes how an agent updates its internal states and when it can do, and hence how it progresses within an ALICA program. These internal states are mentioned as *agent configurations* and constrained by a set of axioms Σ_B.

Definition 1. *An agent configuration is a tuple* $(B, \Upsilon, \Xi, \theta, R)$, *where:*

- B *is the belief base of agents, it holds the current model of the environment – everything the agent believes to be true,*
- Υ *is the agent's plan base, it captures its current state*
- $\Xi \subseteq B \times, \mathcal{Z}$, *is called the context of behaviors b. The agent executes b together with the state in which b is occupied.*
- θ *a substitution, it holds the current instantiations of plan and behavior parameters,*
- R *is a set of roles assigning to the agent based on its capabilities.*

The plan base of an agent is a set of triples $(\rho,\ \tau,\ z\ )$, showing that the agent is executing the behaviors in state z of task τ in plan ρ. There is at most one triple for each plan in any plan base and it is reflected by a literal In (a, ρ, τ, z) in the belief base.

An ALICA program is structured by functions and relations between elements in a tuple $(\mathcal{P}, \mathcal{Z}, R, \mathcal{T}, \mathcal{W}, \mathcal{B}, Plantype, \rho_0, z_0, \tau_0)$ where $\mathcal{P}$ is a set of plans, $\mathcal{Z}$ a set of sates, R a set of roles, $\mathcal{T}$ a set of tasks, $\mathcal{W}$ a set of transitions, $\mathcal{B}$ a set of behavior.

For the specific ALICA program, the following function are used:

- States: $\mathcal{P} \rightarrow 2^{\mathcal{Z}}$, States$(p)$ denotes the states within a plan.
- Tasks: $\mathcal{P} \rightarrow 2^{\mathcal{T}}$, Task$(\tau)$ denotes the tasks of a plan.

When the ALICA program is implemented, each agent executes the state based on its configuration. Therefore, to inform an agent about the state of the team, we use the following predicates to is reflect in its belief base:

- In(a, p, τ, z) defined to hold iff $(p, \tau, z) \in \text{PBase}(a)$. This indicates the agent's belief about the internal state of other agents. For instance, $Bel_{a1}In(a3, vehicle\_platoon, defaultTask, leading)$ denotes that a1 believes the a3 to be committed to the *defaultTask* in a plan *vehicle_platoon* and currently inhabits state *leading*,
- HasRole(a, r), expressing that the role r is assigned to a,
- Succeeded(a, p, τ), return *true* value iff agent a successfully completed task τ in plan p,
- $Handle_f(p)$ and $Handle_f(b, z)$ which mean to hold if an agent might handle the failure of plan p or behavior b executed in state z, respectively,
- Failed(p, k), plan p failed k-times,
- Failed(b, z, k) in state z, behavior b failed k-times,
- *Alloc(z)* return *true* iff a task allocated to agents in state z is necessary.

Within ALICA, when the logical transformation rules change, the agent configuration also is changed. Explaining all rules is beyond the scope of this paper. The complete rules can be found in [12]. Therefore, we only present two rules applied in A2U translator:

The transition rule controls how and when an agent switches between two states, connected by a transition.

$$Trans: \frac{B \vdash \phi(p, \tau, z) \in \Upsilon(z, z', \phi) \in \mathcal{W}}{(B, \Upsilon, E, \theta, R) \rightarrow ((B - \vartheta_b^-) + \vartheta_b^+, (\Upsilon - \vartheta_p^-) + \vartheta_p^+, E', \theta, R)}$$

If an agent currently occupies in state z and it believes the condition annotating the transition to hold, an agent will follow an outgoing transition from z to z'. Moreover, this transition must not be a synchronization. The following transition only can 'fire' when all plans and behaviors of the agent, executed in the context of z, have finished or been stopped.

The Synchronized Transition Rule triggers a transition within a synchronization set when these transitions can 'fired'. Intuitively, a synchronization models the start of cooperation, depending on the involved agents to act in a tiny time frame. The upper bound on the size of this time frame depends on the latency, reliability of the communication, and the precision with which agents can track their teammates' intentions.

$$STrans: \frac{(\exists A \subseteq A)a \in A(\exists s \in \Lambda)(z, z', \phi) \in s \wedge \psi}{(B, \Psi, E, \theta, R) \to ((B-\vartheta_b^-)+\vartheta_b^+, (\Psi-\vartheta_b^-)+\vartheta_b^+, E', \theta, R)}$$

Here, an agent will follow a synchronized transition, if and only if it can identify that it is part of a group of agents, called A, such that agent a believes that there is a mutual belief in A that all relevant conditions hold.

5   Uppaal Model and Platooning Verification

5.1   Uppaal Model

The Uppaal automaton models are translated from the ALICA plan of vehicle platooning by the A2U tool upgrade version. The A2U tool in [15] can only interpret the ALICA engine's simple plans, but features such as hierarchical states (plans can inhabit in a state), broadcast channels, or synchronized transitions were not allowed. However, the plan for an automotive platoon needs many features of the ALICA engine to function as the designer's requirements. For example, the leader uses the broadcast channel to transmit information to all members, or the followers use *synchronized transitions* to obligate all followers to move from *Follower* state to *Leader_left* state. Furthermore, the dynamic leader is an interesting property of the scenario, so just using a behavior like *Start* in *Start* state is not enough to handle all the cases. Instead, we have to use a hierarchical state and multiple tasks (as shown in Fig. 3) in a plan to deal with the problem.

The A2U tool to solve the multiple tasks in the ALICA plan performs two steps. First, A2U will translate the platoon vehicle plan to Uppaal like [15]. However, for states that contain plans, which have multiple tasks, these tasks will be translated and connected to the corresponding locations instead of creating a new template as in [13]. Second, A2U will delete the duplicate locations or transitions after translating. For example, the behavior that adds the old leader after negotiating between the new candidate and the leader of the existing platoon is identical to the process of merging two platoons. From there, it is possible to limit the explosion of state space.

The Uppaal model consists of nine modes shown in Fig. 4, corresponding to the modes designed on the ALICA plan (Sect. 3). Note that we did not annotate all modes for readability purposes. In order to ensure that the platoon vehicle in Uppaal is functioning as the plan made in ALICA Plan Designer, we have tested a few circumstances, e.g., if the joining time is timeout, does the vehicle candidate move from *joining* to the *discovery* mode? Or do two leaders of two platoons correctly negotiate leadership when they want to merge?

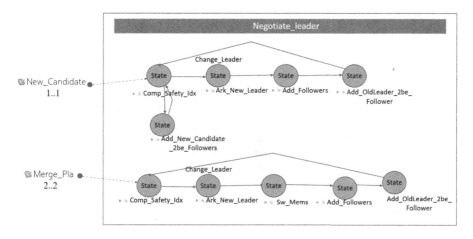

Fig. 3. Multi tasks in the ALICA plan

5.2   Platooning Verification

After translating the vehicle platooning plan, the timed automata of the platoon
is now available to verify their properties using Uppaal. To create this multi-
agents platoon, we used our robots for RoboCup Middle Size League (MSL).
According to the MSL rules [3], robots can communicate with each other via
wifi (also used for the platoon scenario), and each team has at most five members. Therefore, to facilitate the validation of the results from the Uppaal model
checker, we analyze the global and timing properties of the multi-agent platoon
composed of five members. In the following, we configure a few parameters, such
as *joining time* and *leaving time* and set random values for each vehicle's safety
index.

If an agent is a leader, then its safety index must be the highest in all other
vehicles involved in its platoon. This property is formulated for agent v2 as
follows (A$\Box$ φ expresses that φ should be true in all reachable states):

```
A□ (v2.leading) imply
forall (i:ID) v2.safety_idx[2] >= v2.safety_idx[i]
```

where v2 is the agent which is in *leading* location, i.e, the agent has the highest
safety index, array *safety_idx* contains the safety index of all platoon members
of v2.

The next interesting property is whenever the vehicle with the highest safety
index starts joining in the platooning, it always ends up being a leader. To express
this liveness property, we use the *lead to* or *response* form, written $\varphi \rightsquigarrow \psi$ stating
that if φ is satisfied, then ψ will inevitably be satisfied.

```
v1.start --→ v1.leading
```

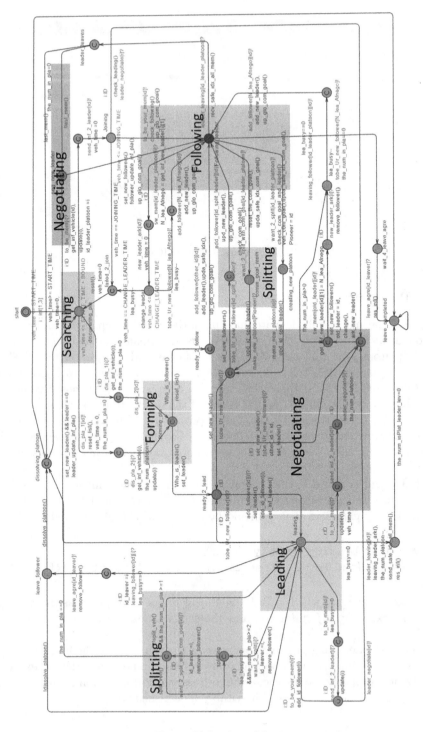

Fig. 4. Uppaal model

Similarly, we check if two platoons want to merge, the leader negotiation is triggered, and the one having a higher safety index will be the new leader.

```
v4.leader_nego && v5.leader_nego
--→ v4.leading && v5.id_new_leader == 4
```

In this scenario, we assume that the vehicle v4 and v5 are the leaders of two platoon and v4 has a higher safety index than v5, variable *id_new_leader* indicates an identify number of the new leader.

To ensure that the platoon is disbanded when the leader (v4) leaves and only one member (v1) is left. At this time, the only or last member v1 must move to the *dissolving_platoon* region.

```
A□ (v4.leave_completed && v4.the_num_in_pla==1
&& (v1.id_leader_pla ==4 || v1.id_new_leader ==4))
imply (a1_leave_completed || a1.dissolving_platoon)
```

The platoon only can initiate to split, if the platoon has at least three members and two of them have the same goal.

```
A□ v1.splitting && v1.the_num_in_pla >=3
imply (v2.creating_new_platoon && v3.comm_goal_mem
&& a2.com_goal ==a3.com_goal)
```

When two platoon want to merger the leadership negotiation is triggered and then the old leader removes one by one its members, at the same time the new leader add one by one to its platoon. We are interested in verifying if the old leader accomplishes joining the platoon within an expected interval.

```
A□ (v2.time_out imply
(v2.chang_leader_time>=7 && v2.chang_leader_time<=21))
```

6 Conclusion and Future Work

Following the idea of verifying multi-agent plans during the modeling process, to save time and help the designers reduce modeling errors and improve the efficiency and consistency of the modeling process, we develop the A2U tool for mapping ALICA plans into Uppaal format. In this paper, we have used the formal verification for the ALICA plan vehicle platooning as the case study to demonstrate that our tool can handle the complicated plans.

As future work, we plan to refine the platoon model by adding ALICA's features such as *rules*, *plantypes* containing many plans, and verify more properties. Therefore, there are many issues remaining for the future. An obvious one is to continue developing the A2U translator so that A2U can map all features of the

ALICA program into Uppaal syntax. In the long term goal we plan to make our own model checker to verify hierarchical state machines without flattening them [2].

References

1. Cooperative dynamic formation of platoons for safe and energy-optimized goods transportation (2017). https://cordis.europa.eu/project/id/610990/en?format=pdf. Accessed 6 May 2020
2. Alur, R., Yannakakis, M.: Model checking of hierarchical state machines. ACM SIGSOFT Softw. Eng. Notes **23**(6), 175–188 (1998)
3. Asada, M., et al.: Middle size robot league rules and regulations for 2012 (2010). https://msl.robocup.org/wp-content/uploads/2018/08/msl-rules-2011-12-29.pdf. Accessed 01 July 2020
4. Behrmann, G., David, A., Larsen, K.G.: A tutorial on UPPAAL. In: Bernardo, M., Corradini, F. (eds.) SFM-RT 2004. LNCS, vol. 3185, pp. 200–236. Springer, Heidelberg (2004). https://doi.org/10.1007/978-3-540-30080-9_7
5. Campbell, J., Tuncali, C.E., Liu, P., Pavlic, T.P., Ozguner, U., Fainekos, G.: Modeling concurrency and reconfiguration in vehicular systems: A π-calculus approach. In: 2016 IEEE International Conference on Automation Science and Engineering (CASE), pp. 523–530. IEEE (2016)
6. Colin, S., Lanoix, A., Kouchnarenko, O., Souquières, J.: Using CSP——B components: application to a platoon of vehicles. In: Cofer, D., Fantechi, A. (eds.) FMICS 2008. LNCS, vol. 5596, pp. 103–118. Springer, Heidelberg (2009). https://doi.org/10.1007/978-3-642-03240-0_11
7. El-Zaher, M., Contet, J.M., Gruer, P., Gechter, F., Koukam, A.: Compositional verification for reactive multi-agent systems applied to platoon non collision verification. Stud. Inform. Univ. **10**(3), 119–141 (2012)
8. Kamali, M., Dennis, L.A., McAree, O., Fisher, M., Veres, S.M.: Formal verification of autonomous vehicle platooning. Sci. Comput. Program. **148**, 88–106 (2017)
9. Mallozzi, P., Sciancalepore, M., Pelliccione, P.: Formal verification of the on-the-fly vehicle platooning protocol. In: Crnkovic, I., Troubitsyna, E. (eds.) SERENE 2016. LNCS, vol. 9823, pp. 62–75. Springer, Cham (2016). https://doi.org/10.1007/978-3-319-45892-2_5
10. Opfer, S., Niemczyk, S., Geihs, K.: Multi-agent plan verification with answer set programming. In: Proceedings of the 3rd Workshop on Model-Driven Robot Software Engineering, pp. 32–39 (2016)
11. Plotkin, G.D.: A structural approach to operational semantics (1981). https://web.eecs.umich.edu/~weimerw/2014-6610/reading/plotkin81structural.pdf. Accessed 04 July 2020
12. Skubch, H.: Modelling and Controlling of Behaviour for Autonomous Mobile Robots. Springer, Heidelberg (2017). https://doi.org/10.1007/978-3-658-00811-6
13. Skubch, H., Wagner, M., Reichle, R., Geihs, K.: A modelling language for cooperative plans in highly dynamic domains. Mechatronics **21**(2), 423–433 (2011)
14. Tang, C.K.F., Ternovska, E.: Model checking abstract state machines with answer set programming. Fundamenta Informaticae **77**(1–2), 105–141 (2007)
15. Van, T.N., Fredivianus, N., Tran, H.T., Geihs, K., Huynh, T.T.B.: Formal verification of alica multi-agent plans using model checking. In: Proceedings of the Ninth International Symposium on Information and Communication Technology, pp. 351–358 (2018)

16. Witsch, A., Opfer, S., Geihs, K.: A formal multi-agent language for cooperative autonomous driving scenarios. In: 2014 International Conference on Connected Vehicles and Expo (ICCVE), pp. 546–551 (2014)
17. Yin, H., Carlson, J., Hansson, H.: Towards mode switch handling in component-based multi-mode systems. In: Proceedings of the 15th ACM SIGSOFT symposium on Component Based Software Engineering, pp. 183–188 (2012)

Contextual Defeasible Reasoning Framework for Heterogeneous Systems

Salwa Muhammad Akhtar[1] and Hafiz Mahfooz Ul Haque[2](✉) (iD)

[1] Department of Computer Science, University of Lahore, Lahore, Pakistan
salwaakhtar0728@gmail.com
[2] Department of Software Engineering, University of Lahore, Lahore, Pakistan
mahfoozul.haque@se.uol.edu.pk

Abstract. This paper presents a contextual defeasible reasoning based multi-agent formalism to model heterogeneous systems using the notion of a multi-context system. This framework relies on the semantic knowledge sources which allow us to model context-aware non-monotonic reasoning agents to infer the desired goals using the extracted rules from the ontologies and handles inconsistencies using conflicting contextual information. We illustrate the validity and correctness of the proposed formalism using a simple case study of a smart healthcare system with the prototypal implementation of the system.

Keywords: Multi-context systems · Context-awareness · Defeasible reasoning · Semantic knowledge representation

1 Introduction

Context-aware systems and applications have gained significant attention in mobile and pervasive computing paradigms to model heterogeneous knowledge sources. These systems facilitate users by providing customized information or services at any time and anywhere using personalized smart devices. The customized information can be provided according to the environment in a specified contextual format. The smart devices acquire contextual information autonomously, perform reasoning, interact with other users or devices, and adapt their behavior in the rapidly changing environment. Literature has revealed different notions of the context so far. In this work, we follow the approach proposed by Dey et al. [9] for modeling contextual information to be used by context-aware reasoning agents. Context modeling and reasoning has been considered to be the most promising and fundamental research area in context-aware computing. When these context-aware smart devices interact with each other to fulfill the user's desires, they usually perform context modeling and reasoning [12]. In the literature, numerous context-aware frameworks have been proposed incorporating different context modeling and reasoning approaches including ontology-based systems, rule-based reasoning, etc. [5,21,22]. Formal modeling of such systems are mostly based on client-server architecture or centralized in nature but

P. C. Vinh and A. Rakib (Eds.): ICCASA 2020/ICTCC 2020, LNICST 343, pp. 16–30, 2021.
https://doi.org/10.1007/978-3-030-67101-3_2

perform distributed reasoning using different smart devices and/or agents. How-ever, the imperfect nature of contextualized information in a heterogeneous envi-ronment is often become a very challenging task due to the inconsistent behav-ior of the system. As a result, these systems often become useless and unable to draw a plausible conclusion due to inconsistent and incomplete information to be shared among the heterogeneous environment. To resolve this issue in a real context-aware deployment setting, the coalition of heterogeneous domain modeling could be useful to exchange contextual information. In this connec-tion, the multi-context system can be used for interlinking different knowledge sources using a predefined communication mechanism to preserve the identity and independence of each of the knowledge sources. A multi-context system (MCS) consists of a set of contexts where each context is a self-contained knowl-edge source having a set of contextual information (facts) and a set of inference rules and allows the flow of information among different contexts [11].

In the literature, several approaches have been proposed using multi-context systems [6,8,13,16,17]. In [8], Brewka et al. have proposed a multi-context rea-soning framework to combine arbitrary monotonic and nonmonotonic logics. They model the flow of information among different contexts using bridge rules. In [6], the authors have focused on a distributed reasoning approach for model-ing ambient agents to form a peer-to-peer system. In this framework, distributed algorithm based preference ordering has been used to handle inconsistencies. The authors in [13] have used mapping rules to govern the flow of information among different contexts in an MCS. They have used defeasible rules to man-age the inconsistencies in the MCS. In [17], the authors have proposed an MCS based framework to handle inconsistencies for modeling the heterogeneous sys-tem. The communication flow among different contexts is modeled using bridge rules for semantic knowledge sharing. However, authors in [16] used mapping rules to model communication among different contexts. In contrast with the previous work, this approach is novel in a sense that context-aware agents use contextual defeasible reasoning based formalism to model the flow of information among different contexts and handle inconsistencies using a defeasible reasoning approach. This formalism relies on semantic knowledge sources where domains are modeled using ontologies. The rules used by agents are extracted from corre-sponding ontologies to model the system to infer the desired goals. We illustrate the use of the proposed framework using a simple example and its prototypal implementation using Python programming.

The rest of the paper is organized as follows. In Sect. 2, we briefly review the core notions of the multi-context system and contextual defeasible reasoning. Section 3 presents the semantic knowledge formulation to contextualize hetero-geneous knowledge sources. In Sect. 4, we present contextual defeasible reasoning based multi-agent formalism for heterogeneous systems. In Sect. 5, the prototy-pal implementation of the proposed framework is provided using a simple case study of the smart healthcare system. Section 6 briefly presents the related work, and finally concludes in Sect. 7.

2   Preliminaries

2.1   Multi-Context System

A multi-context system consists of a set of contexts (knowledge sources) where each context has its own knowledge base, a set of inference rules, and a logic used to perform reasoning. Multi-context systems have been considered as one of the most suitable approaches for interlinking different contexts where each context may be formalized using formal knowledge representation languages. The multi-context system has applications in different areas such as data integration, argumentation, multi-agent systems. The knowledge representation model based on the multi-context system paradigm uses inference rules for local and distributed reasoning to exchange information among different contexts. Non-monotonic features can be included in the multi-context system to resolve potential inconsistencies in distributed contextual knowledge sources [6,8,10,13]. MCS is mainly used to express the individualized domain-specific knowledge as well as the inter-contextual flow of information among different contexts [10]. Formally speaking, a multi-context system $\mathbb{C} = \{\mathbb{C}_1, \ldots, \mathbb{C}_n\}$ is a collection of contexts where each context in MCS is a triple; $\mathbb{C}_i = \{L_i,\ KB_i,\ R_i\ \}$ where L_i is a logic, KB_i is a knowledge base and R_i is a set of local and mapping rules. There are two types of rules in MCS: local rules and mapping rules. The body of the local rules is a conjunction of contextualized information from the local context and these rules can either be strict rules or defeasible rules or a combination of both. Mapping rules perform reasoning by conjoining local contextual information with the foreign contextual information and infer the derived goals considering local contextual information.

Inconsistency is one of the major issues in the multi-context systems, as an inconsistent MCS produces no results and thus inconsistency renders the whole system useless. Another issue being dealt with in multi-context systems is the availability of incomplete information. This type of issue arises when the system is unable to generate the required information due to some software or hardware malfunction. When such incomplete information arrives in the system, due to the unavailability of complete information the system is unable to infer the desired results and thus the system becomes useless. In this work, we intend to solve the inconsistency issue due to which the system losses its state of Equilibria, i.e., the system as a whole does not have a belief state. This happens when the contextual information received by the system is contradictory or inconsistent. In such situations, the multi-context system becomes incapable of deriving plausible results which renders it useless. This becomes a serious issue, especially in the safety-critical system such as in healthcare systems.

2.2   Contextual Defeasible Logic (CDL)

Contextual defeasible logic has emerged from multi-context systems and defeasible reasoning. CDL is based on the rule-based reasoning technique following the principles of defeasible logic to handle incomplete and inconsistent information.

Due to its low computational complexity, defeasible logic has been considered as one of the most promising techniques in non-monotonic reasoning. It is a simple and efficient reasoning technique to perform reasoning monotonically as well as non-monotonically when developing expert decision making systems [2]. This reasoning is useful for deriving plausible conclusions even with partial or conflicting information. The conclusions drawn from this reasoning are tentative, therefore a conclusion can be withdrawn when more authentic information is obtained. CDL essentially supports two kinds of reasoning, local reasoning, and global reasoning. Local reasoning is performed by strict rules or defeasible rules or both, while global reasoning is performed by mapping rules. Strict rules state that if the premises of the rule are true, so is the conclusion whereas defeasible rules can be defeated by contrary evidence. Both the strict and defeasible rules define the local contextual knowledge acquired from a single ontology [13]. Strict rules are of the form:

$$r_i^s : a_1^i, a_2^i, \ldots, a_{n-1}^i \rightarrow a_n^i.$$

whereas defeasible rules are of the form:

$$r_i^d : a_1^i, a_2^i, \ldots, a_{n-1}^i \Rightarrow a_n^i.$$

On the other hand, mapping rules are constructed from different knowledge sources (contexts). These rules coalition the local contextual information ($a_1^i \in \mathbb{C}_i$) and the foreign contextual information ($a_3^j \in \mathbb{C}_j$) to model the system. Local contextual knowledge consists of facts and rules of the same ontology, while foreign contextual knowledge consists of the facts and rules of other ontology. Mapping rules are interpreted as defeasible rules, and are of the form:

$$r_i^m : a_3^j, a_1^i, \ldots, a_{n-1}^i \Rightarrow a_n^i.$$

The above rule $\Re^m$ is a set of mapping rules and $\mathcal{T}_i$ is a preference ordering on the $\mathbb{C}$. Modeling of local rules can be done using a single ontology however modeling of mapping rules requires multiple ontologies.

3   Contextualizing Semantic Knowledge Sources

In recent years, literature has revealed significant contributions in modeling and reasoning heterogeneous systems using semantic knowledge representation formalisms. To model the domains of real-time environment, knowledge engineers opt for different knowledge representation formalisms according to the requirements and define a set of facts and relationships to perform reasoning in order to model a knowledge-based system. Knowledge-based systems use knowledge representation techniques to resolve human-like assisted decision making using inference rules. Literature has revealed several languages to develop knowledge-based systems [23]. Among others[4], the ontology-based approach has been advocated as the most promising ones in the pervasive computing environment due to its simplistic and efficient reasoning capability, flexibility, and expressiveness. In addition, ontology-based systems provide semantic knowledge interoperability

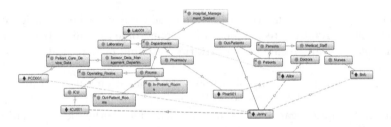

Fig. 1. A fragment of smart hospital ontology

with the pervasive systems to perform distributed reasoning using contextual modeling techniques [12,18]. Gruber et al. [14] define ontology as "*an ontology is a formal specification of a conceptualization.*" In the semantic web, ontology is an explicit conceptualization of the domain that can be used to model the system using language constructors in the form of classes (concepts) with their predefined relationships, axioms and rules to support inferencing, store the conceptualized information in a structured manner, and query the information. In the literature, ontology has been classified in two different versions by World Wide Web Consortium (W3C) as OWL 1 (Web Ontology Language) and OWL 2. OWL 1 has three sub-languages named as OWL Lite, OWL DL and OWL Full. OWL 2 has also three sub-languages named as OWL 2 EL, OWL 2 QL and OWL 2 RL. Each of the sub-languages in OWL 1 and OWL 2 can be used according to reasoning capability, expressivity, and scalability of the system.

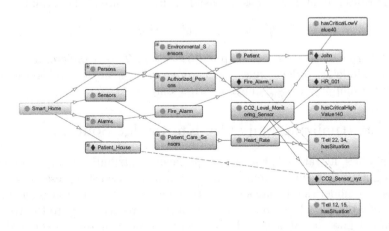

Fig. 2. A fragment of smart home ontology

In [15,21,25], it has been shown how the semantic knowledge sources (ontologies) can be used for context modeling and reasoning using context-aware rule-based reasoning agents. According to Brewka et al. [8], a single context in MCS can be represented in the form of ontology which is an independent domain itself.

Benslimane et al. [5] describe ontology as an independent knowledge source having a set of axioms and inference rules. In contrast, the multi-context system consists of a set of contexts having a set of rules used in the ontology. The formalism proposed in this work empowers the distributed knowledge sources to be interpreted in a heterogeneous fashion and enables the information flow among different contexts. In this work, we consider the semantic knowledge-based context modeling approach. As the proposed framework is heterogeneous in nature using the notion of multi-context system and domains are modeled in ontologies. For this, we develop two ontologies of smart home and smart hospital systems. These are very comprehensive ontologies and it is very hard to show these in this paper. However, fragments of these ontologies can be seen in Fig. 1, Fig. 2 and class hierarchies of both ontologies are shown in Fig. 3. To model the system, we extract contextual information independently form both ontologies with the intention of preserving the identity and independence of each specialized domain. We choose OWL 2 RL and Semantic Web Ontology Language (SWRL) due to its reasoning capability, genericity, extensibility, and expressiveness. Using OWL 2 RL and SWRL, we develop complex rules for each specialized domain that can be transformed into horn-clause rules format and is suitable for the design and development of a rule-based reasoning system [16,17].

(a) Smart Home Ontology   (b) Smart Hospital Ontology

Fig. 3. Class hierarchies of smart healthcare system

4　Contextual Defeasible Reasoning Based Multi-agent Formalism

In this section, we present a contextual defeasible reasoning based multi-agent formalism to model heterogeneous systems using the notion of a multi-context system. In a context-aware multi-agent system (MAS), each agent in the system consists of a knowledge-base having a set of strict and defeasible rules along with a set of contextualized information and a reasoning strategy. These context-aware agents acquire contextualized information from their corresponding knowledge sources. The contextualized information (the set of facts and the set of rules) may either be obtained from a single ontology or multiple ontologies. These agents perform reasoning based on the set of rules. If the reasoning is being performed on the rules which are obtained from a single ontology, then it is known as local reasoning. If the agents perform reasoning on the set of rules and set of facts which are extracted multiple ontologies, then it is known as distributed reasoning [7,20]. To model a centralized system, agents may use individualized knowledge source whereas, in case of a decentralized heterogeneous system, agents acquire information from different knowledge sources using a set of mapping rules along with the set of strict and defeasible rules to perform reasoning, share information among agents and then adapt their behavior accordingly (Fig. 4).

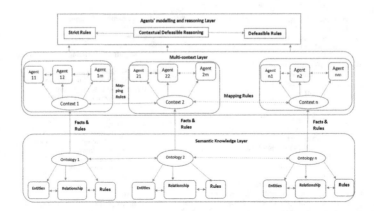

Fig. 4. Proposed framework of the system

In a multi-context setting, every context is composed of a group of agents where each agent has the capability to perform its specified tasks as designated by its corresponding knowledge source (context). To suitably model a heterogeneous system, we define MCS as $\mathbb{C} = \{\mathbb{C}_1, \ldots, \mathbb{C}_n\}$ where $\mathbb{C}$ represents the heterogeneous system in which each context $\mathbb{C}_i$ is considered as a sub-domain of $\mathbb{C}$, for all $i \in \mathbb{C}$. Each context in MCS includes a triple (V_i, R_i, T_i), where contextual knowledge in C_i is represented by vocabulary V_i, R_i represents a set of rules and T_i is a preference ordering on C. In each context in MCS, we develop multi-agent system consisting of $n_{Ag}(\geq 1)$ agents, i.e., $A_g = \{1, 2, \ldots, n_{Ag}\}$, where each agent is expressed as a triple $(\Re, \mathcal{F}, \succ)$. In the set, $\Re$ represents the set of all rules derived from multiple ontologies, $\mathcal{F}$ is a finite set of facts that are stored in the working memory of the agents and $\succ$ is the superiority relation on $\Re$. As the proposed framework runs in a highly decentralized environment, therefore there is a need of different kinds of rules for modeling and reasoning.

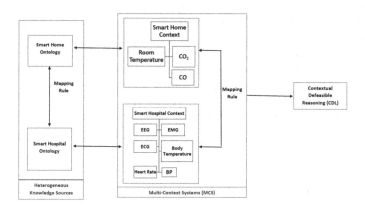

Fig. 5. Framework reasoning process

In the system, the set $\Re = \{\Re^s, \Re^d, \Re^m, \Re^c\}$ is a finite set of rules including strict, defeasible, mapping rules and communication rules respectively. Strict rules ($\Re^s$) follow the straightforward reasoning approach and these rules are non-contradictory in nature whereas defeasible rules ($\Re^d$) can be defeated based on contrary evidence. Mapping rules ($\Re^m$) associate contextual information from different contexts and perform reasoning to derive the results for the local context. The set of facts from local or foreign context are formed to make the mapping rules and these rules are interpreted defeasibly. Mapping rules can change the perception based on conflicting information in order to reduce the inconsistency and suitable mechanism for the coalition of different contextual data from different contexts, to model heterogeneous systems. Hence the set $\Re$ which is $\langle \Re^s \cup \Re^d \cup \Re^m \cup \Re^c \rangle$ may be also contradictory. The superiority relation $\succ$ in the rules can be used to prioritize the set of rules in case if conflicting information arrives in the working of agents at the same time interval. Rules are of the form $P_1, P_2, \ldots, P_n \hookrightarrow P$. In a rule instance, the antecedents $P_1, P_2, \ldots, P_n$ and the consequent P are contextual data. In the rest of this logic, we assume $\to$ arrow for strict rules and communication rules, and $\Rightarrow$ arrow for defeasible and mapping rules respectively. To model the communication, agents usually exchange information via message passing and coordinate among themselves in order to infer the desired goals. In our model, agents use special communication primitive; i.e., "*Tell(i, j, C)*" which means that agent i shares a context C with the agent j. As the proposed formalism follows the rule-based reasoning strategy, so argument "*Tell(i, j, C)*" may appear either in the antecedent or in the consequent of the rule. Whenever *"Tell(i, j, C)"* appears in the consequent, then the rule is said to be a communication rule. All other rules including strict, defeasible, and mapping rules are known as deduction rules. Even if the argument *"Tell(i, j, C)"* appears in the antecedent, then it is also known as deduction rules. Due to the heterogeneity of the proposed model, mapping rules can also be used for the exchange of information among different agents in different contexts. In the system, a multi-context system is composed of a set of rule-based agents that perform three core actions: *(a) Rule, (b) Copy* and *(c) Idle*. *Rule* instances are of different types such as strict rules, defeasible rules, mapping rules, and communication rules. *Copy* action is performed by firing the rule instances of communication rules whenever agents exchange the contextual information. *Idle* action allows agents to remain in an idle state but transit to the next state is triggered by the system. The system performs defeasible reasoning non-deterministically, and the rule priorities are static and set by the system designer at the design time of the system in order to avoid inconsistent behavior of the system.

5   Case Study: Prototypal Implementation of the System

To illustrate the use of proposed formalism, we model a comprehensive smart healthcare system considering two independent domain ontologies, namely Smart Hospital System and Smart Home. This case study specifically focuses on Parkinson's disease patients who mostly stay at home and can't escape themselves immediately in hazardous situations. The core purpose of developing this case study is to model the heterogeneous system using context-aware reasoning agents for sharing knowledge across different domains. The system can be installed in the patient's house to detect abnormalities in the patient's condition and to allow the continuous monitoring of the patient's physiological situation, and generate alerts in the form of messages, emails and notifications, and send them automatically to the doctor or caregiver. After considerable deliberation, two different domains (contexts) are developed to implement the multi-context system based formalism. We assume the proposed system consists of CO_2, CO and room temperature monitoring sensors embedded in the patient's home, and a smart device is attached with the patients to monitor the vital signs using sensors such as heart rate, blood pressure, body temperature, EEG, ECG, and EMG and provide the required information to the agents modeled in the system. A set of facts and rules are extracted from different domain ontologies and assigned to each agent in the system correspondingly. As the system is heterogeneous in nature and runs a highly decentralized environment, therefore it is assumed that the agents in this system acquire and share contextual information in an autonomous manner. Each of these agents has its own knowledge-base consisting of a set of rules along with the set of facts, and a reasoning mechanism. These agents perform three main actions: *(a) Rule, (b) Copy* and *(c) Idle*. *Copy* actions are triggered by firing communication rules instances to exchange the information among agents and *Idle* actions are triggered for the transition to the next states while leaving agents configuration unchanged. For *Rules* actions, there are three kinds of rules which are triggered by firing the rule instances. However, their interpretations are different for strict rules and defeasible rules. Mapping rules are interpreted defeasibly by associating the facts from different contexts (domains). Agents use these actions for modeling and reasoning to represent the overall behavior of the system as shown in Fig. 5.

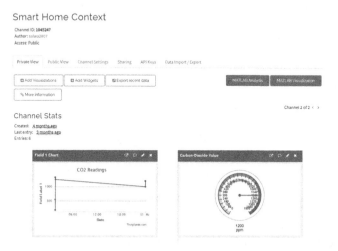

Fig. 6. Thingspeak channels with their access

In a multi-context setting, three agents (room temperature agent, carbon dioxide monitoring agent, and carbon monoxide monitoring agent) are developed for smart home and six agents (heart rate monitoring agent, body temperature agent, blood pressure agent, EEG monitoring agent, ECG monitoring agent, and EMG monitoring agent) are developed for the smart hospital context. These agents are programmed in Python language using Notepad++ editor. In both contexts, context-aware agents are developed for acquiring contextual information, processing data and perform distributed reasoning accordingly. These agents generate values based on the acquired information using the Thingspeak channel. As the system starts execution, agents start performing the reasoning process no-deterministically in order to achieve the desired goals. A total of nine agents are developed which are sending data to the Thingspeak platform. In order to receive data on the Thingspeak platform, an account was first made for the Thingspeak website. After signing into Thingspeak, two channels are developed for each context namely, smart home and smart hospital. These channels received the data generated by the virtual agents. These channels have the ability to store the received data in the Thingspeak cloud until the user deletes the data. Figure 6 shows the channels created on the Thingspeak platform for implementing the prototype of the proposed framework. Thingspeak react is a Thingspeak application that allows us to trigger actions in the form of sending emails, notifications, SMS, etc. when the data received by a Thingspeak channel. For the sake of this work, three reacts were developed which sent email, notification, and SMS respectively whenever the data met certain conditions. Figure 7 shows the Thingspeak reacts created on Thingspeak platform for implementing the prototype of the proposed framework.

Apps / React / High CO Rate		Apps / React / High heart rate	
Edit React		Edit React	
Name:	High CO Rate	Name:	High heart rate
Condition Type:	Numeric	Condition Type:	Numeric
Test Frequency:	On data insertion	Test Frequency:	On data insertion
Last Ran:	2020-05-17 22:18	Last Ran:	2020-05-29 20:24
Channel:	Smart Home Context	Channel:	Smart Hospital Context
Condition:	Field 2 (Field Label 2) is greater than 110	Condition:	Field 1 (Values) is greater than 120
MATLAB Analysis:	Read Channel to Trigger Email 2	ThingHTTP:	High_Heart_Rate
(a) Smart Home Context		(b) Smart Hospital Context	

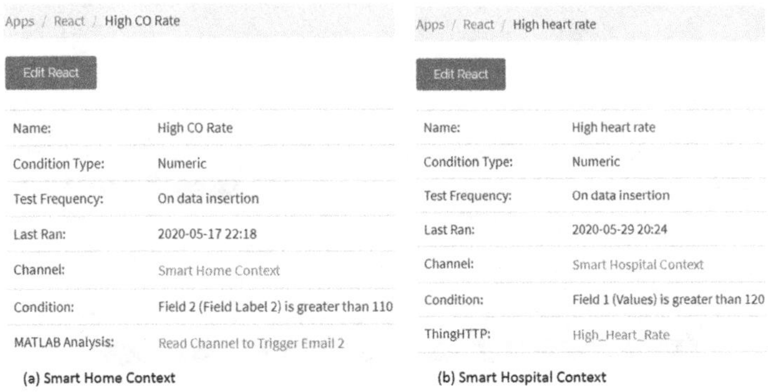

Fig. 7. Thingspeak reacts

Thingspeak HTTP is a Thingspeak application that allows us to connect services and applications to a Thingspeak channel using the HTTP protocol. We use two services; Twilio and IFTTT for SMS and notification respectively. MATLAB software has been integrated with Thingspeak and can be used to write the source code for email generation [24]. Figure 9 shows the source code used to send the email. An Account on the IFTTT platform is required to access its services. Once an account has been created it can be used on multiple devices to interconnect them. IFTTT has access to many services including Webhook, a technique using a callback function to access and alter an application's behavior. This framework uses IFTTT's webhook access to send notifications. An account on the Twilio website is required to utilize its services. This framework uses Twilio to send an SMS. Twilio uses the SMS gateway and the SMPP protocol to send an SMS to the specified number.

After developing agents, connecting them to Thingspeak platform, and then connecting to other services for the alert generation, the prototype of the proposed framework is started to perform actions to check the validity of the system. As a result, it is noticed that the agents successfully transfer data to Thingspeak channels. For determining whether the system will generate an SMS when required, agents have been programmed for this. Whenever the heart rate monitoring agent is activated and it starts generating random values between 0 bpm and 200 bpm. When the system detects the values below the 120 bpm threshold the system behaves normally. However, as the system detects the value above the normal range, for example; 120 bpm, the system automatically generates a notification and sends the notification to the user's specified device. Figure 8 shows

Table 1. Example rules for smart healthcare system

Agent 1: Smart Home Care Agent
Initial facts: Location('Home), CO2Level('1300), currentCO2Level('Home, '1300), CO2GreaterThan ('1300, '1000), COLevel('17), currentCOLevel('Home, '17), COGreaterThan ('17, '15)
R11: Location(?l), currentCO2Level(?l, ?co2), CO2Level(?co2), CO2GreaterThan (?co2, '1000) → CarbonDioxideSituation (?l, "Dangerous")
R12: Location(?l), currentCOLevel(?l, ?co), COLevel(?co), COGreaterThan (?co, '15) → CarbonMonoxideSituation (?l, "Dangerous")
R13: CarbonDioxideSituation (?l, "Dangerous") → Tell (1, 4, (CarbonDioxideSituation (?l, "Dangerous"))
R14: CarbonMonoxideSituation (?l, "Dangerous") → Tell (1, 4, (CarbonMonoxideSituation (?l, "Dangerous"))
Agent 2: Heart Rate Monitoring Agent
Initial facts : Person ('Alice), HeartRate('127), hasHeartRate('Alice, '127), GreaterThanEqual('127, '100)
R21: person(?p), hasHeartRate(?p, ?hr), HeartRate(?hr), GreaterThanEqual(?hr, '100) → hasHeartBeat (?p, "Abnormal")
R22: person(?p), hasHeartRate(?p, ?hr), HeartRate(?hr), LessThanEqual(?hr, '60) → hasHeartBeat (?p, "Abnormal")
R23: hasHeartBeat (?p, "Abnormal") → Tell (2, 4, (hasHeartBeat (?p, "Abnormal"))
Agent 3: EEG Monitoring Agent
Initial facts : Person ('Alice), EEG('5), hasEEG('Alice, '5), LessThanEqual('5, '8)
R31: person(?p), hasEEG(?p, ?eeg), EEG(?eeg), GreaterThanEqual(?eeg, '8) → PatientEEG(?p, "Abnormal")
R32: person(?p), hasEEG(?p, ?eeg), EEG(?eeg), LessThanEqual(?eeg, '8) → PatientEEG(?p, "Abnormal")
R33: PatientEEG(?p, "Abnormal") → Tell (3, 4, (PatientEEG(?p, "Abnormal"))
Agent 4 : Smart Hospital Control Agent
Initial facts : Person ('Alice), PatientID('P1), hasPatientID ('Alice, 'P1), PatientCondition ('critical), Location('Home)
R41: Person(?p), hasPatientID(?p, ?PID), PatientID(?PID) → Patient(?p)
R42:'Tell(1,4,(CarbonMonoxideSituation(?l,"Dangerous")) → CarbonMonoxideSituation(?l,"Dangerous")
R43: 'Tell (1,4,(CarbonDioxideSituation(?l, "Dangerous")) → CarbonDioxideSituation(?l, "Dangerous")
R44: 'Tell (2, 4, (hasHeartBeat(?p, "Abnormal")) → hasHeartBeat (?p, "Abnormal")
R45: 'Tell (3, 4, PatientEEG(?p, "Abnormal")) → PatientEEG(?p, "Abnormal")
R46: hasHeartBeat (?p, "Abnormal") ⇒ PatientCondition(?p, Critical)
R47: PatientEEG(?p, "Abnormal") ⇒ PatientCondition(?p, Critical)
R48: hasHeartBeat (?p, "Abnormal"), PatientEEG(?p, "Abnormal") ⇒ PatientCondition(?p, Critical)
R49: CarbonMonoxideSituation (?l, "Dangerous") ⇒ LocationCondition(?l, "Critical")
R410: CarbonDioxideSituation (?l, "Dangerous") ⇒ LocationCondition(?l, "Critical")
R411: CarbonMonoxideSituation (?l, "Dangerous"), CarbonDioxideSituation (?l, "Dangerous") ⇒ LocationCondition(?l, "Critical")
Superiority Relation: R48 ≻ R46, R411 ≻ R410, R411 ≻ R49

Fig. 8. Thingspeak channel field receiving data from corresponding agents

```
alert_body = 'CO Level is not in normal range.';
alert_subject = 'CO Level Danger';
alert_api_key = 'TAK3H92UP1852CRXX';
alert_url= "https://api.thingspeak.com/alerts/send";
jsonmessage = sprintf (['{"subject": "%s", "body": "%s"}'], alert_subject, alert_body);
options = weboptions ("HeaderFields", {'Thingspeak-Alerts-API-Key', alert_api_key; 'Content-Type',
'application/json'});
result = webwrite (alert_url, jsonmessage, options);
```

Fig. 9. Matlab code for email generation

the notification received in the notification panel and int the IFTTT mobile application respectively. Some example rules of the smart healthcare system can be seen in Table 1 to show the reasoning process of the system. These rules are extracted from ontologies and can be used by the agents in the development of a preference model to support customized preferences in order to defeat the contrary evidence.

6   Related Work

In the literature, a significant effort has been made to resolve inconsistencies in heterogeneous systems using defeasible reasoning with the incorporation of multi-context systems to leverage human lively situations. In [6], the authors proposed a multi-context systems based argumentation framework incorporating the non-monotonic features that use the preference information to resolve conflicts, and a distributed algorithm for query evaluation. They have proposed a framework to resolve the potential conflicts caused by the interaction of different contexts through mappings. To resolve potential inconsistencies, they have used a mobile phone-based application to evaluate the contextual information received from various sources and determined the preferences based decision support mechanism in order to avoid conflicts. Antoniou et al. in [3] proposed a semantic knowledge-based context-aware meeting alert application. This application acquires different types of contexts such as location, environment, time, calendar information, and whether services. The user's calendar uses the contextual information stored in the server. They use DR-Prolog defeasible reasoning engine to perform reasoning based on the user's rules to infer the appropriate decisions and notifies the user by showing an alert message about the upcoming scheduled event. In [1], the authors proposed a defeasible logic-based framework for multi-context distributed systems and distributed reasoning processes. The authors, in this work, extended the defeasible logic theory using the notion of meta-rules to perform reasoning over theories for checking the validity and correctness of the system. The inconsistencies occurring in the framework were dealt with using defeasible logic. In [19], the authors have presented a rule-based contextual reasoning framework for ambient intelligence and demonstrated its use in ambient assisted living environment, by developing an application using the Kevoree software development platform. It uses the information from a sensor embedded smart home and a smartwatch worn by the patient to determine his/her current situation. In case of an emergency, the application sends the alert message on the caretaker's mobile phones.

The proposed framework and application differ from other approaches in the sense that it captures the effects of handling the conflicts in the form of inconsistencies and incompleteness using contextual defeasible logic. It provides a semantic knowledge-based sound inferencing system to stipulate distributed reasoning in multi-agent systems using mapping rules and the consistency of the system is attained in order to achieve the desired goals correctly and efficiently. The prototypical implementation using Thingspeak, IFTTT, Twilio, and MAT-LAB platforms reveals the validity and correctness of the proposed formalism.

7 Conclusion

In this paper, we proposed ontology-driven contextual defeasible reasoning based multi-agent formalism to handle inconsistent information in a highly decentralized environment. We develop a simple case study considering two different domains (contexts) ontologies with the prototypal implementation of the system and show the validity, correctness, and verify the non-conflicting contextual information. In future work, we plan to develop a state-of-the-art mobile application for smartphone users to tailor the specific need and verify the correctness properties of the system suitable for the smart spaces.

References

1. Al-Anbaki, N.S., Obeid, N., Sabri, K.E.: A defeasible logic-based framework for contextualizing deployed applications. Work **10**(9) (2019)
2. Antoniou, G.: A nonmonotonic rule system using ontologies. In: RuleML, vol. 60 (2002)
3. Antoniou, G., Bikakis, A., Karamolegou, A., Papachristodoulou, N.: A context-aware meeting alert using semantic web and rule technology-preliminary report. In: Semantic Web Technology for Ubiquitous and Mobile Applications (SWUMA 2006), vol. 23 (2006)
4. Baldauf, M., Dustdar, S., Rosenberg, F.: A survey on context-aware systems. Int. J. Ad Hoc Ubiquitous Comput. **2**(4), 263–277 (2007)
5. Benslimane, D., Arara, A., Falquet, G., Maamar, Z., Thiran, P., Gargouri, F.: Contextual ontologies. In: Yakhno, T., Neuhold, E.J. (eds.) ADVIS 2006. LNCS, vol. 4243, pp. 168–176. Springer, Heidelberg (2006). https://doi.org/10.1007/11890393_18
6. Bikakis, A., Antoniou, G.: Defeasible contextual reasoning with arguments in ambient intelligence. IEEE Trans. Knowl. Data Eng. **22**(11), 1492–1506 (2010)
7. Borgida, A., Serafini, L.: Distributed description logics: directed domain correspondences in federated information sources. In: Meersman, R., Tari, Z. (eds.) OTM 2002. LNCS, vol. 2519, pp. 36–53. Springer, Heidelberg (2002). https://doi.org/10.1007/3-540-36124-3_3
8. Brewka, G., Eiter, T.: Equilibria in heterogeneous nonmonotonic multi-context systems. In: Proceedings of the Twenty-Second AAAI Conference on Artificial Intelligence, vol. 7, pp. 385–390. AAAI Press (2007)

9. Dey, A.K.: Understanding and using context. Pers. Ubiquit. Comput. **5**(1), 4–7 (2001). https://doi.org/10.1007/s007790170019
10. Eiter, T., Fink, M., Schüller, P., Weinzierl, A.: Towards diagnosing inconsistency in nonmonotonic multi-context systems. Logic-Based Interpretation, p. 9 (2009)
11. Eiter, T., Fink, M., Schüller, P., Weinzierl, A.: Finding explanations of inconsistency in multi-context systems. Artif. Intell. **216**, 233–274 (2014)
12. Esposito, A., Tarricone, L., Zappatore, M., Catarinucci, L., Colella, R.: A framework for context-aware home-health monitoring. Int. J. Auton. Adapt. Commun. Syst. **3**(1), 75–91 (2010)
13. Grau, B.C., Parsia, B., Sirin, E.: Working with multiple ontologies on the semantic web. In: McIlraith, S.A., Plexousakis, D., van Harmelen, F. (eds.) ISWC 2004. LNCS, vol. 3298, pp. 620–634. Springer, Heidelberg (2004). https://doi.org/10.1007/978-3-540-30475-3_43
14. Gruber, T.R., et al.: A translation approach to portable ontology specifications. Knowl. Acquis. **5**(2), 199–220 (1993)
15. Haque, H.M.U., Khan, S.U.: A context-aware reasoning framework for heterogeneous systems. In: 2018 International Conference on Advancements in Computational Sciences (ICACS), pp. 1–9. IEEE (2018)
16. Haque, H.M.U., Khan, S.U., Hussain, I.: Semantic knowledge transformation for context-aware heterogeneous formalisms. Int. J. Adv. Comput. Sci. Appl. (IJACSA) **10**(12), 664–670 (2019)
17. Mahfooz Ul Haque, H., Rakib, A., Uddin, I.: Modelling and reasoning about context-aware agents over heterogeneous knowledge sources. In: Cong Vinh, P., Tuan Anh, L., Loan, N.T.T., Vongdoiwang Siricharoen, W. (eds.) ICCASA 2016. LNICST, vol. 193, pp. 1–11. Springer, Cham (2017). https://doi.org/10.1007/978-3-319-56357-2_1
18. Hong, M.W., Cho, D.J.: Ontology context model for context-aware learning service in ubiquitous learning environments. Int. J. Comput. **2**(3), 172–178 (2008)
19. Moawad, A., Bikakis, A., Caire, P., Nain, G., Le Traon, Y.: R-core: a rule-based contextual reasoning platform for AmI. In: Joint Proceedings of the 7th International Rule Challenge, the Special Track on Human Language Technology and the 3rd RuleML Doctoral Consortium Hosted at the 8th International Symposium on Rules (RuleML2013) (2013)
20. Noy, N.F., McGuinness, D.L., et al.: Ontology development 101: A guide to creating your first ontology (2001)
21. Rakib, A., Haque, H.M.U.: A logic for context-aware non-monotonic reasoning agents. In: Gelbukh, A., Espinoza, F.C., Galicia-Haro, S.N. (eds.) MICAI 2014, Part I. LNCS (LNAI), vol. 8856, pp. 453–471. Springer, Cham (2014). https://doi.org/10.1007/978-3-319-13647-9_41
22. Rakib, A., Ul Haque, H.M., Faruqui, R.U.: A temporal description logic for resource-bounded rule-based context-aware agents. In: Vinh, P.C., Alagar, V., Vassev, E., Khare, A. (eds.) ICCASA 2013. LNICST, vol. 128, pp. 3–14. Springer, Cham (2014). https://doi.org/10.1007/978-3-319-05939-6_1
23. Sowa, J.F.: Knowledge Representation: Logical, Philosophical and Computational Foundations. Cole Publishing Co., Pacific Grove (2000)
24. Sun, D., Toh, K.C., Yuan, Y., Zhao, X.Y.: SDPNAL+: a Matlab software for semidefinite programming with bound constraints (version 1.0). Optim. Methods Softw. **35**(1), 87–115 (2020)
25. Uddin, I., Rakib, A., Haque, H.M.U., Vinh, P.C.: Modeling and reasoning about preference-based context-aware agents over heterogeneous knowledge sources. Mob. Netw. Appl. **23**(1), 13–26 (2018). https://doi.org/10.1007/s11036-017-0899-5

Abnormality Bone Detection in X-Ray Images Using Convolutional Neural Network

Hiep Xuan Huynh[1](✉), Hang Bich Thi Nguyen[3], Cang Anh Phan[2], and Hai Thanh Nguyen[1]

[1] College of Information and Communication Technology, Can Tho University, Can Tho, Vietnam
hxhiep@ctu.edu.vn, nthai@cit.ctu.edu.vn
[2] Faculty of Information Technology, Vinh Long University of Technology Education, Vinh Long, Vietnam
cangpa@vlute.edu.vn
[3] Department of Multimedia, Vinhlong Radio and Television Station, Vinh Long, Vietnam
nguyentbichhang41@gmail.com

Abstract. Medical imaging plays a role as a crucial source of data for disease detection and diagnosis. Recent advancements in machine learning and deep learning have become an efficient tool for medical image analysis. Medical image research laboratories are rapidly creating machine learning systems to achieve the professional performance of humans. However, both machine learning and deep learning methods are complex and require a lot of expertise, resources, knowledge, and time to train. Those create a significant barrier for researchers. In this study, we propose a convolutional neural network architecture to detect abnormalities in bone images. The proposed method provides insight into medical images and explains in detail how the model supports the diagnosis.

Keywords: Abnormality detection · Musculoskeletal radiographs · X-ray images · Convolutional neural network

1 Introduction

In recent years, abundant and expandable data sources in the field of health and the rapid development of technologies have contributed to improving the effectiveness of diagnosis and treatment. Health data is very various, the most common of which is medical images. Medical images include Computerized tomography(CT), MRI, and radiography images that perform the internal organs visually.

With features such as faster, cheaper, readily available, and easy to use, bone X-rays are one of the initial clinical measures used for doctors to make a

P. C. Vinh and A. Rakib (Eds.): ICCASA 2020/ICTCC 2020, LNICST 343, pp. 31–43, 2021.
https://doi.org/10.1007/978-3-030-67101-3_3

diagnosis or detect other abnormalities for the different parts of the body. The musculoskeletal conditions affect more than 1.7 billion people worldwide [1] and are the second most common cause of serious disabilities, and have the 4th greatest impact on the overall health of the world population when considering both death and disability. The treatment for osteoarthritis is long and costly. The causes of musculoskeletal problems may be due to external influences such as trauma, accidents, or playing sports, but also due to conditions such as genetics, knee arthritis, osteoporosis, and cancer. Proper diagnosis and abnormal findings are very important for treatment. But an increasing number of musculoskeletal patients is a major challenge in diagnosis. Automatic anomaly detection base on the computer can become very useful for diagnosis as well as saving time. Various machine learning processes have played an important role in the classification of medical imaging. Decision Forests [2], Support vector machine [3] or K-Means clustering [4], Integrating spatial fuzzy clustering [5] showed significant results in medical imaging classification. In addition, in deep learning, Convolutional NeuralNetwork (CNN [6] or ConvNet [7]) has been widely used in classifying images and segmentation problems. The improvements in deep learning in medical images have brought many promising results. For instance, analysis of electronic health records [8], bone tumor diagnosis [9], skin cancer detection [10] or most recently discovered COVID-19 [11,12]. However, this process is not only based on medical professional knowledge, medical industry standard, medical system but also requires knowledge in machine learning.

In this study, we present a novel method based on a convolutional neural network to detect abnormalities in musculoskeletal radiographs images. The method is expected to a good tool for disease diagnosis based on medical images.

The remaining of this work is presented as follows. Section 2 covers works related to detecting problems base on bones including bone disease and abnormalities. Section 3 introduces the architecture of our convolutional neural network for detecting abnormalities in bone images. We present details of the used dataset and experimental Scenarios in Sect. 4. Finally, experimental results are discussed in Sect. 5 respectively.

2   Related Work

Musculoskeletal disorders include many types of abnormalities in the bones, soft tissues, and joints. Finding an anatomical X-ray abnormality is not an easy task, so it is also an attractive topic in medical image classification. There have been many studies on bone images based on machine learning methods: diagnosing bone tumors by Naïve Bayesian model [9], detecting knee bone tumors by fractional method Seg-Unet [13] uses multi-tasking deep learning architecture, or estimates the probability for primary malignant bone tumors [14], detect abnormality in lower extremity radiographs [15] uses convolution neural networks (CNNs) and evaluates bone age [16].

MURA [17] is a large dataset containing images of musculoskeletal x-rays. In the MURA dataset, a 169 layer neural network (densenet) is used to predict anomalies. MURA provides better performance in comparison to the best radiologist performance in detecting abnormalities on finger and wrist studies. This model performs lower than best radiologist performance in case of detecting the abnormality in elbow, forearm, hand, humerus, and shoulder studies. To improve model performance, various network structures are proposed. [18] uses Deep Convolutional Neural Network, [19] uses Multi-Network Model to Detect Abnormalities in Musculoskeletal Radiographs.

3 Deep Learning Architecture for Detecting Abnormalities in Bone Images

3.1 Data Preprocessing and Normalizing

Because the radiographs are of different sizes, resizing is needed to have an equal image size. First, they are resized to 64 × 64 pixels. Then, they were resized to 128 × 128 pixels and finally to 224 × 224 pixels. In the first case, when the image size is 64 × 64 pixels, the image is of poor quality, and most features are lost. In the second case, with an image size of 128 × 128 pixels, the image quality is improved compared to the first case. In the last case, when the image size is 224 × 224 pixels, the feature maps are lost less, thus improving accuracy and reducing losses, but training time is higher. Considering the image quality and training time in the second and third cases, the final 150 × 150 pixels image was chosen for model training. Hence Fig. 1 is a presentation of the image after resizing.

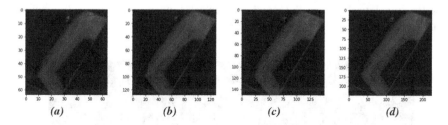

Fig. 1. When the image size is increased, more features are included: (a) image size 64 × 64 (b) image size 128 × 128 (c) image size 150 × 150 (d) image size 224 × 224.

3.2 The Proposed Convolutional Neural Network Architecture

We chose on humerus studies in the MURA dataset for our Convolutional Neural Networks model. And then we compare the results obtained with the results of training humerus studies by a 169-layer DenseNet baseline model [17]. Our Convolutional Neural Networks with structures are illustrated in Fig. 2. The CNN contains two Convolutional layers, followed by a MaxPooling layer and a Fully Connected layer.

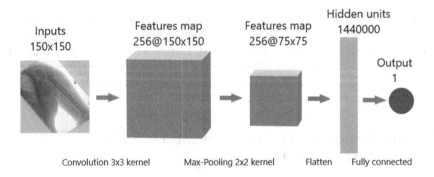

Fig. 2. A shallow convolutional neural network architecture.

For more details, in Fig. 3, CNN receives input data that is 150 × 150 pixels in size. The first convolution layer contains 64 filters or kernels, the filter itself being a 3 × 3 integer matrix. The second convolution layer contains 256 filters or kernels. The Convolutional Layer is a set of feature maps and each of these feature maps is a scanned copy of the original input but extracted into specific features/properties. How to scan depends on the Convolution Filter or the kernel. Here, we use a 3×3 size kernel, scans the input data matrix, from left to right, top to bottom, and multiplies each value of the input matrix with the kernel matrix and then adds up. Via the activation function "relu", we get the feature map. The Max-Pooling layer is used to reduce the dimensions of the generated feature maps. We used the Max-Pooling layer with a size of 2 × 2. The output from the Max-Pooling layer will be flattened to convert tensor in the multidimensional form to tensor 1D.

```
Model: "sequential_3"
_____
Layer (type)                 Output Shape              Param #
=================================================================
conv2d_5 (Conv2D)            (None, 150, 150, 64)      640
_____
conv2d_6 (Conv2D)            (None, 150, 150, 256)     147712
_____
max_pooling2d_3 (MaxPooling2 (None, 75, 75, 256)       0
_____
flatten_3 (Flatten)          (None, 1440000)           0
_____
dense_3 (Dense)              (None, 2)                 2880002
=================================================================
Total params: 3,028,354
Trainable params: 3,028,354
Non-trainable params: 0
_____
```

Fig. 3. A convolutional neural network implementation.

Moreover, CNN is implemented with Adam optimizer [20] with a batch of size 32. To avoid overfitting, we use Early stopping to stop the algorithm before the loss function reaches a value too small. The loss function is built to compare the difference between the predicted output and the actual output. Cross-entropy is a loss function, and its value can be minimized. This helps neural networks evaluate the probability of predicting a data sample corresponding to a class. For binary classification tasks, we computed binary cross-entropy loss during training by the formula 1.

$$-\frac{1}{N}\sum_{i=1}^{N} y_i \log\left(\hat{y}_i\right) + (1 - y_i)\log(1 - \hat{y}_i) \tag{1}$$

3.3 Tools

All experiments were implemented in Keras, trained and tested on a 64-bit Windows system equipped 8 GB of memory. Keras is an open source for neural networks written in python language. It is a high-level API that can be used together with famous deep learning libraries such as Tensorflow, CNTK, and Theano. Keras has some advantages such as: easy to use, fast model building, can run on both CPU and GPU, support to build CNN, RNN, and can combine both 2. Compared to other libraries, Keras is simple, user-friendly, yet very powerful. So, we choose Keras for our study.

4   Experiments

4.1   Dataset Description

MURA [17] is a large dataset of bone X-rays, collected by the Stanford ML group. Algorithms are tasked with determining whether an X-ray study is normal or abnormal. MURA dataset was published with 40,561 images from 14,863 studies including seven body tissues (elbow, finger, hand, humerus, forearm, shoulder, and wrist). Each study was labeled as either normal or abnormal by radiologists. The data set was separated into two parts, including the training set and validation set. MURA is one of the largest public radiographic image datasets (Fig. 4).

4.2   Evaluation Metrics

We have calculated the Training and Validation Accuracy, Training and Validation Loss, Cohen-kappa Score, Area Under the Receiver Operating Characteristic Curve (ROC-AUC) [22] for a general assessment of classifications. While the accuracy metric directly reflects the performance of the model, the Cohen-kappa score [21] is a metric that measures inter-rater agreement for qualitative or categorical items. In the case of musculoskeletal research, kappa statistics provide

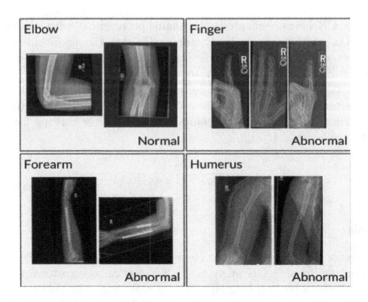

Fig. 4. MURA dataset contains 14,863 musculoskeletal studies of the upper extremity including the shoulder, humerus, elbow, forearm, wrist, hand, and finger. These examples show a normal elbow study (top left), an abnormal finger study (top right), an abnormal forearm study (bottom left), and an abnormal humerus study with a fracture (bottom right). The dataset is freely available at https://stanfordmlgroup.github.io/competitions/mura/

much more valuable information because k often considers random consensus. The formula to calculate Cohen's kappa for two raters is:

$$K = \frac{P_0 - P_e}{1 - P_e} \qquad (2)$$

where P_0 represents consensus values observed among the evaluation variables and P_e represents probability assumptions ability consensus.

ROC is a graph of one axis is Sensitivity (or true positive rate), the other is Specificity (true negative rate) for a binary classification system. ROC is a probability curve and AUC represents a level or measure of separation. With TP represents true positive, TN represents true negative, FP represents false positive, and FN represents false negative; True positive rate (TPR) and true negative rate (TNR) are presented by the following formula:

$$\text{TPR} = \frac{\text{TP}}{\text{TP} + \text{FN}} \qquad (3)$$

$$\text{TNR} = \frac{\text{TN}}{\text{TN} + \text{FP}} \qquad (4)$$

Besides, we use the confusion matrix to visualize model performance. Each row of matrices represents instances in a predictive class while each column represents instances in an actual class (or vice versa). The confusion matrix makes it easy to see if the system is confusing two layers (usually mislabeled as another layer). Here, we label the two layers normal (0) and abnormal (1) as Table 1.

Table 1. Confusion matrix.

		Predicted class	
Actual class		Normal	Abnormal
	Normal	TN	FP
	Abnormal	FN	TP

Accuracy is defined as:

$$ACC = \frac{TP + TN}{TP + TN + FP + FN} \tag{5}$$

4.3 Experimental Scenarios

The learning rate is an important metric for the model. It controls how quickly the pattern is adjusted to the problem. A learning rate that is too large can cause the model to converge too quickly to a non-optimal solution, while a learning rate that is too small can make the process difficult. Therefore, we choose four different model scenarios to compare accuracy by changing the learning rate hyperparameter of the optimizer that implements the Adam algorithm. First, we train the model with a default learning rate of 0.001. After that, we in turn reduced the learning rate to 0.0001; 0.00001 and finally 0.000001. In addition, we also train the model with epochs of 12, 50, and 100. For each learning rate, the epoch with higher accuracy will be chosen. We compared accuracy in four learning rate scenarios in Table 2 to achieve good performance on our problem.

Table 2. Comparison of model accuracy in 4 scenarios.

Scenarios	Learning rate	Epoch		
		12	50	100
Scenario 1	0.001	0.635	0.514	0.597
Scenario 2	0.0001	0.576	0.674	0.684
Scenario 3	0.00001	0.604	0.625	0.615
Scenario 4	0.000001	0.563	0.608	0.604

In scenario 1, we train our model with the default learning rate hyperparameter of optimizer Adam is 0.001. We got a model accuracy of 0.635 at epoch 12. This accuracy is higher than that of the MURA model (0.600) on humerus study. Continue to train the model with epoch 50 and 100, the model's accuracy is 0.514 and 0.597, respectively, lower than MURA model's accuracy.

In scenario 2, the learning rate hyperparameter is reduced to 0.0001. We achieve higher accuracy than scenario 1 at epoch 50 (0.674) and epoch 100 (0.684). However, the model has low accuracy at epoch 12 (0.576) compared to scenario 1 (0.635).

Continue to reduce the learning rate hyperparameter to 0.00001 in scenario 3 and 0.000001 in scenario 4, we get the highest accuracy for each scenario of 0.625 and 0.608 respectively. Both of these precision is higher than the MURA model but lower than the accuracy in scenario 1 and 2. The successive precision drops in scenarios 3 and 4, so we stop reducing the learning rate. Comparing all 4 scenarios (Fig. 5), we choose the one with the highest accuracy to use for the training model.

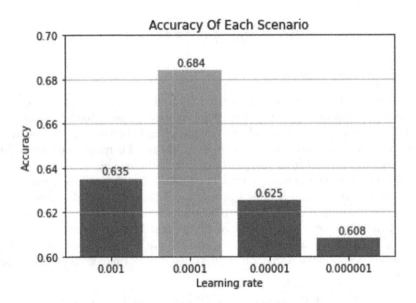

Fig. 5. Using the best accuracy of each scenario for comparison, scenario 2 with learning rate 0.0001, accuracy 0.684 is chosen to train the model.

5   Conclusion

5.1   Results

Our CNN model reached the overall 67.33% of training and 68.4% validation accuracy. The humerus image was correctly classified 64.28% for the abnormal class and 72.29% for the normal class. The training and validation accuracy is visualized in Fig. 6.

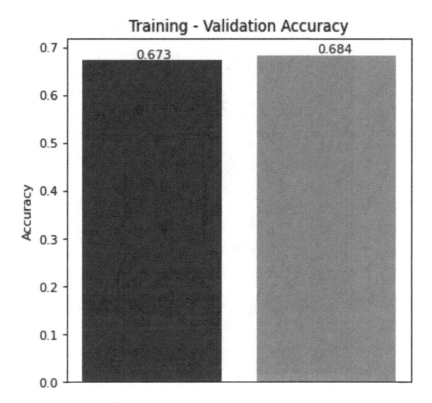

Fig. 6. The visualization of accuracy during training.

In the case of an unbalanced data set, the ROCAUC appears to be a more efficient measure than accuracy to evaluate performance. Our model achieved 0.659 and 0.655 for AUC training- validation respectively. The AUC is illustrated in Fig.7.

With 1,272 images in the training data, 288 images in valuation data, and 727 studies cases of humerus; We have shown the training results using a confusion matrix (Fig. 8). The humerus is correctly classified with 197/288 images. 90/140 images correctly predicted to be abnormal (TP); 50/140 abnormal images that are incorrectly predicted as normal (FN). 107/148 correctly predicted images are normal (TN) images; 41/148 normal images are incorrectly predicted to be abnormal (FP).

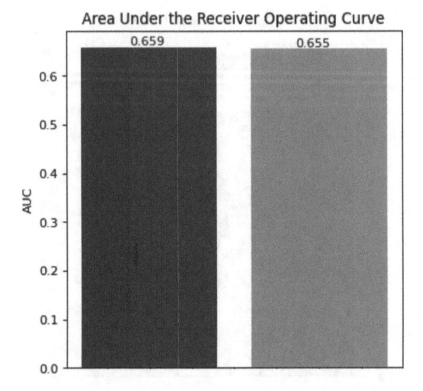

Fig. 7. The visualization of AUC during training.

The result of our model is better than the result of training on humerus studies by a 169-layer DenseNet baseline model (60.0%)[17]. In Table 3, MURA's model compares performance between 3 radiologists and model on the Cohen's kappa statistic. We highlight the result of MURA's model (red) and our model (green) on humerus studies to express performances.

Table 3. Comparison between MURA's model and our CNN model.

	Radiologist 1	Radiologist 2	Radiologist 3	MURA's Model	our model
Humerus	0.867	0.733	0.933	0.600	0.684

5.2 Discussion

Detecting abnormalities in musculoskeletal x-rays has important clinical applications. An abnormality detection model can be used to support the radiologist for faster review and approval. Besides, the detection of normal musculoskeletal

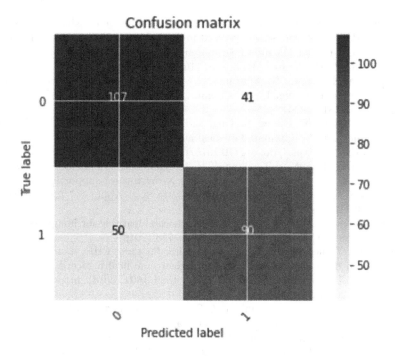

Fig. 8. 197/288 images of humerus are accurately classified at 68.4%.

helps to save time, treatment costs for patients. Therefore a computer-based automatic anomaly detection model can lead to disease interpretation through diagnostic imaging, removal of reducing agents, and standardization of quality.

We presented an approach to use Convolutional Neural Network to detect abnormality in musculoskeletal radiographs.

Due to a limited number of computational resources, we only implemented a shallow CNN architecture for image classification tasks on humerus in large MURA data sets. We hope our framework can help to classified musculoskeletal x-ray images to be better and contribute to the development of more diagnostic imaging methods. There are still many other machine learning methods and more in-depth research is needed on larger sets of images in the future.

References

1. Weinstein, S.L., Yelin, E.H., King, S.: The Burden of Musculoskeletal Diseases in the United States (BMUS), 3rd edn., p. 12 (2016)
2. Nedjar, I., El Habib Daho, M., Settouti, N., Saïd, M., Chikh, M.: Random forest based classification of medical x-ray images using a genetic algorithm for feature selection. J. Mech. Med. Biol. **15**(02), 1540025 (2015). https://doi.org/10.1142/S0219519415400254

3. Çamlica, Z., Tizhoosh, H.R., Khalvati, F.: Medical image classification via SVM using LBP features from saliency-based folded data. In: 2015 IEEE 14th International Conference on Machine Learning and Applications (ICMLA), Miami, FL, pp. 128–132 (2015). https://doi.org/10.1109/ICMLA.2015.131
4. Shrivastava, K., Gupta, N., Sharma, N.: Medical image segmentation using modified K means clustering. Int. J. Comput. Appl. **103**, 12–16 (2014). https://doi.org/10.5120/18157-9341
5. Li, B.N., Chui, C.-K., Chang, S., Ong, S.: Integrating spatial fuzzy clustering with level set methods for automated medical image segmentation. Comput. Biol. Med. **41**, 1–10 (2010). https://doi.org/10.1016/j.compbiomed.2010.10.007
6. Nguyen, H.T., Huynh, H.T., Tran, T.B., Huynh, H.X.: Explanation of the convolutional neural network classifying chest X-ray images supporting pneumonia diagnosis. EAI Endorsed Trans. Context-Aware Syst. Appl., 1–7 (2020). https://doi.org/10.4108/eai.13-7-2018.165349
7. He, K., Zhang, X., Ren, S., Sun, J.: Deep residual learning for image recognition. In Proceedings of the IEEE CVPR, pp. 770–778 (2016)
8. Shickel, B., Tighe, P.J., Bihorac, A., Rashidi, P.: Deep EHR: a survey of recent advances in deep learning techniques for electronic health record (EHR) analysis. IEEE J. Biomed. Health Inform. **22**(5), 1589–1604 (2018). https://doi.org/10.1109/JBHI.2017.2767063
9. Do, B.H., Langlotz, C., Beaulieu, C.F.: Bone tumor diagnosis using a Naïve Bayesian model of demographic and radiographic features. J. Digit. Imaging **30**(5), 640–647 (2017). https://doi.org/10.1007/s10278-017-0001-7
10. Ascalu, A., David, E.O.: Skin cancer detection by deep learning and sound analysis algorithms. A prospective clinical study of an elementary dermoscope. EBioMedicine **43**, 107–113 (2019). https://doi.org/10.1016/j.ebiom.2019.04.055
11. Toğaçara, M., Ergenb, B., Cömert, Z.: COVID-19 detection using deep learning models to exploit Social Mimic Optimization and structured chest X-ray images using fuzzy color and stacking approaches. Comput. Biol. Med. **121**, 103805 (2020). https://doi.org/10.1016/j.compbiomed.2020.103805
12. Wang, S., et al.: A fully automatic deep learning system for COVID-19 diagnostic and prognostic analysis. Eur. Respir. J., 1399–3003 (2020). https://doi.org/10.1183/13993003.00775-2020
13. Do Nhu, T., Joo, S.-D., Yang, H.-J., Jung, S., Kim, S.H.: Knee bone tumor segmentation from radiographs using Seg-Unet with dice loss. In: 25th International Workshop on Frontiers of Computer Vision (IW-FCV2019), Gangneung, South Korea, pp. 1–3 (2019)
14. Benndorf, M., Neubauer, J., Langer, M., Kotter, E., et al.: Bayesian pretest probability estimation for primary malignant bone tumors based on the Surveillance, Epidemiology and End Results Program (SEER) database. Int. J. Comput. Assist. Radiol. Surg. **12**, 485–491 (2017). https://doi.org/10.1007/s11548-016-1491-3
15. Varma, M., Lu, M., Gardner, R., et al.: Automated abnormality detection in lower extremity radiographs using deep learning. Nat. Mach. Intell. **1**, 578–583 (2019). https://doi.org/10.1038/s42256-019-0126-0
16. Larson, D.B., Chen, M.C., Lungren, M.P., Halabi, S.S., Stence, N.V., Langlotz, C.P.: Performance of a deep-learning neural network model in assessing skeletal maturity on pediatric hand radiographs. Radiology **287**(1), 313–322 (2017). https://doi.org/10.1148/radiol.2017170236. RSNA
17. Rajpurkar, P., et al.: MURA: large dataset for abnormality detection in musculoskeletal radiographs. In: 1st Conference on Medical Imaging with Deep Learning (MIDL 2018), pp. 1–10. arXiv:1712.06957 [physics.med-ph]

18. Panda, S., Jangid, M.: Improving the model performance of deep convolutional neural network in MURA dataset. In: Somani, A.K., Shekhawat, R.S., Mundra, A., Srivastava, S., Verma, V.K. (eds.) Smart Systems and IoT: Innovations in Computing. SIST, vol. 141, pp. 531–541. Springer, Singapore (2020). https://doi.org/10.1007/978-981-13-8406-6_51

19. Liang, S., Gu, Y.: Towards robust and accurate detection of abnormalities in musculoskeletal radiographs with a multi-network model. Sensors (Basel, Switzerland) **20**(11), 31–53. https://doi.org/10.3390/s20113153

20. Kingma, D.P., Ba, J.L.: Adam: a method for stochastic optimization (2014). arXiv:1412.6980v9

21. McHugh, M.L.: Interrater reliability: the kappa statistic. Biochem. Med. (Zagreb) **22**(3), 276–282 (2012)

22. Park, S.H., Goo, J.M., Jo, C.-H.: Receiver operating characteristic (ROC) curve: practical review for radiologists. Korean J. Radiol. **5**(1), 11–18 (2004)

Statistical Properties and Modelling of DDoS Attacks

Pheeha Machaka[1(✉)] and Antoine Bagula[2]

[1] School of Computing, University of South Africa,
Unisa Science Campus, Christiaan de Wet Road & Pioneer Avenue,
Johannesburg 1709, Florida, South Africa
machap@unisa.ac.za
[2] University of the Western Cape, Robert Sobukwe Road, Bellville 7535,
Cape Town, South Africa
abagula@uwc.ac.za

Abstract. The work presented in this paper is an implementation of a design of a DDoS simulation testbed that uses parameter estimation and probability fitting of source IP address features of a network. We explored the issue of lack of adequate and recent evaluation datasets, we therefore designed a way that can be used to generate synthetic data that simulates a DDoS attack. We found that the Gaussian probability distribution best represents the normal operations of a network, while the Poisson probability distribution represents the operations of a network under a DDoS attack.

Keywords: DDoS · EWMA · CUSUM · Attack modelling · Probability fitting

1 Introduction

The rapid transition in information technology has made information more easily available by quicker and cheaper means. The use of these innovations has now changed from the conventional desktop computer to the cellphone and unexpectedly to the Internet of Things (IoT). With this technology, numerous devices that exist in homes, shopping malls, and workspaces will be linked to the internet.

The increased use and reliance of internet technology on society has contributed to a major increase in vulnerabilities. Consequently, large facets of society are directly impacted by any breakdown and damage to the services rendered by these systems. This disturbance can be felt intensely and some can last longer than can be bearable. For example, disruption of an enterprise or government infrastructure can have a major effect on their daily activities [1].

The internet has created a better platform of communication and offered benefits and greater advantages for individuals, organizations and businesses. The proliferated use of the diverse internet devices and products also presents increased security challenges. The internet did not have "security" in its initial design; therefore, attackers have taken advantage of this design glitch. Attackers use easily available malicious tools to carry out attacks on Internet services and products. These attackers have

P. C. Vinh and A. Rakib (Eds.): ICCASA 2020/ICTCC 2020, LNICST 343, pp. 44–54, 2021.
https://doi.org/10.1007/978-3-030-67101-3_4

exploited and taken advantage of devices that are not secured and used these devices as a means to carry out a large scale attack [2].

Recently, Amazon Web Services reported one of the largest DDoS attack in history. In February 2020, they observed and mitigated a 2.3Tbps DDoS attack. In their research they also indicated that there was a 23% increase in DDoS attacks observed in Q1 2020 compared to Q1 2019. Induced disruptions can be caused by efforts of a hacker to harm a system using Denial of Service (DoS) attacks. This is a malicious endeavor by an attacker to interrupt a service provider in order to render it inaccessible to customers. The large-scale variation is the Distributed Denial of Service (DDoS). Such intrusions could have catastrophic consequences on an organisation. This can contribute to dissatisfied clients and substantial damages; this can also see forfeiture of intellectual property, which then affects the longevity of corporations and governments in economic and commercial sustainability. Therefore, it is necessary for organizations and governments to adopt strategies that will help them effectively identify the start and frequency of DDoS attacks [3].

There are two types of NIDS, firstly, signature-based detection systems seek to describe a collection of templates that determine if a specified network traffic sequence is an intrusion. If the traffic pattern fits the classification in the database, then it can be accurately detected. Consequently, in detecting intrusions, signature-based systems achieve high levels of accuracy and low false positive rate. However, they are not able to accurately identify new attacks or modifications of known attacks. Therefore, the impetus for the development of anomaly-based NIDS was the shortcomings of signature-based intrusion detection. The second anomaly based intrusion detection systems (ABIDS) identify events based on a 'natural' system's activity that tend to be anomalous. An intrusion is reported when an abnormality from standard network activity has been detected. There are some inherent drawbacks to anomaly-based detection. First, advanced attackers could observe the network traffic in order to train the attacking systems. Second, the intricacy of establishing the optimum threshold contributes to a rise in the false positive rate. Finally, I can be challenging to abstract valid and anomalous network activity characteristics both qualitatively and accurately [4].

A significant number of DDoS attacks assume the format of a constant attack rate. The attack agent generates attack packets that are dispatched at a consistent and continuous pace from the outset of this form of attack. Attack agents create packets without breaking or changing the attack rate. The effect on a victim of such an attack is rapid, persistent and sudden. Signature-based identification strategies make it simple to identify these forms of attacks.

In order to avoid detection, attackers have adapted their attack tactics and have planned low-rate attacks strategy. This strategy will steadily increase to deplete all machine resources. By steadily weakening the services of the victim over an extended period, this technique obstructs the identification of the attack. Depending on the response of the victim to the attack, these kinds of attacks will change their attack rate. In this type of assault, the victim will encounter a periodic interruption of operation since the attack will often alleviate the victim's attack impact in order to avoid detection.

While a large number of systems were developed in the past to address this problem, there are still challenges in research. Some of them being the issue of (1) dimensionality in traffic features; and (2) choosing a better statistical probability distribution that is best fits for modelling traffic data using of synthetic dataset due to the lack of good quality datasets.

Therefore, this paper attempts to answer the following research question: (1) Researchers have used features of incoming packets source IP address as a helpful metric to identify the start of an attack. However, high dimensionality in IP address features and the complicated correlation between them causes heavy computational overheads and make the detection task challenging. We therefore question how the onset of the DDoS attack can be identified on the basis of simple features of the source IP address? (2) Current DDoS attacks datasets have constraints: these are privacy and legal concerns involved with the sharing of recorded datasets. Thus, there is a lack of actual intrusion data that could be used to simulate attacks and to test and validate new detection techniques. From this challenge, we therefore ask: What are the key statistical features of a DDoS attack? How do we model the characteristics of DDoS attacks so that we can simulate and produce practical attack traffic datasets?

2 DDoS Attacks Detection

Kaspersky Lab's 2020 s quarter report showed that the most common attack technique was the TCP SYN flooding attack. The TCP SYN flood accounted for 94.7%, while the ICMP attacks accounted for 4.9%, and other types of DDoS attacks were sidelined [5]. It is for this reason that the TCP SYN attack is the main subject of investigation this paper. The attack methods of the TCP SYN DDoS attack are further elaborated below. This is followed by a background research on detection techniques that use the IP address, and their challenges are also explored.

2.1 TCP SYN Flooding Attack

This is the most common and effective network layer flooding attack. The susceptibilities of the normal TCP three-way handshake are exploited; as shown in the figure below. The client will initiate the connection on a standard TCP connection by sending a SYN packet to the server requesting a connection. The server will open a session after receiving the request and replies with a SYN-ACK; it records the information of the initiated TCP connection in the database while it allocates resources to that session [6].

The session will carry-on in a half-open state, the SYN RECVD state. To finalise the connection with the server, the client will need to approve the connection and reply to it with an ACK packet. The server then scans the memory for a current request for a connection and transfers the TCP connection from the SYN RECVD state to the ESTABLISHED state. If no ACK packet is sent within a given time, the link will be delayed and the allocated resources will not be released [7].

The intruder floods the victim server with SYN packets in this attack. These packets usually contain IP addresses that are spoofed, these are addresses do not exist or unused. It is also possible to initiate TCP SYN floods using corrupted agents with valid IP addresses, but the agents need to be positioned so that the victim server does not respond or recognize it. In this way, the server for the partially open connection request will not be in receipt any acknowledgement packets from the clients (Fig. 1).

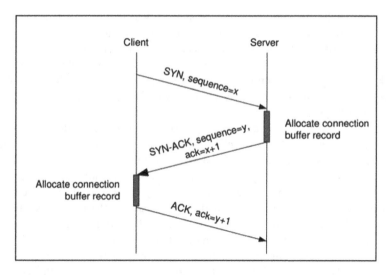

Fig. 1. TCP Three-way Handshake

The server maintains a significant amount of incomplete three-way handshake during the high-rate flooding attack and allocates resources to fake connection requests for a period of time. More fake requests will be collected by the server and its resources will inevitably be depleted. This will prevent further processing of new requests, plus legitimate client requests, by the server [8]. The section that follows explores the use of the IP address for detecting DDoS attacks and the benefits and challenges faced with using IP address as a detection feature.

2.2 DDoS Attack Detection Using IP Address

For information exploration in machine learning, feature selection is important. In the selection of features, researchers pick a subset of relevant data features to develop robust and powerful machine learning models for the detection of intrusions. By finding significant data characteristics and how they correlate, this allows to create a deeper understanding of the data. This will boost the learning model 's efficiency in many ways and help reduce the effect of the issue of high dimensionality. New DDoS attacks have come to light with the emergence of big data and the consequent criteria for successful machine learning techniques, and creative detection approaches are in demand [9].

The importance of feature selection cannot be underemphasized. It is central to any detection method and algorithm because it helps identify those features that are intrinsic of a network attack traffic, and normal network traffic. However, the main challenge that researchers face in designing an effective detection technique is the issue of high dimensionality in network traffic data and the high computational costs it incurs. High dimensionality in network traffic data and the complicated correlation between the features causes heavy computational overheads and make the design of an anomaly detection particularly challenging.

The major challenge with using IP address for a detection technique is the issue of scalability. For an IPv4, the researcher need to compute and store statistical information for 232 elements of the IP address space. This requires large computational and storage overheads, and requires monitoring fewer IP addresses during normal traffic and during an attack. The design of detection technique become even more challenging when it relates to an IPv6 address space were the quantity of elements in the address space increases to 2128 [10].

Over time, researchers have used different features related to IP addresses to design detection techniques for DDoS attacks. Efforts have been made to use IP address characteristics such as IP address traffic volume, adjust the number of different network flows, i.e. a grouping of destination and source IP, destination and source port, and the protocol type [11]. The work of researchers in [12] focus their detection efforts on using incoming traffic volumes and IP address distribution. The researchers also used entropy to further measure IP address distribution and uniformity. They group traffic flows according to the destination IP addresses and they compare each group's traffic volumes to the predicted chi-square statistic. A divergence from the expected traffic profile will signify an attack. The work of researchers in [13, 14] also evaluated entropy measures across IP header features. These use of entropy is a measure of features distribution to detect when there is a deviation in the network traffic performance.

Some researchers have used historical database mechanisms to maintain a list of valid IP addresses. These are IP addresses for whom a three-way TCP handshake has been completed. In order to maintain a recent IP addresses database, this technique uses a sliding window update. During an attack or when the network is overloaded, only those packets from IP addresses listed in the database are accepted [15]. This technique can be outwitted by a crafty attacker by establishing a TCP handshake for the purpose of launching an attack later with various IP addresses.

Some researchers have tried to differentiate flash events from DDoS attacks using the IP address. Flash events (FE) occur when a network server encounters a sudden growth in traffic requests from genuine and authentic clients, however, this sudden increase can be likened to a high rate DDoS attack. In order to differentiate FE's and to also detect DDoS attacks, researchers in [16] used an IP address aggregation technique. The technique makes the assumption that during an FE, most clients' IP addresses will be geographically nearby, while for a DDoS attack, IP addresses will be widely distributed. The section that follows will explore the use of IP address and probability distribution fitting for the purpose of modelling a DDoS attack.

3   DDoS Attack Modelling

In this research, we aim to present methods that can be used for modelling DDoS attacks for the purpose of designing detection techniques against these attacks. We first explore the type of datasets that are used by researchers, the benefits and challenges that researchers face using these datasets. We also explore the probability distributions that are used for differentiating and fitting normal network traffic and network traffic under a DDoS attack. We further explore how researchers can generate synthetic data using that emulates a DDoS attack.

3.1   Datasets Used for Modelling

The research area of network anomaly detection continues to develop, and with good datasets, it is important to evaluate developed detection methods. There are several network intrusion datasets that were created by prominent research groups. The efforts were to assist with the assessing and validating developed techniques and algorithms. A superior dataset assists researchers to identify the efficacy of developed methods to detect attacks when implemented in actual operating environments.

Researchers have used several public dataset, private datasets and network simulated datasets. However most researcher have referenced the publicly available datasets like the DARPA Dataset, KDD Cup dataset, NSL-KDD Cup dataset, DEFCON dataset and the CAIDA dataset. These are yardstick datasets produced using experimental environments [9]. For this research the DARPA dataset was used for its popularity of use in the field of DDoS attack detection. However, this dataset has its own challenges.

For researchers, the natural problem with evaluating the designed techniques for detecting DDoS attacks is the insufficiency of openly obtainable real-word network traffic datasets. The datasets that normally earn reference are usually out of date for correctly demonstrating the latest traffic directions. Due to the legal and privacy issues, they have been removed off sensitive data. Therefore, the majority of research on this topic are evaluated using open-source traffic generators, testbeds based on simulations and publicly available datasets. Each of these evaluation strategies have their own limitations. Therefore, these limitations have lead researchers to developing testbeds that are low cost, customizable and scalable [17].

3.2   Probability Distribution Functions for DDoS Attack Detection (Modelling)

In anomaly-based detection systems, researchers design detection systems by modelling the normal behavior of an attack free network traffic. In the event that a abnormality from the standard behavior is detected, then an attack would be detected. A DDoS attack brings about unexpected changes in the network traffic. Likewise, an unexpected variation in the statistical features of network traffic performance can be noticed. Should there be a DDoS occurrence at a particular time λ, the data will depict a substantial statistical variation about or from the time larger than λ [18].

The literature [19] has shown that statistical and mathematical behavior of these attacks is usually regarded as entropy and the information theory of network traffic characteristics. These metrics capture the unusual distributional changes of the traffic data features in a single value. Therefore, sufficient observations of the changes in the value can distinctly reveal the anomalies in the network therefore distinguishing attack traffic from normal traffic. Researchers have studied various probability distributions to capture the intricacy of the statistical properties of a DDoS attacks. The Weibull, Gaussian and Logistic distributions are the most popular. The Weibull probability distribution function is generally used to represent and to model traffic features. To represent network traffic data, the Gaussian probability distribution model is often commonly used, while logistic regression distribution models are often used in the field of network traffic and attack modeling [20].

It is important for researchers to further understand which distribution model is best suitable for DDoS attack detection. This will assist with building and designing more accurate detection techniques and algorithms. The work of researchers in [20] looked at implementing probability fitting and parameter estimation on many features of a DDoS attack. They provided probabilistic behavior of traffic features of DDoS attacks. They found that the best fitted probability distribution for TCP SYN DDoS attacks is the Weibull, Gaussian and Logistic distribution. This is further confirmed by the work of researchers in [21]. Based on their analysis, they found that under normal legitimate network traffic, where humans were participating, and the probabilistic characteristics of the network data was that of a Gaussian distribution. In the instance were a DDoS attack is launched, where the network traffic data is auto-generated by bots or agents, the probabilistic character of the network data resembled that of a Poisson distribution. For the design of the DDoS attack testbed, we used the Poisson distribution for generating synthetic attack data.

3.3 Synthetic Network Traffic Modelling

Researchers are faced with the challenge of obtaining realistic datasets, and the datasets that are currently available are too old and do not reflect the latest trends. To overcome this challenge many researchers have developed a customized traffic generation testbed simulation in order to evaluate designed techniques. It is for this reason that we used a similar approach in this research.

For the purpose of modelling attack traffic data, in this research we analyzed the attack-free data from various source IP addresses in the DARPA dataset. This is a dataset from the MIT Lincoln Laboratory that was compiled using real traffic data. The data includes trace data from network traffic collected in normal network operation. We examined traffic data in this experiment where there were noteworthy traffic operations. Thus, from 08h00–19h00, so 11 h of traffic data was considered. The dataset was filtered by the source IP address and TCP protocol and the TCP SYN was collected. When investigating the onset of a TCP SYN flood attack, we considered SYN packets.

The examination considered the calculation of SYN packets at intervals of 10 s. This was done so that these attacks were synthetically created to enable investigations of the performance of an algorithm across various attack characteristic scenarios. They were produced using a homogenous Poisson process that generates independent and exponentially distributed delays between packet arrivals. The attack was designed to extend over 30 time intervals (each time interval is 10-s) for 300 s (five minutes). Every five-minute traffic period was injected with attack data to contemplate all potential attacks used for these experiments. We consider and model two kinds of attack characteristics in these experiments: high and low intensity attacks. The particulars of these traffic features will be explained next.

Those attacks whose intensity gradually increases until all resources are depleted are low intensity (or low rate) attacks. By steadily weakening the services of the victim over a prolonged period of time, this technique delays the identification of the attack. For the experiments, we found that a low-intensity attack has its mean amplitude at 50 percent higher than the mean of the normal traffic in a five minute attack interval. Figure 2 reflects this. Between intervals of 20–40, attacks were synthetically injected.

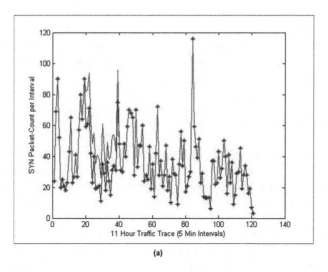

(a)

Fig. 2. Low intensity attacks (red line) seen on interval 20–40. (Color figure online)

High rate attacks were found to have an abrupt increase and reach the highest amplitude in a single attack interval. During the attack, packets are directed at a stable and continuous rate, without a halt or deviation in the attack rate. The victim impact is rapid and abrupt [22]. In our experiments, high rate attacks 250% above the mean packet rate in that given interval. This can be noticed between the same interval 20 and interval 40 of Fig. 3.

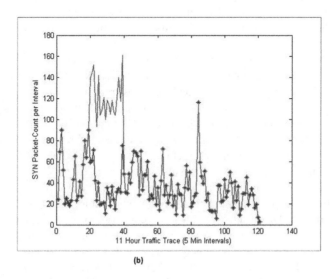

(b)

Fig. 3. High Intensity attacks (red line) seen on intervals 20–40. (Color figure online)

In these experiments, we used the Poisson distribution flow to simulate a DDoS attack traffic, and we assumed a Gaussian distribution for normal network traffic. The Poisson distribution flow used the function: $f_P(k; \lambda)$ were the non-negative integer $k \in [0; \infty]$ and the positive real number λ is the average packet rate per second for a given time interval.

4 Implementation Results and Discussions

The implementation and development of this testbed was in MATLAB. To test the efficacy of the testbed, two change point detection algorithms were deployed. We use the Cumulative Sum (CUSUM) and the Exponentially Weighted Moving Averages (EWMA) algorithms. The implementation details of these algorithms are further elaborated below.

The CUSUM and EWMA belong to a family of change point detection techniques [23, 24]. These algorithms based on the assumption of statistical testing and were developed for independent and identically distributed random variables $\{y_i\}$. In the approach, a sudden change arising at a given time can be modeled using two hypothesis, θ_0 and θ_1. θ_0 represents the statistical properties before the sudden deviation; θ_1 represents the statistical properties after the sudden deviation. The hypothesis testing in our experiments depend on the condition of the network, attack or normal condition. Thus, this is defines as follows:

- θ_0: There is no DDoS attack and has the probability distribution f_0,
- θ_1: There is a DDoS attack and has the probability distribution f_1.

These simulations examined the functioning of the CUSUM and the EWMA algorithms performance against DDoS attacks both low and high rate attacks. We also investigated the balance amongst the algorithms' detection rate, false alarm rate and detection delay.

For the EWMA simulation experiments, and for high intensity DDoS. The algorithm was able to detect high intensity DDoS attack with a detection accuracy of 100%, although the false positive rate continued at an average of 30%. The experiments further revealed that the detection delay was on average between 11–23 s. Thus the algorithm was able to detect, with accuracy, high rate attacks 11–23 s after its onset. For low rate attacks, the EWMA algorithm detects attack with 100% accuracy, however, the false positive rate increased to between to 40%–60%. The EWMA algorithm was able to accurately detect a low intensity attack, on average, 40 s from its onset. More details and results can be found in this publication paper [25].

For the CUSUM algorithm simulation experiments, and for high rate DDoS attacks, the algorithm detects DDoS attacks with a detection rate of 100% whereas having a false positive rate that is between 0% and 7%. The CUSUM algorithm had accurately detected high rate DDoS attacks on average between 26 s to 45 s from its onset. For the case of low rate DDoS attacks, the CUSUM algorithm yielded 14%–81% detection rate but maintaining a low false positive rate that is from 0% to 7%. Even though the CUSUM algorithm could not reach a full detection accuracy, the fastest detection delay was recorded as 73 s detection delay from the onset of an attack. More details and results of this simulation can be found in this publication [26].

The results of the simulation testbed has shown that the algorithms were able to accurately detect high intensity attacks with a fairly reasonable false positive rate and detection delays. However, these algorithms have drawbacks when a low intensity DDoS attack presents itself in network. This further indicates that there is room for improvement in terms of accurately detecting the cunning techniques of a low intensity DDoS attack.

5   Conclusion and Future Work

The work presented in this paper is an implementation of a design of a DDoS simulation testbed that uses parameter estimation and probability fitting of source IP address features of a network. We explored the issue of lack of adequate and recent evaluation datasets, we therefore designed a way that can be used to generate synthetic data that simulates a DDoS attack. We found that the Gaussian probability distribution best represents the normal operations of a network, while the Poisson probability distribution represents the operations of a network under a DDoS attack.

Researchers have often used source IP address in combination with other network traffic features to design DDoS attack detection algorithms. However, this has often lead to the issue of high dimensionality in data. In these experiments we used the source IP address only to find out if a single network traffic feature can be used for the detection of DDoS attacks. We used various scenarios of network attacks were we considered high intensity attacks and low intensity attacks.

To further evaluate the testbed, we deployed two change-point detection algorithms, namely the EWMA and the CUSUM algorithms. The deployment yielded positive results and also indicated areas of improvement. We plan to further intend to implement a deep learning algorithm on this testbed to further evaluate it with more complex and recent detection algorithm so that we can learn more about the efficacy of the testbed for future use.

References

1. Gluhak, A., et al.: A survey on facilities for experimental internet of things research. Commun. Mag. IEEE **49**(11), 58–67 (2011)
2. Mirkovic, J., Reiher, P.: A taxonomy of DDoS attack and DDoS defense mechanisms. ACM SIGCOMM Comput. Commun. Rev. **34**(2), 39–53 (2004)
3. Forrester Consulting. "The trends and Changing Landscape of DDoS Threats and Protection" (2009)
4. Bhattacharyya, D.K., Kalita, J.K.: DDoS Attacks: Evolution, Detection, Prevention, Reaction, and Tolerance (2016)
5. Kupreev, O., Badovskaya, E., Gutnikov, A.: Kaspersky Report: DDoS attacks in Q2 2020 (2020)
6. Douligeris, C., Mitrokotsa, A.: DDoS attacks and defense mechanisms: classification and state-of-the-art. Comput. Netw. **44**(5), 643–666 (2004)

7. Bhuyan, M.H., et al.: Detecting distributed denial of service attacks: methods, tools and future directions. Comput. J. **57**, bxt031 (2013)
8. Mirkovic, J., Reiher, P.: D-WARD: a source-end defense against flooding denial-of-service attacks. IEEE Trans. Dependable Secure Comput. **2**(3), 216–232 (2005)
9. Bhuyan, M.H., Bhattacharyya, D.K., Kalita, J.K.: Network traffic anomaly detection techniques and systems. In: Network Traffic Anomaly Detection and Prevention (2017)
10. Ahmed, E., et al.: Use of ip addresses for high rate flooding attack detection. In: IFIP International Information Security Conference (2010)
11. Barford, P., Plonka, D.: Characteristics of network traffic flow anomalies. In: Proceedings of the 1st ACM SIGCOMM Workshop on Internet Measurement (2001)
12. Feinstein, L. et al.: Statistical approaches to DDoS attack detection and response. In: Proceedings DARPA Information Survivability Conference and Exposition (2003)
13. Lakhina, A., Crovella, M., Diot, C.: Mining anomalies using traffic feature distributions. ACM SIGCOMM Comput. Commun. Rev. **35**(4), 217–228 (2005)
14. Wagner, A., Plattner, B.: Entropy based worm and anomaly detection in fast IP networks. In: 14th IEEE International Workshops on Enabling Technologies: Infrastructure for Collaborative Enterprise (WETICE'05) (2005)
15. Peng, T., Leckie, C., Ramamohanarao, K.: Protection from distributed denial of service attacks using history-based IP filtering. In: IEEE International Conference On Communications, ICC 2003 (2003)
16. Le, Q., Zhanikeev, M., Tanaka, Y.: Methods of distinguishing flash crowds from spoofed DoS attacks. In: 2007 Next Generation Internet Networks (2007)
17. Bhatia, S., et al.: A framework for generating realistic traffic for distributed denial-of-service attacks and flash events. Comput. Secur. **40**, 95–107 (2014)
18. Tartakovsky, A.G., Polunchenko, A.S., Sokolov, G.: Efficient computer network anomaly detection by changepoint detection methods. IEEE J. Select. Topics Signal Process. **7**(1), 4–11 (2013)
19. Bhuyan, M.H., Bhattacharyya, D., Kalita, J.K.: An empirical evaluation of information metrics for low-rate and high-rate DDoS attack detection. Pattern Recog. Lett. **51**, 1–7 (2015)
20. Erhan, D., Anarım, E.: Statistical properties of DDoS attacks. In: 2019 6th International Conference on Control, Decision and Information Technologies (CoDIT) (2019)
21. Li, K. et al.: Effective DDoS attacks detection using generalized entropy metric. In: International Conference on Algorithms and Architectures for Parallel Processing (2009)
22. Machaka, P., Nelwamondo, F.: Data mining techniques for distributed denial of service attacks detection in the internet of things: a research survey. In: Data Mining Trends and Applications in Criminal Science and Investigations (2016)
23. Page, E.: Continuous inspection schemes. In: Biometrika, pp. 100–115 (1954)
24. Roberts, S.: Control chart tests based on geometric moving averages. Technometrics **1**(3), 239–250 (1959)
25. Machaka, P., Bagula, A., Nelwamondo, F.: Using exponentially weighted moving average algorithm to defend against DDoS attacks. In: 2016 Pattern Recognition Association of South Africa and Robotics and Mechatronics International Conference (PRASA-RobMech) (2016)
26. Machaka, P., et al.: Using the cumulative sum algorithm against distributed denial of service attacks in internet of things. In: International Conference on Context-Aware Systems and Applications (2015)

Estimating Land Surface Temperature from Landsat-8 Images Based on a Cloud-Based Automated Processing Service

Phan Hien Vu[1,3], Tan-Long Le[2,3], and Cuong Pham-Quoc[2,3(✉)]

[1] International University (HCMIU), Ho Chi Minh City, Vietnam
[2] Ho Chi Minh City University of Technology (HCMUT),
Ho Chi Minh City, Vietnam
cuongpham@hcmut.edu.vn
[3] Vietnam National University - Ho Chi Minh City (VNU-HCM),
Ho Chi Minh City, Vietnam

Abstract. As the biggest city in Vietnam, Ho Chi Minh City (HCMC) usually suffers from a number of environmental issues such as traffic jam, subsidence and inundation, river and air pollution, high temperature, etc. Therefore, a hazard maps system helps the city government and population understand well environmental risks. The main data sources for such system is a combination of in-situ measurements in ground and remotely sensed images from space. Popular satellite data products available and free of charge are used to environmental monitoring, consisting of Sentinel, Landsat, and Terra/Aqua MODIS. In this paper, we focus on estimating land surface temperature (LST) from Landsat-8 images based on a cloud-based automated processing service. The LST image is computed from red, near-infrared and thermal infrared bands. The service can be integrated as a part of a hazard map system when its data are collected from different sources.

Keywords: Lansat · LST · Cloud-based service · HCMC

1 Introduction

During the 30 last years, urbanization significantly increases in major cities in Asia, e.g. Tokyo, Japan; Chongqing, China; Mumbai, India; Kuala Lumpur, Malaysia; Taipei, Taiwan; Singapore, Singapore; and Ho Chi Minh, Vietnam [1,2]. Most of the cities focus on large investments in urban infrastructure development such as water supply, electric supply, roads, railways, ports, and airports to promote their economic growth [2]. This causes shrinking green urban space, increasing imperious area, vehicle, the amount of waste, etc. and then, urban environment has been affected seriously, e.g. increased emission and noise, or polluted air and water resources. Therein, urban heat is one of negative

© ICST Institute for Computer Sciences, Social Informatics and Telecommunications Engineering 2021
Published by Springer Nature Switzerland AG 2021. All Rights Reserved
P. C. Vinh and A. Rakib (Eds.): ICCASA 2020/ICTCC 2020, LNICST 343, pp. 55–64, 2021.
https://doi.org/10.1007/978-3-030-67101-3_5

impacts on human health. Thus, providing a state of land surface temperature (LST) in cities as a hazard map to their citizen is necessary.

Since the 1960s, remote sensing technique has been developed to observe natural resources and environment from space, e.g. GOES, NOAA, METEOSAT, TERRA, AQUA, Landsat satellite missions. These missions also provide basic data sources for an analysis of LST at global scales, e.g. AVHRR and MODIS images, and regional scales, e.g. TM and TIR images. Particularly, the TM, ETM and TIR sensors of the Landsat satellite program has provided continuously thermal images in the 10.5–12.5 µm wavelength bands with moderate spatial resolution since 1982 [3]. They are suitable for studying urban heat.

Ho Chi Minh City (HCMC) is the biggest city of Vietnam in a term of socioeconomic development. During the last three decades, urban expansion and industrialization have occurred significantly. These lead many issues of urban environment, and meanwhile an increase of LST in HCMC's urban area occurs. The city government would like to develop a hazard map system to provide environmental information to the citizen, e.g. temperature, water and air quality, as a website. The urban heat is one of indicators of the system where its input data is a combination of in-situ ground measurements and satellite images. At present, available satellite thermal images free of charge, consisting of MODIS and Landsat, are suitable for urban heat monitoring. Here this paper focus on exploiting Landsat-8 images to estimating LST as an indicator in the hazard map system in HCMC, where a cloud-based service is developed to automatically download and process Landsat data.

The rest of the paper is organized as follows. Section 2 introduces the study area, fundamental background of Landsat data as well as the approach to estimate LST and Emissivity used in the paper. We present our cloud-based service for automatically download and process data in Sect. 3. The experimental results used to validate the approach are shown in Section 4. Finally, Sect. 5 concludes our paper.

2   Study Area and Method

In this section, we present our study area as well as the remote sensing image source which are used for our service. We also discuss the method used to estimate the LST of HCMC.

2.1   Study Area

HCMC is one of densely urban areas of Vietnam, occupying the total area of approximately 2,095.01 km^2 and the population of about 8.6 million people. It includes 19 urban and 5 rural districts, enclosed by Binh Duong in the north, Tay Ninh in the north-west, Dong Nai in the east, Ba Ria - Vung Tau in the south-east, Tien Giang in the south-west and Long An in the west, as described in Fig. 1 [4]. This region has a tropical climate with two wet and dry seasons.

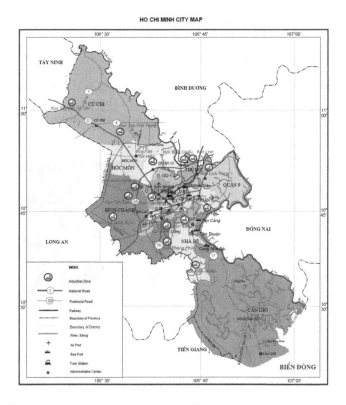

Fig. 1. The administrative map of Ho Chi Minh City, Vietnam

The rainy or wet season from May to November, with a precipitation of approximately 159 rainy days per year while the sunny or dry season from December to consecutive April, with a sunshine of average 2,490 h per year. The average humidity is 75% and the average temperature is 28 0C with little variation throughout the year [4].

2.2 Landsat Images

Landsat-8 is the latest satellite of the Landsat program of the National Aeronautics and Space Administration (NASA) and the United States Geological Survey (USGS), launched in February, 11th 2013. The key mission of this satellite program is to collect multispectral imagery in medium spatial resolution, thereby distributing for public users to bring benefits for many sectors such as agriculture, science, government and so much more [5]. The Landsat-8 data is acquired from two sensors, including The Operational Land Imager (OLI) providing 9 visible, near infrared, and shortwave-infrared band images with 30-m spatial solution, and the Thermal Infrared Sensor (TIRS) providing 2 thermal band images with 100-m spatial resolution. The temporal resolution is 16 days.

Landsat-8 datasets are available and free of charge in the USGS Earth Explorer website [6].

In this study, to cover the whole HCMC, we need to collect three censes at the Path-Row locations of 125-052, 125-053, and 124-053. The two scenes in Path 125 are captured nearly while the scene in the Path 124 is captured before 4 days from the path 125. Figure 2 shows the locations of three Landsat scenes and the composite color image in HCMC after atmospheric calibration and mosaicking.

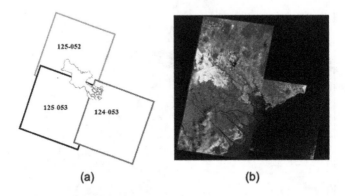

(a)   (b)

Fig. 2. (a) The locations of three Landsat scenes to cover the whole HCMC, and (b) the composite color image after mosaicking three Landsat scenes

2.3 Derivation of LST from Landsat Images

The derivation of LST requires main steps as described in Fig. 3, where LST is determined from TIR band-10 and OLI band-4, 5 band images. The steps of Landsat-8 image processing referred to the Landsat-8 data users handbook [8].

Processing Landsat-8 TIRS Images. *At Sensor Radiance:* Convert the Digital Number (DN) to Top-of-Atmospheric (ToA) Spectral Radiance. Typically, the standard product pixel values of Landsat-8 data are represented in 16-bit unsigned integer format, which is range from 0 and 65536. We need to convert those value to the ToA Spectral Radiance and/or Reflectance to quantize and calibrate for high-accuracy in processing. The Landsat-8 product metadata file (MTL) provides a bunch of parameters and coefficients used for describing band images. In this process, we leverage the radiometric rescaling coefficients to convert the DN values to ToA Spectral Radiance, as described in Eq. 1.

$$L_\lambda = M_L \times Q_{cal} + A_L \tag{1}$$

where, L_λ is the ToA Spectral Radiance in W/m^2 srad μm, Q_{cal} is the DN value of Band 10 or Band 11 Image, M_L is the Band-specific multiplicative rescaling

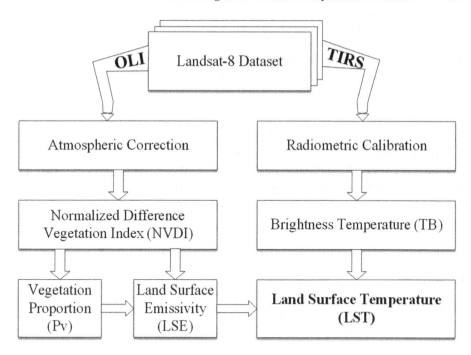

Fig. 3. Land surface temperature

factor from MTL, and A_L is the Band-specific additive rescaling factor from MTL.

Brightness Temperature: Convert the ToA Spectral Radiance to Brightness Temperature. Once having the ToA Spectral Radiance for TIRS band data, we can conduct the ToA Brightness Temperature by using Eq. 2.

$$T_B = \frac{K2}{ln(\frac{K1}{L_\lambda+1})} \qquad (2)$$

where, T is the ToA Brightness Temperature in Kelvin, K_1 and K_2 are the Thermal Conversion Constant and 2 from MTL.

Then, to convert from Kelvin unit to Celsius unit, we apply the following equation (Eq. 3).

$$T_B{}^\circ C = T_B - 273 \qquad (3)$$

Processing Landsat-8 OLIRS Images. *Land Surface Reflectance:* Convert the DN values to ToA Spectral Reflectance and ToA Spectral Reflectance with the sun angle correction, and then apply the MODTRAN atmospheric calibration module to receive Spectral Reflectance in land surface. We convert the DN values to ToA Spectral Reflectance, using Eq. 4.

$$\rho'_\lambda = M_\rho \times Q_{cal} + A_\rho \qquad (4)$$

where, $\rho_{\lambda'}$ is ToA Spectral Reflectance; M_ρ is Band-specific multiplicative rescaling factor from MTL file; Q_{cal} is DN value of OLI Bands Image; and A_ρ is Band-specific additive rescaling factor from MTL file.

Then, the Eq. 5 is used to correct for the sun angle of ToA Reflectance:

$$\rho_\lambda = \frac{\rho_{\lambda'}}{cos(\theta_{SZ})} \tag{5}$$

where, ρ_λ is the ToA Spectral Reflectance with a correction for the sun angle, and θ_{SZ} is the local solar zenith angle from MTL.

Normalized Different Vegetation Index (NDVI): The value of NDVI is used to evaluate the density of vegetation on land surface by observing visible and near-infrared solar radiance reflectance. NDVI is calculated in Eq. 6.

$$NDVI = \frac{\rho_{NIR} - \rho_{RED}}{\rho_{NIR} + \rho_{RED}} \tag{6}$$

where, ρ_{NIR} and ρ_{RED} are the Land Surface Reflectance of the Near-Infrared Band (Band 5) and the Visible Red Band (Band 4).

Vegetation Proportion (P_v): P_v is the fraction of vegetation in each pixel of satellite imagery, which is used to examine the role of vegetation in mixed land over. The Pv estimation is done by applying Eq. 7.

$$P_v = (\frac{NDVI - NDVI_{min}}{NDVI_{max} - NDVI_{min}})^2 \tag{7}$$

where, $NDVI_{max} = 0.5$ and $NDVI_{min} = 0.2$ are the maximum (dense vegetation) and minimum (bare land) NDVI values, respectively [7].

Land Surface Emissivity (ϵ): Land surface emission ϵ is seen as the key factor in the process of retrieving land surface temperature, using Eq. 8 [7]. The land surface emission affects the accuracy of the LST estimation. The value ranges from 0 to 1 representing perfect reflector and perfect emitter, respectively. It means that the lower emission value is, the colder temperature the land surface has, and inversely the higher the emissivity, the more heat was emitted or absorbed.

$$\epsilon = \epsilon_v P_v + \epsilon_s (1 - P_v) \tag{8}$$

where, ϵ_v, and ϵ_s are the emissivity of homogenous pixels of vegetation and bare soil, respectively.

Determining Land Surface Temperature (LST): At final stage, the retrieval of LST value from Landsat-8 imagery is based on the following expression:

$$LST = \frac{T_B}{1 + (\frac{\lambda(T_B)}{\rho})ln\epsilon} \tag{9}$$

where, λ is the wavelength of emitted radiance, and $\rho = h \times c/\sigma$ while $\sigma = 1.38 \times 10^{23} J/K$ is the Stefan Boltzmann's constant; $h = 6.626 \times 10^{34} J.s$ is the Plank's constant; and $c = 2.998 \times 108 m/s$ is the speed of light.

As a result, Fig. 4 presents the NDVI and LST images, derived from Landsat-8 image captured on 19/01/2019.

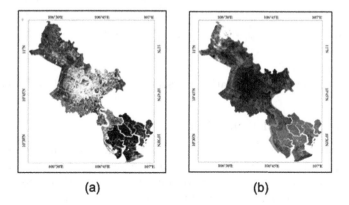

Fig. 4. (a) NDVI and (b) LST images derived from the Landsat-8 image, captured on 19/01/2019.

3 Cloud-Based Service for Estimating LST and Emissivity in HCMC

In this section, we present a cloud-based automated processing system for remote sensing satellites data. The innovative idea of our system is to apply state-of-the-art IT technologies to bring intuitive and visuality for monitoring environmental issues as aforementioned.

3.1 Overview of the Remote Image Processing Service

Figure 5 depicts an overview of our system, which composes of three main sides described as follows.

- *Satellite Imagery Providers:* provide remote sensing of Landsat-8 and MODIS data for the cloud server. Both of the data sources are freely available to find and download.
- *Image Processing Cloud Server:* provides the ability to automatically search and download up-to-date imagery data from providers in associated with fast and reliable data processing in retrieving LST, AOT
- *Client Applications*: provide user-friendly interfaces such as dashboard website or mobile applications with the integration with...from the cloud server.

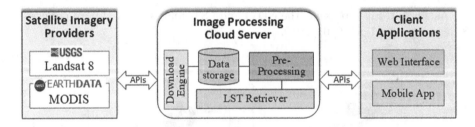

Fig. 5. Cloud-based automated processing system for satellites imagery

3.2   Design and Implementation

The key features of our processing system is to provide an automated mechanism for searching and bulk downloading up-to-date satellite data, and apply fast and reliable processing tasks to retrieve important factors that cause change in temperature of the Earth's surface. Our system is designed and implemented using Python programming language and a wide range of utilize libraries for handling satellite data. The workflow of main classes in the implementation is depicted as Fig. 6.

Download Engine: We design and implement a download engine to acquire images from Landsat-8 and MODIS satellites. The engine is responsible for finding the latest imagery sources, and download to a temporary storage in the cloud server if available. Typically, the Landsat-8 satellites captures the entire of Earth's surface once every two weeks, while MODIS does the same task every 1 to 2 days.

For processing purpose, we check the data source from providers instantaneously every 16 days to get up-to-date satellite images. We use the APIs provided by USGS's Earth Explorer [9] to work with Landsat-8 data, and leverage NASA EarthData Search APIs [10] to download MODIS land data products. All imagery will be converted into the GeoTiff, which is a popular format for satellite images.

Pre-Processing and LST Retriever: Once the Download Engine updates a new imagery, the LST Retriever will be acknowledged to process the data to derive land surface temperature. If the imagery is captured from Landsat-8, it has to be extracted into two type of bands (i.e. OLI and TIRS) to apply the Atmospheric Correction and Radiometric Calibration processes first. Those processes are encapsulated in a *MetadataReader* and *CalibrateLandsatBand* classes as shown in Fig. 6. Otherwise, if the server receives MODIS images, it will extract the LST values from Land Surface Temperature/Emissivity (MOD11) products.

The LST Retriever then calculate land surface temperature using the retrieval algorithm described in above sections. The results in this process will be packaged and provided for end-user applications which can be web interfaces or mobile applications.

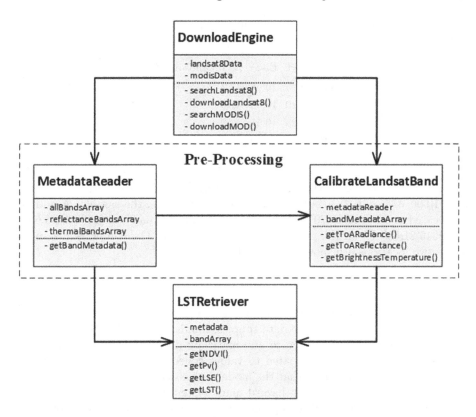

Fig. 6. The class diagram of image processing cloud server

4   Experimental Results

In this section, we present our experiments to estimate LST of HCMC. The LST measurements were performed with the 30 s interval in a range of approximately

Fig. 7. The samples A on the road and B on the grass

Table 1. The estimation of LST at the impermeable surface A and B the method in this paper

Date	Start	End	LST Landsat ($^\circ C$)	Surface
02 Oct., 2019	10:25	10:55	42.2	A
18 Oct., 2019	10:20	10:55	41.6	A
03 Nov., 2019	10:25	10:55	33.8	B
19 Nov., 2019	10:25	10:50	31.3	B

30 min, corresponding to the Landsat and Terra satellite acquisitions at local time 10.00 AM and 10.30 AM, respectively. In this case, the samples A and B are located at (106039′25.70″ N, 10046′19.70″ E) on the road and (106039′33.65″ N, 10046′21.55″ E) on the grass, as presented in Fig. 7. The comparison results of the two locations are shown in Table 1.

5 Conclusion

In this paper, we presented our approach to estimate the LST and Emissivity of Ho Chi Minh City using two data sources, Landsat and MODIS images. We developed a cloud-based service to automatically download and process data. The estimated values are compared to values collected a thermometer device. The comparison results show that the model we used provide good results. The service can be integrated into a hazard maps system where different sources of data can be collect to provide comprehensive information related to environmental issues in Ho Chi Minh City.

Acknowledgement. This research is funded by Department of Science and Technology of Ho Chi Minh City under grant number 09/2018/HD-QKHCN.

References

1. United Nations. https://population.un.org/wup/Country-Profiles/
2. Sheng, Y.K., Thuzar, M.: Urbanisation in Southeast Asian Countries. Institute of Southeast Asian Studies, Singapore (2012)
3. NASA. https://www.nasa.gov/
4. Ho Chi Minh City. http://www.hochiminhcity.gov.vn/
5. Landsat Program. https://landsat.gsfc.nasa.gov/
6. Earth Explorer. https://earthexplorer.usgs.gov/
7. Valor and Caselles: Mapping land surface emissivity from NDVI: application to European, African, and South American areas. Remote Sens. Environ. **57**(3), 167–184 (1996)
8. USGS, Landsat 8 Data Users Handbook. https://www.usgs.gov/core-science-systems/nli/landsat/landsat-8-data-users-handbook
9. U. G. Survey. Usgs/eros inventory service documentation (machine-tomachine api). https://m2m.cr.usgs.gov/api/docs/json/
10. N. Earthdata. Earthdata developer portal. https://earthdata.nasa.gov/collaborate/open-data-services-andsoftware/api

A Comparison Between Stacked Auto-Encoder and Deep Belief Network in River Run-Off Prediction

Bui Tan Kinh$^{(\boxtimes)}$, Duong Tuan Anh, and Duong Ngoc Hieu

Faculty of Computer Science and Engineering, HCM University of Technology,
Ho Chi Minh, Vietnam
tankinhlk@gmail.com, dtanhcse@gmail.com, dnhieu@hcmut.edu.vn

Abstract. The application of deep neural networks in forecasting hydrological time series data is increasingly popular, aiming to improve prediction accuracy in this challenging problem. As for river runoff prediction, Deep Belief Network (DBN) and Stacked Autoencoder (SAE) are two kinds of deep neural networks which are commonly used for extracting meaningful features from the data before prediction. In this study, we aim to compare the prediction performance of SAE model with that of DBN model on the runoff data of Srepok River in Central Highlands of Vietnam. Experiments are conducted by using historical data of the Srepok River that were collected in 11 years. The experimental results in this case study show that SAE brings out better prediction accuracy than DBN in terms of three evaluation criteria: correlation, root mean square error, and mean absolute percentage error.

Keywords: Runoff prediction · Stack autoencoder · Deep belief network · Srepok river

1 Introduction

Time series analysis includes methods for analyzing time series data, from which meaningful statistical attributes and data characteristics can be extracted to serve some purposes such as: prediction, classification, clustering for time series. Time series prediction is the use of a model to predict time events based on known events in the past and thereby predicting data points before they occur (or are measured).

The prediction of river run-off is very important in water resource planning and management. In this research, we focus on river run-off prediction of Srepok River (Vietnamese: Sêrêpok) which is a major tributary of Mekong River in the Central Highlands of Vietnam.

In general, there are two main approaches to solving the river runoff prediction problem: physical-based model and data-driven model [1]. The main disadvantage of the physical-based method is that it requires diverse kinds of

P. C. Vinh and A. Rakib (Eds.): ICCASA 2020/ICTCC 2020, LNICST 343, pp. 65–81, 2021.
https://doi.org/10.1007/978-3-030-67101-3_6

data, ranging from climate, water resource to soil map data. In contrast, data-driven model requires little information, are easy to implement, and do not need experienced specialists.

Among several methods used to forecast hydrological time series data such as rainfall, reservoir inflow, and river runoff, Artificial Neural Networks (ANNs) have been applied commonly [2–5]. But forecasting in hydrological time series data is still a challenging task since forecasting power on this kind of time series with some proposed methods is limited. As for ANN, river runoff time series will increase the feature learning difficulties and the network computation complexities.

Deep neural network models, such as Deep Belief Networks (DBNs), Long Short Term Memory Networks (LSTMs) and Stacked Auto-encoders (SAEs), have recently attracted the interest of many researchers in some applications on big data analysis. For recent years, there have been several researches of applying deep neural networks to predict time series data in various fields. Particularly, some research works on forecasting rainfall and runoff time series can be listed as follows. Gope et al. (2016) [6] employed Stacked Autoencoder in rainfall prediction. Tri et al. (2016) applied Deep Belief Network in daily runoff prediction for a river in Vietnam [7]. Hernandez et al. (2016) applied stacked auto-encoder networks in rainfall prediction [8]. Li et al. in (2016) [9] applied Deep Belief Network in reservoir inflow forecasting. Kratzert et al. (2018) [10] employed Long Short-Term Memory (LSTM) network in rainfall-runoff modeling. Lee et al. (2020) applied Long Short Term Memory Network in runoff analysis for Red River in Vietnam [11]. From these above mentioned research works, DBN model and SAE model are the two kinds of deep neural networks which are commonly-used in river runoff prediction. However, so far there exists no work to answer the question that between DBN model and SAE model which one performs better in river runoff prediction.

In this study, we aim to compare the prediction performance of SAE model with that of Deep belief network (DBN) on the daily runoff data of Srepok River in Vietnam. Experiments are conducted by using historical data of the Srepok River that were collected in 11 years. The experimental results in this case study show that SAE brings out better prediction accuracy than DBN in terms of three evaluation criteria: coefficient of correlation (R), root mean square error (RMSE), mean absolute percentage error (MAPE).

The remainder of the paper is organized as follows. Section 2 provides some basic backgrounds about Deep Belief Network and Stacked Autoencoder. In Sect. 3, the proposed architectures of DBN and SAE for runoff prediction are introduced. Section 4 reports the experiments to compare the prediction accuracy of SAE and that of DBN model in runoff prediction. Finally, Sect. 5 gives some conclusions and future works.

2   Theoretical Background

2.1   Deep Belief Network

Deep Belief Networks have been proposed by Hinton [12] with remarkable success in image processing and AI areas. DBN models are based on stacking of Restricted Boltzmann Machines (RBMs) [13].

RBM is a kind of stochastic artificial neural network with two connected layers: a layer of binary visible units (v, whose states are observed) and a layer of binary hidden units (h, whose states cannot be observed). The hidden units act as latent variables (features) that allow the RBM to model probability distribution over state vectors (see Fig. 1). The hidden units are conditionally independent given visible units.

Given an energy function $E(v, h)$ on the whole set of visible and hidden units, the joint probability is given by:

$$p(v, h) = \frac{e^{-E(v,h)}}{Z} \tag{1}$$

where Z is a normalization partition function, which is obtained by summing up the energy of all possible (v, h) configurations.

$$Z = \sum_{v,h} e^{-E(v,h)} \tag{2}$$

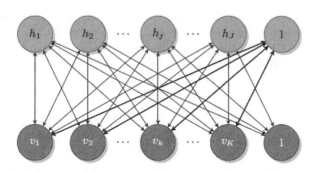

Fig. 1. Restricted Boltzmann Machine (RBM)

For the binary units $h_i \in \{0, 1\}$ and $v_i \in \{0, 1\}$, the energy function of the whole configuration is:

$$E(v, h) = -cv^T - bh^T - hWv^T$$
$$= -\sum_{k=1}^{K} c_k v_k - \sum_{j}^{J} b_j h_j - \sum_{j}^{J}\sum_{k=1}^{K} W_{jk} v_k hj \tag{3}$$

where W is $J \times K$ matrix of RBM weights connecting hidden and visible units, $c = [c_1, c_2, ..., c_K]$ is the bias of the visible units and $b = [b_1, b_2, ..., b_J]$ is the bias of the hidden units. The marginal distribution over v is:

$$p(v) = \sum_h (v, h) \tag{4}$$

The posterior probability of one layer given the other is easy to compute by the two following equations:

$$p(h, v) = \prod_j p(h_j = 1|v)$$
$$\text{where } p(h_j = 1|v) = \sigma(b_j + \sum_k W_{jk} v_k) \tag{5}$$

$$p(v, h) = \prod_k p(v_k = 1|h)$$
$$\text{where } p(v_k = 1|h) = \sigma(c_k + \sum_j W_{jk} h_j) \tag{6}$$

Notice that σ is the sigmoid function. Inference of hidden factor **h** given the observed **v** can be done because **h** is conditionally independent given **v**.

A DBN is a generative model with an input layer and an output layer, separated by l layers of hidden stochastic units. This multilayer neural network can be efficiently trained by composing RBMs in such a way that the feature activations of one layer are used as the training data for the next layer.

An energy-based model of RBMs can be trained by performing gradient ascent on the log-likelihood of the training data with respect to the RBM parameters. This gradient is difficult to compute analytically. Gibbs sampling method is well-suited for RBMs. One iteration of the Gibbs sampling works well and corresponding to the following sampling procedure:

$$v_0 \xrightarrow{p(h_0|v_0)} h_0 \xrightarrow{p(v_1|h_0)} v_1 \xrightarrow{p(h_1|v_1)} h_1...h_{k-1} \xrightarrow{p(h_{k-1}|v_k)} v_k \tag{7}$$

where the sampling operations are schematically described. It is known that Gibbs sampling is very time-consuming. Rough estimation of the gradient using the above procedure is denoted by CD-k, where CD-k represents the Contrastive Divergence algorithm [12] for performing k iterations of Gibbs sampling up to v_k.

The weight parameter is updated with the rate of change as shown in the following formula:

$$\nabla W_{jk} = \eta(\langle v_k h_j \rangle_0 - \langle v_k h_j \rangle_k) \tag{8}$$

where η represents the learning rate.

2.2   Stacked Auto-Encoder

Autoencoder

Autoencoder (AE) is a deep learning neural network model, in which it tries to recreate the input. The Autoencoder basic network is an unsupervised one layered neural network where the input is $X = x_1, x_2, x_3, ..., x_n$. as a characteristic vector with n dimensions. The network output is calculated using the following formula:

$$h_{W,b}(X) = f(W^T X) = f(\sum_{i=1}^{n} W_i X_i + b) \tag{9}$$

where $f: \mathbb{R} \mapsto \mathbb{R}$ is the nonlinear conversion function, W and b are the weights and bias of the corresponding network. The goal is to try to approximate the function $h_{W,b}(X) \approx X$ in order to learn the characteristics of X and recreate it.

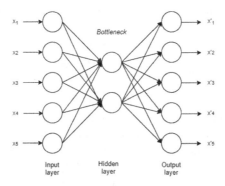

Fig. 2. Autoencoder neural network

Figure 2 describes the Autoencoder network which has two basic components:

- Encoder: The first layer is an encoder, which is simply a group of fully connected layers or convolution layers taking the input and compressing it into a smaller representation with a smaller size. The smaller representation of input is called the bottleneck. Here knowledge or features from the input will be compressed, retained important features and used to pass through the decoder.
- Decoder: The decoder also has the same architecture as the encoder, but the difference is that it takes the knowledge from the bottleneck then tries to reconstruct the input by using the fully connected layers or convolution layers.

The loss function of the Autoencoder network with a hidden layer is as follows:

$$J(W, b) = [\frac{1}{m} \sum_{i=1}^{m} \frac{1}{2} \|h_{W,b}(x_i) - x_i\|^2] + \frac{\lambda}{2} \sum_{i}^{n} \sum_{j}^{nhid} (W_{j,i})^2 \qquad (10)$$

where m is the number of training examples, *nhid* considered only one hidden layer is the number of units in the hidden layer and λ is the weight decay parameter.

The goal of autoencoder network is to learn how to represent the features of a dataset, by training the network to reduce noise from input in order to retain valuable information and features from the input data. There are many variations of autoencoder networks such as: Denoising Autoencoder, Sparse Autoencoder, Stacked Autoencoder, Convolutional Autoencoder, etc. Depending on the different goals of the problem, we use different models to solve the problem.

Stacked Autoencoder
The Stacked Autoencoder (SAE) is formed by stacking autoencoder to make a deep neural network, where each autoencoder is independently trained, and the output of each hidden layer of autoencoder is connected to the input of the next hidden layer, Fig. 3 illustrates how to stack an autoencoder neural network.

The hidden layers are trained by an unsupervised algorithm and then refined by a supervised method. The Stack autoencoder network is trained as follows:

1. Train the first autoencoder with input data and obtain the feature vector.
2. Feature vector of the previous layer is used as input to the next layer and the process is repeated until the training is completed.
3. Use the output of the last layer as input for prediction layer.
4. After all the hidden layers have been trained, the backpropagation algorithm is used to minimize the cost function and updated the weights with the training set labeled to achieve fine-tuning in a supervised way.

Based on the advantages of the Stacked autoencoder network, the model can create new data with more compressed knowledge and features which are used to train a new model to classify or predict, to find greater accuracy than using the original data. There have been studies showing that the use of Stacked autoencoder network instead of Autoencoder in preprocessing data can improve the accuracy of the classification model [14].

3   Two Model Architectures

3.1   Deep Belief Network

The DBN model that will be used in this work has the structure given in Fig. 4. In Fig. 4 the DBN model consists of only two RBMs and one MLP but in general, we can add some more RBMs into the DBN model to make the model deeper. The number of RBMs in DBN model is one of the important hyper-parameters of this deep learning model. Notice that in DBN model, the hidden layer of one

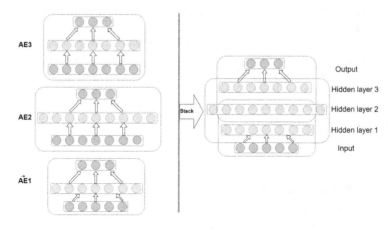

Fig. 3. How to stack autoencoder neural network

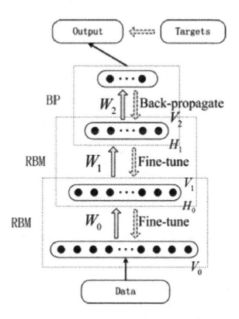

Fig. 4. The DBN model with two RBMs

RBM plays the same role of the visible layer of the RBM at the next (higher) level.

The training algorithm for our proposed DBN consists of two stages: an unsupervised learning and a supervised learning.

The unsupervised learning stage is the Contrastive Divergence (CD) algorithm [12] used for training the RBM(s). The CD algorithm progresses on a layer-by-layer basis. First, a RBM is trained directly on the input data. Hence, the neurons in the hidden layer of the RBM can capture the important features of the input data. The activations of the trained features are then used as "input data" to train a second RBM.

The supervised learning stage is the back-propagation algorithm used for training the MLP.

3.2 Stacked Auto-Encoder

In this section, we describe the general architecture of our proposed SAE model which can predict runoff data of the river for the following days.

The architecture of the model consisting of some stacked autoencoders, which is built by stacking the autoencoders together in order to extract meaningful features from the data. How to design the SAE model architecture for prediction will be discussed in the next section. We will try different configurations, the number of different encoders, the size of the sliding window, and so on to find the model with the best performance. A block diagram of our SAE model is shown in Fig. 5

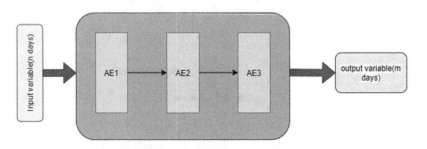

Fig. 5. Proposed stacked autoencoder architecture

In this work, we will test the number of input nodes with eight different values which will be reported later.

3.3 Sliding Window Technique

In order to preprocess the runoff data before entering a deep learning model, we use sliding window technique. From the initial time series $X = x_1, x_2, x_3, ..., x_n$ where n is the number of points (days), the data will be converted into $y_i = x_i, x_{i+1}, x_{i+2}, ..., x_{i+m}$ where m is the size of the sliding window. We will have a new input data is $Y = y_1, y_2, ..., y_n$. Then we apply Y to the predictor model.

3.4   Performance Evaluation

To evaluate the performance of a predictive model, the three statistical criteria applied are root mean square error (RMSE) and coefficient of correlation (R) and mean absolute percentage error (MAPE). The three criteria are computed as follows:

$$RMSE = \sqrt{\frac{1}{n}\sum_{i=1}^{n}(O_i - P_i)^2}$$

$$R = \frac{\sum_{i=1}^{n}(O_i - \overline{O})(P_i - \overline{P})}{\sqrt{\sum_{i=1}^{n}(O_i - \overline{O})^2(P_i - \overline{P})^2}} \tag{11}$$

$$MAPE = \frac{100}{n}\sum_{i=1}^{n}|\frac{O_i - P_i}{O_i}|$$

where n is the number of observations, O_i is the actual value at time point i, $\overline{O}$, is the average actual value and P_i is the forecast value for time point i and $\overline{P}$ is the average predicted value. Notice that R value is higher, the prediction accuracy is better. *RMSE* or *MAPE* value is lower, the prediction accuracy is better. RMSE is an absolute performance measure while MAPE is a relative measure.

4   Experimental and Evaluation

4.1   Study Area

For this study, the Srepok River in Viet Nam has been selected as the study region. The runoff data are collected from Cau14, BuonHo and DucXuyen measurement stations (Fig. 6). They are three measurement stations of the Srepok river in three different locations. A data point is representative of the flow collected at a fixed time of day in a given river basin. With Cau14 and BuonHo measurement stations, we collected 4000 data points corresponding to 4000 days (approximately 11 years) of runoff, while with DucXuyen measuring station we collected 3000 data points. The evaluation criteria of the models' performances are also given Sect. 3.4.

Srepok river [15] (the Khmer name Tonlé Srepok) is an important tributary of the Mekong river. The river originates in Dak Lak, then Dak Nong provinces of Vietnam, and flows through Ratanakiri and Stung Treng provinces, Cambodia. In Vietnam there is a river section called the Dak Krong River. Its length varies about 406 km in which the last 281 km course is in Cambodian territory. The Srepok River, in turn, has three main tributaries: the Krông Nô, Krông Ana, and Ea H'leo Rivers. Before joining the Mekong, the Srepok also merges with the Sesan River and Kong River in Stung Treng province.

The data collected will be divided into two subsets which are training and testing sets. We normalized the time series values to between zero and one interval in order to avoid effects of scale to our deep learning architecture. Data

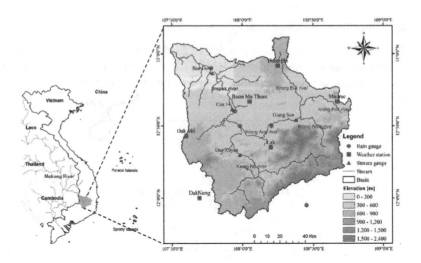

Fig. 6. The location of study area [20]

normalization method is shown in Eq. 12, where x_i represents a value to normalize at the i_{th} time point, min_{x_i} is the minimum value for the time series in the training set/testing set and max_{x_i} is the maximum value for the time series in the training set/testing set. We will normalize separately for training set and testing set.

$$x_i = \frac{x_i - min_{x_i}}{max_{x_i} - min_{x_i}} \tag{12}$$

4.2   Experimental Results

In this section, we will evaluate the performance of SAE model in river runoff prediction by comparing its performance with that of DBN model on the same dataset. The evaluation criteria given in Sect. 3.4 will be used to measure prediction performance.

We will build DBN model based on the best hyper-parameters selected for the DBN prediction model reported in the previous work by Tri et al. [7]. In sum, the good DBN model consists of 4 hidden layers and 5 neurons per layer.

We will not compare the two deep neural network models with ANN since through experiment some previous works [7,9] pointed out that DBN model always outperforms ANN in runoff prediction.

The two comparative deep learning models were implemented in Python with open-source framework Keras [16]. The experiments on four time series datasets were conducted on the PC with CPU Intel(R) Core(TM) i7-8750H CPU @ 2.20 GHz, 16 GB RAM, NVIDIA GeFore GTX 1050Ti. To evaluate the performance of the models and their configurations, we used Cau14 dataset as the standard dataset. The dataset is divided into two parts, the first 10 years (3672 days) for training and the remaining year (328 days) for testing.

To assess the impact of sliding window size on the overall performance of the prediction model, we applied the manual trial-and-error strategy to find out which window size brings out the best performance [17]. For the parameter in the SAE model, the number of epochs was set to 1000 times for sufficient learning of the neural network. Three AE layers are used to extract features and for each AE layer, the corresponding number of nodes in the hidden layer is in turn set to 200, 400, 200. Finally, to consider the temporal continuity of the runoff on Srepok River, the sequence length was changed via eight cases: 2 days, 5 days, 7 days, 8 days, 14 days, 15 days, 20 days and 28 days to investigate the reproducibility of the prediction results according to the length change of the sliding window. Table 1 summarizes the evaluation results in varying the sliding window size m. The lowest error result of RMSE is 45,401 ($m = 7$) and MAPE is 13,897 ($m = 14$). The highest correlation R is 0.9771 ($m = 5$, $m = 7$).

Table 1. Experimental results of SAE model in varying sliding window size.

	Size of sliding window	RMSE	R	MAPE
1	2	48.345	0.9760	14.932
2	5	52.993	**0.9771**	16.208
3	7	**45.401**	0.9771	**14.039**
4	8	49.467	0.9766	15.417
5	14	47.525	0.9763	13.897
6	15	50.060	0.9753	15.600
7	20	50.347	0.9756	14.549
8	28	55.711	0.9732	17.232

We found out that the best case for the length of sliding window is $m = 7$. From the analysis on Table 1, the larger sliding window size has an effect on the prediction performance of the model but it does not mean that the larger the window slide, the higher the prediction performance.

In addition to the effect of sliding window size on prediction, selecting the network size also affects to the predictive performance greatly. This is a typical problem for all neural network design. Tables 2, 3 and 4 show the results of changing the number of hidden nodes per layer and the number of AEs for predictions. Table 2 shows the results of varying the number of hidden nodes per layer when sliding windows with a length of 7 and three AEs are used in this experiment. From Table 2 we can discover the best results in terms of RMSE, R, MAPE measures. In this experiment two sets of values (200, 400, 200) and (200, 600, 200) are the optimal choices. Therefore, we will pick (200, 400, 200) for the number of hidden nodes per layer in our SAE model.

Tables 3 and 4 show the analysis results when changing the number of AEs, we find that the number of AEs has an impact on the prediction performance and the large number of AEs does not mean that the prediction performance

Table 2. Experimental results in varying the number of nodes in one layer of SAE model (Cau14 dataset).

	Nodes on one layer	RMSE	R	MAPE
1	200, 200, 200	54.289	0.9765	16.383
2	400, 400, 400	46.052	0.9766	13.863
3	400, 200, 400	46.158	0.9760	13.954
4	200, 600, 200	46.036	0.9761	**13.634**
5	200, 400, 200	**45.401**	**0.9769**	14.039

will be high. We select the number of AEs and the number of hidden nodes per layer to give the best predictive performance. From Table 3, with the number of hidden nodes per layer of 400, the best ratings are RMSE = 45,789 (Number of AE layers = 2), R = 0.9766 (Number of AE layers = 3), MAPE = 13.863% (Number of AE layers = 3). From Table 4 with a number of hidden nodes per layer of 200, the best indicators are RMSE = 47.454 (Number of AE layers = 2), R = 0.9766 (Number of AE layers = 4), MAPE = 14,390% (Number of AE layers = 4).

Table 3. Performance results in varying the number of AE layers (each AE layer has 400 nodes per layer) in SAE model.

	Number of AE layers	RMSE	R	MAPE
1	2	**45.789**	0.9761	13.916
2	3	46.052	**0.9766**	**13.863**
3	4	53.078	0.9718	16.625

Table 4. Performance results in varying the number of AE layers (each AE layer has 200 nodes per layer) of SAE model.

	Number of AE layers	RMSE	R	MAPE
1	2	**47.454**	0.9756	14.956
2	3	57.271	0.9763	16.825
3	4	48.471	**0.9766**	**14.390**

To evaluate the prediction performance of the SAE model in river runoff prediction, the Deep Belief Network model as in [7] is built as a comparative model. For SAE model, the number of input nodes is also determined by the experiment results given in Table 1 which shows that the best value for this

Table 5. Comparison of the performance results for two different models on the three datasets with sliding window size 2 (for DBN), 7 (for SAE)

Input	Model	RMSE	R	MAPE
Cau14	DBN	52.783	0.9711	14.236
	SAE	**45.401**	**0.9770**	**14.040**
BuonHo	DBN	**94.158**	**0.9266**	19.861
	SAE	99.536	0.9241	**19.835**
DucXuyen	DBN	**54.303**	0.8495	86.138
	SAE	55.798	**0.8695**	**83.483**

parameter is 7. From the experimental results in Tables 3 and 4, the number of AE layers is set to three, and the number of hidden nodes per layer used in SAE model is (200, 400, and 200). Besides, we reuse a selected model for SAE which is based on Cau14 dataset to experiment the runoff prediction on the two datasets at DucXuyen and BuonHo measurement station. To train the SAE model, we applied back-propagation algorithm. To train the DBN model, we apply Contrastive Divergence (CD-k) algorithm in pre-training stage and back-propagation algorithm in fine-tuning stage.

As shown in Table 5, on the Cau14 dataset, the SAE model outperforms DBN model in all three RMSE, R, MAPE evaluation measures. Furthermore, on the DucXuyen and BuonHo datasets, SAE model is also slightly better. These results prove that the ability of feature extraction in predicting the future runoff value of the SAE model is more powerful than DBN.

To study the relation between the observed and predicted data, the scatter plots are generated with line plot in Fig. 7 and Fig. 8. From the visualization results in Fig. 7a, DBN captures all the change over time of the runoff river, but there are also some small amounts of predicted values to move down, it means that the predicted value is smaller than the observed value. Looking at the Fig. 7a, we see that the points with predictive value move down, they are far from the ideal fit (Fig. 7b). Comparing the Fig. 7a with Fig. 8a, we see that the predicted results of the SAE model are closer to the observed data and compared to the forecast points that have the downward movement of the DBN model, it improves better. So they are closer to the ideal fit (Fig. 8b).

Table 6. Comparison of the training time and testing time (in seconds) of the two models on Cau14 dataset

Times	SAE	DBN
Training	**520.499**	585.914
Testing	**0.0589**	0.134

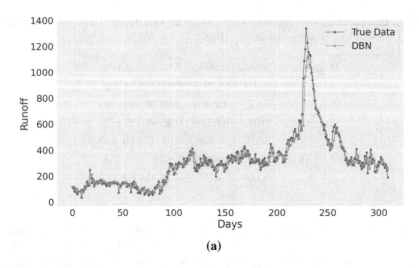

(a)

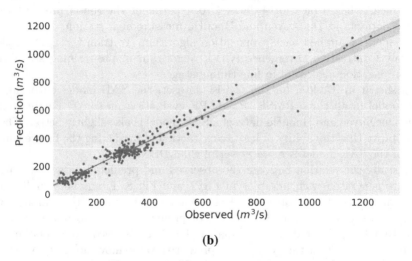

(b)

Fig. 7. (a) Observed (blue) and predicted (red) runoff by DBN in the testing phase. (b) The degree correlation between observed and predicted runoff by DBN in the testing phase. (Color figure online)

We also measured the training times and testing times of the two deep learning forecasting models on the runoff dataset at the Cau14 station and report the results (in seconds) in Table 6. The results in Table 6 indicate that the training/testing time of SAE is slightly shorter than that of DBN.

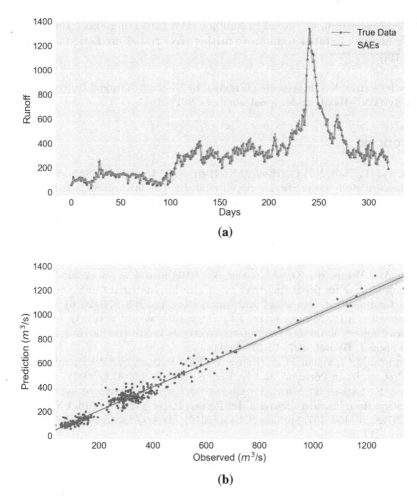

Fig. 8. (a) Observed (blue) and predicted (red) runoff by SAE in the testing phase. (b) The degree correlation between observed and predicted runoff by SAE in the testing phase. (Color figure online)

5   Conclusion and Future Work

River runoff prediction is a challenging forecasting problem. In this paper, we compare the two deep neural network models (SAE and DBN) in river runoff prediction in terms of prediction accuracy. The experimental results show that, SAE brings out better prediction accuracy than DBN on three runoff datasets from Srepok river in Highlands of Vietnam. The results of this work confirm that stacked autoencoder is a promising deep learning approach for runoff time series forecasting. Stacked autoencoder shows the power of feature extraction and gets high accuracy when predicting. Besides, the impact of size of window slides and the architecture of SAE model were also taken into account.

In future research, we intend to combine SAE with Long Short Term Memory (LSTM) network in order to improve further river runoff prediction as suggested in ([18,19]).

Acknowledgement. This research is funded by Vietnam National University Ho Chi Minh City (VNU-HCM) under grant number C2019-20-17.

References

1. Thi, T.T.T., Ngo, N.H.G., Hieu, D.N., Hien, N.T., Hoai, T.V., Nghi, V.V.: A comprehensive study on predicting river runoff. In: The 9th International Conference on Knowledge and Systems Engineering (KSE), Hue, pp. 251–256 (2017)
2. Ngoc Duong, H., Nguyen, Q.N.T., Ta Bui, L., Nguyen, H.T., Snášel, V.: Applying recurrent fuzzy neural network to predict the runoff of Srepok river. In: Saeed, K., Snášel, V. (eds.) CISIM 2014. LNCS, vol. 8838, pp. 55–66. Springer, Heidelberg (2014). https://doi.org/10.1007/978-3-662-45237-0_7
3. Guo, W., Wang, H., Xu, J., Zhang, Y.: RBF neural net-work model based on improved PSO for predicting river runoff. In: International Conference on Intelligent Computation Technology and Automation, pp. 968–971 (2010)
4. Piotrowski, A.P., Napiorkowski, J.J.: Optimizing neural networks for river flow forecasting - evolutionary computation methods versus the Levenberg-Marquardt approach. J. Hydrol. **407**, 12–27 (2011)
5. Demirela, M.C., Venancio, A., Kahya, E.: Flow forecast by SWAT model and ANN in Pracana basin Portugal. J. Adv. Eng. Softw. **40**, 467–473 (2009)
6. Gope, S., Sarkar, S., Mitra, P., Ghosh, S.: Early prediction of extreme rainfall events: a deep learning approach. In: Perner, P. (ed.) ICDM 2016. LNCS (LNAI), vol. 9728, pp. 154–167. Springer, Cham (2016). https://doi.org/10.1007/978-3-319-41561-1_12
7. Tri N. C., Hieu D.N., Hoai, T. V., and Snasel, V.: Predicting daily river runoff by deep belief networks. In: International Conference on Information and Convergence Technology for Smart Society, 19–21 January 2016 in Ho Chi Minh, Vietnam (2016)
8. Hernández, E., Sanchez-Anguix, V., Julian, V., Palanca, J., Duque, N.: Rainfall prediction: a deep learning approach. In: Martínez-Álvarez, F., Troncoso, A., Quintián, H., Corchado, E. (eds.) HAIS 2016. LNCS (LNAI), vol. 9648, pp. 151–162. Springer, Cham (2016). https://doi.org/10.1007/978-3-319-32034-2_13
9. Li, C., Bai, Y., Zeng, B.: Deep learning architecture for daily reservoir inflow forecasting. Water Resour. Manage. **30**, 5145–5161 (2016)
10. Kratzert, F., Klotz, D., Brenner, C., Schulz, K., Herrnegger, M.: Rainfall-runoff modeling using long short-term memory (LSTM) networks. Hydrol. Earth Syst. Sci. **22**, 6005–6022 (2018)
11. Lee, D.E., Lee, G., Kim, S., Jung, S.: Future runoff analysis in the Mekong river basin under a climate change scenario using deep learning. Water **12**, 1556 (2020)
12. Hinton, G.E., Osindero, S., The, Y.W.: A fast learning algorithm for deep belief nets. Neural Comput. **18**, 1527–1554 (2006)
13. Bengio, Y.: Learning deep architectures for AI". Found. Trends Mach. Learn. **2**(1), 1–127 (2009)
14. Katuwal, R., Suganthan, P.N.: Stacked autoencoder based deep random vector functional link neural network for classification. Appl. Soft Comput. **85**, 105854 (2019)

15. Wikipedia. https://vi.wikipedia.org/wiki/SôngSêrêpok. Accessed 10 July 2020
16. Cholett, F., Keras. http://keras.io. Accessed June 2020
17. Azlan, A., Yusof, Y., Mohamad, M., Mohamad, F.: Determining the impact of window length on time series forecasting using deep learning. Int. J. Adv. Comput. Res. **9**, 260–267 (2019)
18. Li, Z., Peng, F., Niu, B., Li, G., Wu, J., Miao, Z.: Water quality prediction model combining sparce auto-encoder and LSTM network. IFAC PapersOnLine **51–17**, 831–836 (2018)
19. Jaseena, K.U., Kovoor, B.C.: A hybrid wind speed forecasting model using stacked autoencoder and LSTM. J. Renew. Substain. Energy **12**, 023302 (2020)
20. Sam, T.T., et al.: Impact of climate change on meteorological, hydrological, and agricultural droughts in the Lower Mekong River Basin: a case study of the Srepok Basin Vietnam. Water Environ. J. (2018). https://doi.org/10.1111/wej.12424

Developing Data Model Managing Residents by Space and Time in Three-Dimensional Geographic Space

Dang Van Pham$^{(\boxtimes)}$ (iD)

Faculty of Information Technology, Nguyen Tat Thanh University,
Ho Chi Minh City, Vietnam
pvdang@ntt.edu.vn, pvdang.tps@gmail.com

Abstract. A major challenge currently of levels of government and construction contractors is how to manage population growth by geographic location and over time. The population increases by geographic location and over time leading to the increase of positive and negative aspects in the community. Managing people living and working on the territory by space and time is a very important and urgent job. The levels of government must regularly manage the people living and working on their localities, which are always associated with the management of permanent populations, temporary populations, blood relations, social relations, previous conviction relations, previous offence relations and birth or death relations that all of this management takes place at a specific geographic location and time. The paper proposes to develop a spatial - temporal - residential data model that is capable of managing human activities at the place of residence, at the workplace and at the location of the relations by geographic location and over time, this model is called STRDM. The paper illustrates empirical results with visual forms through the use of queries by space, time, resident, and search for ancestor and descendant. These empirical results show that it can be applied to residential data management systems in new urban areas.

Keywords: Relations · Spatial - temporal - residential data model · STRDM · Queries · Geographic location · Managing residents

1 Introduction

The increase in population by geographic location will always lead to a society with a strong development in both quality and quantity, in addition to the positive and negative issues in the community lead to archives which store of paper and books increasingly expanding. With large archives, extracting information is extremely difficult because it is difficult to properly and sufficiently extract it. Leaders at all levels and construction contractors can spend a lot of time making excerpts in the archives and not extracting enough material to link to the events, human with events, human with constraints of relations such as blood relations, social relations, previous conviction relations, previous offence relations, birth or death relations and also interested in basic human information that always changes over time. This difficulty has limited

© ICST Institute for Computer Sciences, Social Informatics and Telecommunications Engineering 2021
Published by Springer Nature Switzerland AG 2021. All Rights Reserved
P. C. Vinh and A. Rakib (Eds.): ICCASA 2020/ICTCC 2020, LNICST 343, pp. 82–102, 2021.
https://doi.org/10.1007/978-3-030-67101-3_7

the provision of data, provision of the necessary information for levels of government, for different careers to harness the full potential of human to devise to set forth development policies, also social security policies which appropriate to demands and capabilities of human.

Recognizing the importance and necessity of managing the population according to geographical location and time is to manage the people living and working in the territory and require necessary computerizing the task of residential management, human management to provide timely to the levels of government making decisions and timely supporting information for the task of security protection, ensure social order and safety in the territory. Therefore, we need to focus on building three-dimensional (3D) GIS systems for residential data management, to build this system to adapt to all criteria then the modeling of data models is extremely important and urgent to serve the levels of government or construction contractors in tracing the history of blood relations, the history of social relations, history of previous conviction relations, history of previous offence relations, and history of birth or death relations.

In a blood relation, a person born into a family, also known as a clan, must have an ancestor of grandparents, parents, siblings, etc., called a blood relation. In a social relation, a certain person A and other members participate in a meeting, a seminar, a teach-in, etc., it is called a social relation. With a law relation, person A is a superior of person B, person B is a superior of person C, so person C is a subordinate of person A is called a law relation. In a previous offence relation, a person is referred to as a previous offence relation only when he/she has committed a violation of the law at the warning level, is subject to administrative sanctions, is not convicted by a court and is under the supervision of law. With a previous conviction relation, a person is called a previous conviction relation when he/she commits an offense and is convicted by a court. With a birth or death relation, every person born at birth must be confirmed as a member of a certain household and recorded in that household registration, and a person who dies will be declared dead and deleted in the household [1]. The above-mentioned relationships all took place at the location of defined geographical space and time.

The objective of the paper proposes to develop a STRDM model to manage relations and genealogy by geographic location and over time. This new model is capable of managing human activities at the place of residence, at the workplace and at the location of spatial and temporal relationships. This management will help the levels of government and construction contractors can trace the history of blood relations, the history of social relations, history of previous conviction relations, history of previous offence relations, and history of birth or death relations. The paper presents some experimental results using visual forms through some typical queries. Experimental results show that this new model can be applied to future residential data management systems to assist levels of government and construction contractors in policy making and decision making.

The remainder of this paper will be organized as follows. Part 2 presents an overview of the relevant studies and makes new comments and suggestions. Part 3 presents in detail the spatial, temporal and residential classes from which to propose the spatial, temporal and residential data model and includes some empirical results on the proposed model. Part 4 presents the experimental results on the proposed model using visual forms through a number of queries and search for genealogy. Part 5 presents the results and proposes future development directions. The last part of this paper is for reference.

2 Related Works

The construction of spatial, temporal, semantic and residential data models play an important role in new urban area management systems, especially, data models must participate in the residential data management systems in space, time, and relationships of human with human by events. The paper systemizes spatial and temporal data models according to each type of model.

2.1 The Data Models Based on the Boundary Representation Method

For good representation of 3D objects with boundaries, the boundary representation method (B-REP) is a good choice. This method represents a 3D object based on predefined elements, includes point, line, surface, solid and this method is suitable for representing 3D objects of normal shape. The models proposed by the authors in the past that have applied the B-REP method, include UDM spatial data model was proposed by Coors in 2003 [2]; 3D Cadastral model was proposed by Yuan Ding authors and colleagues in 2017 [3]; TUDM model was proposed by Anh N.G.T authors and colleagues in 2012 [4]; TLODs model was proposed by Dang P.V authors group and his colleagues [5]; VRO-DLOD3D model was proposed by Dang P.V authors and colleagues in 2017 [1]; CityGML model was proposed by Groger authors and colleagues in 2007 [6]; Kolbe authors and colleagues extended the CityGML model in 2009 [7]; Biljecki authors and colleagues improved the CityGML model in 2016 [8]; Dang P.V authors and colleagues proposed the ELUDM for 2.5D objects in 2011 [9]; Dang P.V authors and colleagues proposed the ELUDM for 2.5-3D objects in 2011 [10]; Löwner authors and colleagues proposed a new LoD concept and multi-representational concept for the CityGML model in 2016 [11]; Digital surface model proposed by Abdelkader El Garouani authors and colleagues in 2014 [12]; CityGML-TRKBIS.BI model proposed by Aydar authors and colleagues to meet the need to establish 2-2.5-3D objects at the national level in 2016 [13]; S_EUDM model was proposed by T.V. Phan authors and colleagues in 2020 [14].

2.2 The Data Models Based on Voxel Elements

To represent 3D objects with voxel elements such as pixels in 2D GIS, the voxel method is a good choice. This method represents a 3D object based on the idea of dividing an object into child elements, each of which is called a voxel [15]. An element is considered a geographic space and is assigned an integer [16]. Models proposed by authors in the past applied the voxel method include, 3D Array model proposed by Rahman in 2005 [17, 18]. Models have simple data structures used to represent 3D objects. The elements in the 3D Array have 1 of 2 values 0, 1. In which 0 describes the background value, 1 describes the value that each element in the 3D Array is occupied by the 3D object. If a 3D object is scanned in a 3D array, the elements of array are initialized to 0. After scanning onto the 3D object, the elements with value 1 represent the information for the 3D object. The Octree model was proposed by Gorger authors and colleagues in 2004 [19]. Octree is an extension of a tetrahedron to octal. Octree is a 3D representation model based on block basis. An octal tree gives us an image, which is a method of representing a tree data structure. In general, an octal tree is defined based on the smallest cube containing the 3D object to represent. The original cube will be divided into 8 sub-cubes. An octal tree is based on recursive decomposition.

2.3   The Data Models Based on the 3D Block Composite Method

To represent 3D objects by combining basic 3D blocks proposed by Rahman in 2008 [17]. CSG model represents a 3D object by combining predefined 3D elements. The basic 3D blocks are commonly used as: cube, cylinder, sphere. Relationships between these figures include: transformation and logical operands. Transformations include translations, rotations, and metrics. Logical operands include association, intersection, and difference. CSG is often used in CAD. CSG is very convenient in calculating the volume of objects, CSG is not suitable for representing objects with irregular geometric shapes.

2.4   Comments and Recommendations for the Data Model

To represent spatial features including residential houses, buildings, villas, apartments, etc. in a 3D space, applying modeling is the key to success. The criteria to consider models are the models must be able to represent spatial objects in 3D space, and must be based on the criteria of the outer surface, the inner surface, represents levels of detail but also has the ability to store spatial data, store temporal data, store semantic data, and store residential data. In 2013, Gia T.A.N. authors and colleagues presented a summary of GIS 3D and 4D data models [20], in which this group of authors proposed a summary presentation of the criteria that each GIS 3D and 4D data model must satisfy. These criteria include: representation of surface of objects, representation of inner surface of objects, representation of main elements, representation of data size, applying for applications, spatial data structure, spatial property queries, zero object location queries, semantic queries. Then in 2017, this same group of authors gave a brief survey of the current popular GIS 3D and 4D data models [21] with comparison tables according to characteristic criteria such as representation of face types, representation inner face of objects, capable of triangularization, not capable of triangularization, platform model, data storage size, and applicability to today's applications.

Through systematization and classification of data models has given us a clear view of the development of data models proposed by the authors. We found that these models mainly use B-REP method. This method represents a 3D object based on predefined elements, including: Point, Line, Surface, Solid, Prism, Body and this method is suitable for representing 3D objects of normal shape. From here, the paper proposes to build a STRDM model to manage population data including relationship management, permanent populations, temporary populations, and search for ancestors and descendants.

3 Spatial-Temporal-Residential Data Model Managing Residents

3.1 Temporal Data Class

Time data is an essential element of residential data management systems in 3D geographical space. Time data recorded the start and end times of relationships and basic information about human change. The temporal data class plays an important role in tracing the evolution of human relationships according to geographical location. Based on the factor of time, human can intervene in time to solve urgent problems and see things more precisely and clearly. The element of time can represent the processes taking place in human relationships such as social relations, law relations, previous conviction relations, previous offence relations and birth or death relations attached the geographical location in which takes place human relationships, places of residence, work locations and other basic information of human always change at a point of time or in a period of time.

Time data combined with spatial data and residential data will make the data stored in residential data management systems more abundant and meaningful to meet the needs of users, especially at levels of government and construction contractors. The time data used to trace the history of the beginning and ending of relationships and other information about human activities has become more explicit. Accompanying with three specific types of time data [5, 22, 23] having time data units in Table 3 with the conventions in Table 2. From the time data units in Table 2, the paper classified these time data units into three types of time data in Table 1 and obtained a classification table in Table 3. From the time data units in Table 2, the paper forms the time topology relations in Table 4.

Table 1. Table describing the time data types

Convention	Time data types	Describing the time data types
ET_s	Event time	The time that begins and ended in the real world, the starting yy-mm-dd h:m:s and ending yy-mm-dd h:m:s in real world
LT_s	Legal time	The time that is effective on legal documents, the starting yy-mm-dd h:m:s and ending yy-mm-dd h:m:s in legal documents
DT_s	Database time	The time that is written to the database, the starting yy-mm-dd h:m:s and ending yy-mm-dd h:m:s in the database

Notation: year-month-date hour:minute:second = yy-mm-dd h:m:s

Table 2. Table describing the meaning of time data units

Convention	Describing the meaning of time data units
T_{10}	The starting yy-mm-dd h:m:s took place of the human social relationship in the real world
T_{11}	The ending yy-mm-dd h:m:s took place of the human social relationship in the real world
T_{12}	The starting yy-mm-dd h:m:s took place human law relations in the real world
T_{13}	The ending yy-mm-dd h:m:s took place law relations of human in the real world
T_{14}	The starting yy-mm-dd h:m:s took place previous offence relations of human in the real world
T_{15}	The ending yy-mm-dd h:m:s took place previous conviction relations of human in the real world
T_{16}	The starting yy-mm-dd h:m:s took place previous conviction relations of human in the real world
T_{17}	The ending yy-mm-dd h:m:s took place previous offence relations of human in the real world
T_{18}	The yy-mm-dd h:m:s of human birth in the real world
T_{19}	The yy-mm-dd h:m:s of human death in the real world
T_{20}	The starting yy-mm-dd h:m:s recorded social relations of human in the legal documents
T_{21}	The ending yy-mm-dd h:m:s recorded social relations of human in the legal documents
T_{22}	The starting yy-mm-dd h:m:s recorded law relations of human in the legal documents
T_{23}	The ending yy-mm-dd h:m:s recorded law relations of human in the legal documents
T_{24}	The starting yy-mm-dd h:m:s recorded previous conviction relations of human in the legal documents
T_{25}	The ending yy-mm-dd h:m:s recorded previous conviction relations of human in the legal documents
T_{26}	The starting yy-mm-dd h:m:s recorded previous offence relations of human in the legal documents
T_{27}	The ending yy-mm-dd h:m:s recorded previous offence relations of human in the legal documents
T_{28}	The yy-mm-dd h:m:s of human birth recorded in the legal documents
T_{29}	The yy-mm-dd h:m:s of human death recorded in the legal documents
T_{30}	The starting yy-mm-dd h:m:s recorded social relations of human in the database
T_{31}	The ending yy-mm-dd h:m:s recorded social relations of human in the database
T_{32}	The starting yy-mm-dd h:m:s recorded law relations of human in the database
T_{33}	The ending yy-mm-dd h:m:s recorded law relations of human in the database
T_{34}	The starting yy-mm-dd h:m:s recorded previous conviction relations of human in the database

(continued)

Table 2. (*continued*)

Convention	Describing the meaning of time data units
T_{35}	The ending yy-mm-dd h:m:s recorded previous conviction relations of human in the database
T_{36}	The starting yy-mm-dd h:m:s recorded previous offence relations of human in the database
T_{37}	The ending yy-mm-dd h:m:s recorded previous offence relations of human in the database
T_{38}	The yy-mm-dd h:m:s of human birth recorded in the database
T_{39}	The yy-mm-dd h:m:s of human death recorded in the database
T_{40}	The starting yy-mm-dd h:m:s moving to the permanent population of humans recorded in the legal documents
T_{41}	The starting yy-mm-dd h:m:s registering the permanent population recorded in the legal documents
T_{42}	The starting yy-mm-dd h:m:s deleting the permanent population recorded in the legal documents
T_{43}	The starting yy-mm-dd h:m:s correcting the permanent population recorded in the legal documents
T_{44}	The starting yy-mm-dd h:m:s moving to the temporary population of humans recorded in the legal documents
T_{45}	The starting yy-mm-dd h:m:s registering the temporary population of humans recorded in the legal documents
T_{46}	The starting yy-mm-dd h:m:s deleting register of the temporary population of humans recorded in the legal documents
T_{47}	The starting yy-mm-dd h:m:s correcting the temporary population of humans recorded in the legal documents
T_{50}	The starting yy-mm-dd h:m:s addicting to drugs of human recorded in the legal documents
T_{51}	The ending yy-mm-dd h:m:s addicting to drugs of human recorded in the legal documents
T_{52}	The starting yy-mm-dd h:m:s relapsing into drugs of human recorded in the legal documents
T_{53}	The starting yy-mm-dd h:m:s registering marriage of human recorded in the legal documents
T_{54}	The ending yy-mm-dd h:m:s registering marriage of human recorded in the legal documents
T_{55}	The starting yy-mm-dd h:m:s remarrying of human recorded in the legal documents
T_{56}	The starting yy-mm-dd h:m:s changing full name of human recorded in the legal documents
T_{57}	The starting yy-mm-dd h:m:s changing year birth of human recorded in the legal documents
T_{73}	The starting yy-mm-dd h:m:s moving to the permanent population of human recorded in the database

(*continued*)

Table 2. (*continued*)

Convention	Describing the meaning of time data units
T_{74}	The starting yy-mm-dd h:m:s registering the permanent population of human recorded in the database
T_{75}	The starting yy-mm-dd h:m:s deleting register of the permanent population of human recorded in the database
T_{76}	The starting yy-mm-dd h:m:s correcting the permanent population of human recorded in the database
T_{77}	The starting yy-mm-dd h:m:s moving to the temporary population of human recorded in the database

Notation: year-month-date hour:minute:second = yy-mm-dd h:m:s

Table 3. The table classifies units of time data into three types of time data

Time data types	Describing time data units belonging to three types of time data
ET_s	T_{10}, T_{11}, T_{12}, T_{13}, T_{14}, T_{15}, T_{16}, T_{17}, T_{18}, T_{19}
LT_s	T_{20}, T_{21}, T_{22}, T_{23}, T_{24}, T_{25}, T_{26}, T_{27}, T_{28}, T_{29}, T_{40}, T_{41}, T_{42}, T_{43}, T_{44}, T_{45}, T_{46}, T_{47}, T_{50}, T_{51}, T_{52}, T_{53}, T_{54}, T_{55}, T_{56}, T_{57}
DT_s	T_{30}, T_{31}, T_{32}, T_{33}, T_{34}, T_{35}, T_{36}, T_{37}, T_{38}, T_{39}, T_{73}, T_{74}, T_{75}, T_{76}, T_{77}

Table 4. Table describing the topology relationship of time data units

Relationships	Meaning	Relationships	Meaning
$T_{10} < T_{11}$	T_{10} happen earlier T_{11}	$T_{73} < T_{74}$	T_{73} happen earlier T_{74}
$T_{12} < T_{13}$	T_{12} happen earlier T_{13}	$T_{75} < T_{76}$	T_{76} happen later T_{75}
$T_{14} < T_{15}$	T_{14} happen earlier T_{15}	$T_{76} < T_{74}$	T_{76} happen earlier T_{74}
$T_{16} < T_{17}$	T_{16} happen earlier T_{17}	$T_{42} < T_{40}$	T_{42} happen earlier T_{40}
$T_{18} < T_{19}$	T_{18} happen earlier T_{19}	$T_{42} < T_{43}$	T_{43} happen later T_{42}
$T_{22} < T_{23}$	T_{22} happen earlier T_{23}	$T_{43} < T_{41}$	T_{43} happen earlier T_{41}
$T_{26} < T_{27}$	T_{26} happen earlier T_{27}	$T_{44} < T_{45}$	T_{44} happen earlier T_{45}
$T_{28} < T_{29}$	T_{28} happen earlier T_{29}	$T_{45} < T_{46}$	T_{45} happen before T_{46}
$T_{30} < T_{31}$	T_{30} happen earlier T_{31}	$T_{46} > T_{47}$	T_{46} happen later T_{47}
$T_{32} < T_{33}$	T_{32} happen earlier T_{33}	$T_{50} < T_{51}$	T_{50} happen earlier T_{51}
$T_{34} < T_{35}$	T_{34} happen earlier T_{35}	$T_{53} < T_{54}$	T_{53} happen earlier T_{54}
$T_{36} < T_{37}$	T_{36} happen earlier T_{37}	$T_{40} = T_{41}$	T_{40} happen coincidentally T_{41}
$T_{38} < T_{39}$	T_{38} happen earlier T_{39}	$T_{44} = T_{45}$	T_{44} happen coincidentally T_{45}
$T_{40} < T_{41}$	T_{40} happen earlier T_{41}	$T_{73} = T_{74}$	T_{73} happen coincidentally T_{74}
$T_{41} < T_{56}$	T_{41} happen earlier T_{56}	$T_{77} = T_{76}$	T_{77} happen coincidentally T_{76}

3.2   Residential Data Class

Residential data records relationships, permanent populations, temporary populations, stay populations, and other basic human information. Therefore, the residential class plays a very important role in organizing the storage classes of residential data. The residential data class was built to answer questions related to human activities at the place of residence, at the workplace, at the place of living and at the place of happening social relations, previous conviction relations, previous offence relations, birth or death relations. Levels of government or construction contractors often focus on questions related to human activities including spatial - temporal - residential location. Thus, this residential data class must be capable of answering the user's questions as follows. To answer question for what is that relationship? Which people or groups of people were involved in that relationship accompanied by the spatial location of the relationship at what time? To answer the question for what time it took place - who involved - what that relationship was - the spatial location of that activity. Also, from this residential data class can answer questions for the blood relationship or called the person's genealogy relationship (Figs. 1 and 2).

Fig. 1. A relationship representation consists of people - spatial - temporal – residential relation

Fig. 2. A relationship representation of space – people - time

3.3   Spatial Data Class

Spatial data records the shapes, sizes, and locations of objects in space. The spatial data class does an important task in residential data management systems. Spatial data class is used to manage the position, shape, and size of houses, buildings, bridges, and apartments, etc. but in houses, buildings, apartments, and villas is the place where human relationships usually take place at the living position, the working position and the position of taking place relationships. Nowadays, spatial position places spatial objects that are understood by humans in two aspects. Aspect 1, the coordinates of the spatial objects located in the 3D domain. Aspect 2, addresses are attached to spatial objects including houses, buildings, apartments, bridges, etc.

To store spatial data including spatial coordinates and interpretation semantics for spatial objects. The spatial object is a bridge, house, building, apartment, villa, etc. So, the spatial data class is built on top of the five base objects that are Point, Line, Surface, Body, Prism and two element objects, Node and Face [2]. In which, each Face is defined by three Nodes, each Surface is defined by four Nodes, each Body is defined by four Nodes and one height, each Prism is also defined as four Nodes and a height [2, 5, 24]. From the five base objects Point, Line, Surface, Body, Prism help us to efficiently store spatial and semantic data and very suitable for application in the management of residential data in space and time because it supports the representation of faces and blocks based on triangulation.

The analysis and researches on the data models in the above sections of related studies are suitable for future urban management. Because models mainly manage 3D objects such as houses, apartments, apartment buildings, etc. but does not manage residential data, does not keep track of changing history of relationships and does not manage basic human information that changes over time and space and human genealogy. In residential data management, the levels of government or construction contractors are particularly interested in two properties, the spatial and the temporal property. Therefore, the incorporation of the spatial data class, the temporal data class into the management of the residential data class is extremely important and is an urgent job for levels of government and construction contractors.

3.4   Combining Spatial, Temporal and Residential Data Class to Build New Model

Regarding the management of residential data, information about residential data is collected and stored in the residential data class including properties such as full name, year of birth, place of birth, gender, origin, nationality, ethnicity, portrait, identity card, occupation, and relationship with head of household. Levels of government or construction contractors find that people include properties that do not change over time and also have properties that always change over time. Properties that don't change over time, like citizenship number, blood type, fingerprints, place of death, and DNA. Properties that change over time include full name, year of birth, place of birth, gender, origin, nationality, ethnicity, portrait, identity card, occupation, and relationship with head of household. To describe the full name changing over time, we use numeric properties, citizen identifier, full name, event time type, legal time type, and database time type. To describe the social relationship that changes over time, we use house code property, citizen identifier, social relationship, event time type, legal time type, and database time. To describe the change of previous conviction relation over time, we use house code properties, citizen identifier number, previous conviction relation, event time type, legal time type, and database time, court sanction, count, judgment handling and enforcement results.

Regarding the management of time data, to describe the time data types, we use the time data type code properties and the semantics of the time data type. To describe the time units, we use the properties of time data unit code, the time data type code, the name and the description. To describe the representations of year, month, day, hour, minute, and second for units of time data, we use the code properties representing the time data units, the code of the time data units is year, month, day, hour, minute and second. To describe time marks can be a point of time or a period of time, if the code representing the units of beginning time data is equal to the code representing the units of ending time data that is described as a point of time, but if the code representing the units of beginning time data is different from the code representing the units of ending time data that is described as a period of time.

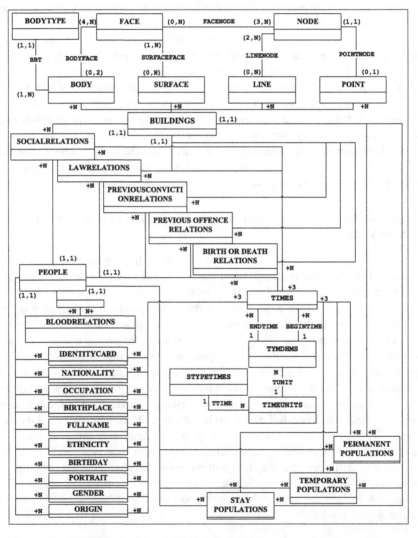

Fig. 3. The STRDM model manages the residential data in the 3D geographic space

Regarding spatial data, the spatial objects to be managed include buildings, apartments and villas, which are collectively called buildings for short. Buildings are where people live and work, and are also places where relationships take place. A building is a 3D master block constructed from various blocks that have or are defined as a set of bodies, which may contain more complex sub-shapes such as complex shape, prism shape, etc. In addition to these blocks, buildings can also contain other special geometrical objects such as lines, points, surfaces, etc. A building has many different levels of detail to be represented called 3D spatial detail levels in the 3D and 4D GIS [5, 8–11, 24].

Through the above analysis, the paper combines the spatial data class, the temporal data class and the residential data class to be a STRDM model (see Fig. 3). The new model is capable of storing and managing 3D spatial objects such as buildings, apartments, roads, houses, light lamps, bridges, relations, generations, and people over time and space. In addition, this data model also has the ability to query by time, to query by resident, to query space by time, to find ancestors and to find descendants, to trace the history of human relationships. Below, this is a summary of the relations for this data model and shows the size of a row (see Table 5).

Table 5. Decomposing the STRDM model into relations

No	Relations name	Bytes	No	Relations name	Bytes	No	Relations name	Bytes
01	Point	60	14	People	120	27	Origin	58
02	Line	70	15	Bloodrelation	110	28	Ethnicity	48
03	Surface	80	16	Buildingbody	48	29	Nationality	35
04	Body	100	17	Buildingsurface	48	30	Occupation	40
05	Bodytype	30	18	SRelations	80	31	Portrait	50
06	Face	30	19	LRelations	80	32	Identitycard	20
07	Node	34	20	PCRelations	80	33	PPopulations	90
08	Surfaceface	20	21	PORelations	80	34	TPopulations	90
09	Linenode	28	22	PDRelations	80	35	SPopulations	90
10	Facenode	28	23	Fullname	50	36	Times	90
11	Surfacenode	28	24	Birthday	40	37	Tymdhms	60
12	Facesurface	20	25	Birthplace	58	38	Timeunits	70
13	Buildings	180	26	Gender	48	39	Stypetimes	130
Total		**708**	**Total**		**922**		**Total**	**871**

3.5   Querying in Residential Data Management

Query 1: Finding and displaying the social relationship is "Meeting for dividing specialty for students of Faculty of Information Technology - Nguyen Tat Thanh University in June 2020" at the time "12/06/2020 09:00 AM" $\in T_{10}$ and is the starting ET_s, the information displayed includes: name of social relationship, space (buildings location and buildings shape), point of time, and composition of attendees.

Query 2: Finding and displaying the previous offence relation is "Illegal drug use" at the time "13/05/2020 11:55 AM" $\in T_{14}$ and is the starting ET_s, the information displayed includes: name of previous offence relation, space (buildings location and buildings shape), point of time, and composition of users.

Query 3: Finding and displaying the permanent populations of the householder is named "Dang Thi Van", the information displayed includes: space (house location and house shape), householder, populations along with the householder relationship.

Query 4: Finding and displaying the descendants of a person's lives have a citizen identification number "11" and named "Vinh" (see Fig. 4), the information displayed includes: descendants of a person's lives and generations (Table 6).

Query 5: Finding and displaying the ancestors of a person's lives have citizen identification number "53 or 51" and named "Khoi or Yen" (see Fig. 4), information displayed includes: ancestor of a person's lives and generations (Table 7).

Query 6: Finding and displaying the children of a person named "Nguyen", information displayed includes: parents and children.

Query 7: Finding and displaying father and mother of a person named "Khoi", the information displayed includes: parents and child.

Query 8: Finding and displaying the temporary populations in a house of the householder named "Tran Anh Minh", information is displayed including: space (including house location and house shape), householder, members along with the relationship with the householder.

Query 9: Finding and displaying where "Pham Thao Nguyen" was born, the information displayed includes: place of birth (house location and house shape) and full name.

Query 10: Finding and displaying where Pham Minh Ngo died, the information displayed includes: place of birth (house location and house shape) and full name.

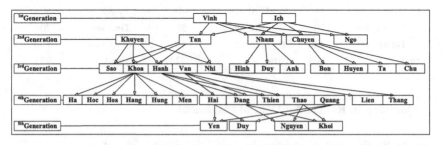

Fig. 4. Describing a family tree including ancestors and descendants of a lineage

Table 6. The table listing of generations by each generation of the person named "Vinh"

Input data	Output data *(Description the results found the descendants of a person named "Vinh")*	
"Vinh" *(In ^{1st} Generation)*	2nd Descendant (^{2nd} Generation)	Tan, Nham, Chuyen and Ngo
	3rd Descendant (^{3rd} Generation)	Sao, Khoa, Hanh, Nhi, Hinh, Duy, Anh, Bon, Huyen, Ta and Chu
	4th Descendant (^{4th} Generation)	Ha, Hoc, Hoa, Hang, Hung, Men, Hai, Dang, Thien, Lien and Thang
	5th Descendant (^{5th} Generation)	Yen, Duy, Nguyen and Khoi

Table 7. The table listing of generations by each generation of the person named "Khoi"

Input data	Output data *(Description the results found the ancestor of a person named "Khoi")*	
"Khoi" *(In ^{5th}Generation)*	4th Ancestor (^{4th} Generation)	Dang and Thao
	3rd Ancestor (^{3rd} Generation)	Hanh and Van
	2nd Ancestor (^{2nd} Generation)	Tan and Khuyen
	1st Ancestor (^{1st} Generation)	Vinh and Ich

3.6   Recursive Query Techniques in Residential Data Management

Input data	Recursive query	Output data	
Applying query 4: Citizen identification number: 11 of the person named "Vinh" (In ^{1st}Generation)	**Select** **Sys_Connect_By_Path** (Name, '- > ') **As** FamilyTree, **Lpad**(' ',6*level-1,'-')‖ Name Descendant, Level + 1 As Generation **From** Bloodrelations br, People p, tblName n **Where** br.Idchil = p. Idcin and p.Idcin = n.Idcin **Connect by** Idpar = **Prior** Idchil **Start With** Idpar = **'11'** **Order Siblings by** Name **Desc**;	2nd Descendant (^{2nd} Generation)	Tan, Nham, Chuyen, Ngo
		3rd Descendant (^{3rd} Generation)	Sao, Khoa, Hanh, Nhi, Hinh, Duy, Anh, Bon, Huyen, Ta, Chu
		4th Descendant (^{4th} Generation)	Ha, Hoc, Hoa, Hang, Hung, Men, Hai, Dang, Thien, Lien, Thang
		5th Descendant (^{5th} Generation)	Yen, Duy, Nguyen, Khoi

(continued)

(continued)

Input data	Recursive query	Output data	
Applying query 5: Citizen identification number: **53** of the person named **"Khoi"** (In [5th]Generation)	**Select Sys_Connect_By_Path** (Name, '- > ') **As** FamilyTree, **Lpad**(' ',2*level-1,'-')‖ Name as Ancestor, Level + 1 As Generation **From** Bloodrelations br, People p, tblName n **Where** br.Idpar = p.Idcin and p.Idcin = n.Idcin **Connect by Prior** Idpar = Idchil **Start with** Idchil = **'53'** **Order Siblings by** Name **Desc**;	[4th] Ancestor ([4th] Generation)	Dang and Thao
		[3rd] Ancestor ([3rd] Generation)	Hanh and Van
		[2nd] Ancestor ([2nd] Generation)	Tan and Khuyen
		[1st] Ancestor ([1st] Generation)	Vinh and Ich

4   Experiment

The paper has detailed the spatial data class, the temporal data class and the residential data class, then combine these three classes together to build a STRDM model. The paper uses Oracle database management system [25, 26] to install STRDM model, using Oracle's spatial data type to store spatial data. This spatial data type makes the time displaying spatial data of buildings in a 3D geospatial space faster and more intuitive. It is then combined with the C# programming language [5, 24, 27] to visually represent some forms with typical queries. The paper selects presenting five visual forms through five queries to find and display relationships, permanent population, and find ancestors and descendants. In each form the user must provide input and output parameters.

Form 1: Applying query 1 to find and display social relationships based on the name of relationship and point of time (see results in Fig. 5 and Fig. 6)

Input: The name of relationship is "Meeting for dividing specialty for students of Faculty of Information Technology - Nguyen Tat Thanh University in June 2020" at the time "12/06/2020 09:00 AM" $\in T_{10}$.

Output: The information displayed includes: name of social relationship - buildings space - time – attendees and ET_s.

Form 2: Applying query 2 to find and display previous offence relations based on the name of relationship and point of time (see results in Fig. 7).

Input: The name of previous offence relation is "Illegal drug use" at the time point "13/05/2020 11:55 AM" $\in T_{14}$.

Output: The information displayed includes: previous offence relation - space including buildings position and buildings shape – time – attendee and ET_s.

Form 3: Applying query 3 to find and display permanent populations based on citizen identification number and householder's name (see results in Fig. 8).

Input: Householder with identification number and full name "Dang Thi Van".

Output: The information displayed includes: relationship with householder - space including house position and house shape - people.

Form 4: Applying query 5 to find and display the ancestor of a person's lives having citizen identification number and full name (see results in Fig. 10 and Fig. 11).

Input: Citizen identification number "53 or 51" and first name "Khoi or Yen"

Output: Ancestor of person's lives named "Khoi" or "Yen"

Form 5: Applying query 4 to find and display the descendants of a person's lives having a citizen identification number "11" and first name (see results in Fig. 9).

Input: Citizen identification number "11" and first name "Vinh"

Output: The information displayed the descendants of a person named "Vinh".

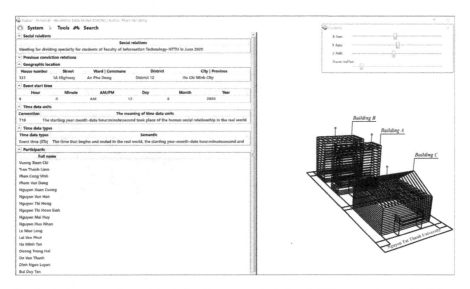

Fig. 5. An instance of a social relationship - space including buildings position and buildings shape - time – people (*view A*)

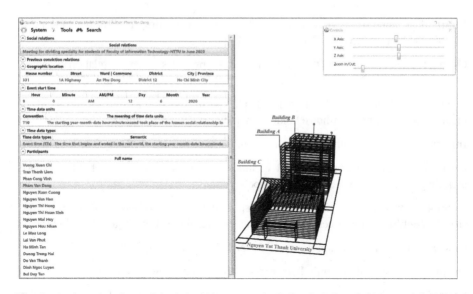

Fig. 6. An instance of a social relationship - space including buildings position and buildings shape - time – people (*view B*)

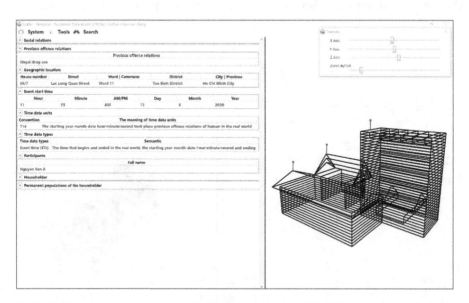

Fig. 7. An instance of a previous offence relation - space including buildings position and buildings shape - time – people

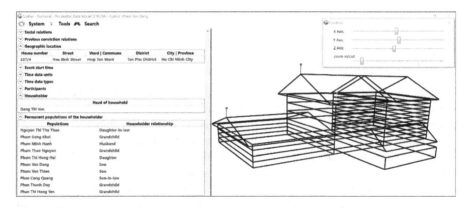

Fig. 8. An instance including relationship with householder - space including house position and house shape – people

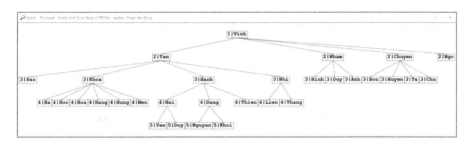

Fig. 9. An instance of descendants of a person named "Vinh"

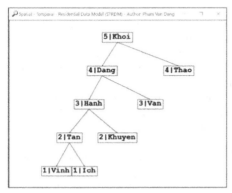

Fig. 10. An instance of ancestors of a person's lives named "Khoi"

Fig. 11. An instance of ancestors of a person's lives named "Yen"

5   Conclusion

The paper presented an overview of the spatial and temporal data models and then gave some comments and suggestions. The paper details the construction of the spatial data class, the temporal data class, and the residential data class, then combines these three classes into a STRDM model. This model showed its availability and opened up new directions in supporting the method of storing residential data over space and time. This model is not only capable of querying relationships, querying permanent and temporary populations, querying space and querying process change basic human information over time but also have the ability to find ancestors and descendants. The paper also illustrated some visual forms whose results are derived from the above queries, in these queries, there are instances of point of time, period of time and semantics of describing residential data. In addition, this model can also develop and expand the semantic inheritance classes for both the space and the residence and other classes such as colors, patterns, styles for spatial objects which are buildings in 3D geospatial space intending to serve other extended storage purposes without affecting the structure of this model.

References

1. Dang, P.V., Phuoc, T.V., Phuoc Tuyen, H.N.: Visual representation of geographic objects in 3D space at levels of different details. Presented at the FAIR - Fundamental and Applied Information Technology (2017)
2. Coors, V.: 3D-GIS in networking environments. Comput. Environ. Urban Syst. **27**, 345–357 (2003)
3. Ding, Y., Jiang, N., Yu, Z., Ma, B., Shi, G., Wu, C.: Extrusion approach based on non-overlapping footprints (EABNOF) for the construction of geometric models and topologies in 3D cadasters. ISPRS Int. J. Geo-Inf. **6**(8), 232 (2017)
4. Anh, N.G.T, Tran, V.P., Huynh, K.D.: A study on 4D GIS spatio-temporal data model. In: Proceedings of IEEE 4th Conference on Knowledge and Systems Engineering, Danang, Vietnam. IEEE Computer Society Order Number P4670 (2012)
5. Van Pham, D., Vinh Tran, P.: Visually analyzing evolution of geographic objects at different levels of details over time. In: Cong Vinh, P., Alagar, V. (eds.) ICCASA/ICTCC -2018. LNICSSITE, vol. 266, pp. 98–115. Springer, Cham (2019). https://doi.org/10.1007/978-3-030-06152-4_9
6. Gröger, G., Kolbe, T.H., Czerwinski, A., Nagel, C.: City Geography Markup Language (CityGML) Encoding Standard. Open Geospatial Consortium Inc. (2007)
7. Kolbe, T.H.: Representing and exchanging 3D city models with CityGML. In: Lee, J., Zlatanova, S. (eds.) 3D Geo-Information Sciences. Lecture Notes in Geoinformation and Cartography, pp. 15–31. Springer, Heidelberg (2009). https://doi.org/10.1007/978-3-540-87395-2_2
8. Biljecki, F., Ledoux, H., Stoter, J.: An improved LOD specification for 3D building models. Comput. Environ. Urban Syst. **59**, 25–37 (2016)

9. Van Pham, D., Tuan Anh, N.G., Vinh, P.T.: Levels of detail for surface in urban data model. In: International Conference on Future Information Technology – ICFIT, pp. 460–464 (2011)

10. Tuan Anh, N.G., Vinh, P.T., Vu, T.P., Van Pham, D., Sy, A.T.: Representing multiple levels for objects in three-dimensional GIS model. Presented at the 13th International Conference on Information Integration and Web-based Applications & Service (iiWAS 2011) (2011)

11. Löwner, M.O., Gröger, G., Benner, J., Biljecki, F., Nagel, C.: Proposal for a new LOD and multi-representation concept for CITYGML. ISPRS Ann. Photogramm. Remote Sens. Spat. Inf. Sci. **IV-2/W1**, 3–12 (2016)

12. El Garouani, A., Alobeid, A., El Garouani, S.: Digital surface model based on aerial image stereo pairs for 3D building. Int. J. Sustain. Built Environ. **3**(1), 119–126 (2014)

13. Ates Aydar, S., Stoter, J., Ledoux, H., Demir Ozbek, E., Yomralioglu, T.: Establishing a national 3D geo-data model for building data compliant to CITYGML: case of Turkey. ISPRS – Int. Arch. Photogramm. Remote Sens. Spat. Inf. Sci. **XLI-B2**, 79–86 (2016)

14. Phan, T.V., Anh Nguyen, G.T., Do Quoc, T.T.: Management of buildings with semantic and 3D spatial properties by S_EUDM data model. In: Reddy, J.N., Wang, C.M., Luong, V.H., Le, A.T. (eds.) ICSCEA 2019. LNCE, vol. 80, pp. 931–940. Springer, Singapore (2020). https://doi.org/10.1007/978-981-15-5144-4_89

15. Swanson, J.: The Three Dimensional Visualization and Analysis of Geographic Data, 24 March 2020. http://maps.unomaha.edu/Peterson/gis/Final_Projects/1996/Swanson/GIS_Paper.html

16. Lieberwirth, U.: 3D GIS voxel-based model building in archaeology. In: Proceedings of the 35th International Conference on Computer Applications and Quantitative Methods in Archaeology (CAA), Berlin (2007)

17. Abdul-Rahman, A., Pilouk, M.: Spatial Data Modelling for 3D GIS. Springer, Heidelberg (2008). https://doi.org/10.1007/978-3-540-74167-1

18. Rahman, A.A.: Developing Three-dimensional topological model for 3D GIS. Project Report, UTM (2005)

19. Gröger, M.R.G., Plümer, L.: Representation of a 3D city model in spatial object-relational databases. In: XXth ISPRS Congress, Geo-Imagery Bridging Continents, Commission 4 (2004)

20. Gia, T.A.N., Tran, P.V., Khac, D.H.: Overview of three and four-dimensional GIS data models. In: Park, J.J.(Jong Hyuk), Ng, J.K.-Y., Jeong, H.Y., Waluyo, B. (eds.) Multimedia and Ubiquitous Engineering. LNEE, vol. 240, pp. 1013–1020. Springer, Dordrecht (2013). https://doi.org/10.1007/978-94-007-6738-6_125

21. Nguyen Gia, T.A., Dao, M.S., Mai Van, C.: A comparative survey of 3D GIS models. Presented at the 2017 4th NAFOSTED Conference on Information and Computer Science (2017)

22. Andrienko, N., Andrienko, G.: Spatio-temporal visual analytics: a vision for 2020s. J. Spat. Inf. Sci. **20**, 87–95 (2020)

23. Peuquet, D.J.: It's about time: a conceptual framework for the representation of temporal dynamics in geographic information systems. Ann. Assoc. Am. Geogr. **84**(3), 441–461 (1994)

24. Van Pham, D., Phan, V.C.: Proposing storage structures and interpolation algorithms of 3D spatial data. In: Cong Vinh, P., Alagar, V. (eds.) ICCASA/ICTCC -2018. LNICSSITE, vol. 266, pp. 81–97. Springer, Cham (2019). https://doi.org/10.1007/978-3-030-06152-4_8

25. Greener, S.: SpatialDB Advisor: Elem_Info_Array Processing: An alternative to SDO_UTIL.GetNumRings and querying SDO_ELEM_INFO itself. http://www.spatialdbadvisor.com/oracle_spatial_tips_tricks/89/sdo_utilget_numrings-an-alternative. Accessed Dec 2019

26. Oracle Spatial User's Guide and Reference, Release 9, Part Number A88805-01, June 2001. https://docs.oracle.com/cd/A91202_01/901_doc/appdev.901/a88805/sdo_uglb.htm.   Accessed Jan 2020

27. Xuesong, W.: A Tool for Visualizing 3D Geometry Models (Part 1), 11 October 2009. https://www.codeproject.com/Articles/42992/A-Tool-for-Visualizing-3D-Geometry-Models-Part-1. Accessed Feb 2020

Trigger2B: A Tool Generating Event-B Models from Database Triggers

Hong Anh Le$^{(\boxtimes)}$

Hanoi University of Mining and Geology, 18 Pho Vien, Bac Tu Liem, Hanoi, Vietnam
lehonganh@humg.edu.vn

Abstract. Triggers are commonly used many traditional database applications that can be checked if they are correct after execution or manual inspection. Formal methods are techniques complementing to testing that ensure the correctness of software. In practical aspect, one limitation of formal techniques is the complexity that makes software developers lazy to use in the development. This paper introduces a tool named Trigger2B which partly supports for translating DML triggers to Event-B models. From the targeted model, we can verify the data constraints and detect infinite loops of trigger execution with RODIN. Finally, we take an example for illustration purpose. The proposed tool overcomes the complexity of formal modeling and makes them practical in the development.

Keywords: Trigger · Event-B · Formal modeling · Generation

1 Introduction

Database is one of the most important and essential aspects in software development. The relational database has shown preeminent advantages as simple structure, easy access, and high performance. Nowadays, relational database become the most widely used in many software and the number of Database Management Systems (DBMS) increase such as MySQL, PostgreSQL, SQLite, SQL server, Oracle, etc. DBMS are passive as they execute commands when applications or users perform appropriate queries. However, in many cases, we want DBMS perform some tasks, for example, we want to record login and logout of table users. For that reason, most of modern DBMS include these features as triggers (or active rules) that monitor and react to specific events happened in and outside the system. They also use triggers to implement automatic tasks when a predefined event occurs.

DBMS usually have two types of triggers: data manipulation language (DML) and system triggers. The former is fired whenever the DML statements such as *deleting*, *updating*, and *insert* statements are executed, the latter is performed in case that system events or data definition language (DDL) ones occur. A trigger has the form of an Event-Condition-Action (ECA) rule informally written as "if a set of *events* occur and a set of *conditions* hold, then perform *actions*".

© ICST Institute for Computer Sciences, Social Informatics and Telecommunications Engineering 2021
Published by Springer Nature Switzerland AG 2021. All Rights Reserved
P. C. Vinh and A. Rakib (Eds.): ICCASA 2020/ICTCC 2020, LNICST 343, pp. 103–112, 2021.
https://doi.org/10.1007/978-3-030-67101-3_8

It is made of a block of code and has a syntax, for example, an Oracle trigger is similar to a stored procedure containing blocks of PL/SQL code. Trigger codes are human readable and do not have any formal semantic. The fact that the main purpose of trigger is maintaining the integrity of the information on the database. These weaknesses come from informal semantic of the trigger. Therefore, we only can verify that if a trigger terminates or conflicts to integrity constraints after executing it or with human inspection step by step. As a result, we cannot verify the correctness of the data system as we do not have any supported tool which used to prove triggers. Then, the problem needed to resolve is that how to specify and verify database system formally.

Many researchers have been working on analyzing triggers (or active rules). The research results of [14,15], proposed in the early 90's, transformed ECA rules to some types of graphs and applied various static analysis techniques to check properties such as *redundancy, inconsistency, incompleteness*, and *termination*. [6] proposed a technique, based on relational algebra, to check if active rules are terminated or confluent. Formal methods for techniques to mathematically build rigorous models of software and hardware systems. Complement to system testing, formal methods use mathematics proofs to verify the system behavior correctness. In this direction, Eun-Hye Choi et al. [10] and Chavarria et al. [7] addressed to both *termination* and *confluence* properties using model checking techniques.

Our previous work [13] initially proposed to use Event-B to formalize and verify a database triggers system at early design phase. The main idea of the method comes from the similar structure and working mechanism of Event-B events and database triggers. We presented a set of translation rules to translate a database system including triggers to an Event-B model. In practical aspect, however, one limitation of formal techniques is the complexity that makes software developers lazy to use in the development. In this paper, we present the design and implementation of a tool called Trigger2B which partly supports automatic modeling process with the RODIN. In the supporting tool Rodin, almost proofs are discharged automatically, hence it reduces complexity in comparison with manual proving. The tool makes the proposed method feasible in the database development process.

The remainder of this paper is organized as follows. Section 2 provides background of database triggers and Event-B. In Sect. 3, we present the architecture of the tool. In Sect. 4, we present the tool Trigger2B, which supports for partly automatic translation. Section 6 summarizes the related work. We conclude the paper and present the future work in Sect. 7.

2   Background

In this section, we first briefly introduce about database triggers and their SQL syntax. Then we give an overview of Event-B formal method.

2.1   Database Triggers and ANTLR

A relational database system, based on the relational model, consists of collections of objects and relations, operations for manipulation and data integrity for accuracy and consistency. Modern relational database systems include active rules as database triggers which response to events occurring inside or outside of the database. Triggers are commonly used in some cases: to audit the process, to automatically perform an action, and to implement complex business rules. The structure of a trigger has the form: *rule_name:: Event(e) IF condition DO action.*

The definition of SQL:1999 trigger has the syntax as follows:

```
CREATE [OR REPLACE] TRIGGER <trigger_name>

{BEFORE|AFTER} {INSERT|DELETE|UPDATE}
ON <table_name>

[REFERENCING [NEW AS <new_row_name>]
[OLD AS<old_row_name>]]

[FOR EACH ROW
[WHEN (<trigger_condition>)] ]

<trigger_body>
```

ANTLR [1] stands for ANother Tool for Language Recognition that is a powerful parser generator for text or binary files. It uses an input user-defined grammar to create a parse tree or abstract syntax tree. ANTLR v4 supports several languages such as Java, C#, Python, etc. The following snippets show a basic grammar named Hello

```
grammar Hello;
r : 'hello' ID;
ID : [a-z]+ ;
WS : [ \t\r\n]+ -> skip ;
```

2.2   Event-B and Rodin

Event-B [3] is a formal method for system-level modeling and analysis. Key features of Event-B are the use of set theory as a modeling notation, the use of refinement to represent systems at different abstraction levels, and the use of mathematical proof to verify consistency between refinement levels. A basic structure of an Event-B model consists of MACHINE and CONTEXT.

An Event B CONTEXT describes a static part where all the relevant properties and hypotheses are defined. A CONTEXT consists of carrier sets, constants, axioms. Carrier sets, denoted by s, are represented by their names, and are nonempty. Different carrier sets are completely independent. The constants c are defined by means of a number of axioms $P(s, c)$ also depending on the carrier sets s.

A MACHINE is defined by a set of clauses. A machine is composed of variables, invariants, theorems and events. Variables v are representing states of the model. Invariants $I(v)$ yield the laws that state variables v must always be satisfied. Each event has the form $evt = $ any x where $G(x, v)$ then $A(x, v, v')$ end where x are local variables of the event, $G(x, v)$ is a guard condition and $A(x, v, v')$ is an action. An event is enabled when its guard condition is satisfied. The event action consists of one or more assignments. We have three kinds of assignments for expressing the actions associated with an event: (1) a deterministic multiple assignment ($x := E(t, v)$), (2) an empty assignment (skip), or (3) a non-deterministic multiple assignment ($x : |P(t, v, x')$).

Rodin [4], built on top a Eclipse, is a part of European Deploy project. It is customizable by a sets of plug-ins tools which support for modeling and analyzing with Event-B. A Rodin project contains seven file XML-based divided into three groups shown in Table 1 Group unchecked files contain user input text, and files in two group static checked and proof are automatically generated by static checker and provers, respectively.

Table 1. Rodin project file types

File extension	Root element type	Contents	Group
.bum	IMachineRoot	Event-B machine	Unchecked
.buc	IContextRoot	Event-B context	Unchecked
.bcm	ISCMachineRoot	Event-B checked machine	Static checked
.bcc	ISCContextRoot	Event-B checked context	Static checked
.bpo	IPORoot	Event-B proof obligations	Proof
.bpr	IPRRoot	Event-B proofs	Proof
.bps	IPSRoot	Event-B proof statuses	Proof

3   Translating Triggers to Event-B

In this section, we recall translation rules from database trigger system to Event-B models which have been defined in our previous work [13]. A database trigger is translated to an Event-B event where trigger conditions are guards of the event.

The rules translating the *Action* part of a trigger are described as follows:

- Insert: This statement has the form "Insert into T values $(val1, ..valn)$", where $val1, .., valn$ are column values of the new record of the table T. We encode this new row as a parameter $r \in T$ of the event. More specifically, the translated event has the form $Evt=$ **Any** r **Where** $r \in T \land e \land c$ **Then** $t := t \cup r$.

– Delete: This statement is generally written in the form: "Delete from T where $column1 = some\_value$". It will delete the record that has the first column's value equal to $some\_value$. We add a parameter for the event representing the value $some\_value$. The event is specified in detail as follows $Evt=$ **Any** v **where** $v \in TYPE_1 \wedge e \wedge c$ **Then** $t := t - f(v)$.

– Update: The general syntax of this statement is "Update T set $column1 = value1$, $column2 = value2$ where $column1 = some\_value$". This statement will update a record where value of the first column is equal to $some\_value$, similar to the case of delete statement, we encode the input values as parameters of the event. The description of the translated event is as follows: $Evt=$ **Any** $v1, v2$ **where** $v1 \in TYPE_1 \wedge v2 \in TYPE_2 \wedge e \wedge c$ **Then** $t := \{1 \mapsto v1, 2 \mapsto v2\} \oplus t$.

4 Architecture and Design

Following the method presented in Sect. 3, we implement a tool called Trigger2B[1] to support designing and modeling a database system including trigger. In this section, we present the architecture and detailed design of the tool.

4.1 Architecture

This tool can generate multiples XML-based format output which can be used later in verification phase with Event-B supporting tools such as RODIN platform. The architecture of this tool is illustrated in Fig. 1. The UI provides a graphic interface for users. Module Data Adapter is responsible connect to the database and extract metadata that is SQL statements describe about given database schema. SQL extractor is the module recognize SQL structure then extract database model. Translator component is the heart of our tool. It translates database models to event-b models. Shared Component shares common libraries is used by different modules. Module Event-B Builder exports handles exporting event-b model received from previous module into Rodin project. Finally, system is handled and logged error by System Handler & Logging module.

Figure 2 below described process of translating between models of this tool has been implemented. The processing is done through the six major steps as in figure. Firstly, users browse a database want to verify. Then, our tools will connect to database and dump the database in an SQL text format. After that, SQL structure is parsed to extract database model. The result of the previous process is used as input in the translation process. Finally, the Trigger2B tool will export results into a Rodin project. Users can import the archived project into Rodin platform and continue to perform the verification and modeling.

---

[1] The Trigger2B source code can be found at: https://github.com/anhfit/Trigger2B.

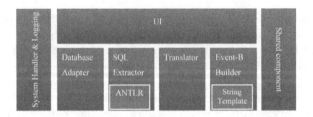

Fig. 1. Architecture of the proposed tool

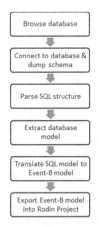

Fig. 2. Processing flow of the tool

4.2 Component Design

Database Adapter. Database Adapter component, based on JDBC technology, connects to the DBMS and extracts database schema. For each DBMS, we need to define a specific JDBC driver. Subsequently, Trigger2B is flexible enough to handle with various DBMS.

SQL Extractor. The input of this component is text-based values of database schema received from Database Adapter component. SQL Extractor makes this value in standard form, removes redundant or duplicated data, parses SQL statements, and extracts needed information. The process of extraction is illustrated in Fig. 3.

Translator. Translator component is the most important part of the tool following the method presented in Sect. 3. This component translates database model achieved from SQL Extractor to Event-B models using the proposed rules.

Event-B Builder. This component exports constructed Event-b models into Rodin project. Basically, a Rodin project contains seven XML-based file types illustrated in Sect. 2. Group unchecked files contain user input text, and files in two group static checked and proof are automatically generated by static checker and provers, respectively. So we only need to export into .bum and .buc files. The Event-B Builder component uses a template engine named StringTemplate [2] that provides features like combining one or more templates with a data model to produce target Rodin documents. This engine is provided as the ANTLR library built-in.

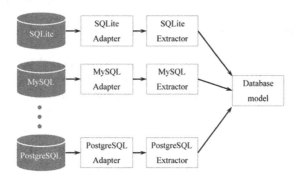

Fig. 3. Constructing database model

5   Implementation and Results

The Trigger2B tool is implemented in Java programming language and structured several packages corresponding to specific component mentioned above. In order to parse trigger statements, we define grammar files which contains grammars and rules for trigger SQL syntax. The snippet codes below show a part of grammar file for defining SQLite trigger parser.

```
grammar SQLite;

create_trigger_stmt

    : CREATE ( TEMP | TEMPORARY )? TRIGGER ( IF NOT EXISTS )?

      ( database_name '.' )? trigger_name

    ( BEFORE | AFTER | INSTEAD OF )?

    ( DELETE | INSERT | UPDATE ( OF column_name ( ',' column_name )* )? )

    ON ( database_name '.' )? table_name

    ( FOR EACH ROW )?

    ( WHEN expr )?
```

```
      BEGIN ( ( update_stmt
| insert_stmt
| delete_stmt
| select_stmt ) ';' )+

END

;
```

Even though, ANTLR provides an automatic tree-walking mechanism, Trigger2B uses -visitor option to generate a visitor interface from the defined a grammar and invokes explicitly interface *ParseTreeVisitor.visit(node)* method on child nodes.

Figure 4 depicts the results when we run Trigger2B tool in a case study of human resource management. It shows the parsed tree from trigger statements and Rodin project files which are generated automatically.

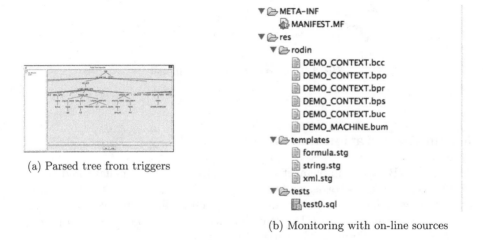

(a) Parsed tree from triggers

(b) Monitoring with on-line sources

Fig. 4. Generated Rodin project

6   Related Work

From theoretical aspect, there are a number of works proposed for checking and verifying database trigger. In [14,15], Sin-Yeung Lee and Tok-Wang introduced algorithms to detect the correctness of updating triggers. R. Manicka Chezian and T. Devi [17] introduced a new algorithm which does not pose any limitation on the number of rules but it only emphasizes on algorithms detecting the termination of the system. Baralis [6] improved existing techniques and proposed propagation algorithms, based on relational algebra, to statically check if active rules are terminated or confluent. This approach, can be applied widely for active database rule languages and for trigger language (SQL:1999). Zang *et al.* [18] proposed an approach to checking structural errors such as inconsistency, circularity, and redundancy of ECA rule-based systems. Their method classifies three different levels of verification and builds an EA tree to check each level. These works focused on theoretical aspects and did not propose any practical tool.

Another direction is using model checking techniques such as Tarek and Huth [11] presented an abstract modeling framework for active database management systems and implemented a prototype of a Promela code generator. Choi *et al.* [9] proposed a general framework for modeling active database systems and rules. Their framework is feasible by using a model checking tool, e.g., SPIN. Ksystra [12] proposed a method to express and verify safety properties of reactive rules which also are ECA rules. It provides verification mechanism of termination, confluence and safety properties using CafeOBJ method. With these direction, practical tools have been mentioned and proposed, but they required users to specify the model manually.

Chavarria and Li [7,8,16] have had a series of work which focus on verifying active rules by using conditional colored Petri nets. They also proposed a tool called ECAPNSim which supports to achieve rules from a text file, then translate them to a Petrinet automatically. Our tool is different because we use Event-B and Rodin for modeling and verification.

Regarding to support tools for modeling in Event-B and Rodin. Most of tools are in the reversed direction, i.e., code generation from Event-B. Most related work is UB2DB [5] which assists users on incremental database design with Rodin. It generates database models from Event-B ones. To the best of our knowledge, Trigger2B is the first tool for translating SQL-based statements to Event-B.

7   Conclusions and Future Work

Support tools for formal modeling and verification are significantly important in software development. These tool will help engineers to ease the complexity of formalization. In this paper, we presented the Trigger2B tool for modeling and checking database triggers. The proposed tool accesses DBMS and automatically generates the Event-B models and corresponding Rodin project. The database developers using Trigger2B do not need much skills and do not have to spend time in detail modeling with Event-B. The current implementation, however, works only with SQLite. The tool needs to be improved with more complex cases and more DBMS. We intend to make it available as a Rodin plug-in. Enhancing the translation rules to only triggers but also a database schema is one of our future work.

Acknowledgments. This work is supported by the project no. CT.2019.01.05 granted by Ministry of Education and Training (MOET).

References

1. Anltr (2014). http://www.antlr.org
2. String template (2014). http://www.stringtemplate.org
3. Abrial, J.-R.: Modeling in Event-B - System and Software Engineering. Cambridge University Press, Cambridge (2010)
4. Abrial, J.-R., Butler, M., Hallerstede, S., Voisin, L.: An open extensible tool environment for Event-B. In: Liu, Z., He, J. (eds.) ICFEM 2006. LNCS, vol. 4260, pp. 588–605. Springer, Heidelberg (2006). https://doi.org/10.1007/11901433_32
5. Al-Brashdi, A., Butler, M., Rezazadeh, A.: UB2DB Rodin plug-in for automated database code generation. In: 6th International ABZ Conference ASM, Alloy, B, TLA, VDM, Z, 2018Programme (2018)
6. Baralis, E.: Rule analysis. In: Paton, N.W. (ed.) Active Rules in Database Systems. MCS, pp. 51–67. Springer, New York (1999). https://doi.org/10.1007/978-1-4419-8656-6_3
7. Chavarría-Báez, L., Li, X.: Verification of active rule base via conditional colored petri nets. In: SMC, pp. 343–348 (2007)
8. Chavarriéa-Baéez, L., Li, X.: Termination analysis of active rules - a petri net based approach. In: IEEE International Conference on Systems, Man and Cybernetics, SMC 2009, pp. 2205–2210, October 2009
9. Choi, E.-H., Tsuchiya, T., Kikuno, T.: Model checking active database rules. Technical report, AIST CVS, Osaka University, Japan (2006)
10. Choi, E.-H., Tsuchiya, T., Kikuno, T.: Model checking active database rules under various rule processing strategies. IPSJ Digit. Cour. **2**, 826–839 (2006)
11. Ghazi, T., Huth, M.: An abstraction-based analysis of rule systems for active database management systems. Technical report, Kansas State University, April 1998. Technical report KSU-CIS-98-6, pp15
12. Ksystra, K., Triantafyllou, N., Stefaneas, P.: On verifying reactive rules using rewriting logic. In: Bikakis, A., Fodor, P., Roman, D. (eds.) RuleML 2014. LNCS, vol. 8620, pp. 67–81. Springer, Cham (2014). https://doi.org/10.1007/978-3-319-09870-8_5
13. Le, H.A., Truong, N.T.: Modeling and verifying DML triggers using Event-B. In: Selamat, A., Nguyen, N.T., Haron, H. (eds.) ACIIDS 2013, Part II. LNCS (LNAI), vol. 7803, pp. 539–548. Springer, Heidelberg (2013). https://doi.org/10.1007/978-3-642-36543-0_55
14. Lee, S.-Y., Ling, T.-W.: Are your trigger rules correct? In: Proceedings of the 9th International Workshop on Database and Expert Systems Applications, DEXA 1998, pp. 837–842. IEEE Computer Society, Washington, D.C. (1998)
15. Lee, S.-Y., Ling, T.-W.: Verify updating trigger correctness. In: Bench-Capon, T.J.M., Soda, G., Tjoa, A.M. (eds.) DEXA 1999. LNCS, vol. 1677, pp. 382–391. Springer, Heidelberg (1999). https://doi.org/10.1007/3-540-48309-8_36
16. Li, X., Medina, J., Chapa, S.: Applying petri nets in active database systems. IEEE Trans. Syst. Man Cybern. Part C Appl. Rev. **37**(4), 482–493 (2007)
17. Manicka Chezian, R., Devi, T.: A new algorithm to detect the non-termination of triggers in active databases. Int. J. Adv. Netw. Appl. **3**(2), 1098–1104 (2011)
18. Zhang, J., Moyne, J., Tilbury, D.: Verification of ECA rule based management and control systems. In: IEEE International Conference on Automation Science and Engineering, CASE 2008, pp. 1–7, August 2008

Predicting the Level of Hypertension Using Machine Learning

Pham Thu Thuy[1], Nguyen Thanh Tung[2(✉)] [iD], and Chu Duc Hoang[3]

[1] Science and Technology Department, Vietnam National University,
Hanoi, Vietnam
phamthuthuy@vnu.edu.vn
[2] International School, Vietnam National University, Hanoi, Vietnam
tungnt@isvnu.vn
[3] Ministry of Science and Technology, Hanoi, Viet Nam
hoangcd@gmail.com

Abstract. In recent years, data mining has been put into research and application in many different areas in the world such as economy, education, sports, telecommunications, etc. And the health - health care [1] sector is not out of this trend. If it is possible to successfully analyze the data [2–4] from the huge amount of data of diseases, patients and hospitals every day, it can help a lot of doctors in the process of diagnosis, examination and treatment of diseases for patients. The problem raised here is whether we can accurately diagnose the patient's disease based on the information provided. The information provided may be age, gender, occupation, symptoms, test information, etc. from which it is necessary to achieve the most accurate diagnosis possible to minimize the work pressure for the medical team as well as minimize the time of diagnosis.

Keywords: Machine learning · Data mining · Healthcare · Hypertension

1 Introduction

We has chosen hypertension to test this problem because in the future, hypertension will be very popular because of the aging of the population worldwide. Input data will be the information of patients related to hypertension, and the output information is the result of predicting the level of hypertension patients based on the information given. Details are given in Sect. 3.

There are numerous factors which can cause hypertension [5].

To begin with, aging plays a role and aged people have higher risk of hypertension. Gender is another cause of high blood pressure. Although women of productive age are more likely to suffer from cardiovascular disease than men, the proportion of men under 45 years with high blood pressure is higher than that of women.

In addition, secondary hypertension is also the result of a consequence of several conditions such as: kidney disease, thyroid disease, adrenal adenoma, neurological diseases such as mental disorders, diabetes, and atherosclerosis and so on.

Moreover, hypertension also results from unhealthy lifestyles. First, overweight and obesity increases the risk of hypertension. Obesity is when people's bodies excess their

© ICST Institute for Computer Sciences, Social Informatics and Telecommunications Engineering 2021
Published by Springer Nature Switzerland AG 2021. All Rights Reserved
P. C. Vinh and A. Rakib (Eds.): ICCASA 2020/ICTCC 2020, LNICST 343, pp. 113–122, 2021.
https://doi.org/10.1007/978-3-030-67101-3_9

body weights (BMI in men is more than 25, women are over 30). The formula for calculating BMI is as follows: weight (kg) divides (height × height) (meters). Others factors include: sedentary lifestyle, unhealthy eating, too salty eating (the amount of salt exceeds 5 g/day), too much alcoholic drinking, smoking, dyslipidemia and diabetes, frequent stress and social factors which cause urban people to have higher chances of having urban diseases than the ones living in rural areas due to stressful and urgent life styles.

Research has proved that early symptoms of hypertension can be recognized by some related tests such as blood biochemical tests (blood urea, blood uric acid, blood creatinine, blood electrolytes) to determine the diagnosis of kidney-related diseases - kidney disease increases the likelihood of hypertension. Other tests include Blood glucose test which relates to diabetes. Test index which evaluates blood lipid disorders (Cholesterol, Triglyceride, HDL-C, LDL-C, XN: Electrolyte Na; Potassium) also helps monitor and detects some diseases such as blood lipids, Atherosclerosis and hypertension [6].

2 Related Works

There are more and more researches related to diagnosing patients from the medical records received. We can model the classification problem so each class is a diagnostic result of the disease for the patient. The method of identification given here is to use machine learning [7] method. The algorithms used are specialized algorithms for classification problems such as Naïve Bayes, Association Rule, KNN, Decision Tree. Specifically, with this problem, information about patients will play an important role in classification. So we will have to consider which information is needed for classification, which information to keep and which information should be removed. Thus, we have the machine learning training process [8, 9] to carry out the diagnostic test described in Fig. 1:

Fig. 1. Training process

In which:

- **Data** is the original data set of the disease, including multiple data streams with many information about patients.
- **Feature Filter** is the process of filtering and retrieving features from data. Only those features that are needed will be retained for later training.
- **Training Data** is the data set for training, after removing unnecessary features in the original data set.
- **Training** is the training process based on the training data set using a machine learning algorithm (SVM, Naïve Bayes, etc.).

- **Model** is a file that retains the information and training results after using the training machine algorithm on the data set. This file will be used to predict future results.

After the training is complete, we will make predictions for the data we want to label. The prediction process is described as in Fig. 2:

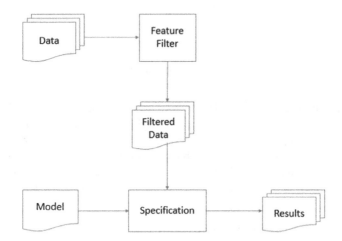

Fig. 2. The process of labeling predictions

In which:

- **Model** is the model file we get from the training process.
- **Data** is the input data that we want to classify.
- **Feature Filter** is the process of filtering and retrieving features from data. Only those features that are needed will be retained.
- **Filtered Data** is the data set retained after the features that are not necessary for the classification have been removed.
- **Specification** is the process of labeling the data after it has been filtered and given the results.
- **Results** is a set of label results corresponding to the input data set.

3   Select and Build Data to Test the Diagnosis of Hypertension

All the data for the paper is collected from the medical records for hypertension patients from Son La province hospital in the national project "Application and deployment of software system for integrating and connecting biomedical electronic devices and communication networks to support the monitoring of health and epidemiology in the Northwest region" [10]. Initial data for the test is a set of statistical data for hypertension collected by the author from the hospital. All of the data is the hypertension medical records in the paper form. Data was collected, processed and stored in excel file in tables, with each line containing information for each patient. On each line, each column will represent an information about that patient such as birth date, province, district, information about the patient's health, status at admission, etc. (Fig. 3).

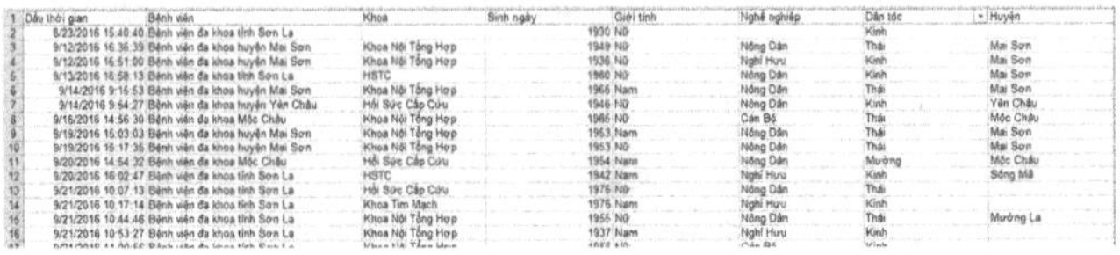

Fig. 3. Data is stored in excel file

The data of hypertension include a total of 2594 data streams, of which 1868 are labeled for diagnosis. As been classified by World Health Organization, there are 3 types of hypertension patients that we will use as classification labels for hypertension data sets [11]. We also have other labels but the proportion of the data is negligible, so we ignore them in the model because we are only interested in the hypertension patients who already went to the hospital in this paper. Labels are listed in Table 1:

Table 1. Classification labels for hypertension

Label	Quantity	Percentage (%)
Hypertension level III (Systolic $\geq$ 180 and Diastolic $\geq$ 110)	336	17.99
Hypertension level I (Systolic 140–159 and Diastolic 90–99)	700	37.47
Hypertension level II (Systolic 160–179 and Diastolic 100–109)	665	35.60

After having input data of hypertension, we filtered training data to test the diagnosis of this disease. Accordingly, we will build the data in SVMlight form, with each line corresponding to one line in the original data. The line will contain numbers representing the features of the data. For example, with the third feature of value 2, we will represent "3: 2". If the feature has a value of 0, we will not represent it. For features with numerical values we will take that numerical value as a value for the features. As for features with many textual values, we turn that feature into multiple columns corresponding to the value that the feature can receive. If any value is used, that column will be worth one.

For example, "Age" is the 10th feature and has a value of 24. Since "Age" is a number, we always convert the value to "10:24". But "Gender" has 2 values: "Male" and "Female" and being the 11th feature, we need to convert into 2 columns of 11 and 12. When we receive the value "Nam", we save it as "11: 1 12: 0", and when we receive the value "Nữ", we save it as "11: 0 12: 1". But since we will then remove columns with a value of 0, we can save it straight into "11: 1" or "12: 1".

Each training data line will have a classification label and with the SVMlight data structure, we need to put its label value at the beginning of the line. With the data set, each label has its corresponding value. For example, if there are 6 label values, they will be numbered 1 to 6 respectively.

"Classification" is considered the data label and be converted into the first column. Because the "classification" column has 3 different values as shown in Table 1, it corresponds to numbers 1 to 3. The remaining columns will be numbered the same way as described above.

Since there are many columns with very little data or no value, we only build 2 sets of data based on columns with information greater than or equal to 50% and 70% to conduct the test.

Specifically, in Table 2, columns with the amount of data greater than or equal to 50% of hypertension are used as features of the training data set as follows:

Table 2. Statistics of columns with data amount of $\geq 50\%$

Name of column	Amount of data (%)	Type of data
Age	100.00	Natural number
Hospital	100.00	Text
Department	99.85	Text
Gender	100.00	Text
Occupation	86.40	Text
Ethnic:	94.95	Text
District	53.81	Text
City	82.63	Text
Province	100.00	Text
Do you have diabetes yourself, blood lipid disorder, coronary artery disease, kidney disease, or smoke?	56.93	Text
Age of high blood pressure	87.60	Natural number
Body weight	97.61	Real number
Body height	97.61	Real number
Temperature	97.50	Real number
Low blood pressure	98.15	Real number
High blood pressure	98.11	Real number
Breathing	95.45	Natural number
Blood glucose	90.83	Real number

(*continued*)

Table 2. (*continued*)

Name of column	Amount of data (%)	Type of data
Urea	91.64	Real number
Uric acid	56.32	Real number
Creatinine	91.14	Real number
Cholesterol	81.39	Text
Triglyceride	77.04	Text
HDL-C	52.54	Text
LDL-C	51.69	Text

Training data after being completed will look like following:

```
1 1:86 2:1 20:1 32:1 43:1 45:1 52:1 54:110 55:36.8 56:120 57:200 58:25 59:13.89 60:20.67 61:336.9 62:1 65:1
1 1:67 3:1 8:1 20:1 33:1 43:1 45:1 52:1 54:90 55:36.7 56:140 57:200 58:20 59:4.9 60:4.3 61:65 63:1 65:1
1 1:80 3:1 8:1 20:1 23:1 32:1 43:1 45:1 52:1 54:74 55:36.6 56:130 57:180 58:22 59:5.8 60:3.8 61:61 63:1 65:1
1 1:56 2:1 9:1 20:1 22:1 32:1 43:1 45:1 52:1 54:85 55:37 56:120 57:220 58:21 59:7.15 60:4.73 61:56.7 62:1 65:1
2 1:51 3:1 8:1 21:1 22:1 33:1 43:1 45:1 52:1 54:59 55:60 56:90 57:140 58:18 59:5.1 60:3.8 61:169
3 1:70 4:1 10:1 20:1 22:1 32:1 43:1 45:1 52:1 54:80 55:37 56:110 57:185 58:20 59:5.6 60:4.9 61:75 63:1
2 1:51 5:1 8:1 20:1 24:1 33:1 45:1 53:1 54:75 55:37 56:100 57:160 58:20 59:5.8 60:6.8 61:91 62:1 65:1
3 1:63 3:1 8:1 21:1 22:1 33:1 43:1 45:1 52:1 54:100 55:36.8 56:100 57:160 58:20 59:15.1 60:5.53 61:94 63:1 66:1
1 1:63 3:1 8:1 20:1 22:1 33:1 43:1 45:1 52:1 54:90 55:36 56:100 57:180 58:20 59:13.5 60:8.1 61:100 63:1 65:1
3 1:62 5:1 10:1 21:1 32:1 34:1 43:1 45:1 52:1 54:95 55:37 56:120 57:180 58:19 59:6.8 60:11.3 61:111
1 1:74 2:1 9:1 21:1 23:1 32:1 45:1 52:1 54:90 55:37 56:100 57:180 58:22 59:8.84 60:9.1 61:116.5 63:1 65:1
2 1:57 3:1 8:1 20:1 25:1 33:1 43:1 45:1 52:1 54:86 55:36.5 56:90 57:150 58:19 59:6.85 60:6.01 61:154 63:1 66:1
3 1:52 3:1 8:1 21:1 25:1 33:1 43:1 45:1 53:1 54:68 55:36.8 56:100 57:170 58:20 59:4.6 60:4.8 61:72 63:1 66:1
4 1:52 3:1 20:1 25:1 33:1 43:1 45:1 53:1 54:96 55:36.5 56:80 57:130 58:21 59:6.47 60:3.61 61:75 63:1 65:1
4 1:87 3:1 8:1 20:1 25:1 33:1 43:1 45:1 52:1 54:130 55:36.8 56:80 57:130 58:24 59:5.8 60:4 61:80 63:1 66:1
3 1:86 3:1 8:1 20:1 25:1 33:1 43:1 45:1 52:1 54:80 55:36.8 56:100 57:170 58:20 59:5.24 60:4.63 61:86 63:1 65:1
1 1:49 3:1 8:1 20:1 22:1 33:1 45:1 52:1 54:86 55:37 56:110 57:200 58:22 59:5.58 60:4.3 61:73 63:1 65:1
2 1:48 3:1 8:1 21:1 22:1 33:1 43:1 45:1 53:1 54:07 55:37 56:90 57:140 58:20 59:4.41 60:3.6 61:102 63:1 66:1
2 1:76 5:1 8:1 21:1 22:1 33:1 45:1 52:1 54:78 55:37 56:80 57:160 58:20 59:8.5 60:7.1 61:98 62:1 66:1
1 1:53 2:1 9:1 21:1 22:1 32:1 43:1 45:1 52:1 54:100 55:37 56:100 57:180 58:21 59:6.52 60:4.3 61:81 63:1 66:1
2 1:71 2:1 8:1 21:1 24:1 32:1 43:1 45:1 52:1 54:82 55:37 56:90 57:140 58:20 60:5.4
2 1:82 2:1 8:1 21:1 23:1 32:1 43:1 45:1 52:1 54:113 55:37 56:90 57:140 58:22 59:4.8 60:3.6 61:81 63:1 66:1
2 1:74 2:1 9:1 20:1 23:1 32:1 43:1 45:1 54:80 55:32 56:90 57:150 58:20 59:12.42 60:14.76 63:1 65:1
1 1:42 2:1 8:1 21:1 23:1 33:1 43:1 45:1 54:84 55:37 56:80 57:180 58:20 59:4.07 60:4.47 61:79 63:1 66:1
2 1:54 2:1 8:1 20:1 24:1 32:1 43:1 45:1 52:1 54:78 55:37 56:90 57:150 58:18 59:9.23 60:7.39 61:66.7 62:1 66:1
3 1:65 2:1 8:1 20:1 23:1 33:1 43:1 45:1 54:78 55:37 56:80 57:120 58:20 59:3.3 60:4.7 61:94 63:1 65:1
2 1:74 2:1 8:1 21:1 23:1 32:1 43:1 45:1 52:1 54:37 55:82 56:90 57:150 58:20 59:5.44 60:5.15 61:95.6 63:1 65:1
3 1:51 2:1 8:1 21:1 22:1 32:1 43:1 54:80 55:37 56:70 57:160 58:20 59:7.5 60:4.8 61:9.5 63:1 66:1
2 1:61 2:1 8:1 20:1 22:1 32:1 43:1 45:1 54:80 55:37 56:80 57:150 58:20 59:5.92 60:5.66 61:77.1 63:1 66:1
```

Training data structure

4 Test Data Set Developed Using Weka

We conducted the test using the data set developed, using four algorithms that are SVM, Naive Bayes, Decision Tree and KNN. The tool used to support the test is Weka, a machine learning software developed by Waikato University, New Zealand in Java. Weka is free software released under the GNU General Public License.

Weka [12] is a synthesis of machine learning algorithms for data mining. Algorithms can be used directly on data sets or can be called from Java code. Weka also includes data pre-processing, classification, regression, clustering, association rules and visualization tools.

In order to use Weka for the test, we follow these steps:

- Step 1: conduct data pre-processing:

  We put in the training data set and select the data as shown in Fig. 5 (Fig. 4).

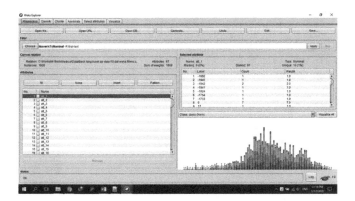

Fig. 4. Data pre-processing.

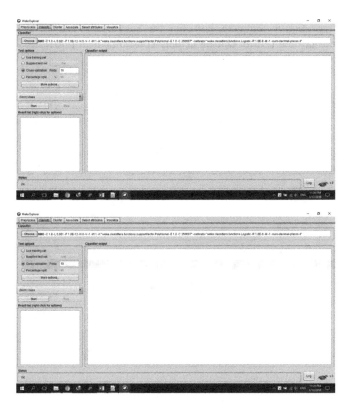

Fig. 5. Test configuration.

- Step 2: Configure the test settings:

Click on the Classify tab and set Cross-validation to 10 and other algorithms to conduct the test as shown in Fig. 6.

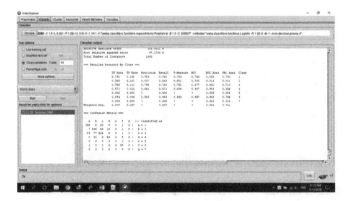

Fig. 6. Test configuration.

- Step 3: run the test

After configuration is complete, just click the Start button and the Weka tool will perform the test and the results will be displayed as shown in Fig. 7.

Fig. 7. Test running screen.

In running the test, we will use 2 models. One model uses features with data amount of $\geq 70\%$ and a model with data amount of $\geq 50\%$. Based on the test results of the two models, we assess the influence of the features on the classification of labels.

Test model 1 performed using features with data amount of $\geq 70\%$ and we have results in the following Table 3:

Table 3. Results of test model 1.

Algorithm	Accuracy (%)
SVM	80.19
Naïve Bayes	74.18
Decision Tree	82.49
KNN	65.36

Test model 2 performed using features with data amount of $\geq 50\%$ and we have results in the following Table 4:

Table 4. Results of test model 2.

Algorithm	Accuracy (%)
SVM	80.67
Naïve Bayes	66.54
Decision Tree	83.29
KNN	61.29

Some detailed results of predictive algorithms with hypertension data with Model 1 (Tables 5 and 6):

Table 5. Detailed results for each predictive label of Decision Tree algorithm for hypertension data with model 1

Label	Precision	Recall	F1
Hypertension level III (Systolic $\geq$ 180 and Diastolic $\geq$ 110)	0,855	0,842	0,849
Hypertension level I (Systolic 140–159 and Diastolic 90–99)	0,835	0,873	0,853
Hypertension level II (Systolic 160–179 and Diastolic 100–109)	0,819	0,823	0,821

Table 6. Detailed results for each predictive label of Decision Tree algorithm for hypertension data with model 2

Label	Precision	Recall	F1
Hypertension level III (Systolic $\geq$ 180 and Diastolic $\geq$ 110)	0,791	0,789	0,790
Hypertension level I (Systolic 140–159 and Diastolic 90–99)	0,836	0,851	0,844
Hypertension level II (Systolic 160–179 and Diastolic 100–109)	0,785	0,791	0,788

So, based on the results we can see that using both models, Decision Tree always gives the highest results with accuracy of 82.49% and 83.29% respectively for the data of hypertension in 2 models. And using more features gives higher results. SVM algorithm also gave quite good results, with accuracy of 80.19% in models 1 and 80.67 in model 2 on the same set of data of hypertension. The remaining two algorithms Naïve Bayes and KNN gave poor results, with KNN giving the worst results for both models, with an accuracy of 70% the highest.

5   Conclusion

In this paper, we has explored and analyze data on hypertension disease using machine learning methods with the test supporting tool of Weka. Based on the results of this test, we can more or less assess the ability to predict hypertension using the information obtained from patients, thereby helping doctors in the process of medical examination and treatment. In the future, we can continue to test using with more accurate and complete data sets in order to be able to improve the accuracy rate of disease prediction.

References

1. Machine Learning in Healthcare. https://emerj.com/ai-market-research/machine-learning-in-healthcare-executive-consensus/
2. Nguyen, L.L., Su, S.: Neural network approach for non-invasive detection of hyperglycemia using electrocardiographic signals (2014)
3. Lyon, A., Mincholé, A., Martínez, J.P., Laguna, P., Rodriguez, B.: Computational techniques for ECG analysis and interpretation in light of their contribution to medical advances. J. R. Soc. Interface **15**, 20170821 (2018)
4. Kachuee, M., Fazeli, S., Sarrafzadeh, M.: ECG heartbeat classification: a deep transferable representation (2018)
5. Causes of hypertension. https://www.vinmec.com/vi/tin-tuc/thong-tin-suc-khoe/suc-khoe-tong-quat/cac-xet-nghiem-sinh-hoa-mau-chan-doan-benh-cao-huyet-ap/
6. Diagnose of hypertension. https://www.dieutri.vn/sinhhoalamsang/xet-nghiem-sinh-hoa-trong-tang-huyet-ap
7. Machine Learning for Medical Diagnostics. https://emerj.com/ai-sector-overviews/machine-learning-medical-diagnostics-4-current-applications/
8. Zhu, Q.-Y., Qin, A.K., Suganthan, P.N.: Evolutionary extreme learning machine. Pattern Recogn. **38**(10), 1759–1763 (2005)
9. Gondra, I.: Applying machine learning to software fault-proneness prediction. J. Syst. Softw. **81**(2), 186–195 (2008)
10. Thanh Tung, N.: Application and deployment of software system for integrating and connecting biomedical electronic devices and communication networks to support the monitoring of health and epidemiology in the Northwest region. National research project funded by Ministry of Science and Technology
11. WHO Information about hypertension. https://www.who.int/health-topics/hypertension/#tab=tab_1
12. Weka. https://www.cs.waikato.ac.nz/ml/weka/

Can Blockchain Fly the Silver Fern?
Exploring the Opportunity in New Zealand's Primary Industries

Mahmudul Hasan and Johnny Chan[(✉)]

University of Auckland, Auckland, New Zealand
{mahmudul.hasan,jh.chan}@auckland.ac.nz

Abstract. Blockchain is an emerging technology perceived as ground-breaking. Yet, technology service providers are not realising the untapped market potential as quick as it was predicted. New Zealand is not any different. Currently, the number of blockchain-based solutions available in the country is rather limited. A clear understanding of the market of blockchain is critical for service providers to recognise the opportunities and the challenges. It has been suggested that multiple industries could utilise blockchain technology to attain numerous benefits. The primary industries of New Zealand will be one of them that remains underexplored. Therefore, in this study, we use total addressable market (TAM), a technique to estimate the market size, to explore the available economic opportunity of blockchain-based solutions in New Zealand's primary industries. Our estimation suggests that it may be close to NZ$1.65 billion per year, including self-employed enterprises; or NZ$496 million per year, excluding self-employed enterprises. Besides, our review of secondary sources indicates that blockchain technology could tackle some of the challenges the primary industries are facing like food fraud and foodborne illness. However, lack of strong and practical use cases, lack of streamlined practice for data management, lack of understanding of the technology and its implication to business, and lack of regulation and legislation are the major impediments to blockchain adoption.

Keywords: Blockchain · Total addressable market · Primary industries · New Zealand

1 Introduction

New Zealand has an open and competitive economy with a population of about 5 million. The primary industries (e.g. agriculture, forestry, horticulture, and seafood) play a vital role in economic growth. They consist of enterprises that produce, process and move goods domestically and internationally. Together, they contribute to more than 70% of all merchandise exports, representing NZ$46.5 billion of annual revenue [1]. At the same time, the primary industries are facing several challenges, including food fraud and foodborne illness [2]. They pose significant risk to the safety of the goods and the reputation of New Zealand [3]. At a global level, food fraud is estimated to cost the food industry US$49 billion (NZ$82 billion) a year [4]. On the other hand, we have 420,000

P. C. Vinh and A. Rakib (Eds.): ICCASA 2020/ICTCC 2020, LNICST 343, pp. 123–130, 2021.
https://doi.org/10.1007/978-3-030-67101-3_10

people die every year worldwide due to food contamination [5]. The Ministry of Primary Industries estimates New Zealand to have 200,000 cases of foodborne illness per year [2]. With the addition of the ongoing COVID-19 pandemic, it is fair to assume both the local and global customers would only demand more accuracy and transparency of information from the suppliers. The traditional approach of tracking and tracing goods for quality control (e.g., recording, verifying, securing and distributing data like the provenance of ingredients, freshness and safety information) has always been costly and time-consuming. Therefore, some suppliers around the world have started to experiment and adopt various blockchain solutions to tackle these challenges.

A blockchain is a record of transactions built upon distributed ledger technologies which is secure, imputable, anonymised and decentralised. When a new transaction occurs (i.e. an event), it is timestamped and recorded chronologically in a block, which is then connected to previous blocks in the chain. Once the transaction is verified and validated, the updated ledger is copied across all participants in the peer-to-peer network [6]. That distributed ledger acts as a trusted single point of truth tracking all identity, status, ownership and authority information among the participants. It eliminates the need of intermediaries, which could massively reduce transaction costs.

Therefore, blockchain technology is a promising innovation that enables trust through visibility among stakeholders [6, 7], and it has many user cases for incremental improvements and disruptive changes, ranging from technical, social, political, cultural and economic aspects. However, the full market potential of blockchain technology specifically in New Zealand is yet to be realised. Currently the number of blockchain-enabled products and services available in New Zealand is rather limited. We believe that the understanding of market potential of blockchain is critical to draw interests from technology service providers, because that helps them to recognise the opportunities and challenges, and they could customise their existing solution while minimising development costs and associated risks. In this paper, we use total addressable market (TAM) to explore the available opportunity for blockchain-enabled services in New Zealand. It is a technique to estimate the market size which enables a single service provider to define the holistic opportunity from their offering. Through the study, our hope is to get more blockchain service providers on board, so they could supply various solutions to the primary industries of New Zealand and enhance their capacity in providing accurate and transparent information to the customers.

2 Blockchain and the Primary Industries of New Zealand

2.1 Opportunities

Being the predominant source of wealth generation for New Zealand, the primary industries are comprised of multiple enterprises from different sectors (see Fig. 1). Blockchain-enabled services can be used by the goods producers, distributors and suppliers to track and trace the goods from production to consumption (i.e. farm to plate) and be in compliance with government regulations. As an exporting nation of meat, dairy, agri-food and seafood products, blockchain-enabled services in New Zealand could boost transparency, ensure goods safety, minimise the risk of errors, and reduce potential fraud.

As a result of increased transparency, some customer behaviour towards product consumption could be improved (e.g. healthy diet). Besides, blockchain-enabled services can facilitate a more resilient and efficient supply chain solutions to face unexpected events (e.g. a pandemic).

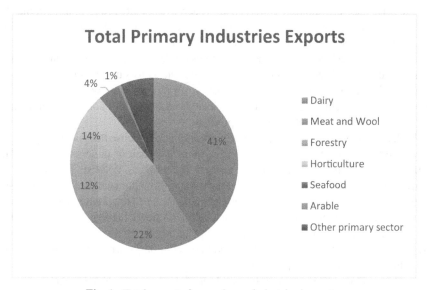

Fig. 1. Total exports from primary industries by sector

New Zealand has numerous enterprises producing non-branded high-quality homogenous products, and typically they sell their products through intermediaries. Blockchain-enabled services could create more value for these enterprises specifically. For example, the domestic market of organic products is growing rapidly in New Zealand [8]. Blockchain-enabled services could enable customers who place a high premium on food to buy organic products directly from the producers rather than through the intermediaries. New Zealand is one of the very few countries exporting chilled lamb around the world. While the local and global customers are valuing fresh and quality meat products, producers are facing increasingly tight shipping deadlines [9]. As a result, maintaining the freshness of meat is often difficult due to the short shelf time on arrival to supermarket chillers. Counter-intuitively, the fresher the product the more paperwork is needed and that slows down the shipping process. Blockchain-enabled services could potentially reduce the time and cost in product verification and expedite the shipping deadlines without sacrificing the freshness and quality of the product.

2.2 Challenges

Although blockchain-enabled services possess numerous potential benefits, they are not without limitations. Several technical, organisational and social factors could hinder the acceptance of blockchain-enabled services in the primary industries of New Zealand.

First, typical blockchain application is not originally developed to handle massive amount of data. However, the primary industries generate a large volume of data from multiple stakeholders. For example, enterprises in the food industry need to manage multiple levels of data including purchase orders, stock keeping unit (SKU) information, details of the distributors, and more. Thus, technology service providers must understand the individual use case and employ a layered approach to data storage (e.g. integrating the blockchain solution with the traditional solution of centralised database). Still, managing such continuous integration could be costly and risky.

Second, there is a lack of streamlined practices for data entry among the enterprises in primary industries. Different enterprises from different sectors use various applications, generate multiple forms of data (including paper format), and follow a diversity of data storing methods. Technology service providers should carefully consider some smart solution to streamline the data capturing process.

Third, although many sectors in the primary industries realise the potential transformative effect of blockchain-enabled services, there is a lack of understanding of how exactly that would change their business process and practice. Polarising views and the absence of strong visible use case could be the main reasons for such barrier. Even some studies suggest that enterprises in the primary industries of New Zealand are generally quick adopters of new technology [10], such adoption never happens overnight and in most cases the adoption is incremental and dependent on existing technology. Having some strong and practical use cases of blockchain technology with linkage to the status quo could be helpful for enterprises to adopt.

Fourth, there is a lack of regulation and legislation to recognise blockchain application like digital currency in New Zealand [11], which may undermine the confidence of enterprises to adopt blockchain technology. For example, how should goods and services tax (GST) be collected if some enterprises accept digital currency for business transaction? The exchange rates among popular digital currencies in the world have not been as stable as most fiat money from developed countries.

3   Economic Opportunity of Blockchain in New Zealand

Blockchain has been forecasted to generate an annual business value of over US$175 billion (NZ$293 billion) globally by 2025 [12]. In the Asia-Pacific region, blockchain technology market is expected to grow and earn an annual revenue of US$4.59 billion (NZ$7.68 billion) by 2023 [13]. It has the potential to contribute to the rising digital economies in Australia and New Zealand, which are worth AU$139 billion (NZ$149 billion) combined [14]. According to the Ministry of Business, Innovation and Employment (MBIE) in New Zealand, if all businesses are more digitally engaged, they could generate 20% more revenue and collectively lift the national GDP by NZ$34 billion per year [2]. Gartner predicts that spending on technology products and services in New Zealand will reach NZ$13.9 billion [15]. Although these statistics show the high-level potential of blockchain technology, they may not be adequate for technology service providers to jump into the bandwagon. Recent report also warns that 90% of blockchain-based initiatives will suffer 'blockchain fatigue' by 2023 due to a lack of strong use cases [16]. Therefore, technology service providers must understand the prospective market before launching their blockchain-enabled services.

4   Total Addressable Market for Primary Industries in New Zealand

Total addressable market (TAM) is a market size metric representing the potential revenue opportunity for a single service provider, assuming the full market is being captured by their service [17]. For example, if the food industry is the subject of our study, then every food producer is assumed to use blockchain-enabled services to support their daily transactions. The TAM of blockchain-based services in this case will be a cumulative value of operations in the food industry as if the total demand from the market could be fulfilled by blockchain-enabled services. TAM could also be used to eliminate potential blockers and irrelevant industries.

TAM can be determined in two ways: (1) a top-down approach, and (2) a bottom-up approach. The top-down approach mainly relies on secondary research data and reports. The results of top-down approach are typically presented in the form of "according to this study, it is a $X dollar market" and shows how a service provider could share a percentage of that market. One disadvantage of the top-down approach is the tendency of overestimation, as the secondary data source may not be framed specifically to a localised subject or case. On the contrary, the bottom-up approach is very specific, but it requires a granular look at the market to identify potential customers. When potential customers are identified within a market segment, revenue per customer is a prerequisite for estimating the TAM. In either approach, it is important to build end-user (e.g., individual or organisation) profile. Additionally, it is vital for technology service providers to carefully consider their pricing models (e.g., mixed subscription) when building the end-user profile. Below we estimate the TAM for primary industries in New Zealand.

4.1   Building End User Profile

We consult the latest New Zealand Business Demography Statistics (NZBDS) that shows an annual snapshot of the structure and characteristics of New Zealand enterprises to build the end-user profile (Statistics New Zealand 2019). NZBDS are limited to those enterprises with GST turnover greater than NZ$30,000 per year. Enterprises can either be self-employed individual, company, incorporated society, local government body or central government body that is engaged in the production of goods and services in New Zealand. As shown in Fig. 2, there are a total of 546,735 enterprises in New Zealand as of 2019 financial year, among which 64,779 (11.12%) are in the primary industries. Moreover, 123,800 employees work among primary industries enterprises.

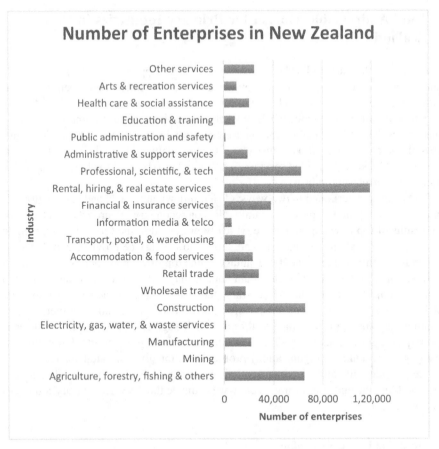

Fig. 2. New Zealand business demography statistics in 2019

Table 1 summarises the number of enterprises and corresponding employees involved in the primary industries of New Zealand.

Table 1. New Zealand business demography statistics for primary industries

Industry		Size of enterprise (Group by employee count)							
		0	1–5	6–9	10–19	20–49	50–99	100+	Total
Agriculture, forestry, fishing and others	Number of enterprises	45,258	14,925	2,301	1,362	669	171	90	64,779
	Number of employees	0	33,600	16,500	17,900	20,200	11,500	24,100	123,800

4.2 Calculating TAM

The general equation to calculate TAM is:

TAM = Total number of potential customer × annual contract value per customer (ACV)

As abovementioned, the spending on technology products and services in New Zealand will reach NZ$13.9 billion. Therefore, we estimate the average spending by each enterprise to be NZ$25,424 per year (i.e. 13,900,000,000/546,735) or NZ$2,119 per month (i.e. 25,424/12).

The estimated TAM for the primary industries is around NZ$1.65 billion per year, assuming the total number of enterprises is 64,779 and the ACV per enterprise is NZ$25,424 per year:

$$TAM = 64,779 \times NZ\$25,424 \approx NZ\$1.65 \text{ billion per year including self}$$
$$-\text{employed enterprises}$$

It is fair to assume that self-employed enterprises will show less interest to adopt blockchain-enabled services. Thus, if we exclude them from our calculation, the estimated TAM for primary industries is close to NZ$496 million per year:

$$TAM = (64,779 - 45,258) \times NZ\$25,424 = NZ\$496 \text{ million per year excluding self}$$
$$-\text{employed enterprises}$$

We could further narrow down the TAM for primary industries by specific target group. For example, if a target group is defined as enterprise that has at least 10 employees, then the estimated TAM is NZ$58 million per year:

$$TAM = (1,362 + 669 + 171 + 90) \times NZ\$25,424 = NZ\$58 \text{ million per year excluding}$$
$$\text{enterprises with less than 10 employees}$$

Technology service provider could also follow a clustered approach to estimate TAM if they have defined multiple target groups, and each of them may have a different pricing model (i.e. ACV).

5   Conclusion

The opportunity for blockchain technology in New Zealand is promising. Through our estimation of the total addressable market in the primary industries for blockchain-enabled services, we believe it may be close to NZ$1.65 billion per year including self-employed enterprises, or NZ$496 million per year excluding self-employed enterprises. Additionally, the characteristics of blockchain technology are suitable to tackle some of the challenges the primary industries are facing like food fraud and foodborne illness. The current pandemic may even further increase the demand for various blockchain solutions as the accuracy, trustworthiness and transparency of shared data is a matter of health and safety for everyone. Yet, we observe a number of potential impediments to adoption, including the lack of strong and practical use cases, the lack of streamlined practice for data management, the lack of understanding of the technology and its implication to the business, and the lack of regulation and legislation.

References

1. Ministry for Primary Industries: Situation and Outlook For Primary Industries. Ministry for Primary Industries (2020)
2. Ministry for Primary Industries: Strategic Intentions 2018–2023. Ministry for Primary Industries (2018)
3. New Zealand Herald: Counterfeit manuka honey causing legal headaches in the US (2018). https://www.nzherald.co.nz/business/news/article.cfm?c_id=3&objectid=12114712
4. Skerrett, A.: Food fraud: Should we be worried? (2019). https://www.newshub.co.nz/home/rural/2019/08/food-fraud-should-we-be-worried.html
5. World Health Organization: Food safety (2020)
6. Saberi, S., Kouhizadeh, M., Sarkis, J., Shen, L.: Blockchain technology and its relationships to sustainable supply chain management. Int. J. Prod. Res. **57**, 2117–2135 (2019). https://doi.org/10.1080/00207543.2018.1533261
7. Bai, C.A., Cordeiro, J., Sarkis, J.: Blockchain technology: business, strategy, the environment, and sustainability. Bus. Strategy Environ. **29**, 321–322 (2020). https://doi.org/10.1002/bse.2431
8. Piddock, G.: New Zealand organic sector now a half a billion dollar industry (2018). https://www.stuff.co.nz/business/farming/104863640/new-zealand-organic-sector-now-a-half-a-billion-dollar-industry
9. Rennie, R.: Blockchain speeds agri processes (2018). https://farmersweekly.co.nz/section/agribusiness/view/blockchain-speeds-agri-processes
10. Macaulay, S.: Positioning New Zealand's Primary Industry to Take Advantage of Opportunities Presented With New and Emerging Technologies Occurring in the Production And Marketing Of Food Products. Winston Churchill Memorial Trust (2018)
11. Sims, A., Kariyawasam, K., Mayes, D.: Regulating Cryptocurrencies in New Zealand. The Law Foundation New Zealand (2018)
12. Gartner. Blockchain Potential and Pitfalls (2020). https://www.gartner.com/en/webinars/3878710/blockchain-potential-and-pitfalls
13. Marketresearchinc. Asia-Pacific Blockchain Technology Market (2018–2023) (2018). https://www.marketresearchinc.com/technology-and-media/Asia-Pacific-Blockchain-Technology-Market-2018-2023--7681
14. Deloitte Australia. Australia's Digital Pulse (2019). https://www2.deloitte.com/au/en/pages/economics/articles/australias-digital-pulse.html
15. Paredes, D.: NZ Tech Spending To Reach $13.9 Billion In 2020 - Gartner (2019). https://www.cio.com/article/3510088/nz-tech-spending-to-reach-13-9-billion-in-2020-gartner.html
16. Gartner. Gartner Predicts 90% Of Blockchain-Based Supply Chain Initiatives Will Suffer 'Blockchain Fatigue' By 2023 (2019). https://www.gartner.com/en/newsroom/press-releases/2019-05-07-gartner-predicts-90--of-blockchain-based-supply-chain
17. Vascik, D., Jung, J.: Assessing the impact of operational constraints on the near-term unmanned aircraft system traffic management supported market. In: 16th AIAA Aviation Technology, Integration, and Operations Conference, American Institute of Aeronautics and Astronautics, Reston, Virginia (2016). https://doi.org/10.2514/6.2016-4373

Design and Implementation of a Real-Time Web Service for Monitoring Soil Moisture and Landslide in Lai Chau Province, Viet Nam

Hong Anh Le, Bao Ngoc Dinh, and Dung Nguyen[✉]

Hanoi University of Mining and Geology, 18 Pho Vien, Bac Tu Liem, Hanoi, Vietnam
{lehonganh,baongocdinh}@humg.edu.vn

Abstract. Web service technology has been recognized as one of key factors for developing natural hazards monitoring systems. This study proposes an open source web service solution for monitoring soil moisture in Lai Chau, a northern province of Vietnam. The system supports a real-time mechanism for data communication with gateway and mobile applications via http-based protocol. It receives structured data packets from the gateway, then makes the visualization on map and immediately alerts users if data is in warning range. Mobile applications are also capable to retrieve web map services by using provided RESTful APIs. The system has made a great contribution to the local government for natural disasters monitoring and management in Lai Chau province.

Keywords: Real-time · Monitoring · Landslide · Web service

1 Introduction

Environmental and natural resources monitoring systems collect, measure, and analyze the data to evaluate changes and predict the up coming events. These systems play an important role in protecting environment and preventing natural hazards. In Feb 2020, Vietnamese government approved a national master plan to build nationwide systems for monitoring environmental and natural resources including land, water, air,.. This plan also consists of many tasks such as developing laboratories, implementing frameworks and platforms for analyzing and sharing data from localities. Lai Chau is a mountainous province in Northwest region of Viet Nam with population is around 403,200 and approximately 9068 km2 in square. This region has high risk of landslide and flooding which cause many damages in both economy and human death every year. Developing a system which monitors landslide and soil moisture in Lai Chau is essential. It is even more important if such system supports local government for monitoring natural resources at real-time, therefore they can give better decisions that reduce potential damages. Web services are well-known technologies which allow to reuse software's resources and functionalities over the Internet using XML-based

© ICST Institute for Computer Sciences, Social Informatics and Telecommunications Engineering 2021
Published by Springer Nature Switzerland AG 2021. All Rights Reserved
P. C. Vinh and A. Rakib (Eds.): ICCASA 2020/ICTCC 2020, LNICST 343, pp. 131–140, 2021.
https://doi.org/10.1007/978-3-030-67101-3_11

protocol. Based on this technology, many software systems developed in various languages and platforms can communicate and transfer data easily over the networks. Web services contribute significantly to developing systems which act as management center and share resources for the other systems [9,11]. Zhou *et al.* [10] applied web service technology to develop a personal digital assistant (PDA) forest fire monitoring system. The system showed the advantages of using web services for sharing and realizing the forest fire data. S. Lee *et al.* [4,5] implemented a project which collects sensor data about soil, atmosphere, ecology, etc. and makes them sharable using a common platform. This study presents a soil moisture and landslide real-time monitoring web service system which is designed and deployed for Lai Chau Province. Based on open source technologies, this system has several advantages such as reducing the deployment cost, supporting various communication protocols with hardware devices and mobile-based applications which are specifically designed for Lai Chau's observation stations.

The structure of this paper is organized as follows. Section 2 presents the technologies used for developing the platform and the study area. Followed by Sect. 3, we present methodologies of the platform development including system design and functionalities. In Sect. 4, the system implementation and results are described. Section 5 summarizes and compares our work with related ones. Finally, Sect. 6 concludes the paper and discusses the future work.

2 Technologies and Study Area

In this section, we present the open source technologies which are used for developing the system and brief information of Lai Chau province.

2.1 Node.Js

Node.js [1] is a open source, cross platform which provides a lot of modules in for developing server-side and network applications. Node.js application are written in JavaScript, a light weight, interpreted, and most well-known script language for web pages, and can be run in various operating systems such as OS X, MS Windows, or Linux. Node.js has a bunches of built-in modules which users can use such as events to handle events of applications, net to create servers and clients, https to make it available as a HTTPS server. In order to use a built-in module, users just need to specify module name using statement require.

2.2 Data Technologies

In order to store data received from monitoring stations, the proposed platform use PostgreSQL [2] which is a powerful, open source object- relational database with reliability, security, and high robustness. The applications connect to PostgreSQL over TCP/UP network connection to perform database operations. PostgreSQL has many advanced features such as user-defined types, table inheritance, asynchronous replication, etc. JSON and GeoJSON which are data interchange formats used in the proposed system. JSON consists of an unordered set of name/value pairs. A JSON text is sequence of tokens.

2.3   Socket.io

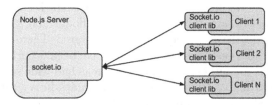

Fig. 1. Communication between server and clients with Socket.io

Socket.io [3], built on top of WebSocket and Node.js, has two components which are a Node.js server and a Javascript client library (web browser or Node.js client). It provides real-time directional event-based communication mechanism between client and server that means whenever an event occurs the server will be notified and can push messages to the client. The communication between server and clients is illustrated in Fig. 1.

2.4   Study Area

Fig. 2. Lai Chau areas with high risk of landslide

Lai Chau is a poor province situated at approximately 1,5 km latitude above the sea where floods and landslides cause many damages every year. Lai Chau has eight districts with population density is 53 people/km2 that is the sparest province in Vietnam. According to statistics of Vietnam Disaster Management Authority, in recent 17 years, there are nearly 600 floods and 850 landslide sites causing around 673 deaths and 41.436 houses devastated. There were around 905 sites at which landslides possibly happen while have been occurred at nearly 970 locations. Among these, authorities defined 28 areas had wide scale of landslides (Fig. 2). The hazard in Lai Chau usually accompanies heavy rains or volcanic eruptions. Table 1 shows the number of landslide, flash flooding, and eroding bank sites in Lai Chau in 2013.

Table 1. Lai Chau landslides statistics in 2013

No	District	Landslide sites	Flash flood	Eroding bank
1	Muong Te	203	5	7
2	Nam Nhum	106	5	6
3	Phong Tho	80	5	10
4	Sin Ho	334	1	12
5	Tam Duong	24	1	1
6	Tan Uyen	101	0	2
7	Lai Chau City	7	0	0
8	Than Uyen	115	18	42

3 Methodologies

3.1 The System Design

Figure 3 shows the architecture of the proposed platform. It consists of four main components including Communication, Core, and GUI services.

- **Communication**: Monitoring stations use sensors getting soil moisture, soil temperature then push data to the Communication module in the format of JSON or GEOJSON via HTTP RESTful. This component also handles queries from other external systems then forward the query content to the **Core** component.
- **GUI services**: It allows end users (e.g., local government or residents in Lai Chau) to access monitoring and administrative features such as viewing maps of landslide sites, real-time data and charts from stations, updating warning from the decision support system.

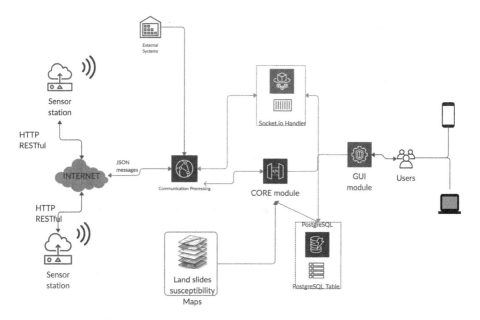

Fig. 3. Architecture of the platform

- **Core**: It is the main component of the platform that acts as a bridge linking other components. It receives data or request from **Communication** component, manipulates data store in PostSQL, then send back the results to the **Communication** and **GUI** component.

Messages exchanged between the platform with other clients including sensor stations, mobile client, web client are defined as follows.

```
{
    "station_id": identification of monitoring station,
    "device_id": identity of device ,
    "gps_lati": lattitude value of the station,
    "gps_long": longtitude value of the station,
    "time_stamp": time of data collecting,
    "param": parameter name,
    "value": parameter value
}
```

where *param* field represents parameter that sensors in the monitoring station can collect such as air moisture, soil moisture, soil temperature, etc. and *value* is the value of corresponding parameter.

Web service provider implemented in Node.JS and Socket.io listens events from PostgreSQL whenever new data is updated, then notify to service subscribers (web or mobile applications). In order to store the data transferred from monitoring stations, the database of this platform is designed with four main

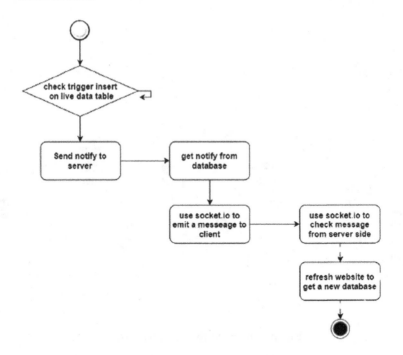

Fig. 4. Real-time communication flow

tables including stations, stations_params, live_data, and params. The purposes of each specific table is described as follows

- Stations: storing data of each stations equipped with IoT sensors containing station identifier, name, and location of the station.
- Params: defining monitoring parameters that sensors in stations can achieve. It allows users flexibly configure in each specific applied area.
- live_data: store data from each station with specific time stamp.
- stations_params: contains data packet structures which ingested by the station.

In order to support real-time communications between this platform and clients, we propose to use postgresql trigger and socket.io to implement this feature. Figure 4 depicts the real-time mechanism of the platform. The designed trigger which is fired when soil moisture and landslide are inserted by monitoring station will notify the server. The platform then send messages to clients using socket.io framework. After getting messages from platforms, clients will be refreshed.

3.2 Functionalities

The proposed platform provides both graphical interfaces to users and services to programmers. The former is intended to for local authorities and residents who can use this platform to monitor live data of soil moisture and landslide of five stations in Lai Chau. The later are for developers who want to use the live data from stations to build their own applications, for example, Android applications can use the provided services to collect data at real-time. There are three actors including users (i.e., local residents), administrators (i.e., local authorities), and service subscribers. Functionalities for each actor are described as follows.

- Users:
  - Viewing live data for soil moisture and landslide from monitoring stations
  - Viewing live charts for the specific stations
- Administrators:
  - Managing the configuration of the platform such as stations, data packet parameters, etc.
- Service subscribers:
  - Gateway and mobile applications can exchange data in bi-direction using published services with HTTP REST API

4 System Implementation and Results

4.1 Implementation

Recall that we make use of PostgreSQL's triggers and socket.io to implement real-time notification described in Sect. 2. The snippets below show the content of the trigger.

```
CREATE TRIGGER watch_realtime_table_trigger AFTER INSERT ON live_data
FOR EACH ROW EXECUTE PROCEDURE notify\_trigger ();
CREATE FUNCTION notify_trigger () RETURNS trigger AS $$
DECLARE
BEGIN
PERFORM pg_notify ('watch_realtime_table', row_to_json (NEW): : text);
RETURN new;
END;
```

Trigger *watch_realtime_table_trigger* declares if there is any update on table *live_data*, it emits an event *watch_realtime_table* to the system. The listener service developed in Node.js receives the emitted event and pushes to the clients via HTTP REST APIs. Monitoring stations are able to push data to the system using HTTP POST method with data package defined in Sect. 3.1. Mobile and other external applications can get data from the system using HTTP GET method and custom queries. Custom queries allows users to define parameters to filter expected data.

4.2 Results

The monitoring system is deployed on the Internet for public usage[1]. Figure 5a shows the susceptible landslide sites and status of five monitoring stations located in Lai Chau. Users can observe the real-time data in each station and receive warnings from the decision support system. Figure 5b depicts the observation maps integrated with real-time online data sources from Weather Map[2].

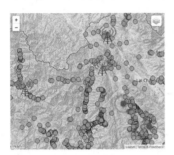

(a) Susceptible land-slide sites

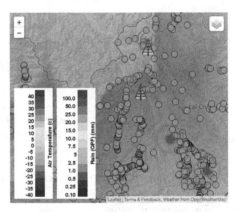

(b) Monitoring with on-line sources

Fig. 5. Land-slides monitoring system in Lai Chau

Besides the visualized and interactive map, the system allows local residents and officers monitoring real-time data from each station with a time line (Fig. 6). They can choose which station to observe in the interval of date. This would help local officers and experts give decision before natural hazard.

5 Related Work

VietNam Ministry of Natural Resources and Environment conducted a project that accomplished the susceptible landslide map in some provinces including Lai Chau. This project implemented a webGIS[3] for visualizing the information. This product, however, lacks of real-time factors such as sensors data.

Muandar *et al.* [6] presented a mobile-based real-time weather monitoring system. It also uses sensor in Automatic Weather Station to collect data. The advantages of our system in comparison to their system is that real-time communication between web server and mobile applies in their approach via FTP,

---

[1] http://103.145.62.106:3000.

[2] https://openweathermap.com.

[3] https://canhbaotruotlo.vn.

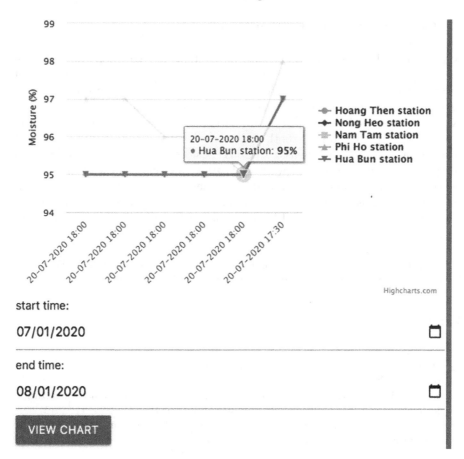

Fig. 6. Data monitoring in time-line charts

then Android applications read files and display the information. Their approach makes more delay than using socket and trigger mechanism. Their system is mobile-based while the proposed system is web service-based.

Song *et al.* [8] developed a real-time environment monitoring using Open GIS Specifications and Open Source GeoSpatial Software with low-cost sensors. There are several commons between their system and our one, for example, using sensors to retrieve air temperature and humidity and PostgreSQL for storage. Their approach, however, just provided a web-based feature and did not focus on landslide.

Recently, Rahmat *et al.* [7] used smart sensors to collect pH, soild moisture, air humidity, and light intensity for rice plants. However, the monitoring information are sent to users in form of SMS. It did not show the extension of the monitoring eco-systems including web and mobile applications.

6   Conclusions and Future Work

Natural hazard prediction and monitoring systems are vital for every country that help to reduce damages of both economy and human life. Such kind of systems depends much on characteristics of monitoring areas. In this study, we presented the system for monitoring landslide and soil moisture in Lai Chau. This system is developed using open source technologies such as Node.Js, socket.io and PostgreSQL. It provides both end users (local residents and government) to monitor live data from sensor stations. Besides, the system also offers web services interfaces for other software application can reuse. In the future, we will develop the mobile applications and components to control sensors remotely. Integrating GIS as a component which allows to flexibly manage maps of vulnerable areas with flooding and landslide in Lai Chau province is also another future work.

Acknowledgments. This work is supported by the project no. CT.2019.01.05 granted by Ministry of Education and Training (MOET).

References

1. Node.js (2020). https://Node.JS
2. Postgresql (2020). https://www.postgresql.org
3. Socket.io (2020). https://socket.io
4. Lee, S., Jo, J.Y., Kim, Y.: Restful web service and web-based data visualization for environmental monitoring. Int. J. Softw. Innov. (IJSI) **3**(1), 75–94 (2015)
5. Lee, S., Jo, J., Kim, Y., Stephen, H.: A framework for environmental monitoring with arduino-based sensors using restful web service. In: 2014 IEEE International Conference on Services Computing, pp. 275–282 (2014)
6. Munandar, A., Fakhrurroja, H., Rizqyawan, M.I., Pratama, R.P., Wibowo, J.W., Anto, I.A.F.: Design of real-time weather monitoring system based on mobile application using automatic weather station. In 2017 2nd International Conference on Automation, Cognitive Science, Optics, Micro Electro-Mechanical System, and Information Technology (ICACOMIT), pp. 44–47 (2017)
7. Rahmat, R.F., Pujiarti, T.Z.L., Hizriadi, A.: Implementation of real-time monitoring on agricultural land of rice plants using smart sensor. In: 2019 3rd International Conference on Electrical, Telecommunication and Computer Engineering (ELTICOM), pp. 40–43 (2019)
8. Song, X., Wang, C., Kagawa, M., Raghavan, V.: Real-time monitoring portal for urban environment using sensor web technology. In 2010 18th International Conference on Geoinformatics, pp. 1–5 (2010)
9. Thumtuan, P., Chub-Uppakarn, T., Chalermyanont, T.: Real time monitoring of soil moisture content for landslide early warning: wn experimental study. In: MATEC Web Conference, vol. 192, pp. 02032 (2018)
10. Zhou, Y., Liu, P., Tang, X.: Application of PDA forest fire monitoring based on web service technology. Front. For. China. **4**, 358–362 (2009)
11. Zhou, Y., Liu, P., Tang, X.: Environmental sensor monitoring with secure restful web service (2009)

Optimizing the Operational Time of IoT Devices in Cloud-Fog Systems

Nguyen Thanh Tung[(⊠)]

International School, Vietnam National University, Hanoi, Vietnam
tungnt@isvnu.vn

Abstract. With the increasing number of connected devices, sensors, data generated need to be analyzed. The current cloud computing model, which concentrate on computing and storage resources in a few large data centers, will inevitably lead to excessive network load, end-to-end service latency, and overall power consumption. This leads to the creation of new network architectures that extend computing and storage capabilities to the edge of the network, close to end-users. The emerging problem is how to efficiently deploy the services to the system that satisfies service resource requirements and QoS constraints while maximizing resource utilization.

In this paper, we investigate the problem of IoT services deployment in Cloud Fog system to provide IoT services with minimal energy consumption. We formulate the problem using a Linear Programming (LP) model to maximize the operational time of Cloud-Fog system as well as the IoT services specific requirements [1]. We propose a new heuristic algorithm to simplify the problem. We compare the lifetime of the proposed algorithm with the optimal solution solved by Linear Programming. The experimental results show that our proposed solution is very close to optimum solutions in terms of energy efficiency.

Keywords: IoT · Cloud-Fog system · Battery constraint · Operation time · Linear Programming

1 Introduction

Along with the development of connected devices and smart environments, the Internet of Things (IoT) has been receiving attention for years because of the growth in the number of devices.

Recently, Cisco has introduced Cloud Fog computing as a new paradigm which takes advantage of the extensive resources in the cloud while being able to expand computing power to the edge of the network, close to end-users. Figure 1 illustrates the architecture of a Cloud-Fog system with three hierarchical layers. At the edge most of the network is the device layer which contains numerous sensor devices. They can be widely distributed at various public infrastructures to monitor the environment over time. Each node either collects data (i.e., video, temperature, noise) or performs a certain function (i.e., sprinkle, smart light). Data generated by IoT devices can be sent to and processed and deployed at the fog nodes near by the data sources. The fog nodes can be micro clouds, access network devices or even user devices, which located in a

© ICST Institute for Computer Sciences, Social Informatics and Telecommunications Engineering 2021
Published by Springer Nature Switzerland AG 2021. All Rights Reserved
P. C. Vinh and A. Rakib (Eds.): ICCASA 2020/ICTCC 2020, LNICST 343, pp. 141–147, 2021.
https://doi.org/10.1007/978-3-030-67101-3_12

wide-spread geographical area, together they form the fog layer that lies between the device layer and the cloud layer. Each fog node is connected to and responsible for a group of IoT devices, performing data analysis in a timely manner. On top of the architecture is cloud layer consists of a number of powerful servers allocated in a few data centers. The cloud layer is considered as an unlimited resource pool providing an ability to process computational-intensive tasks, store a massive amount of data [2, 3].

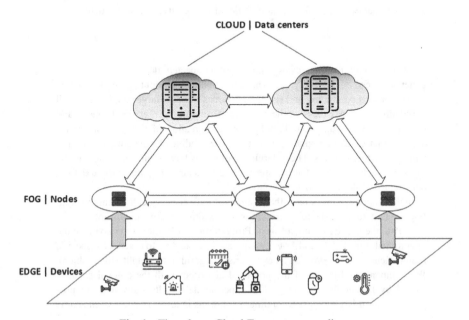

Fig. 1. Three-layer Cloud-Fog system paradigm.

The Cloud-fog system is considered to be an efficient solution for providing resources to handle newly emerging IoT services with tightly QoS constraints. However, the computing intensive functions of IoT services can not be deployed to the devices due to its limitations on computing power and battery life.

2 Linear Programming Model for Optimizing the Operational Time of IoT Devices with Multiple Fog Nodes (Fns)

To model the energy consumption of the FN problem, the full wireless radio energy dissipation model is not used. A very simple energy usage model is given below. The validation of the simulation results is not affected.

$$E(S) = d^2, E(D) = 0 \tag{1}$$

where S is the energy to transmit data, D is the destination node. In other words, the energy to transmit a unit of data is equal to the square of the distance to a destination, and the energy to receive data is equal to zero [5].

We define a round of operation of a IoT device as the time the device must transmit a unit of data to the closest FN. It is also assumed that only k FNs from N FNs (k < N) as the FNs in each round of transmission and the role is reallocated among all FNs so the system lifetime is maximized. The linear programming model needs to calculate the optimal usage of FNs under the battery constraint of every IoT device [5–7].

Given a Cloud Fog network with k Fog Nodes (FNs) in the set of N FNs, each IoT device connect to the closest FN of the k FNs provides the optimal lifetime for the Cloud Fog network.

In more detail, we have n IoT devices located in the Cloud Fog system. We define W as the set of ways to choose k FNs in the given set of N FNs. If every FN is different to the remaining $N - 1$ FNs, the number of items in W is $\binom{N}{k}$. The energy c_i^j is equal to the energy dissipation of Device j to send a unit of data to the closest FN in the ith element in W. We define n_i as the number of rounds, the ith item in W is chosen as the active FNs. We define E_j as the initial energy of Device j. We also define O as the optimal solution of the following Linear Programing problem:

Maximize:

$$\sum_{i=1}^{\binom{N}{k}} n_i$$

Subject to:

$$\sum_{i=1}^{\binom{N}{k}} n_i c_i^j \leq E_j : \forall j \in [1\ldots n] \tag{2}$$

$$n_i \in Z^+ : \forall i \in [1\ldots \binom{N}{k}]$$

3 Proposed Heuristic Algorithm

The solution given by the above LP model for the IoT devices networks is not simple for calculation. Each time, there is a change in the network, the solution needs to be recalculated. Also, IoT devices are too small to solve the LP model. Furthermore, it is infeasible to calculate an optimum solution for the big cloud fog network. We need to find out a heuristic algorithm to calculate the FN pattern.

In the heuristic algorithm, the FNs pattern needs to be reallocated among the IoT nodes so that the minimum residual energy of all IoT device is maximized. As the process is rerun in every round, the energy consumption of active FNs is reasonably distributed among all FNs so that the operational time lasts until a IoT device dies. The heuristic method is called Modified-LEACH (M-LEACH) and can be stated as below [4, 8, 9].

M-LEACH:

In every round, select k FNs randomly from all N FNs in Cloud Fog networks.
Given:
N The number of FNs indexed from 1 to N
s: The current FN pattern
For every round of data transmission
i = Random (1..N) Repeat for k different FNs
Result: s is the FNs pattern for the current round
Repeat until the first IoT device dies

4   Simulation Results

Visual Studio C++ is used to simulate the efficiency of M-LEACH. For the calculation of the optimum solution, we use the LP solver mentioned in [10]. The coefficients of the analytical model for different Cloud Fog topologies are generated from a C++ application. In the program, every possible combination of k FNs from N FNs is generated and the energy usages of sending data from all IoT devices to each combination active FNs are calculated.

In our experiments, 100 random 100-node IoT networks are generated. Initially, each node has 3,000,000 units of energy. The algorithm M-LEACH is run over the network topologies while the number of FNs k is set to 3 and N is set to 5, and the operational time is calculated for every Cloud Fog topology. The Cloud Fog networks are given below. The IoT device positions and the FNs position are described as in Fig. 2 and Fig. 3.

Network size $(100m \times 100m)$

Fog Nodes (0,120); (50,120);(100,120);(120,50);(120,0)
Number of IoT devices   100 nodes
Position of IoT device: Uniform placed in the area
Energy model: $E_t = d^2$ where d is the distance between the source IoT device and the destination IoT device

---

Fig. 2. IoT devices and Fog Nodes.

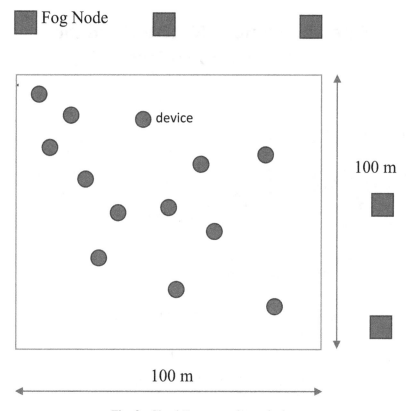

Fig. 3. Cloud Fog network topologies.

The performance of the heuristic M-LEACH and the optimum solution from the analytical model is compared. For the optimum solution, the analytical model in Sect. 2 is used where k is set to 3 and N is set to 5. Both methods are run over the above 100 network topologies and the ratio between the lifetime of M-LEACH and the optimum is calculated. Figure 4 shows that M-LEACH simulation result is very close to the optimum solution (Table 1).

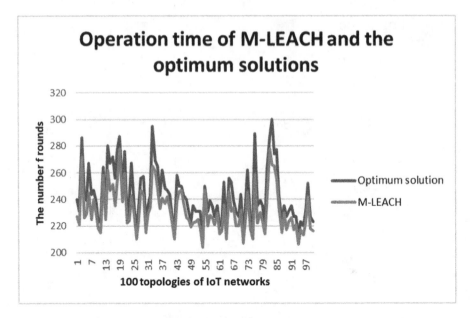

Fig. 4. Simulation results compared M-LEACH and the optimum solution.

Table 1. Results for Fig. 4.

Statistics	M-LEACH/Optimum solution
Mean	**0.89**
Variance	**0.0005**

5 Conclusion

In this paper, we model the IoT services deployment in Cloud Fog system using a Linear Programming (LP) model taking into account the characteristics of energy resources in Cloud-Fog system and IoT devices. However, it is impractical to find the solution of large Cloud Fog network. Therefore, heuristic algorithms are needed to solve the problem. A new heuristic method M-LEACH is then proposed. 100 random 100-node networks are used to evaluate the performance of the methods. Simulations show that M-LEACH provides performance very close to the optimum solutions.

References

1. Dastjerdi, A.V., Gupta, H., Calheiros, R.N., Ghosh, S.K., Buyya, R.: Fog computing: principles, architectures, and applications. In: Internet of Things, pp. 61–75. Elsevier, Amsterdam (2016)

2. Bonomi, F., Milito, R., Zhu, J., Addepalli, S.: Fog computing and its role in the internet of things. In: Proceedings of the First Edition of the MCC Workshop on Mobile Cloud Computing, pp. 13–16. ACM (2012)
3. Hajibaba, M., Gorgin, S.: A review on modern distributed computing paradigms: cloud computing, jungle computing and fog computing. J. Comput. Inf. Technol. **22**(2), 69–84 (2014)
4. Chang, R., et al.: An energy efficient routing mechanism for wireless sensor networks. In: Proceedings of the 20th International Conference on Advanced Information Networking and Applications (AINA 2006) (2006)
5. Tung, N.T.: Energy-efficient routing algorithms in wireless sensor networks. Ph.D. thesis, Monash University, Australia (2009)
6. Tung, N.T., Thanh Binh, H.T.: Base station location -aware optimization model of the lifetime of wireless sensor networks. Mobile Netw. Appl. (MONET), May 2016. https://doi.org/10.1007/s11036-015-0614-3
7. Tung, N.T., Nguyen, V.D.: Optimizing the operating time of wireless sensor network. EURASIP J. Wirel. Commun. Netw. (2013). https://doi.org/10.1186/1687-1499-2012-348, ISSN: 1687-1499
8. LourthuHepziba, M.M., Balamurugan, K., Vijayaraj, M.: Maximization of lifetime and reducing power consumption in wireless sensor network using protocol. Int. J. Soft Comput. Eng. **2**(6), 90–95 (2013)
9. Paschalidis, I.C., Wu, R.: Robust maximum lifetime routing and energy allocation in wireless sensor networks. Int. J. Distrib. Sens. Netw. **2012**(523787), 14 (2012)
10. https://www.gnu.org/software/glpk/

Proposing Spatial - Temporal - Semantic Data Model Managing Genealogy and Space Evolution History of Objects in 3D Geographical Space

Dang Van Pham$^{(\boxtimes)}$ (iD)

Faculty of Information Technology, Nguyen Tat Thanh University,
Ho Chi Minh City, Vietnam
pvdang@ntt.edu.vn, pvdang.tps@gmail.com

Abstract. Managing construction projects in new urban areas is an essential work for construction contractors as well as authorities at all levels. In this management, managing the spatial evolutionary history of two-dimensional (2D), two-point-five-dimensional (2.5D) and three-dimensional (3D) spatial objects over time and semantics in 3D geographical space is an urgent and extremely important work. This paper proposes a spatial - temporal - semantic data model (STSDM), spatial queries over time and semantics, and algorithms finding the ancestors and descendants of space objects (ASA and DSA). The paper presents some empirical results about the spatial evolutionary history of spatial objects over time and semantics. The experimental results show that it can completely be used to trace the space evolution history of bridges, houses and apartments at a given time or in a given period in new urban management applications.

Keywords: Spatial - temporal - semantic data model · STSDM · Spatial evolutionary history · Spatial queries · Space objects

1 Introduction

In urban management, especially the management of traces of spatial evolution history of 2D, 2.5D and 3D space objects of constructions in new urban areas is an important and necessary work. In aspects of construction techniques performed by humans, we can sometimes meet with risks as when they were being constructed, they collapsed. In aspects of nature, we can sometimes meet with risks caused by natural disasters such as earthquakes, tsunamis or storms causing space objects to disappear. Therefore, in aspects of managing risks and tracing the spatial evolution history of 2D, 2.5D and 3D spatial objects in new urban areas that is an essential work not only for the construction contractors but also authorities at all levels in managing new urban areas of smart.

When constructing bridges spanning rivers, buildings, smart houses, etc., keeping traces of the current history at different times of construction is an important work for building contractors. This work is aimed at helping construction contractors the opportunity to trace the spatial evolution history of 2D, 2.5D, 3D space objects as

© ICST Institute for Computer Sciences, Social Informatics and Telecommunications Engineering 2021
Published by Springer Nature Switzerland AG 2021. All Rights Reserved
P. C. Vinh and A. Rakib (Eds.): ICCASA 2020/ICTCC 2020, LNICST 343, pp. 148–168, 2021.
https://doi.org/10.1007/978-3-030-67101-3_13

evidence to support the calculation of labors, construction materials as well as time to complete construction items. The management of spatial and genealogy variations of spatial features in construction items is essential for contractors. They can observe in detail the construction items change over time. From there they will make timely adjustments when a project goes into operation. Therefore, people can avoid short-comings and risks during construction.

Currently, the situation of urbanization is happening quickly and complicatedly. Therefore, an information system that manages the development in the field of con-struction becomes even more urgent and necessary. This system not only helps con-struction contractors to closely monitor their construction progress but also assists policymakers to develop new urban in the future. The management focus on methods of storing spatial data, searching and enumerating of construction items according to construction history is very important. Semantics is an essential element of a man-agement information system. The semantic class plays an important role in saving the meaning of each attribute in the space object. Based on this factor, users can understand the types of objects in space. What is the name of the space object? What are its attributes? What properties does it reflect in space objects? Who managed, who owned and who maintained?

Time is essential factor embedded in management information systems. In life, humans always have different relationships (Fig. 1) such as blood relationships, social relationships, previous conviction relationships, previous offence relationships, born/death relationships, etc. These relationships lead to the importance of the spatial and temporal classes and have formed object – space - time relationships [1–3]. The time class plays an important role in saving the spatial change history of object – space - time relationships. Based on the element of time, we can extract history of these relationships to serve different fields of careers. The time element in a paper can represent the history of spatial change occurring at a specified time point or interval.

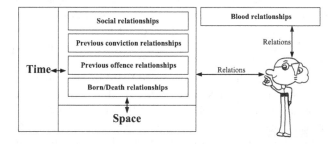

Fig. 1. Expressions of non - temporal relationships, relationships with time and space elements

The objective of this paper is to propose three classes such as spatial, temporal, and semantic classes to construct spatial - temporal - semantic data model (STSDM) for managing spatial evolution history and genealogy of 2D, 2.5D and 3D spatial objects in the new urban area. This new model has the ability to manage and potentially query space over time and semantics, and algorithms finding the ancestors and descendants of space objects. Experimental results simulating the history of spatial evolution and genealogy of spatial objects show that they can be applied to specific applications in the management of construction works in the future.

The remainder of this paper is presented as follows: Part 2 briefly presents the relevant research works, makes comments and encloses new proposals for the application of construction works in new urban areas. Part 3 proposes the STSDM and proceeds to build spatial class, time class, semantic class, algorithms to find genealogy of 3D space objects, and construct spatial and temporal queries. Part 4 presents empirical results simulating the history of space evolution and genealogy of space objects. Part 5 is the conclusion section and suggestion development for future paper. Finally, that is the material reference section.

2   Related Works

Building spatial - temporal - semantic data models plays an important role in tracking the spatial change history of houses, apartments, bridges as well as tracing the length of development history of urban architectures is the key to supporting GIS applications 2-2.5-3-4D time. This paper systematizes data models by type and makes some comments as a premise for a new proposal.

2.1   Overview of Data Model Types

For good representation of 2D, 2.5D and 3D spatial objects with boundaries, the boundary representation method (B-REP) is the most suitable choice. This method represents 3D objects based on predefined elements, including: point, line, surface, solid and this method is suitable for representing 2-2.5-3D objects have regular and scalar shapes. The data models were proposed by the authors from the past to the present that have applied the B-REP method include: The UDM spatial data model was proposed by Coors in 2003 [4]; 3D Cadastral model was proposed by Yuan Ding authors group and his colleagues in 2017 [5]; TUDM model proposed by Anh N.G.T authors group and his colleagues in 2012 [6]; VRO-DLOD3D model was proposed by Dang P.V authors group and his colleagues in 2017 [7]; CityGML model was proposed by Groger authors group and his colleagues in 2007 [8]; Kolbe authors group and his colleagues expanded CityGML model in 2009 [9]; Biljecki authors group and his colleagues improved CityGML model in 2016 [10]; Dang P.V authors group and his colleagues proposed ELUDM model for 2.5D objects in 2011 [11]; Anh N.G.T authors group and his colleagues proposed ELUDM model for 2.5D objects in 2011 [12]; Löwner authors group and his colleagues proposed a new LoD and multi-representational concept for CityGML model in 2016 [13]; CityGML-TRKBIS.BI model Aydar authors group and his colleagues to meet the need to establish 2-2.5-3D objects at the national level in 2016 [14]; TLODs model was proposed by Dang P.V authors group and his colleagues [15].

To represent 3D objects with voxel elements such as pixels in 2D GIS, the voxel method is the most suitable choice. This method represents a 3D object based on the idea of splitting an object into child elements, each of which is called a voxel [16].

An element is referred to as a 3D geospatial and is assigned by an integer [17]. Models proposed by the authors in the past that have applied the voxel method include the 3D Array model proposed by Rahman [18, 19]. The model has the simplest data structure used to represent 3D objects. Elements in 3D Array have one of two values 0 and 1. In which 0 describes the base value, 1 describes the value that each element in the 3D Array is occupied by the 3D object.

If a 3D object is scanned in a 3D array that the elements of the array are initially initialized with a value of 0. After scanning the 3D object, the elements with a value of 1 represent the information for the 3D object. Octree model was proposed by Gorger authors group and his colleagues in 2004 [20]. Octree is an extension of a tetrahedral tree to an octal. Octree is a 3D representation model based on a block platform. The octal tree gives us an image, which is a method represented by a tree data structure. In general, an octal tree is defined based on the smallest cube containing the 3D object to be represented. The original cube will be divided into 8 sub cubes. An octal tree is based on decomposition according to the recursive algorithm. In a tree, each node either leaves or has 8 seedlings. Each seedling will be tested before being divided into 8 other seedlings.

To represent 3D objects in 3D geographical space, we use the combination of basic 3D blocks proposed by Rahman in 2008 is the best choice [18]. CSG model represents 3D objects by combining predefined 3D elements. Basic 3D blocks are often used as cube, cylinder and sphere. The relationships between these figures include: transformations and logical operands. The transformations include translations, rotations, and degrees. Logical operands include union, intersection, and difference. CSG is often used in CAD and CSG is very convenient in calculating the volume of objects, CSG is not suitable for representing objects with irregular geometric shapes.

2.2   Comment and Recommendation Data Models

Through analysis of the above data model types, it is given us a clear view of the developmental history process of data models proposed by the authors groups. We found that these models mainly use the B-REP method, which represents 2-2.5-3D objects based on predefined elements including: point, line, surface, solid. Therefore, this method is suitable for representing 2-2.5-3D objects of regular and scalar shapes.

To represent spatial objects including bridges, residential houses, villas, etc. in 3D geographical space, the application of modeling is the key to success. The criteria to consider models are models that must be able to represent spatial objects in 3D geographical space include the criteria representing outside surface, the criteria representing inside surface, the criteria representing the level of detail but must also be able to store spatial data, time data, and semantic data. In 2013, T.A.N.Gia authors group and his colleagues [21] presented a summary of GIS 3-4D data models, in which this authors group has proposed a presentation that summarizes the criteria that each GIS 3-4D data model must satisfy. Those criteria include surface representation of objects, inside surface representation of objects, representation of main elements, representation of data size applying to applications, spatial data structure, spatial attribute queries, spatial object location queries, semantic queries. After that in 2017, T.A.Nguyen-Gia authors group and his colleagues [22] gave a brief survey of the current popular 3-4D

GIS data models with comparison tables by typical criteria such as representation of surface types, inside surface representation of objects, triangulation capability, triangulation incapability, model platforms, data storage dimensions, and applicability to existing applications now.

Through the systematization and classification of data models and based on the criteria proposed by the authors mentioned above as a premise for this paper to propose the construction of the STSDM to manage spatial evolutionary history, we found that the above models mainly applied B-REP method. In general, these models focus on managing and exploiting spatial, time and relationships objects. However, a major challenge now is how to represent residential houses in urban areas in more detail in the spatial evolutionary history of 2D, 2.5D and 3D space objects, from there the managers have the opportunity to manage spatial objects according to spatial evolutionary history to serve in the planning of future urban development policies. From these challenges, we propose constructing a STSDM to manage spatial evolutionary history and find the genealogy of bridges and residential buildings in new urban areas in 3D geographical space.

3   Spatial – Temporal – Semantic Data Model

3.1   Time Class

Time is an essential element of an information system that manages construction items. The time class plays an important role in tracking the spatial variation of objects in space. Based on the time element, people can intervene in time to resolve urgent issues and recognize the situation more clearly. The time element in the paper can represent spatial changes that occur at a time point or a given time segment. In order to manage spatial objects according to time and semantics which had studies suggesting three types of time data as shown in Table 1 [15, 23]. The time element is attached to spatial data, which makes the stored data more abundant and more meaningful to use. Happened events are causes of the spatial changes of objects that also presented in this

Table 1. Detailed description of time data types

No	Time data type	Meaning describes the time data types
1	Event time (ET_s)	Event time is the time that begins to occur and ends in the real world. There is day – month – year - hour: minute: second beginning to occur and day – month – year - hour: minute: second ending in the real world
2	Legal time (LT_s)	Legal time is the effective time on legal documents. There is day – month – year - hour: minute: second beginning to occur and day – month – year - hour: minute: second ending in documents
3	Database time (DT_s)	Database time is the time to write to the database. There is day – month – year - hour: minute: second beginning to occur and day – month – year - hour: minute: second ending in database

paper. Time is used to trace the beginning and ending history of an object in space. Time is divided into three specific time data types (see Table 1) having nine-time data units located on the time axis (see Fig. 2) with the convention in Table 2. In the nine-time data units described in Table 2, people are mainly interested in the four-time data units as T_1, T_3, T_5 and T_8. From the nine-time data units we form the time topology relations in Tables 3, 4 and 5 as follows (Figs. 3, 4, 5 and 6).

Table 2. The table describes nine - time data units

No	Convention	Meaning describes the time data types
1	T_1	The start time of the object in the real world
2	T_2	The end time of the object in the real world
3	T_3	The time people start the owner or manager of the object
4	T_4	The time people end the owner or manager of the object
5	T_5	The time people start to maintain the object according to regulations
6	T_6	The time people end to maintain the object according to regulations
7	T_7	Time people maintain the object periodically
8	T_8	The time people start to write objects to the database
9	T_9	The time people end to write objects to the database

Table 3. The table classifies time data units into time data types

No	Convention	Meaning describes the time data types
The event time type consists of two - time data units:		
1	T_1	The start time of the object in the real world
2	T_2	The end time of the object in the real world
The legal time type consists of five - time data units:		
3	T_3	The time people start the owner or manager of the object
4	T_4	The time people end the owner or manager of the object
5	T_5	The time people start to maintain the object according to regulations
6	T_6	The time people end to maintain the object according to regulations
7	T_7	Time people maintain the object periodically
The database time type consists of two - time data units:		
8	T_8	The time people start to write objects to the database
9	T_9	The time people end to write objects to the database

Table 4. The table describes the relationship before and after between time data units

No	Relationship	Meaning describes the relationship before and after
1	$T_1 < T_2$	T_1 is a unit of time beginning to occur with space objects in real world earlier than the end time unit of the space objects in real world (T_2)
2	$T_1 < T_3$	T_1 is a unit of time beginning to occur with space objects in real world earlier than the time when people start the owner or manager of the space objects according to regulations (T_3)
3	$T_1 < T_4$	T_1 is a unit of time beginning to occur with space objects in real world earlier than the time when people end the owner or manager of the space objects according to regulations (T_4)
4	$T_1 < T_5$	T_1 is a unit of time occurring in the real world earlier than the start time maintaining of space objects according to regulations (T_5)
5	$T_1 < T_6$	T_1 is a unit of time occurring in the real world earlier than the start time maintaining of space objects according to regulations (T_6)
6	$T_1 < T_7$	T_1 is a unit of time occurring in the real world earlier than the time maintaining of spatial objects periodically (T_7)
7	$T_1 < T_8$	T_1 is a unit of time occurring in the real world earlier than the start time recording the change of spatial objects into database (T_8)
8	$T_1 < T_9$	T_1 is a unit of time occurring in the real world earlier than the end time recording the change of spatial objects into database (T_9)
9	$T_5 < T_6$	T_5 is a unit of start time maintaining space objects according to regulations earlier than the unit of time maintaining space objects to regulations (T_6)
10	$T_6 < T_7$	T_7 is a unit time maintaining space objects periodically later than the end time unit maintaining space objects to regulations (T_6)
11	$T_8 < T_5$	T_8 is a unit of time recording the database earlier than the time unit maintaining on legal documents (T_5)
12	$T_8 < T_9$	T_9 is a unit of end time recording the changes of space objects into the database later than the start time recording the changes of space objects into the database (T_8)

Table 5. Table describes the overlapping relationship between time data units

No	Relationship	Meaning describes the overlapping relationship
1	$T_1 = T_8$	T_1 is a unit of time occurring in real world overlapping with the time recording into database (T_8)
2	$T_1 = T_5$	T_1 is a unit of time occurring in real world overlapping with the time maintaining on legal documents (T_5)
3	$T_8 = T_5$	T_8 is a unit of time recording into database overlapping the time maintaining on legal documents (T_5)

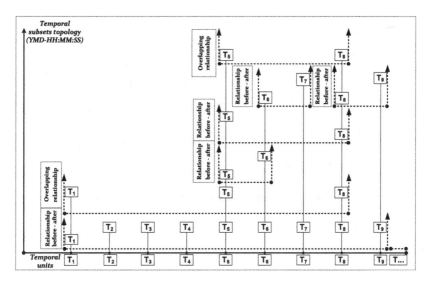

Fig. 2. Topology relational diagram of nine - time units

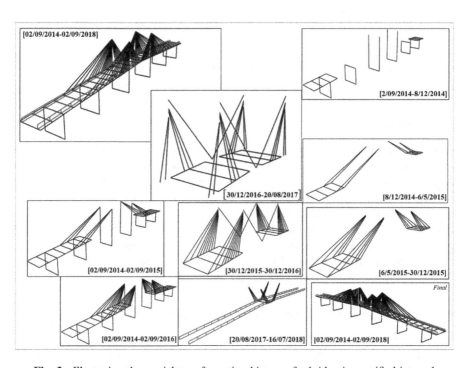

Fig. 3. Illustrating the spatial transformation history of a bridge in specified interval

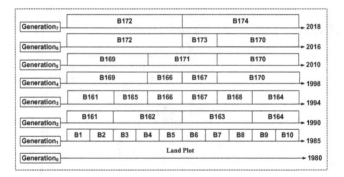

Fig. 4. Illustrating the history of using the land plot

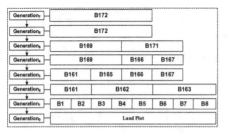

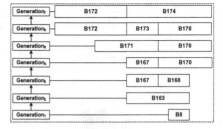

Fig. 5. Ancestor of a house with code "B172"

Fig. 6. Descendants of a house with code "B8"

3.2   Semantic Class

Semantic data is integrated into spatial and temporal objects to express the meaning of using objects. Semantics are attributes that contain phrases used to explain a phenomenon, a thing, an event, a happening occurred on space and time objects. For example, when we say the type of time is the type of event time, so must be accompanied by semantic attributes to explain the type of event time is like? When we say the object, we have to explain what kind of object it is? What is this object's name? What geographical region does this object belong to? Who is the owner, who is the manager or the maintainer? The semantic attribute is also used to explain what causes an object to change in space. What makes objects lose in the real world as well as in database.

3.3   Combine Spatial, Temporal and Semantic Class into STSDM

After combining three spatial - temporal - semantic class and then becoming a spatial - temporal - semantic data model and called spatial - temporal - semantic data model (STSDM). STSDM has the ability to store and manage 2D, 2.5D and 3D spatial objects in time and semantics and is illustrated by the spatial, temporal and semantic data sets shown in the section of experimental result. In addition, STSDM also has the ability to query space over time, has the ability to query space by semantics, has the ability to query space by time and semantics, and can find ancestors and children grandchildren of space objects and especially the history of space evolution is applied to specific spatial objects such as bridges that are 2-2.5D objects and apartments are 3D objects located on new urban areas.

Entity group belongs to space class. To answer which space object is located on? We have the following entities: there are 6 main entities Point, Line, Surface, Surfacetype, Body, Bodytype and there are 2 sub entities Node, Face. Entity group belongs to time class. To answer what kind of time those space objects born and lost belong to? At what time or period that object was it born and lost? We have the following entities: Stypetime, Timeunits, Tymdhms, Times. Entity group belongs to semantic class. To answer what is the type of object? And what is the name of object? We have the following entities: Objectstype and SObjects. To answer how is that object? Which geographical region does that object belong to? Who is the owner of that object? Who is the manager or maintainer? What event causes the object to change? We have the following entities: Owners, RegionaS, RegionbS, RegioncS, Eventstype, Events. To answer what is the semantics of each attribute in that space object? We have entities attributes. Below, this is a summary of the relations for the STSDM model and shows the size of a record for each relation that we have decomposed the STSDM model (see Fig. 7) into relations in Table 6.

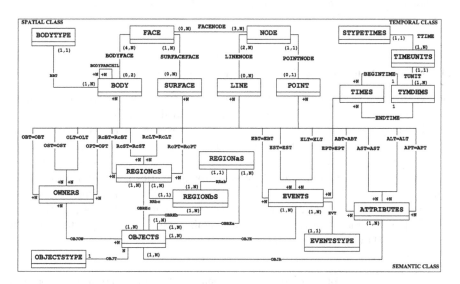

Fig. 7. Spatial – Temporal – Semantic Data Model (STSDM) managing spatial objects of 2D, 2.5D and 3D

Table 6. Decomposing the STSDM into the relations

No	Relations name	Bytes	No	Relations name	Bytes	No	Relations name	Bytes
1	Stypetimes	70	18	Surparchil	40	35	Rcbt	68
2	Timeunits	60	19	Lineparchil	60	36	Rcst	58
3	Tymdhms	80	20	Pointparchil	48	37	Rclt	35
4	Times	30	21	Objectstype	48	38	Rcpt	40
5	Node	30	22	Objects	86	39	Ebt	50
6	Point	30	23	Owners	76	40	Est	20
7	Line	34	24	Objow	66	41	Elt	69
8	Linenode	20	25	Obja	50	42	Ept	64
9	Face	28	26	Obje	40	43	Attributes	62
10	Facenode	28	27	Obt	50	44	Regionas	69
11	Surfacetype	28	28	Ost	58	45	Regionbs	67
12	Surface	20	29	Olt	60	46	Regioncs	75
13	Surfaceface	58	30	Opt	48	47	Obrea	48
14	Bodytype	54	31	Abt	38	48	Obreb	34
15	Body	78	32	Ast	58	49	Obrec	57
16	Bodyface	92	33	Alt	64	50	Eventstype	50
17	Bodyparchil	69	34	Apt	50	51	Events	48
Sum of bytes:		**809**	**Sum of bytes:**		**940**	**Sum of bytes:**		**914**

3.4   Building Some Spatial Queries Over Time and Semantics

Through the analysis and combinations of the above classes, STSDM has query abilities, has ability to find ancestors and ability find descendants with a variety of criteria to help construction contractors as well as government levels seize opportunities, promptly handle incidents occurring during the construction process, carry out completion plans and carry out traces of spatial evolutionary history of 2D, 2.5D and 3D objects. These capabilities are expressed through queries and two algorithms for finding ancestors and finding descendants that we described and implemented by experiments on Oracle 11G database management system and the C# programming language [24–26], the empirical results show that they are completely practical and can be applied to 3D GIS systems to manage construction works in new urban areas for practical implementation.

Query 1: Find and display the spatial evolutionary history of the construction process of the bridge "Phu My" over time and semantics. The periods of construction of the "Phu My" bridge are as follows: [Sep 02, 2005 $\in T_1$ - Dec 08, 2005 $\in T_2$] (Fig. 8); [Dec 30, 2006 $\in T_1$ - May 01, 2008 $\in T_2$] (Fig. 9); [Dec 30, 2007 $\in T_1$ - Feb 2, 2009 $\in T_2$] (Fig. 10); [Sep 02, 2005 $\in T_1$ – Sep 02, 2009 $\in T_2$] (Fig. 11) and is the type of ET_s

Query 2: Find and display houses owned by Ms. Pham Thao Nguyen during the period [Sep 8, 1998 $\in T_3$ - Jun 12, 2008 $\in T_4$] and is the type of LT_s.

Query 3: Find and display the space of houses according to each event and time period: (Planning, [Sep 8, 1998 $\in$ T_8 - June 12, 2012 $\in$ T_9]); (Storms, [Sep 8, 1998 $\in$ T_8 - June 12, 2012 $\in$ T_9]); (Landslide, [Sep 8, 1998 $\in$ T_8 – June 12, 2016 $\in$ T_9]) and is the type of DT_s.

Query 4: Find and display houses by time points, houses built during the years: 1985 $\in$ T_8; 1990 $\in$ T_8; 1994 $\in$ T_8; 1998 $\in$ T_8; 2010 $\in$ T_8; 2016 $\in$ T_8; 2018 $\in$ T_8 and is the type of DT_s.

Query 5: Find and display the bridge space "Can Tho" before Sep 26, 2007 $\in$ T_1 had an accident and is the type of ET_s.

Query 6: Find and display the bridge space "Can Tho" after the period of time [Sep 26, 2007 $\in$ T_1- Aug 25, 2008 $\in$ T_2] had an accident and is the type of ET_s.

Query 7: Find and display the bridge space "Phu My" was built in the period from Sep 2, 2005 $\in$ T_8 to Sep 2, 2009 $\in$ T_9 and according to the event "Planning" and is the type of DT_s.

Query 8: Find the ancestor of the house with the code "B172". Applying the ASA and DSA algorithms to find the ancestors below, the found result is the order of generations for each generation of house "B172" in Table 7.

Query 9: Find descendants of the house with code "B8" (Fig. 15 and 16). Applying the ASA and DSA algorithms to find descendants below, the found result is the order of genealogy for each generation of house "B8" in Table 8.

Table 7. List the orders of the generations of the house "B172"

Input Data	Output Data *(The found result is the ancestral house of the house having the code "B172".)*	
"B172" *(In generation 6)*	Ancestral generation $5_{(5th\ generation)}$	B171
	Ancestral generation $4_{(4th\ generation)}$	B169
	Ancestral generation $3_{(3rd\ generation)}$	B165, B166, B167
	Ancestral generation $2_{(2nd\ generation)}$	B161, B162, B163
	Ancestral generation $1_{(1st\ generation)}$	B1, B2, B3, B4, B5, B6, B7, B8

Table 8. List the orders of the generations of the house "B8"

Input Data	Output Data *(The found result is the descendant house of the house having the code "B8")*	
"B8" *(In generation 1)*	Descendants of generation $2_{(2nd\ generation)}$	B163
	Descendants of generation $3_{(3rd\ generation)}$	B167, B168
	Descendants of generation $4_{(4th\ generation)}$	B170
	Descendants of generation $5_{(5th\ generation)}$	B171
	Descendants of generation $6_{(6th\ generation)}$	B172, B173, B170
	Descendants of generation $7_{(7th\ generation)}$	B174

3.5 Designing Algorithms Find Ancestors and Descendants (ASA and DSA)

- **ASA (Ancestors Search Algorithm)**

Create the tblAncestors table to contain ancestors

Global declaration: i=0, j=0, gcount=0, arrAncestors, arrParDirect, arrParAll

Input   : bodychild

Output : arrAncestors

01: **Function AncestorsSearch** (bodychild) **return arrAncestors**

02: **Is**

03:        cstop Exception;

04:        Cursor nCur(parameters are bodychild) is query ancestorbody;

05: **Begin**

06:        Open nCur(bodychild);

07:        Get the ancestral body of some generation from nCur;

08:        While nCur data discovery

09:        Loop

10:            arrParAll(i):= bodyparent;

11:            arrParDirect(j):= bodyparent;

12:            Increase the index i of the arrParAll array to one unit;

13:            Increase the index j of the arrParDirect array to one unit;

14:            Get the ancestral body of some generation from nCur;

15:        End loop;

16:        Count the gcount generation to one unit;

17:        If discovered out of data arrParDirect Then

18:            raise cstop;

19:        End if;

20:        for direct in 1..arrParDirect

21:        Loop

22:            tblAncestors ⇐ arrParDirect(direct);

23:            return **AncestorsSearch**(bodychild);

24:        End loop;

25:        return arrParDirect;

26:        Exception when cstop then

27:            return arrParAll;

28: **End function;**

- **DSA (Descendants Search Algorithm)**

Create the tblDescendants table to contain descendants

Global declaration: i=0, j=0, gcount=0, arrDescendants, arrChildDirect, arrChildAll

Input   : bodyparent

Output : arrDescendants

01: **Function DescendantsSearch**(bodyparent) **return arrDescendants**

02: **Is**

03:    cstop Exception;

04:    Cursor nCur(parameters are body parents) Is query descendantsbody;

05: **Begin**

06:    Open nCur(bodyparent);

07:    Get the the descendant of some generation from nCur;

08:    While nCur data discovery

09:    Loop

10:        arrChildAll(i):= bodychild;

11:        arrChildDirect(j):= bodychild;

12:        Increase the index i of the arrChildAll array to one unit;

13:        Increase the index j of the arrChildDirect array to one unit;

14:        Get the descendant body of some generation from nCur;

15:    End loop;

16:    Count the gcount generation to one unit;

17:    If discovered out of data arrChildDirect Then

18:            Raise cstop;

19:    End if;

20:    For direct In 1..arrChildDirect

21:    Loop

22:            tblDescendants ⇐ arrChildDirect(direct);

23:            return **DescendantsSearch**(bodyparent);

24:    End loop;

25:    return arrChildDirect;

26:        Exception when cstop then

27:            return arrChildAll;

28: End function;

---

4 Experiment

In this section, we perform installation the STSDM in Oracle 11G and combine with C# programming language [24–26] to represent the spatial change history of the 2D, 2.5D and 3D spatial objects in 3D geographical space through the use of queries and the two ancestral and descendant search algorithms presented above (ASA and DSA). Empirical results show this STSDM is capable of answering questions related to the topic of managing the evolutionary history of spatial objects in 3D geographical space. The queries require the user to provide input parameters, output parameters are the results of the spatial evolutionary history and the semantics of spatial objects. Here are some empirical results obtained from the execution of queries and two algorithms for finding ancestors and descendants.

4.1   Query Spatial Evolutionary History Over Time and Semantics of Object 2-2.5D

Experiment 1: Apply to query 1 above to find and display the spatial evolution history of the bridge construction process "Phu My" at given intervals and semantics. We get the result shown in Fig. 8, 9, 10 and 11.

- **Input:** The bridge "Phu My" and the periods [Sep 2, 2005 $\in$ T_1 – Dec 08, 2005 $\in$ T_2]; [Dec 30, 2006 $\in$ T_1 - May 01, 2008 $\in$ T_2]; [Dec 30, 2007 $\in$ T_1 - Feb 2, 2009 $\in$ T_2]; [Sep 02, 2005 $\in$ T_1- Sep 02, 2009 $\in$ T_2] and is the type of $\in$ ET_s.
- **Output:** Image of bridge and semantic description of the bridge.

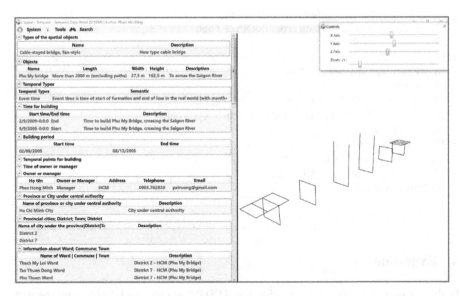

Fig. 8. Display semantics and image of bridge with construction time [Sep 2, 2005 $\in$ T_1 – Dec 8, 2005 $\in$ T_2] $\in$ ET_s.

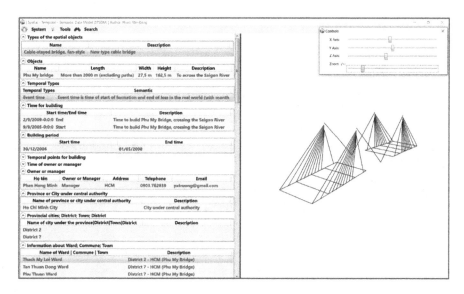

Fig. 9. Display semantics and image of bridge with construction time [Dec 30, 2006 ∈ T_1 - May 01, 2008 ∈ T_2] ∈ ET_s.

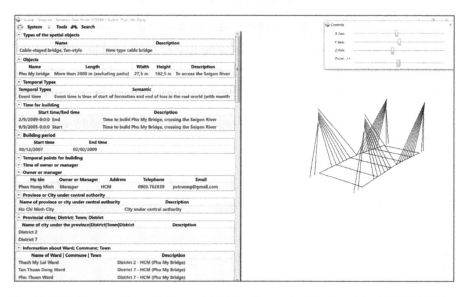

Fig. 10. Display semantics and image of bridge with construction time [Dec 30, 2007 ∈ T_1 – Feb 2, 2009 ∈ T_2] ∈ ET_s.

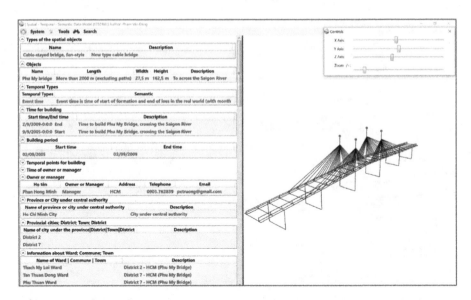

Fig. 11. Display semantics and image of bridge with construction time [Sep 2, 2005 $\in$ T$_1$ – Sep 2, 2009 $\in$ T$_2$] $\in$ ET$_s$.

4.2   Query Space Over Time and Semantics of 3D Objects

Experiment 2: Apply to query 2 above to find and display houses owned by Ms. Pham Thao Nguyen in the period of time and is the type of given legal time. We get the result shown in Fig. 12.

- **Input:** Ms. Pham Thao Nguyen and the period of time [Sep 08, 1998 $\in$ T$_3$ – June 12, 2012 $\in$ T$_4$] and is the type of LT$_s$.
- **Output:** Images of houses and semantics describing houses owned by Ms. Pham Thao Nguyen.

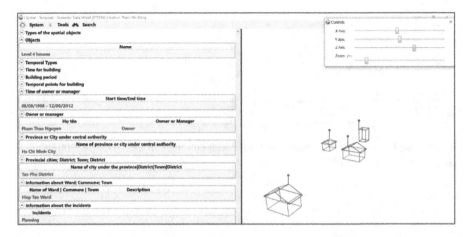

Fig. 12. The houses were owned by Ms. Pham Thao Nguyen in the period of time [Sep 08, 1998 $\in$ T$_3$ - June 12, 2012 $\in$ T$_4$]. $\in$ LT$_s$

Experiment 3: Apply to query 3 above to find and display the space of houses by event, period of time and is the type of database time. We get the result shown in Fig. 13 and 14.

- **Input:** Types of events such as (Storm, [Sep 08, 1998 $\in$ T_8 - June 12, 2012 $\in$ T_9]) or ([Landslide, Sep 08, 1998 $\in$ T_8 - June 12, 2012 $\in$ T_9]) $\in$ DT_s.
- **Output:** Houses images and semantics describing houses after events occurred.

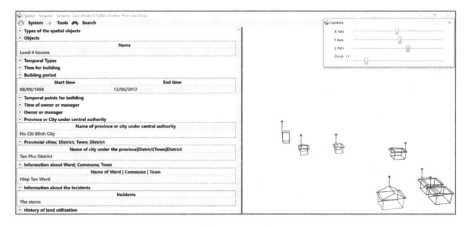

Fig. 13. Incident due to the storm and the period of time [Sep 08, 1998 $\in$ T_8 – June 12, 2012 $\in$ T_9] $\in$ DT_s

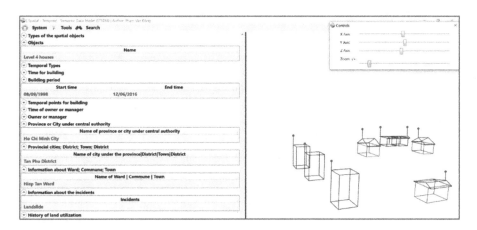

Fig. 14. Incident due to the Landslide and the period of time [Sep 08, 1998 $\in$ T_8 – June 12, 2012 $\in$ T_9] $\in$ DT_s

4.3   Query Each Generation of Descendant Houses of a Father House

Experiment 4: Apply to query 9 above to find each generation of descendant houses of father house with code "B8". We have the results of finding generations of descendant houses of father house in Fig. 15 and Fig. 16.

- **Input:** the house with code "B8"
- **Output:** Images of descendant houses of a father house with code "B8"

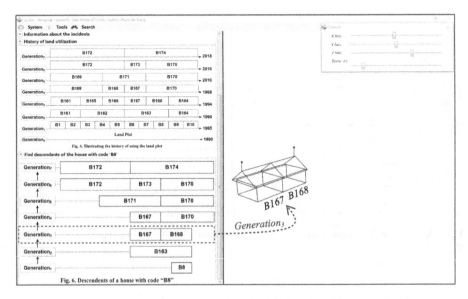

Fig. 15. There are two houses B167 and B168 just found in generation 3.

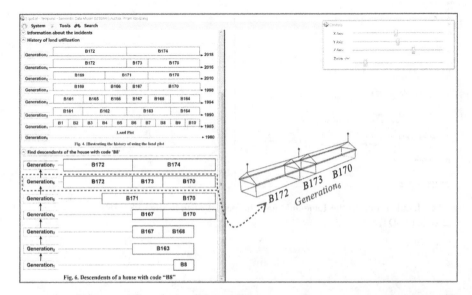

Fig. 16. There are three houses B172, B173 and B170 just found in generation 6.

5 Conclusion

This paper has systematized and analyzed in detail the spatial and temporal data models proposed by the authors over the years and the paper made new comments and proposals. The paper presents the necessity of three spatial, temporal and semantic classes to cater to construction works management in new urban areas and describe in detail how to incorporate these three new classes into construction works management to implement the construction of spatial - temporal - semantic spatial data model and this new model is called STSDM. STSDM is capable of managing spatial evolutionary history of 2D, 2.5D and 3D spatial objects, capable of spatial queries over time and semantics, capable of spatial queries over time, capable of semantic queries, and capable of finding ancestors and descendants of space objects. The above experimental results show that it is possible to apply the capabilities of the STSDM in managing the spatial evolutionary history of construction works in new urban management in the future. In addition, this STSDM is capable of managing various and rich objects in terms of colors, shapes, dimensional numbers and more diversified semantic integration.

References

1. Andrienko, N., Andrienko, G.: Spatio-temporal visual analytics: a vision for 2020s. J. Spat. Inf. Sci. **2020**(20), 87–95 (2020)
2. Ott, T., Swiaczny, F.: Time-Integrative GIS. Springer, Heidelberg (2001). https://doi.org/10. 1007/978-3-642-56747-6. p. 234
3. Peuquet, D.J.: It's about time: a conceptual framework for the representation of temporal dynamics in geographic information systems. Ann. Assoc. Am. Geogr. **84**(3), 441–461 (1994)
4. Coors, V.: 3D-GIS in networking environments. Comput. Environ. Urban Syst. **27**(4), 345–357 (2003)
5. Ding, Y., Jiang, N., Yu, Z., Ma, B., Shi, G., Wu, C.: Extrusion approach based on non-overlapping footprints (EABNOF) for the construction of geometric models and topologies in 3D cadasters. ISPRS Int. J. Geo-Inf. **6**(8), 232 (2017)
6. Anh, N.G.T., Tran, V.P., Huynh, K.D.: A study on 4D GIS spatio-temporal data model. In: Proceedings of IEEE 4th Conference on Knowledge and Systems Engineering, Danang, Vietnam, IEEE Computer Society Order Number P4670 (2012)
7. Dang, P.V., Phuoc, T.V., Phuoc Tuyen, H.N.: Visual representation of geographic objects in 3D space at levels of different details. Presented at the FAIR - Fundamental and Applied Information Technology (2017)
8. Gröger, G., Kolbe, T.H., Czerwinski, A., Nagel, C.: City Geography Markup Language (CityGML) Encoding Standard. Open Geospatial Consortium Inc., Wayland (2007)
9. Kolbe, T.H.: Representing and exchanging 3D city models with CityGML. In: Lee, J., Zlatanova, S. (eds.) 3D Geo-Information Sciences. LNGC, pp. 15–31. Springer, Heidelberg (2009). https://doi.org/10.1007/978-3-540-87395-2_2
10. Biljecki, F., Ledoux, H., Stoter, J.: An improved LOD specification for 3D building models. Comput. Environ. Urban Syst. **59**, 25–37 (2016)

11. Van Pham, D., Tuan Anh, N.G., Vinh, P.T.: Levels of detail for surface in urban data model. In: International Conference on Future Information Technology – ICFIT, pp. 460–464 (2011)
12. Tuan Anh, N.G., Vinh, P.T., Vu, T.P., Van Pham, D., Sy, A.T.: Representing multiple levels for objects in three-dimensional GIS model. Presented at the The 13th International Conference on Information Integration and Web-based Applications & Service (iiWAS2011) (2011)
13. Löwner, M.O., Gröger, G., Benner, J., Biljecki, F., Nagel, C.: Proposal for a new LOD and multi-representation concept for CITYGML. ISPRS Ann. Photogramm. Remote Sens. Spat. Inf. Sci. **IV-2/W1**, 3–12 (2016)
14. Ates Aydar, S., Stoter, J., Ledoux, H., Demir Ozbek, E., Yomralioglu, T.: Establishing a national 3D geo-data model for building data compliant to CITYGML: case of Turkey. ISPRS Int. Arch. Photogramm. Remote Sens. Spat. Inf. Sci. **XLI-B2**, 79–86 (2016)
15. Van Pham, D., Vinh Tran, P.: Visually analyzing evolution of geographic objects at different levels of details over time. In: Cong Vinh, P., Alagar, V. (eds.) ICCASA/ICTCC 2018. LNICSSITE, vol. 266, pp. 98–115. Springer, Cham (2019). https://doi.org/10.1007/978-3-030-06152-4_9
16. Swanson, J.: The Three Dimensional Visualization and Analysis of Geographic Data, 24 March 2020. http://maps.unomaha.edu/Peterson/gis/Final_Projects/1996/Swanson/GIS_Paper.html
17. Lieberwirth, U.: 3D GIS voxel-based model building in archaeology. In: Proceedings of the 35th International Conference on Computer Applications and Quantitative Methods in Archaeology (CAA), Berlin (2007)
18. Abdul-Rahman, A., Pilouk, M.: Spatial Data Modelling for 3D GIS. Springer, Heidelberg (2008). https://doi.org/10.1007/978-3-540-74167-1
19. Rahman, A.A.: Developing three-dimensional topological model for 3D GIS. Project report, UTM (2005)
20. Gröger, M.R.G., Plümer, L.: Representation of a 3D city model in spatial object-relational databases. In: XXth ISPRS Congress, Geo-Imagery Bridgeing Continents, Commission 4 (2004)
21. Gia, T.A.N., Tran, P.V., Khac, D.H.: Overview of three and four-dimensional gis data models. In: Park, J.J.(Jong Hyuk), Ng, J.K.-Y., Jeong, H.Y., Waluyo, B. (eds.) MUE 2013. LNEE, vol. 240, pp. 1013–1020. Springer, Dordrecht (2013). https://doi.org/10.1007/978-94-007-6738-6_125
22. Nguyen Gia, T.A., Dao, M.S., Mai Van, C.: A comparative survey of 3D GIS models. Presented at the 2017 4th NAFOSTED Conference on Information and Computer Science (2017)
23. Dang, P.V., Phuoc, T.V.: Developing TPS data model in 3D GIS for management the population data. Presented at the The 9th National Conference on Fundamental and Applied IT Research (2016)
24. Xuesong, W.: A Tool for Visualizing 3D Geometry Models (Part 1), 11 October 2009. https://www.codeproject.com/Articles/42992/A-Tool-for-Visualizing-3D-Geometry-Models-Part-1. Accessed Feb 2020
25. Greener, S.: SpatialDB Advisor: Elem_Info_Array Processing: An alternative to SDO_UTIL.GetNumRings and querying SDO_ELEM_INFO itself. http://www.spatialdbadvisor.com/oracle_spatial_tips_tricks/89/sdo_utilget_numrings-an-alternative. Accessed Dec 2019
26. Oracle Spatial User's Guide and Reference, Release 9, Part Number A88805-01, June 2001. https://docs.oracle.com/cd/A91202_01/901_doc/appdev.901/a88805/sdo_uglb.htm. Accessed Jan 2020

Modelling Situation-Aware Formalism Using BDI Reasoning Agents

Kiran Saleem[1] and Hafiz Mahfooz Ul Haque[2(✉)] (iD)

[1] Department of Computer Science, University of Lahore, Lahore, Pakistan
kiransaleem26@gmail.com
[2] Department of Software Engineering, University of Lahore, Lahore, Pakistan
mahfoozul.haque@se.uol.edu.pk

Abstract. Natural or man-made disasters are unavoidable situations that can occur anytime and anywhere. Timely disaster response plays a vital role in reducing its after-effects and can save countless lives. Over the years, people have been developing the guidelines and processes to cope up with such kinds of hazardous situations. In recent years, situation-awareness has been considered to be the most fascinating approach for the situation assessment and provides decision support accordingly. Situation-aware systems observe/perceive dynamic changes in the environment, understand/comprehend the situation, and perform actions according to the environment. Although state-of-the-art formalisms have been developed to handle such kinds of hazardous situations intelligently and rescue the victims. However, there are still many uncontrolled challenging issues. In this paper, we present a Belief-Desire-Intention (BDI) based multi-agent formalism to model the context-aware decision support system dynamically in order to achieve the desired goals. To illustrate the use of the proposed formalism, we develop a simple case study in which BDI agents are modeled and simulated to present results in terms of agents' reasoning processes. The behavior of the system has been tested using the NetLogo simulation environment to rigorously evaluate the validity of the system.

Keywords: Situation-awareness · BDI · Multi-agent system · Netlogo

1 Introduction

A natural disaster is an inevitable situation that can occur at any time and anywhere. It has varied forms such as earthquakes, floods, hurricane, wildfire, etc., and different level of occurrences has been recorded from mild to an intense level. A severe level of disasters usually deprives everything including people from their homes and even from their relatives. Numerous affected people become helpless and they wait for getting help to escape themselves from such kinds of vilest situations. Earthquake is considered to be the most dangerous natural disaster in the world and much effort has been made to predict the earthquake but unable

© ICST Institute for Computer Sciences, Social Informatics and Telecommunications Engineering 2021
Published by Springer Nature Switzerland AG 2021. All Rights Reserved
P. C. Vinh and A. Rakib (Eds.): ICCASA 2020/ICTCC 2020, LNICST 343, pp. 169–181, 2021.
https://doi.org/10.1007/978-3-030-67101-3_14

to find prolific results so far. On the other hand, with the technological advancements and growing interest in smart and intelligent devices, significant efforts have been made to escape and/or avoid such kinds of hazardous situations using these tiny smart devices along with the intelligent decision support systems.

In recent years, with the advent of the pervasive computing environment, context-awareness has gained significant attention, as context-aware systems acquire/sense information from distant locations using smart mobile devices, perform reasoning, and adapt behavior to take the right decision at the right time and in right place accordingly. The recent notion of situation-awareness has emerged from context-awareness. Context-aware systems have a very broad domain of applications for complex problem-solvings in the pervasive environment. In contrast, situation-aware systems perceive the dynamic changes in the environment within a volume of time and space, comprehend the situation, and perform actions according to the situation [20,24]. In recent years, situation-awareness has gained much attention in safety-critical domains and in emergency situations such military command and control operation [3], health care [2], emergency situations [24], navigation [18], and aviation [7]. To model such situations, agent-based technology has emerged as a new paradigm for conceptualizing, designing, and implementing sophisticated software systems. An agent could be a software agent, that perceives its environment and takes actions to perform specifically assigned tasks. According to Chen [6], *"We humans are inherently context-aware agents"*. Context-aware agents sense the environment and perform reasoning in order to achieve the desired goal. Literature has witnessed various multi-agent based complex applications, as multi-agent systems use different reasoning techniques to handle the different nature of problems. Among others, BDI (Belief-Desire-Intention) based reasoning has been advocated as the most optimistic approach due to its simplistic nature and the usage of folk psychological notions which corresponds to the human behavior as humans think, plan and make an intention to meet their desired goals [10]. BDI architecture presents the artificial agents with human-like decision-making strategies, based on their belief, desire, and intention components. Combining these two techniques such as BDI agents and situation-awareness leads a better decision-making mechanism [4]. In the literature, Feng et al. [9] present a situation-awareness based context-aware decision support system using an agent-based approach. In this framework, they incorporated a shared situation-aware model that provides human objects with their customized views and services through collaborative agents' planning to reduce the cognitive load of human objects. They have applied rule-based reasoning to model context-aware decision support systems and simulated command and control domains. The entity agents perform event classification and action recommendations with a high level of accuracy. Valette et al. [22] proposed BDI agents based evacuation model to deal with the disaster situation like a fire. They have used the BDI paradigm to model the cognition of agents along with their communication plan to infer their behavior in terms of emotions. The authors have implemented the model in the simulation environment to analyze the variability of the results. In [1], authors proposed BDI based multi-agent formalism for ontology-driven health-care system. In this model, they have developed an intelligent decision support system using BDI reasoning agents to infer the desired goals dynamically. This work is an extension of the previous work [1] where BDI agents based intelligent decision support system has been developed for an ontology-driven health care system. However, the work in BDI agents based on intelligent decision support systems incorporating the notion of situation-awareness is still in its infancy stage. In this paper, we intend to provide customized services out of shared situation-awareness based on contextual knowledge. We propose BDI agents based context-aware decision support system to assist hazardous situations dynamically in the affected area due to earthquake hit. We use the NetLogo simulator for BDI agents modelling and simulation to monitor the overall behavior of the system and rigorously evaluate the validity of the system.

The rest of the paper is structured as follows. Section 2 discusses the core notions of BDI and NetLogo simulation. Section 3 presents a formalism for BDI reasoning agents to model the context-aware decision support system. In Sect. 4, we discuss a case study of a smart rescue system. For this, we use the NetLogo simulator for the prototypal implementation using BDI agents' modelling and simulation to evaluate the validity of the system and finally conclude in Sect. 5.

2 Preliminaries

2.1 BDI (Belief, Desire, Intention)

BDI (Belief, Desire, Intention) is a classical paradigm to formalize the internal structure of cognitive agents for complex problem-solving in a real-time environment. The BDI paradigm attempts to capture the general understanding of how humans observe and gain knowledge from the environment, have a perception about it, and develop a set of beliefs on it. Based on the existing information and with a newly gained set of hypothetical beliefs, humans intend to take a set of actions in order to achieve the desired goals efficiently. The concept of BDI is based on human decision making strategy, BDI agents acquire information from the environment or other agents and have a set of beliefs on it, perform reasoning to take specifically assigned task, and then make individual or collaborative plan among multi-agent systems to achieve the desired goals [5,8,23]. The BDI reasoning agents consist of a set of predicates having a set of agent's own beliefs, desires, and intentions. A predicate may have a name along with the parameter containing the values according to the situation. For example; *isSmokeDetected('true, GPSLocation('a, 'b))* – meaning that Smoke is detected at location('a, 'b). The architecture of BDI agents has three core components:

- **Beliefs** (what agents think): It is a set of facts stored in the agent's memory or agent's internal knowledge. For example; whenever an agent derives a predicate *isSmokeDetected('true, GPSLocation('a, 'b))*, whatever the predicate that may either be true or false, it will be added to agent's belief set.

- **Desires** (Intending to do): The ultimate objective of an agent is to accomplish the goal, i.e., *isSmokeDetected('false, GPSLocation('a, 'b))* – The desire is to put water to remove smoke. However, the agent's desire may have priority to select new intentions based on the desire and the agent's belief.
- **Intentions** (Act of doingness): The plans or set of actions that agents intend to follow and peruse their desires. Intentions can also be prioritized based on the selected plan to fulfill the desire.

BDI agents have strong roots in philosophy and are extensively used for modelling and simulation of complex systems using intelligent agents. BDI reasoning paradigm allows the systems to design and model a multi-agent system to do complex reasoning.

2.2 NetLogo

In the literature, a significant effort has been done for modelling and simulations using multi-agent systems such as Netlogo [4,14,17], Jason [13], JADE [11], GAMA [22], etc. Among other simulation tools, we opt the NetLogo simulation tool because it is a multi-agent based programming platform to model and simulate natural or unusual phenomena. The NetLogo platform was introduced in 1999 by Uri Wilensky. It is open-source software that includes a graphical development interface, a set of commands to create agent-based models, and a suite of tools to assist the development of the model, and the analysis of simulation results [19,21]. NetLogo can be used to design complex and reactive multi-agent systems by modelling a great number of intelligent agents, operating independently as well as collaboratively. It also powers HubNet participatory simulations [17]. NetLogo is used in different kinds of scenarios for instance in gaming, military purpose and in disaster management scenarios, etc. [4,14]. There are four types of agents in the NetLogo named as turtle, links, patch, and observer. Turtle agents can be used to model the agents' behavior, Link agents establish the connection between agents, patches are stationary agents with a set of predefined activities, and the observer oversees the set of activities.

NetLogo also supports BDI agents modelling and simulation. Authors in [15] introduced additional libraries for BDI agents' reasoning and communication mechanism. The BDI library can be imported in the NetLogo Simulation environment to implement the belief-desire-intention based multi-agent system. We have chosen BDI agents to model the system in NetLogo because it has the capability to capture the complex adaptive behavior using the pro-active goal-seeking approach.

3   BDI Agents Based Situation-Aware Formalism

In this section, we propose a BDI reasoning agents based formalism to provide customized services out of shared situation-awareness based on contextual knowledge. The primary roles of agents are to observe/acquire the environment situation, perform BDI reasoning to model a context-aware decision support system in a command and control setting. The system consists of a set of BDI agents where each agent in the system has a plan consisting of a set of beliefs along with a set of actions. In this formalism, the BDI agents have context-aware capabilities to identify the nature of the problem from the environment, classify the contextual knowledge based on the agent's belief set, recommend suitable action, and select the decision mode. As the system is designed for complex and safety-critical problems in nature, human assistance and support play vital roles to cope up with hazardous situations. However, the system is autonomous in nature and has an intelligent decision-making capability with minimal human involvement. The system is classified into an automated mode and semi-automated mode. In automated mode, group agents plan collaboratively with the set of specified actions, communicate themselves, and select the optimal goals according to the situation. Whereas agents in the semi-automated mode need human assistance due to the high consequences of the situation, as agents do not have the capability to take appropriate action in a rapidly changing environment. For example; severe damages of the earthquake and its after-effects. In such cases, human assistance is continuously required.

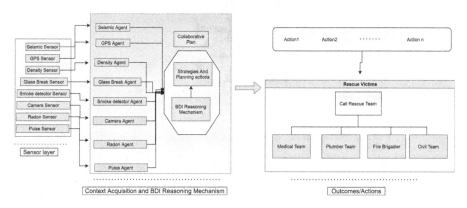

Fig. 1. Layered architecture of the proposed formalism

As shown in Fig. 1, the proposed framework consists of three layers, namely: (a) context acquisition, (b) BDI agents reasoning, and (c) agents modelling and simulation. In the context acquisition layer, we assume that BDI agents acquire the contextual information from sensors that can be installed to monitor the hazardous situation. In this model, every sensor is connected to its corresponding BDI based agent where an agent in the system can have a belief based on the existing knowledge or newly acquired knowledge from other agents/sensors.

BDI Agent's activity is driven by its belief set, intentions, and desires; given below:

- Perception of elements in the current situation: Agent's activity is driven by its belief set, however, the agent's belief set can be revised as the situation varies in the dynamic environment.

– Comprehension of the current situation: Each agent in the system observes the situation in the environment after certain intervals of time, revise its belief set, select the execution plan to attain its goal.
– Projection of future status: After selecting the execution plan, agents trigger the actions and act accordingly in order to achieve its desire objective.

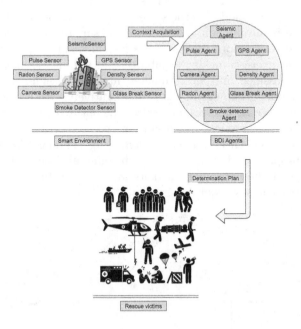

Fig. 2. System flow: BDI agents modelling and simulation

In the BDI agent's reasoning layer, each agent in the system performs the specifically assigned task to achieve the desired goals individually or collaboratively. For this, each agent has a plan consisting of a set of predicates having its own set of beliefs, desires, and intentions for each action. As BDI agents perform goal-directed tasks based on the set of beliefs, where the belief of the agents can be revised dynamically whenever the situation changes. The main inspiration is that each agent updates its belief every time whenever the situation changes keeping the most recent values in the memory. To model the communication among different agents, an agent can communicate with other agents only if it needs to have additional information in its belief set to produce the desired result or to achieve the goal state in order to fulfill the agent's intentions and desires.

4   BDI Agents Modelling and Simulation Using NetLogo

To illustrate the use of the proposed formalism, we present a smart rescue system to observe the after-effects of earthquakes and rescue the victims. For this, we develop a context-aware decision support system for modelling BDI agents and simulate the validity of the results to see whether the system would be able to achieve the desired goals effectively or not? NetLogo has additional libraries for BDI agents' reasoning and communication mechanism that can be imported in the NetLogo simulation environment to implement the belief-desire-intention based multi-agent system [15,16].

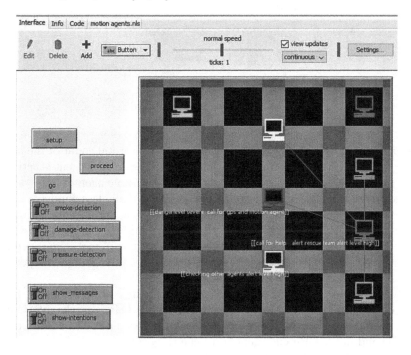

Fig. 3. BDI agents' modeling

We develop a case study of a smart rescue system to illustrate the use of the proposed formalism. A severe earthquake is considered to be the most dangerous disaster that can have a deteriorate after-effects such as fire, building damages if the situation would not handle in time [12]. We consider the earthquake evacuation system to handle the disaster situation. In the system design, we consider a number of intelligent BDI reasoning agents to monitor the current status of the affected area. For example, a number of smart and intelligent devices/sensors are considered to monitor a current situation, which updates their status whenever the situation changes. The Fig. 2 depicts the system flow using BDI agents modelling whereas the Fig. 3 shows the execution process in the NetLogo simulation environment. The description of the BDI agent's task are listed below:

- Seismic Agent: When the earthquake hits, the seismic agent acquires the data from the sensor with earthquake magnitude value and save newly acquired data in its belief set. Then it takes a set of actions to pursue the desire. The seismic agent generates alerts based on the magnitude level which is forwarded to the concerned agents.

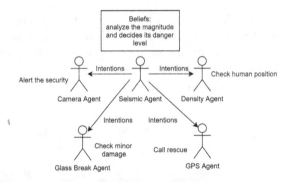

Fig. 4. Seismic agent's design

- Density Agent: The density agents acquire the data (total count of the people nearby the affected area) from a density sensor. The density agent is activated whenever it receives earthquake alerts from the seismic agent.
- Glass Break Agent: This agent ensures the safety of all glass windows and its effects on the people. It notifies RescueAgent to take appropriate action.
- Pulse Agent: Pulse sensor detects the severe building damages by a ratio called inter-story drift. As the earthquake hits, Pulse Agent acquires pulses after certain intervals of time and sends updates to the consequent agents to take suitable action in case of abnormalities.
- Smoke Detector Agent: This agent may alarm in case if smoke or fire is detected. As this information arrives in the agent's belief set, the information is forwarded to the density agent to check the existence and counts of the people and notifies RescueAgent to rescue the people.
- Radon Agent: When the earthquake hits, the density agent alerts the radon agent to detect the gas leakages, thus if the detection would be true then the density agent checks human counts near it. The radon agent performs reasoning on the acquired data by its existing facts, thus plan the actions to achieve its desires according to the situation.
- Camera Agent: The level disaster or severity of the damage can be observed through a Camera agent.
- GPS Agent: It is activated immediately after receiving GPS location requests from other agents. The system detects the exact location of the notified area and tags itself with other agents to call RescueAgents.

As the framework is based on a multi-agent system, agents in the system perform BDI reasoning in order to monitor the hazardous situations, take decisions intelligently based on the existing set of beliefs, and infer the preventive plan to rescue the victims from the disaster situation. As shown in Table 1, the system needs a set of BDI predicates to infer the desired goal. The BDI predicate of each agent has a belief set, intentions, and desires to fulfill agents' desired objectives. NetLogo provides additional library support to design BDI agents. Agents are modeled with their belief sets, intentions, and desires as shown in

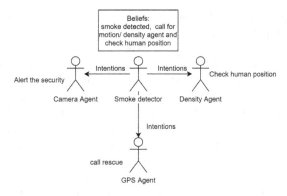

Fig. 5. Smoke agent's design

Fig. 4 and Fig. 5, all other agents are designed in the same pattern as per their set of beliefs and communication plan.

```
if dangerlevel >= 7 [ set agentbelief create-belief "danger level" "severe"
   add-belief create-belief "danger level" "severe"
   print "**********Belief Of Seismic Agent*************************"
   show agentbelief
    print "----------------Invoke Intention----------------"
   call-rescue]
 ; intentions
if dangerlevel >= 7 [
   add-intention "dangerlevel severe " "call for gps and motion agent"
   add-intention "call-to-agents" "true"]
    ;plan
   broadcast-to gpsAgents add-content (list "rescue need as soon as possible for seismic agent" )
   create-message "Earthquake"
   broadcast-to camAgents add-content (list "alert the security" )
   create-message "earthquake"
   broadcast-to motionAgents add-content (list "check for positions via Density/ Motion Agent" )
   create-message "acquire data about humans"
   broadcast-to GlassBreakAgents add-content (list "check the severity on building damage" )
   create-message "check minor damage, earthquake severe"
```

Fig. 6. Seismic agent code

For modelling multi-agent systems in NetLogo, we have created 8 files(nls) of the mentioned agents. Initially, we model all agents with their belief set along with their execution and communication plan in the NetLogo simulator with their specified actions. At the initial stage of the simulation environment, all agents in the system have predefined belief sets and execution plans. As the system proceeds with the dynamic changes, agents revise their belief sets according to the situation, select the best available plan, and execute. So when we simulate the smart rescue system, the Seismic agent observes the situation, earthquake hits with the magnitude value +7. As this magnitude value is high, the system immediately activated and generate alerts to all agents in the system to perform their corresponding tasks. The seismic agent updates its beliefs about magnitude value and communicates with the corresponding agents such as the density agent, GPS agent, glass break agent, camera agent to revise their belief set and act accordingly. The Fig. 6 shows a fragment of the Seismic agent's Netlogo code. As the density agent gets an earthquake alert, it exchanges information with the radon and smoke agents to observe the human presence at the smoked and gas leakage area. The radon agent checks gas mains breakage or pressure detection (site 1), the smoke detector agent activates in case of fire or smoke detected (site 2), the camera agent sends an alert message to the security, the density agent checks human counts, and notify rescue agent. As the radon agent detects the gas mains are broken or any leakage at site 1, the radon agent notifies the density agent. The density agent observes the human presence at site 1, updates its belief set, sends a notification to the GPS agent, and camera agent. In case of fire or smoke detected at site 2, the smoke agent notifies the density agent. Then the density agent counts the human presence at site 2, updates its belief set. The radon agent shares the GPS location of the affected site to rescue the victims. As the Seismic agent shares the magnitude value with the glass break agent, the glass break agent revises its belief and notifies rescue agents. Based on the situation, the rescue agent notifies the rescue team to rescue the victims. This the severity level, rescue action needs to be taken on a priority basis. Figure 7 depicts a few agent's execution processes along with their beliefs, intentions, and executions. We have tried to simulate the system with the maximum possible execution steps in order to test and simulate the designed model of the system. We analyze the behavior of the system and rigorously evaluate the validity of the system.

Table 1. BDI reasoning agent's data model.

BDI agents	Context acquisition	Belief set	Intention	Desire (Goal)
Seismic Agent	Get earthquake magnitude value	- Earthquake magnitude value	- Check human position - Call rescue	- Call rescue agent to help the victims
Density Agent	- Seismic agent alert - Human counts	- Earthquake hit - Building damage detected	- Check for human counts - Call GPS agent - Alert Camera	- Call rescue team - Help victims
Glass Break Agent	- demage level - Minor damage (frequency detection)	- Earthquake hit	- Check damage severity	- Check severity of the building damage
Smoke Detector Agent	- Smoke alert	- Earthquake hit - Smoke detected	- Alert Density agent - Alert GPS agent - Alert Camera agent	- Call rescue team - Check human count - Alert the security - Help victims
Radon Agent	- Gas leakage	- Earthquake hit - Gas leakage detected	- Alert Density agent - Alert GPS agent - Alert Camera agent	- Call rescue team - Check human count - Alert the security - Help victims

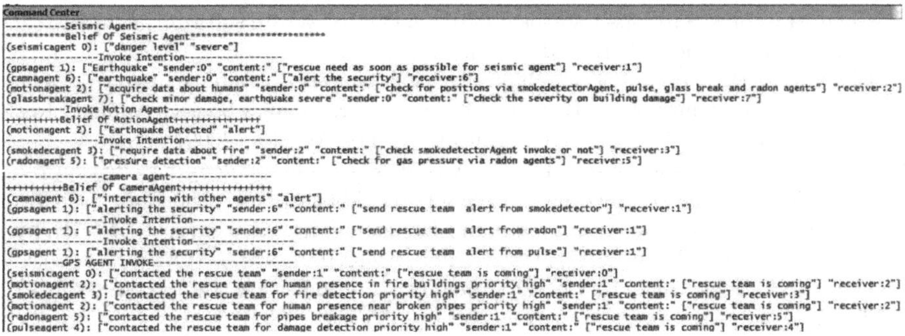

Fig. 7. BDI agents execution process

5   Conclusion

In this paper, we proposed BDI agents based formalism to model the context-aware decision support system to suitably manage the disaster management system. To evaluate the scalability and validity of the system, we tested the proposed system in the NetLogo simulation environment using BDI agents modelling, reasoning, and simulation. Although it is the implementation of a simple case study and early stage in the development process, however, this work has shown promising results using BDI agents. In future work, we will implement the system physically using a comprehensive case study. For this, we will use NetLogo as a middle-ware platform, as it allows the API facility and interoperability with other platforms such as Python, Matlab, Jason.

References

1. Akhtar, S.M., Nazir, M., Saleem, K., Haque, H.M.U., Hussain, I.: An ontology-driven IoT based healthcare formalism. Int. J. Adv. Comput. Sci. Appl **11**(2), 479–486 (2020)
2. Alkhomsan, M.N., Hossain, M.A., Rahman, S.M.M., Masud, M.: Situation awareness in ambient assisted living for smart healthcare. IEEE Access **5**, 20716–20725 (2017)
3. Boril, J., Smrz, V., Mach, O.: Development of experimental methods for testing of human performance in the framework of future millitary pilot's preparation. In: 2017 International Conference on Military Technologies (ICMT), pp. 548–552. IEEE (2017)
4. Buettner, R., Baumgartl, H.: A highly effective deep learning based escape route recognition module for autonomous robots in crisis and emergency situations. In: Proceedings of the 52nd Hawaii International Conference on System Sciences (2019)
5. Caillou, P., Gaudou, B., Grignard, A., Truong, C.Q., Taillandier, P.: A simple-to-use BDI architecture for agent-based modeling and simulation. In: Jager, W., Verbrugge, R., Flache, A., de Roo, G., Hoogduin, L., Hemelrijk, C. (eds.) Advances in Social Simulation 2015. AISC, vol. 528, pp. 15–28. Springer, Cham (2017). https://doi.org/10.1007/978-3-319-47253-9_2

6. Chen, H., Tolia, S.: Steps towards creating a context-aware software agent system. HP. Technical report HPL-2001-231 (2001)

7. Endsley, M.R., Garland, D.J.: Pilot situation awareness training in general aviation. In: Proceedings of the Human Factors and Ergonomics Society Annual Meeting, vol. 44, pp. 357–360. SAGE Publications, Los Angeles (2000)

8. Evertsz, R., Thangarajah, J., Ly, T.: A BDI-based methodology for eliciting tactical decision-making expertise. In: Sarker, R., Abbass, H.A., Dunstall, S., Kilby, P., Davis, R., Young, L. (eds.) Data and Decision Sciences in Action. LNMIE, pp. 13–26. Springer, Cham (2018). https://doi.org/10.1007/978-3-319-55914-8_2

9. Feng, Y.H., Teng, T.H., Tan, A.H.: Modelling situation awareness for context-aware decision support. Expert Syst. Appl. **36**(1), 455–463 (2009)

10. Georgeff, M., Pell, B., Pollack, M., Tambe, M., Wooldridge, M.: The belief-desire-intention model of agency. In: Müller, J.P., Rao, A.S., Singh, M.P. (eds.) ATAL 1998. LNCS, vol. 1555, pp. 1–10. Springer, Heidelberg (1999). https://doi.org/10.1007/3-540-49057-4_1

11. Junger, D., Guinelli, J., Pantoja, C.E.: An analysis of Javino middleware for robotic platforms using Jason and JADE frameworks. In: 10th Software Agents, Environments and Applications School (2016)

12. Little, B.: The deadliest earthquake ever recorded (2020). https://www.history.com/news/the-deadliest-earthquake-ever-recorded

13. Ramirez, W.A.L., Fasli, M.: Integrating NetLogo and Jason: a disaster-rescue simulation. In: 2017 9th Computer Science and Electronic Engineering (CEEC), pp. 213–218. IEEE (2017)

14. Luna Ramirez, W.A., Fasli, M.: Plan acquisition in a BDI agent framework through intentional learning. In: Berndt, J.O., Petta, P., Unland, R. (eds.) MATES 2017. LNCS (LNAI), vol. 10413, pp. 167–186. Springer, Cham (2017). https://doi.org/10.1007/978-3-319-64798-2_11

15. Sakellariou, I., Kefalas, P., Stamatopoulou, I.: Enhancing NetLogo to simulate BDI communicating agents. In: Darzentas, J., Vouros, G.A., Vosinakis, S., Arnellos, A. (eds.) SETN 2008. LNCS (LNAI), vol. 5138, pp. 263–275. Springer, Heidelberg (2008). https://doi.org/10.1007/978-3-540-87881-0_24

16. Sakellariou, I., Kefalas, P., Stamatopoulou, I.: Teaching intelligent agents using NetLogo. In: ACM-IFIP IEEIII, pp. 209–221 (2008)

17. Sakellariou, I., Kefalas, P., Stamatopoulou, I.: MAS coursework design in NetLogo. In: Proceedings of the International Workshop on the Educational Uses of Multi-Agent Systems (EDUMAS 2009), pp. 47–54 (2009)

18. Saus, E.R., Johnsen, B.H., Eid, J., Thayer, J.F.: Who benefits from simulator training: personality and heart rate variability in relation to situation awareness during navigation training. Comput. Hum. Behav. **28**(4), 1262–1268 (2012)

19. Schermer, B.W.: Software agents, surveillance, and the right to privacy: a legislative framework for agent-enabled surveillance (2007)

20. Stanton, N.A., Chambers, P.R., Piggott, J.: Situational awareness and safety. Saf. Sci. **39**(3), 189–204 (2001)

21. Tisue, S., Wilensky, U.: NetLogo: a simple environment for modeling complexity, pp. 16–21, January 2004

22. Valette, M., Gaudou, B., Longin, D., Taillandier, P.: Modeling a real-case situation of egress using BDI agents with emotions and social skills. In: Miller, T., Oren, N., Sakurai, Y., Noda, I., Savarimuthu, B.T.R., Cao Son, T. (eds.) PRIMA 2018. LNCS (LNAI), vol. 11224, pp. 3–18. Springer, Cham (2018). https://doi.org/10.1007/978-3-030-03098-8_1

23. van Oijen, J., van Doesburg, W., Dignum, F.: Goal-based communication using BDI agents as virtual humans in training: an ontology driven dialogue system. In: Dignum, F. (ed.) AGS 2010. LNCS (LNAI), vol. 6525, pp. 38–52. Springer, Heidelberg (2011). https://doi.org/10.1007/978-3-642-18181-8_3
24. Yau, S.S., Huang, D., Gong, H., Davulcu, H.: Situation-awareness for adaptive coordination in service-based systems. In: 29th Annual International Computer Software and Applications Conference (COMPSAC 2005), vol. 1, pp. 107–112. IEEE (2005)

Using Empathy Mapping in Design Thinking Process for Personas Discovering

Waralak Vongdoiwang Siricharoen[(⊠)] [iD]

Silpakorn University, Nonthaburi 11120, Thailand
siricharoen_w2@su.ac.th

Abstract. Exploring user attitudes and behaviors within the domain of interests helps the user experience team to match the user with a deeper understanding. The mapping process also reveals any gap in existing user data. Design thinking is the ground-breaking and cooperative approach to problem-solving that puts the user first to make user-centered products and services. There are many various design thinking activities that use to generate a thoughtful of the users or customer, including the conception of personas. This paper revisits the concept of persona and draws the connection of using empathy map to build persona within the design thinking process. Also showing the benefit of empathizing method to construct the effective persona. This can be used for the benefit in Human Computer Interaction(HCI) designing processes or marketing analysis.

Keywords: Persona · Design thinking · Empathy · HCI · User-centered design

1 Persona Concept

The first step in understanding users is creating a user profile. When the designer developed a detailed user profile. Persona is possible to develop from user profile (role model of end users): is designed to help specific users to focus during the design. Scenario is daily use of the users. Persona helps to test system and build functionality of products that users will want to use [1]. Persona are not real people who have a set of behaviors and requirements designer want to design for, nevertheless represent people throughout the design process. They are the theoretical models of real users. Even if they are imagined however they are determined with significant stability and accuracy. The persona is and gives the user life style and helps the designers feel connected with them. Every team members of designers thinks about the same person instead of the individual's work on their own vision of who is the user. If there is no specific goal to focus on, "(target)users" can be varied from experts to beginners. Main goal of a persona is to help someone imagine the intended users of a system. Their primary purpose is to form designers, researchers, easier lives while designing products. It is important to understand whether the merchandise is going to be useful for this sort of persona before entering the market.

Persona can use it as a tool for discussion about advice, storytelling, role playing, and other use activities such as *"Rosy won't use that device."* Persona can also help new designer in the team learned quickly which users are hypothetical people created to describe specific users, not every end user. Then designer create models that can

© ICST Institute for Computer Sciences, Social Informatics and Telecommunications Engineering 2021
Published by Springer Nature Switzerland AG 2021. All Rights Reserved
P. C. Vinh and A. Rakib (Eds.): ICCASA 2020/ICTCC 2020, LNICST 343, pp. 182–191, 2021.
https://doi.org/10.1007/978-3-030-67101-3_15

represent end users. Personas are also tools that are also used in many parts of interaction design [2] as follows:

- Requirements: Understand the wants and explain user in a clear way.
- Design: understand what this persona needs.
- Evaluation: detect needs that are or are not being encountered.
- Marketing: aim the user needs that have already been recognized and intended for.

Persona are used extensively by Human Computer Interaction (HCI) designers within the design process. To defining the (target) user to explaining the understanding of the persona, helping designing process at different stages of the planning process of the HCI system [3]. To illustrate the design process of the model, in order to reflect organizational problems and to systematically explore design options. By considering differences in expectations, scope, and goals of planning-related processes such as the role of needs, requirements, necessities. The questions that designer need to ask is: Will it characterize the design concept or the HCI design process? [4].

The persona's disadvantage appearances less than scientific (dilemma issue). Designer can use a small number of people; Persona is sometimes an imaginary description of the persona who is truly exist. The persona can be true in real-life [5]. The use of that persona is appropriate if designer create a personality profile that is as detailed as possible for the fictional agent of the target audience. The target audience need to be defined in advance for this to work. Based on empirical data collected with the help of web analytics and character tracing, self-created will be created later. Demographic and socio-economic information should flow into these personality patterns. Social media also provides good insight into the target audience. Many users have profiles that are publicly accessible. These provide accurate insights into various buyers' interests and lifestyles which can be created as persona [6]. With buyers' personalities, designer can tailor the advertising efforts, marketing strategies, and content creation to capture each type of buyer. If designers can have people in their mind, instead of a crowd that does not know the strategy.

Personas are characters that designer simply generate supported the research to point out the sort of users which will use the service or product. But added with real-world features like traits [7], disappointments, and other related characteristics. Personas are people that represent a group of users with different needs, objectives, and expectations. Persona may help designers and merchandise owners decide whether the merchandise or service will slot in their daily lives. Easily which will provide a transparent picture of the person's user experience section. All elements of the character should be chosen carefully, as these are the qualities which will give us the idea that it should be like. This is often a time consuming but worthwhile process. Personas also are very useful once a prototype test has been taken that appears at the end and finds problems that we will face with the system flow.

The reason the persona is so important. when an apps or web applications or maybe a landing page have to be developed, developer would like to understand the users who are getting to use it or see the merchandise that we are designing. Knowing the audience will help developing better solutions and real results that users want from the merchandise. Some interesting inquiries to ask when checking out persona in design concepts are [8, 15]: 1. Who is the ideal customer? 2. what's the present behavior of users? 3. what is going to users look like? 4. What are the requirements and final goals of users? 5. what's the answer to their current problems? 6. Why do they hate current solutions? Understanding the requirements of users well, it can create products that service better. The transparent personality in design thinking will assist designer identify user needs and communicate better with the proper solutions that users need for an extended time. How designer team define user characteristics: before defining the identity of a user, designer want to study the users and their behavior well and gather enough data and organize the info and make the ideal customers (Fig. 1).

Fig. 1. Example of persona (Sources: https://commons.wikimedia.org/wiki/File:New_Readers_User_persona_-_Sandeep_-_India.png)

Attention is a critical element in human-centered design and style. What is consideration? Why is it noteworthy to style solutions that engagement for user/people? It is not only but see what meaning but to determine how it helps designers to make solutions that service. In dissimilar, lack of attention may result in product failures, additionally, empowering ideas can be understood that everybody can understand. As already mentioned, the persona has widespread misunderstanding: many people think that it is the persona who is invented but that is not true. How do we determine what characteristics a character has, what qualities, what are their names, and what is important to them? But designer do not delusion these things out of the head. The basis for all good people is information, data, and insights about the users. designer want to develop a product for particular persona.

Keep the persona to a minimum 3 to 4 good personas. If designer can manage two things better than all. It should not exceed five people, it will be there to clarify the target audience and that will make it more difficult in personality. Even many large online stores that have a diverse product range and a consistent diverse customer base can work with three to four people. For good persona, there are only two criteria:

1. They must live inside the minds of readers when they read their descriptions.
2. They must be correct.

We can easily confirm the first point for good persona:

- Does this description make a good impression on this persona?
- Do we feel like we can recognize them if we meet them on the street?
- Have this coworker neutral and ask these questions if we are not sure who we are. It's a little harder when talking about the second issue. In order to test this, we need to study user research and market research again.
- Do they match the description?

Double check carefully that we haven't created the desired personality.

The persona seemed to feel thoroughly and perfectly designed. For example; *"Willy, 55, an employee in the financial department of the Bank, no children. As a technology supporter, he also gives people advices all the time about using devices."* That persona may exist but most likely not very much in the real life. That is why Willy is not a very good persona. Designer should avoid modeling persona with real people. In the end, the character means the combination of many qualities in one. They do not have the same personality when talking about them (at least not for all). If the character is truly a person, everybody with the real same information, who will feel like being tracked and it should be avoided it at all costs.

This is outline the ten-steps process as described by Lene Nielsen [14], and briefly described in [9].

1. Gather as much knowledge about the users as possible through high quality user research of real users in the target users group.
2. Begin to create general concepts about various users within the focus area. This should include creating assumptions about how different users can use the relationship diagram and attention map to perform this step.
3. The goal at this stage is to decide whether to support or reject assumptions about differences between users.
4. Decide the appropriate number of final persona to build based on the assumptions about different types of users. So how can the target audience be divided into different types of users?
5. Make sure to show enough understanding and attention to the users. It should include necessary details about education, lifestyle, interests, values, goals, needs, limitations, desires, attitudes and behavior patterns. Personal details worn to give the character a realistic personality. 1–2 pages that describe the person in detail.

6. There should be a list of the needs, including a list of situations in which the product or service will be used.
7. Accept by the organization. Reorganize the group at this stage and ensure that as many team members as possible are involved, accepting and acknowledging the development of the person. We can ask the team more broadly for their opinions at this stage or (even better) let them participate in the process.
8. It is important to decide first that we want to share this knowledge with those who are not directly involved in the process - for new employees and external partners in the future.
9. Create a situation for you. It will get a better understanding of the problems that individuals want to solve when we show these situations, which will prove to have a lot of information for the overall design process.
10. Designer should edit the description commonly, as new information, perspectives may affect the way we build or describe the personality. Sometimes designer will have to write an explanation of the existing identity, add a new personality or get rid of outdated words.

2   Empathy in Design Thinking

In general, empathy is the good tool to examine the world through the judgements of others to confirm what they see, feel what they feel and know things while they are doing. Of course, no one can feel what other person do. But we will plan as closely as possible and we will do so by placing prejudiced ideas and selecting to know the thoughts, and desires of others in its place [10].

In design thinking, empathy shown in Fig. 2 is described in the IDEO's human-centered design toolkit [11], which is a deep understanding of the issues and reality of the persona we are designing. Learn about the needs that person face, as well as revealing their hidden needs and wants to explain their behavior. In doing so, it is good to have a sympathetic of person's situation, including the role and collaboration with their environment.

Empathy helps designers gain greater appreciation and insight about person's expressive and physical desires and therefore the way they perceive, realize, and cooperate with the realm around them. It will help knowing how motivating all of their lives are, especially within the context in question. Unlike traditional market research, empathy research does not involve facts about persona. Nevertheless, more about their motivation and ideas (For example, why do they like to watch TV compared to going out to jog) is inherently subjective, as there are many interpretations related to discovery what persona mean instead of what they confirm [12].

Empathy is the first step in the planning thinking process. The next steps are usually summarized as follows: determination, ideal, prototype, and experiment. Within the arena, the goal as a designer is to be aware of the exact sympathetic of the persona which are designed and therefore the problems we are trying to solve. This process involves detecting, appealing, and giving attention to the persona which are designed in

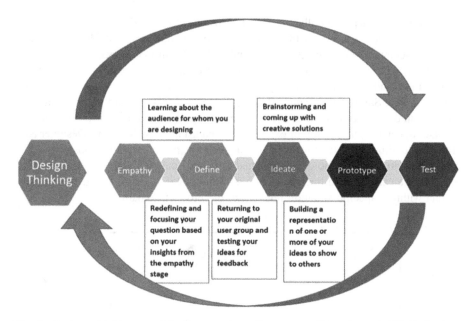

Fig. 2. Design thinking model (Source: https://commons.wikimedia.org/wiki/File:Design_thinking.png [11])

order to get to know their experience and motivation, as well as being occupied in their own physical situation.

Attention is important to the user-centered design process. For example, design thinking and attention will help design thinkers build their expectations about the world in order to understand users and their needs from time to time. The person must gather a lot of information in the thinking planning process. Within the Empathize process of the design process, designer will develop an understanding, experience, experience, insights and observations that the person will use. To create the rest of the design project The designers needed to develop the easiest possible understanding of our users, their needs, and therefore problems arising from the events of the product or service. Actually, designer will design. If designer has time and money, they should consider an expert advisor to find out more. But that person will be surprised that the persona and the team will get through the Empathize method.

Here are some of popular Empathize methods: Assume the idea of a beginner, ask what - why -, ask 5 whys, interviews, sympathetic interviews, build empathy by comparing, take education using photos and videos, use personal journals, photos and videos, very engaged with users, share stories and capture images, body storm, create travel maps. Sympathy, the word that is often confused, is about the power of a person to have or show concern for the well-being of others, while compassion does not need experience. In the deep in what persona. In addition, compassion is often associated with feelings of impartiality and advantage; When we feel compassion, we tend to point out compassion and grief for others.

The Empathy map is a collaborative visualization used to identify what we know about certain types of users. It transmits knowledge about users outside to 1) create common understanding about user needs and 2) help them make decisions.

Empathy Map as example in Fig. 3 for the target group to explain what they think and feel more and more deeply The question consists of 6 topics which are Think and Feel, Hear, See, Say and Do, Pain and Gain. There are users who are more possible to benefit from the service than others. To create more context and insight for these users, to create 'Special layers' on top of existing persona using empathy maps. Designer add a rotation to Empathy Mapping [16] by focusing on personas during post-synthesis workshops with our stakeholders. Renamed Persona Empathy Mapping, this process simplifies the categories to three main issues: Think, Feel, and Do, and zeroes in on a persona within a specific situation relevant to the product domain.

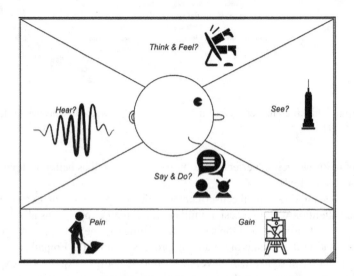

Fig. 3. Empathy map (Source: https://flic.kr/p/puLPuR)

The Empathy map provides in-depth content about what users are saying, thinking, feeling, and doing while accessing the service.

Key benefits I discovered from using the attention map [13]

- Easy to update after each round of research
- They focus on the user experience and behavior in the latest round of photography
- Easy to refer to within the playing field
- Help the team think that our users are real people.

After filling out all the areas of the Empathy map designer get a comprehensive information about the users. It's worth it to transfer this information to the model of the one particular personas. Each persona should include the basic elements reflecting the map's areas, as well as additional, specific information about the imagined user. Every

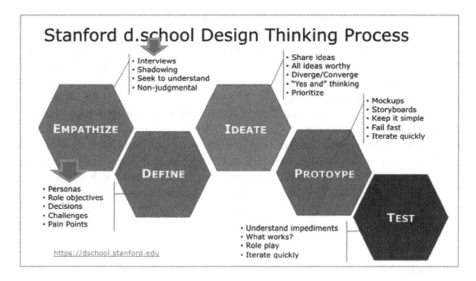

Fig. 4. Design thinking model (Source: adapt from https://dschool.standford.edu)

map character, when turning into a persona, should represent a person which, it will be easier to understand during the design process.

3   Conclusion

In general, an individual is easy for people to understand and care for users. But that person is seen as not detailed and cannot be used as the understanding benefits of an individual should reach out to a wide range of stakeholders. The idea of designing or developing without using a persona can be very difficult. The more we know the users, the better the product or the software will be. That's why people help everyone on the team focus on occupied with users.

User-centered design has greatly benefited people. It just has to make sure that the identity is truly true. Persona development means living in a state that needs it. From then on we can improve very well for these people but if they are unrealistic, real people will not understand or produce or buy the product. Nonetheless if the real data and knowledge of the users form the core, there are every purpose to advance oneself or to improve them.

The benefits of persona are powerful and perfect ways to express design needs, helping the team are designing to easily explain management. It allows designer to see users as a persona instead of a set of design specifications. Of course, the concept of empathy involves the creation of the right self. There is also a way to create Empathy maps, which is useful for synthesizing research data to understand users. Empathy maps are great for creating Personas by identifying users with different intentions. Being a collaborative tool, Empathy Mapping helps the design team focus on users and is a good idea for creating Empathy Mapping workshops with stakeholders as well -

helping to develop user-centric ideas. However, there are simple workshop activities where we can facilitate the stakeholders. (Or whoever is actually responsible for product development) to build awareness for the end users. We call it Persona Empathy Mapping. And also in Stanford "dschool" framework process, in Fig. 4 show that persona can be discovered in defining phase and the process of empathizing is related to how we can determine persona.

Empathy Mapping helps us consider how others think and feel. Research notes are generally categorized according to what research interviewees are thinking, feeling, doing, seeing and hearing when they engage with the product. It helps teams not have to focus on behavior to determine the mood and experience of users as well. Persona Empathy Mapping is a sympathetic workshop activity that aligns with the needs of target users and pain points and connects channels. Interpersonal and design concepts. Designers increase rotation for Empathy Mapping by focusing on the persona during the combination workshops with stakeholders.

References

1. www.grihotools.udl.cat. User profiles. Personas (2014). https://www.slideshare.net/DCU_MPIUA/user-profiles-personas-39303051. Accessed 18 Apr 2020
2. Vaniea, K.: HCI: PERSONA. (2020). http://www.inf.ed.ac.uk/teaching/courses/hci/1617/lects/Lecture09_persona.pdf. Accessed 18 Apr 2020
3. Dahiya, A., Kumar, J.: How empathizing with persona helps in design thinking: an experimental study with novice designers. In: Conference: IADIS International Conference Interfaces and Human Computer Interaction (2018)
4. Culén, A.L., Følstad, A.: Innovation in HCI: what can we learn from design thinking? In: NordiCHI 2014, Helsinki, Finland, 26–30 October 2014. ACM 978-1-4503-2542-4/14/10 (2019). http://dx.doi.org/10.1145/2639189.2654845. Accessed 20 May 2020
5. Meyer, S.: Complete guide: How to create personas based on data. https://www.testingtime.com/en/blog/complete-guide-how-to-create-personas-based-on-data/
6. https://www.ionos.com. Buyer personas (2019). https://www.ionos.com/digitalguide/online-marketing/web-analytics/buyer-personas-for-optimal-targeting/. Accessed 11 May 2020
7. Subramanian.: How Personas shaped our Design thinking? (2019). https://www.customerlabs.co/blog/how-personas-shaped-our-design-thinking/. Accessed 21 May 2020
8. Veal, R.L.: How to Define a User Persona (2019). https://careerfoundry.com/en/blog/ux-design/how-to-define-a-user-persona/. Accessed 11 May 2020
9. Dam, R.F., Siang, T.Y.: Personas – A Simple Introduction (2019). https://www.interaction-design.org/literature/article/personas-why-and-how-you-should-use-them. Accessed 11 May 2020
10. Dam, R.F., Siang, T.Y.: Design Thinking: Getting Started with Empathy (2019). https://www.interaction-design.org/literature/article/design-thinking-getting-started-with-empathy. Accessed 11 June 2020
11. IDEO.: Design Kit: The Human-Centered Design Toolkit (2009). https://www.ideo.com/work/human-centered-design-toolkit/. Accessed 17 June 2020
12. Psychology Today, The Neuroscience of Empathy (2013). https://www.psychologytoday.com/blog/the-athletes-way/201310/the-neuroscience-empathy. Accessed 01 July 2020

13. Thompson, L.: Why I chose to work with empathy maps instead of personas (2019). https://medium.com/hippo-digital/why-i-chose-to-work-with-empathy-maps-instead-of-personas-38934fb38b88. Accessed 19 June 2020
14. Nielsen, L.: 10 Steps to Personas (2007). https://www.kommunikationsforum.dk/lene-nielsen/blog/10-steps-to-personas. Accessed 20 July 2020
15. Jansen, B.J., Salminen, J. O., Jung, S.: Data-driven personas for enhanced user understanding: combining empathy with rationality for better insights to analytics. Data Inf. Manag. **4**(1) (2020). https://doi.org/10.2478/dim-2020-0005. Accessed 20 July 2020
16. Knox, N.: Persona Empathy Mapping (2020). https://www.cooper.com/journal/2014/05/persona-empathy-mapping/. Accessed 20 July 2020

Taiwanese Stock Market Forecasting with a Shallow Long Short-Term Memory Architecture

Phuong Ha Dang Bui[1], Toan Bao Tran[2,3], and Hai Thanh Nguyen[1(✉)]

[1] College of Information and Communication Technology, Can Tho University,
Can Tho 900100, Vietnam
{bdhphuong,nthai}@cit.ctu.edu.vn
[2] Center of Software Engineering, Duy Tan University, Da Nang 550000, Vietnam
tranbaotoan@dtu.edu.vn
[3] Institute of Research and Development, Duy Tan University, Da Nang 550000,
Vietnam

Abstract. The trading of stock in companies holds an important part in numerous economies. Stock Forecast which is popularly published in the public domain in the forms of newsletters, investment promotion organizations, public/private forums, and scientific forecast services is very necessary to contribute successes in financial for individuals or organizations. Leveraging advancements in machine learning, we propose an approach based on Long Short-Term Memory model and compare the performance to the classic machine learning such as Random Forest model and Support Vector Regression model when we do forecast tasks on Taiwanese stock market. The proposed method with deep learning algorithm shows better performance comparing to the classic machine learning in the tasks of forecasting the stock market in Taiwan.

Keywords: Trading of stock · Machine learning · Forecast tasks

1 Introduction

In recent years, the development of Machine learning and Deep learning technique has an influence on the stock market in participate and the finance predictions in general. The prediction of future stock price movement has been widely researched in numerous studies. The existing approaches have focused on the construction of econometric, statistical based on the selection of variables or forecasting models. The stock market forecasting is not a basic task due to the behavior of a stock time series. By using Machine learning techniques can help the market intermediaries to reveal better forecasting stock prices for short term stock price trends. Furthermore, there are numerous factors that produce uncertainty and high volatility in the market affected stock markets definitely which can be considered as the psychology of investors' political events, general economic conditions, or commodity price index [1]. The computation of the

P. C. Vinh and A. Rakib (Eds.): ICCASA 2020/ICTCC 2020, LNICST 343, pp. 192–202, 2021.
https://doi.org/10.1007/978-3-030-67101-3_16

value of stock groups is based on market capitalization. In each country, the estimated economic status are presented by the prices of stocks with high market investment.

In this paper, we propose an approach based on Long Short-Term Memory model and compare the performance to the classic machine learning such as Random Forest model and Support Vector Regression model to forecast the Taiwan Stock Exchange Capitalization Weighted Stock Index (TAIEX) [12]. The proposed method with deep learning algorithm shows better performance comparing to the classic machine learning for forecasting the TAIEX. The rest of this paper is organized as follows. In Sect. 2, we present related work on forecasting the TAIEX. In Sect. 3, we present the forecasting methods based on three models: Random Forest model, Support Vector Regression model and Long Short-Term Memory model. In Sect. 4, we compare the forecasting results of the methods based on three learning models. The conclusion is discussed in Sect. 5.

2   Related Work

Some methods including [2–11] have been presented to forecast the TAIEX [12].

In [2], Cai et al. presented a fuzzy time series model combined with ant colony optimization (ACO) and auto-regression to forecast the TAIEX, where ACO is used to partition the universe of discourse and an auto-regression high-order fuzzy time series model is used to make better using of the historical data. Chen and Chang [3] presented a multi-variable fuzzy forecasting method based on the fuzzy clustering method and fuzzy rule interpolation techniques for forecasting the TAIEX. In [4], Chen and Chen presented a fuzzy time series forecasting method to forecast the TAIEX based on fuzzy variation groups. Chen and Chen [5] presented a method for forecasting the TAIEX based on two-factors second-order fuzzy-trend logical relationship groups and the probabilities of the down-trend, the probabilities of the equal-trend and the probabilities of the up-trend of the two-factors second-order fuzzy logical relationships. Chen and Kao [6] presented a method to forecast the TAIEX based on fuzzy time series, PSO techniques and support vector machines, where the PSO techniques are used to obtain optimal intervals in the universe of discourse and the support vector machine is used to classify the training data set. In [7], Chen et al. presented a method to forecast the TAIEX based on two-factors second-order fuzzy-trend logical relationship groups and PSO techniques, where the PSO techniques are used to get the optimal weighting vector of each group of the fuzzy-trend logical relationship groups. Chen and Phuong [8] presented a method for forecasting the TAIEX based on optimal partitions of intervals in the universe of discourse and optimal weighting vectors of two-factors second-order fuzzy-trend logical relationship groups, where the PSO techniques are used to obtain the optimal partitions of intervals and the optimal weighting vectors simultaneously. Huarng et al. [9] presented a method using a multivariate heuristic model, which can be integrated with univariate fuzzy time-series models to forecast the TAIEX. In

[10] Yu presented a weighted fuzzy time-series method to forecast the TAIEX. Yu and Huarng [11] used neural networks to fuzzy time series forecasting and presented bivariate fuzzy time series models to forecast the TAIEX. In order to increase the forecasting accuracy rates to forecast the TAIEX, we need to propose a forecasting method to obtain better results.

3   Random Forest, Support Vector Regression and Long Short-Term Memory Models for Stock Market Prediction

We use Random Forest [13], Support Vector Regression (SVR) [14] and Long Short-Term Memory (LSTM) [15] models to investigate the performance of stock prices prediction.

3.1   The Random Forest Model

Random Forest is a supervised learning algorithm which uses ensemble learning method for classification and regression. A Random Forest operates by constructing several decision trees at training time and outputting the class or mean prediction of the individual trees. In this paper, we implement Random Forest Regression with the following parameters: the number of trees in the forest is 500, the maximum depth of each tree is 4 and estimate the tree quality by Mean Squared Error (MSE). MSE is the square of RMSE.

3.2   The Support Vector Regression Model

Support Vector Regression is the combination of a Support Vector Machine and Regression. SVR is flexible to define the acceptable error in the model and will find an appropriate hyperplane to fit the data. Furthermore, the stock prices prediction using SVR can gain promising results due to the minimization the error within a certain threshold. In this paper, we implement SVR with the regularization parameter is 0.001, the gamma is 0.1 and Radial Basis Function kernel.

3.3   The Long Short-Term Memory Model

Long Short-Term Memory is a special kind of Recurrent Neural Networks (RNN) and can be used to avoid the long-term dependency problem. The LSTM architecture contains a Long Short-Term Memory layer and a Fully Connected layer. We implement the LSTM with Adam optimizer function [16] and MSE loss function. The learning rate is initiated at 0.001. We train our LSTM on 20 epochs with a batch size of 1. We also illustrate the LSTM in Fig. 1.

```
OPERATION                DATA DIMENSIONS    WEIGHTS(N)    WEIGHTS(%)

  Input    #####        1    3
   LSTM    LLLLL  ------------------     10800         99.5%
   tanh    #####           50
  Dense    XXXXX  ------------------  ∘   51         0.5%
           #####            1
```

Fig. 1. The visualization of LSTM architecture which includes 2 layers LSTM with tanh activation function

Table 1. The performance of Support Vector Regression model over several training years

No. of training years	Training RMSE	Testing RMSE	Training MAE	Testing MAE
9 years	437.9962	403.0504	361.0728	360.5454
10 years	429.9880	419.9105	353.8121	383.4044
11 years	435.1563	392.1609	361.7393	358.0659

Table 2. The further information of TAIEX dataset

Dataset	From year	To year	Min price	Max price	Avg price	Total number of samples
TAIEX	1990	2004	2560.47	12495.34	6053.86	4086

4 Experimental Results

In this section, we compare the forecasting results of the methods based on three learning models: the Random Forest model, the Support Vector Regression model and the Long Short-Term Memory model.

4.1 The TAIEX Dataset

We use the TAIEX dataset in our experiments. The TAIEX dataset includes the stock price on each trading day over several years. The TAIEX were recorded in 15 years, from 1990 to 2004. Further information, e.g. minimum, maximum, average stock prices and the number of total samples of the dataset are described in Table 2. We also visualize the stock prices change of the TAIEX dataset in Fig. 2. The minimum price is 2560.47, whereas the maximum and average are 12495.34 and 6053.86 respectively.

We divide the dataset into two parts, where the first part of dataset is used as the training data and the remaining is used as the testing data. In specific, we use the first 9 years for training, the last 6 years for testing. Besides, we also use the first 10 years for training, the last 5 years for testing and the first 11 years for training, the last 4 years for testing.

We normalize the stock prices by rescaling the values within the range of 0 and 1 due to the differences in the scales across the stock prices. In general, an

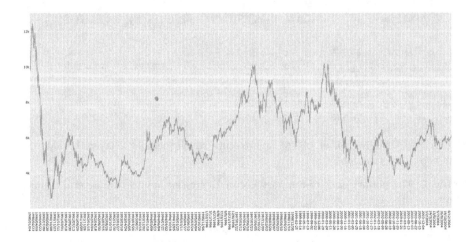

Fig. 2. The visualization of TAIEX dataset from 1990 to 2004

output with a large value may influence negatively to the learning process of the models.

The purposes of data normalization are to enhance the numerical stability of the learning models and to reduce the training time. In other words, the learning models can converge rapidly. Furthermore, accuracy is not affected by normalizing inputs.

4.2 The Metrics for Evaluating the Performance

In order to evaluate the performance of learning models, we use the Mean Absolute Error (MAE) and the Root Mean Squared Error (RMSE). They are both common metrics in regression and define the prediction errors with the range from 0 to ∞. They are negatively-oriented scores, which means lower values are better. The MAE and the RMSE can be computed by the Eq. 1 and Eq. 2.

$$MAE = \frac{\sum_n^{i=1} |y_i - \hat{y}_i|}{n} \tag{1}$$

$$RMSE = \sqrt{\frac{\sum_n^{i=1} (y_i - \hat{y}_i)^2}{n}} \tag{2}$$

where n denotes the number of trading days of the historical testing data, y_i denotes the forecasted value of the historical testing datum of the TAIEX on trading day i, and $\hat{y}_i$ denotes the actual value of the historical testing datum of the TAIEX on trading day i, where $1 \leq i \leq n$.

4.3   The Performance of Random Forest Model

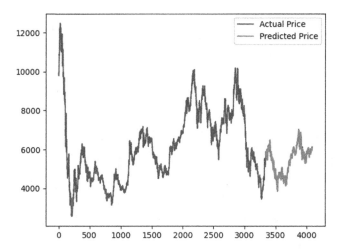

Fig. 3. The visualization of the actual prices and the forecasting prices by using Random Forest model on 11 training years (Color figure online)

Table 3. The performance of Random Forest model over several training years

No. of training years	Training RMSE	Testing RMSE	Training MAE	Testing MAE
9 years	50.5450	115.8137	35.0288	85.0645
10 years	52.4664	94.5714	36.4398	72.0539
11 years	51.6092	91.1585	35.9066	69.8861

The performance of Random Forest model on 9 training years, 10 training years and 11 training years are presented in Table 3. The performance of Random Forest model on 11 training years is better than the others. In specific, the lowest errors obtained are 91.1585 and 69.8861 for the RMSE and the MAE respectively. The performance of that on 10 training years and 9 training years follows closely, with the RMSE are 94.5714 and 115.8137 respectively, and the MAE are 72.0539 and 85.0645 respectively. We also visualize the forecasting prices and the actual prices by using Random Forest model on 11 training years in Fig. 3. The blue line in Fig. 3 stands for the actual prices, whereas the orange line denotes the predicted prices.

4.4 The Performance of Support Vector Regression Model

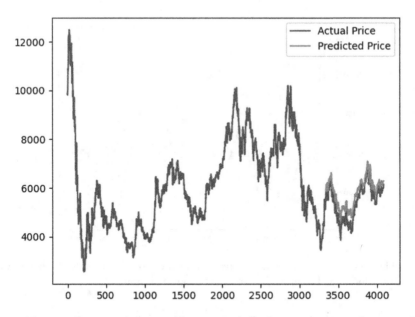

Fig. 4. The visualization of the actual prices and the forecasting prices by using Support Vector Regression model on 11 training years (Color figure online)

We also investigate the performance of SVR model on 9 training years, 10 training years and 11 training years. The SVR model on 11 training years reached the highest performance with the RMSE is 392.1609 and the MAE is 358.0659, followed by that on 9 training years, with the RMSE and the MAE obtained are 403.0504 and 360.5454 respectively. We also present the performance details of SVR model in Table 1. Furthermore, Fig. 4 visualizes the actual prices and forecasting prices by using SVR model on 11 training years. The actual prices is visualized by the blue line, whereas the orange line stands for the forecasting prices.

4.5   The Performance of Long Short-Term Memory Model

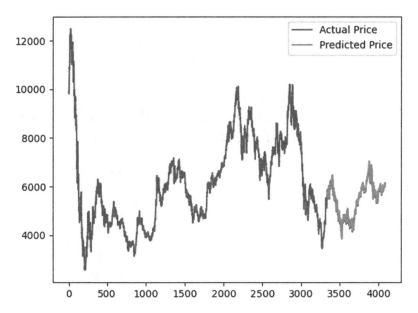

Fig. 5. The visualization of the actual prices and the forecasting prices by using Long Short-Term Memory model on 11 training years (Color figure online)

The optimal performance of LSTM model obtained by using 11 training years with the RMSE is 88.7651 and the MAE is 67.7686, followed by the performance of that by using 10 training years with the RMSE and the MAE are 89.7668 and 69.1916 respectively. We also present the performance details of LSTM model in Table 4. The actual prices and the forecasting prices by using LSTM model on 11 training years are visualized in Fig. 5. The actual prices is visualized by blue line, whereas the orange line stands for the forecasting prices.

Table 4. The performance of Long Short-Term Memory model over several training years

No. of training years	Training RMSE	Testing RMSE	Training MAE	Testing MAE
9 years	122.3369	109.4436	86.2959	80.0706
10 years	125.5805	89.7668	89.2567	69.1916
11 years	121.4129	88.7651	88.2835	67.7686

Table 5. The comparison between the performance of Random Forest model, Support Vector Regression model, and Long Short-Term Memory model in the testing phase on 11 training years

The learning model	RMSE	MAE
LSTM	88.7651	67.7686
Random Forest	91.1585	69.8861
SVR	392.1609	358.0659

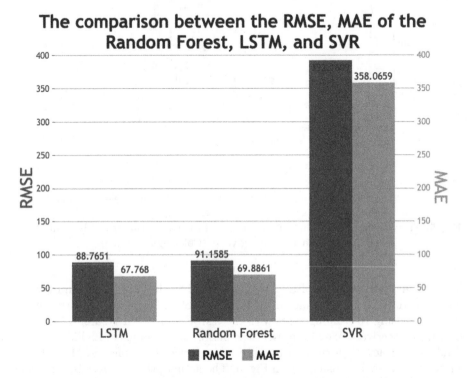

Fig. 6. The visualization of the RMSE and the MAE for comparison between Random Forest model, LSTM model, and SVR model on 11 training years

4.6 The Comparison Between the Learning Models

The comparison between the learning models on 11 training years is presented in Table 5. The LSTM model shows the highest performance with the RMSE is 88.7651 and the MAE is 67.7686, followed by the Random Forest model, with the RMSE and the MAE are 91.1585 and 69.8861 respectively. The performance of SVR model is not good enough in comparison to the others. We also visualize the RMSE and the MAE for comparison between Random Forest model, LSTM model, and SVR model on 11 training years in Fig. 6.

5 Conclusion

In this paper, we propose the approach with a shallow deep learning architecture based on Long short-term memory for forecasting the TAIEX. In order to evaluate the performance for forecasting prices, we divide the dataset into two phases. The first one is the preceded 9–11 years which fetched into the model for the learning and the remaining is for the testing phase. As observed from the tables, we can see that with more than time for training set, we obtain lesser errors in testing phase.

We also compare the performance between deep learning approach and the classic machine learning method for forecasting tasks. The obtained results show that deep learning with Long short-term memory (although only with a shallow architecture) performs an efficient prediction performance comparing to the classic machine learning such as Random Forest model and Support Vector Regression model.

We continue the work with further research on sophisticated architectures to improve the performance in forecasting.

References

1. Miao, K., Chen, F., Zhao, Z.: Stock price forecast based on bacterial colony RBF neural network. J. Qingdao Univ. (Nat. Sci. Ed.) **2**(11) (2007)
2. Cai, Q., Zhang, D.F., Zheng, W., Leung, S.C.H.: A new fuzzy time series forecasting model combined with ant colony optimization and auto-regression. Knowl. Based Syst. **74**, 61–68 (2015)
3. Chen, S.M., Chang, Y.C.: Multi-variable fuzzy forecasting based on fuzzy clustering and fuzzy interpolation techniques. Inf. Sci. **180**(24), 4772–4783 (2010)
4. Chen, S.M., Chen, C.D.: TAIEX forecasting based on fuzzy time series and fuzzy variation groups. IEEE Trans. Fuzzy Syst. **19**(1), 1–12 (2011)
5. Chen, S.M., Chen, S.W.: Fuzzy forecasting based on two-factors second-order fuzzy-trend logical relationship groups and the probabilities of trends of fuzzy logical relationships. IEEE Trans. Cybern. **45**(3), 405–417 (2015)
6. Chen, S.M., Kao, P.Y.: TAIEX forecasting based on fuzzy time series, particle swarm optimization techniques and support vector machines. Inf. Sci. **247**, 62–71 (2013)
7. Chen, S.M., Manalu, G.M.T., Pan, J.S., Liu, H.C.: Fuzzy forecasting based on two-factors second-order fuzzy-trend logical relationship groups and particle swarm optimization techniques. IEEE Trans. Cybern. **43**(3), 1102–1117 (2013)
8. Chen, S.M., Phuong, B.D.H.: Fuzzy time series forecasting based on optimal partitions of intervals and optimal weighting vectors. Knowl. Based Syst. **118**, 204–216 (2017)
9. Huarng, K., Yu, T.H.K., Hsu, Y.W.: A multivariate heuristic model for fuzzy time-series forecasting. IEEE Trans. Syst. Man Cybern. Part B Cybern. **37**(4), 836–846 (2007)
10. Yu, T.H.K.: Weighted fuzzy time-series model for TAIEX forecasting. Physica A **349**(3–4), 609–624 (2004)
11. Yu, T.H.K., Huarng, K.H.: A bivariate fuzzy time series model to forecast the TAIEX. Expert Syst. Appl. **34**(4), 2945–2952 (2008)

12. TAIEX. http://www.twse.com.tw/en/products/indices/tsec/taiex.php
13. Breiman, L.: Random forests. Mach. Learn. **45**(1), 5–32 (2001). https://doi.org/10.1023/A:1010933404324
14. Drucker, H., Burges, C.J.C., Kaufman, L., Smola, A., Vapnik, V.: Support vector regression machines. In: Mozer, M.C., Jordan, M.I., Petsche, T. (eds.) Advances in Neural Information Processing Systems, vol. 9, pp. 155–161. MIT Press, Cambridge (1997)
15. Hochreiter, S., Schmidhuber, J.: Long short-term memory. Neural Comput. **9**(8), 1735–1780 (1997). https://doi.org/10.1162/neco.1997.9.8.1735
16. Kingma, D.P., Ba, J.L.: Adam: a method for stochastic optimization (2014). arXiv:1412.6980v9

A Convolutional Neural Network on X-Ray Images for Pneumonia Diagnosis

Hiep Xuan Huynh[1]([✉]), Son Hai Dang[2], Cang Anh Phan[3],
and Hai Thanh Nguyen[1]

[1] College of Information and Communication Technology, Can Tho University,
Can Tho, Vietnam
hxhiep@ctu.edu.vn, nthai@cit.ctu.edu.vn
[2] Pham Hung High School, Vinh Long, Vietnam
dhsontinhoc@gmail.com
[3] Faculty of Information Technology, Vinh Long University of Technology Education,
Vinh Long, Vietnam
cangpa@vlute.edu.vn

Abstract. The application of AI in general and Deep learning, in particular, is becoming increasingly popular in human life. AI has been able to replace people in many fields, with data already synthesized and stored by computers that will help AI become smarter. One of the areas where AI can be applied very well is the medical field, especially X-ray imaging. In this study, we propose a convolutional network architecture to classify chest X-ray images as well as apply explanatory methods to trained models to support disease diagnosis. The proposed method provides insight into medical imaging to support the diagnosis of Pneumonia.

Keywords: AI · Deep learning · Chest X-ray · X-ray imaging · Pneumonia · Convolutional neural network

1 Introduction

The lungs are a part of the body with the main role of exchanging gases - bringing oxygen from the air into the pulmonary veins, and carbon dioxide from the pulmonary arteries. Besides, the lungs also have some other secondary abilities, which help metabolize some biochemicals, filter some toxins in the blood. The lungs are also a store of blood.

Because the lungs are the organs in direct contact with the external environment, they are very susceptible to bacterial, viruses, etc.: dry cough, cough with phlegm, difficulty breathing, ... with pathologies from pneumonia, bronchial tablets, ... to more severe tuberculosis, lung cancer [1]. In particular, SARS, COVID-19 (a virus causes acute respiratory infections in humans) over 16,601,552 people in the world have been infected and 655,214 people have died. Symptoms of Covid-19 disease appear very quickly within 14 days, if not treated promptly, it will lead to complications such as respiratory failure, arrhythmia,

© ICST Institute for Computer Sciences, Social Informatics and Telecommunications Engineering 2021
Published by Springer Nature Switzerland AG 2021. All Rights Reserved
P. C. Vinh and A. Rakib (Eds.): ICCASA 2020/ICTCC 2020, LNICST 343, pp. 203–215, 2021.
https://doi.org/10.1007/978-3-030-67101-3_17

blood infection, liver failure, kidney failure, ... can lead to death [11]. Early detection and timely treatment are the best way to prevent disease progression and increase the patient's chance of survival.

Chest radiography is one of the most common types of diagnostic radiology exams, which is critical for screening and diagnosis of many different thoracic diseases [13]. Diagnosing abnormalities in an x-ray image requires a lot of expertise and the quality of the diagnosis can sometimes affect the outcome (an error may occur).

Today, the application of AI to human health care is the application that is most concerned today. Machine learning, deep learning has become an effective tool for image classification, image segmentation [9,10]. In particular convolutional networks, have rapidly become a methodology of choice for analyzing medical images [14]. And this is also a very effective tool for doctors to diagnose abnormalities of lung X-ray faster and faster.

2   Related Work

Recently, a deep learning model has been found suitable or superior to human expert radiologists in diagnosing 10 or more pathologies on chest radiography. The success of AI in imaging has fueled growing debate on the future role of radiologists in an era in which deep-learning models are capable of performing diagnostic tasks. Automated critical guessing and speculation around the radiologist's comprehensive diagnostic interpretation skills can be replicated in algorithms. However, AI is also affected by some disadvantages including deviations due to limited training data, lack of cross-population popularity, and the inability of deep learning models to contextualize.

The author in [2] describe to detect lung X-ray images showing signs of tuberculosis or healthy, we use two different machine learning models, AlexNet and GoogLeNet, and use over 1007 back-chest X-rays labeled for distribution. assorted images. As a result, an in-depth study can accurately classify tuberculosis during a chest X-ray with an AUC of 0.99.

The author in [3] describes based on the deep convulsive neural network (CNN) to detect specific diseases such as lymph node or lung cancer through X-ray images, this model is trained on more than 200,000 supervised X-rays. of data sets and achieve certain success.

The author in [4] describes a machine-learning study that uses the CNN network to detect abnormalities in X-ray images of lower extremities for clinical and treatment use in musculoskeletal disorders. The model is based on a large dataset of 93,455 x-rays of the lower extremities of each body part, with each test labeled normal or abnormal. A dense, interconnected CNN dense 161 layer has achieved AUC-ROC of 0.880 (sensitivity = 0.714, specificity = 0.961) in this unusual classification task.

The author in [5] describes research, three types of deep neural networks (e.g., CNN, DNN, and SAE) are designed for lung cancer calcification. Those networks are applied to the CT image classification task with some modification for the benign and malignant lung nodules. Those networks were evaluated on the LIDC-IDRI database. The experimental results show that the CNN network archived the best performance with an accuracy of 84.15%, sensitivity of 83.96%, and specificity of 84.32%, which has the best result among the three networks.

3   Theoretical Modeling

Most clinical techniques are based on anomaly analysis of lung X-ray images for diagnosis and treatment cite 13. Diagnosing anomalies in an x-ray image require a lot of specialist knowledge, and the quality of the diagnosis also sometimes affects the result (error may occur). Diagnosis results are not shared and doctors have to look back from the beginning when there is an image to diagnose. The quality of diagnosis depends on the expertise and experience of each doctor. This is a problem for doctors as the number of X-rays to diagnose increases. In places where access to skilled radiologists is limited, diagnosis of results can be delayed and affect the patient's treatment

We propose a method to classify pneumonia and normal patients from Chest X-ray images with CNN architectural model [7,8]. The intended method will be a good tool for diagnosing medical imaging diseases.

We train a CNN architectural model that contains a Convolutional class followed by a Max-Pooling class of 2 × 2 dimensions connected to the full class. [6]. The output of the Max-Pooling layer will form a 1D, array that forms the matrix input for the fully connected layer. Our convolution layer contains 64 filters or nuclei, the filter itself is a 3 × 3 integer matrix.

Furthermore, CNN was performed with a default learning rate of 0.000001 and ran 100 times over a period 1 day. And we used the input of size 150 × 150, a shallow architecture that should be able to work well in this task.

We calculated binary cross-entropy losses during the training using the formula 1. The goal is to compare the probability distribution volume with the real label.

$$-\frac{1}{N} \sum_{i=1}^{N} y_i \log\left(\hat{y}_i\right) + (1 - y_i) \log(1 - \hat{y}_i) \tag{1}$$

Where y_i and $\hat{y}_i$ denote the label and the predictive results respectively.

After establishing an abnormal detection system on the chest X-ray, the system was evaluated by the following method:

We calculated the overall accuracy, the area according to the characteristic curve (ROC-AUC) [12]. Each row of matrices represents instances in a predictive class while each column represents instances in an actual class (or vice versa). The name of the confusion matrix comes from the fact that it makes it easy to see whether the system is confusing two layers (usually mislabeled as another class).

Model: "sequential"

Layer (type)	Output Shape	Param #
conv2d (Conv2D)	(None, 150, 150, 32)	320
batch_normalization (BatchNo	(None, 150, 150, 32)	128
max_pooling2d (MaxPooling2D)	(None, 75, 75, 32)	0
conv2d_1 (Conv2D)	(None, 75, 75, 64)	18496
dropout (Dropout)	(None, 75, 75, 64)	0
batch_normalization_1 (Batch	(None, 75, 75, 64)	256
max_pooling2d_1 (MaxPooling2	(None, 38, 38, 64)	0
conv2d_2 (Conv2D)	(None, 38, 38, 64)	36928
batch_normalization_2 (Batch	(None, 38, 38, 64)	256
max_pooling2d_2 (MaxPooling2	(None, 19, 19, 64)	0
conv2d_3 (Conv2D)	(None, 19, 19, 128)	73856
dropout_1 (Dropout)	(None, 19, 19, 128)	0
batch_normalization_3 (Batch	(None, 19, 19, 128)	512
max_pooling2d_3 (MaxPooling2	(None, 10, 10, 128)	0
conv2d_4 (Conv2D)	(None, 10, 10, 256)	295168
dropout_2 (Dropout)	(None, 10, 10, 256)	0
batch_normalization_4 (Batch	(None, 10, 10, 256)	1024
max_pooling2d_4 (MaxPooling2	(None, 5, 5, 256)	0
flatten (Flatten)	(None, 6400)	0
dense (Dense)	(None, 128)	819328
dropout_3 (Dropout)	(None, 128)	0
dense_1 (Dense)	(None, 1)	129

Total params: 1,246,401
Trainable params: 1,245,313
Non-trainable params: 1,088

Fig. 1. Model 1

The accuracy of the model is calculated by the ratio between the total number of correctly detected lungs (normal and abnormal lung)/the total number of detected lung images, according to formula 2:

$$ACC\left(M\right) = \frac{TP + TN}{TP + TN + FP + FN} \tag{2}$$

Inside:

TP (True Positive) - the number of abnormal-labeled lung images correctly classified into abnormal layers.

FP (False Positive) - number of normal labeled lung images incorrectly classified into abnormal layers.

FN (False Negative) - the number of abnormal labeled lung images that are incorrectly classified into normal layers.

TN (True Negative) - the number of normal labeled lung images correctly classified into the normal layer.

4   Tool

We experimented with Keras is an open-source neural network written in the Python language. It is run on Windows 64-bit system with 8G memory. Keras has several advantages: simple, easy to use, runs on both CPU and GPU and is very powerful. So we choose Keras to study.

5   Experimental Results

5.1   Dataset

CheXpert is a dataset of 224,316 chest X-ray images of 65,240 patients who underwent an X-ray examination at Stanford University Medical Center from October 2002 to July 2017, both at the control center. Inpatient and outpatient treatment [3]. We used this dataset including 2 folders (Train, Val), and each folder will be the corresponding categories (Pneumonia/Normal). The Train folder contains 7599 images of chest X-rays with 1082 images of normal lungs and 6517 images of patients with pneumonia. The Val folder contains 234 images of chest X-rays with 38 images of normal lungs and 196 images of patients with pneumonia. The sample of chest X-ray image shown in Fig. 2 includes pneumonia (left) and normal (right).

5.2   Scenario 1

We have conducted on model 1 consisting of 5 classes. Coaching and validation in coaching are shown in Fig. 1. The model's performance for the categorical assignment was assessed by an ACC accuracy of 0.84 shown in Fig. 3.

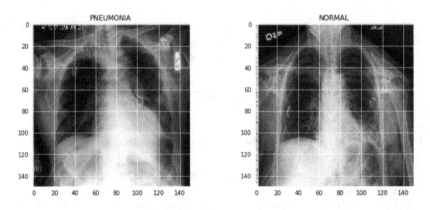

Fig. 2. Image in the dataset

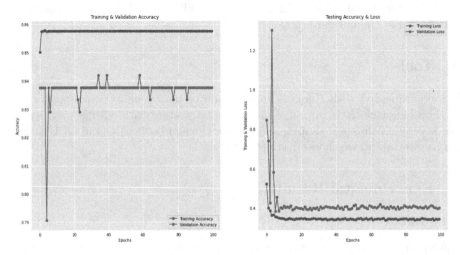

Fig. 3. ACC-Model 1

5.3   Scenario 2

We have conducted on model 2 consisting of 4 classes. Coaching and validation in coaching are shown in Fig. 4. The model's performance for the categorical assignment was assessed by an ACC accuracy of 0.8375 shown in Fig. 5.

```
Model: "sequential"
```

Layer (type)	Output Shape	Param #
conv2d (Conv2D)	(None, 150, 150, 32)	320
batch_normalization (BatchNo	(None, 150, 150, 32)	128
max_pooling2d (MaxPooling2D)	(None, 75, 75, 32)	0
conv2d_1 (Conv2D)	(None, 75, 75, 64)	18496
batch_normalization_1 (Batch	(None, 75, 75, 64)	256
max_pooling2d_1 (MaxPooling2	(None, 38, 38, 64)	0
conv2d_2 (Conv2D)	(None, 38, 38, 128)	73856
dropout (Dropout)	(None, 38, 38, 128)	0
batch_normalization_2 (Batch	(None, 38, 38, 128)	512
max_pooling2d_2 (MaxPooling2	(None, 19, 19, 128)	0
conv2d_3 (Conv2D)	(None, 19, 19, 256)	295168
dropout_1 (Dropout)	(None, 19, 19, 256)	0
batch_normalization_3 (Batch	(None, 19, 19, 256)	1024
max_pooling2d_3 (MaxPooling2	(None, 10, 10, 256)	0
flatten (Flatten)	(None, 25600)	0
dense (Dense)	(None, 128)	3276928
dropout_2 (Dropout)	(None, 128)	0
dense_1 (Dense)	(None, 1)	129

```
Total params: 3,666,817
Trainable params: 3,665,857
Non-trainable params: 960
```

Fig. 4. Model 2

5.4 Scenario 3

We have conducted on model 3 consisting of 3 classes. Coaching and validation in coaching are shown in Fig. 6. The model's performance for the categorical assignment was assessed by an ACC accuracy of 0.8375 shown in Fig. 7.

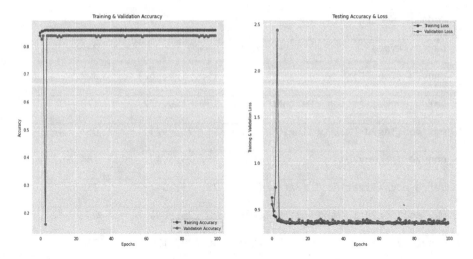

Fig. 5. Accuracy M2

After conducting experiments on 3 models, we have the following summary table: Fig. 8

We see that in the above 3 models CNN, model 1 with ACC has the best accuracy and error is very low. So we have chosen model 1 as the training model. It is quite good for classifying abnormalities on a chest X-ray (Fig. 9).

However, a major downside in medical image processing with deep learning is the limited dataset size compared to the computer vision domain. And due to the similarity between the X-ray images of normal lungs and pneumonia, there is confusion in the classification of X-ray images of normal lungs. Specifically, in Fig. 10, the X-ray image of a normal lung in the episode Val is similar to Fig. 11, which is an X-ray image of pneumonia in Train episode.

```
Model: "sequential"

_____
Layer (type)                    Output Shape              Param #
=================================================================
conv2d (Conv2D)                 (None, 150, 150, 64)      640

batch_normalization (BatchNo    (None, 150, 150, 64)      256

max_pooling2d (MaxPooling2D)    (None, 75, 75, 64)        0

conv2d_1 (Conv2D)               (None, 75, 75, 128)       73856

dropout (Dropout)               (None, 75, 75, 128)       0

batch_normalization_1 (Batch    (None, 75, 75, 128)       512

max_pooling2d_1 (MaxPooling2    (None, 38, 38, 128)       0

conv2d_2 (Conv2D)               (None, 38, 38, 256)       295168

dropout_1 (Dropout)             (None, 38, 38, 256)       0

batch_normalization_2 (Batch    (None, 38, 38, 256)       1024

max_pooling2d_2 (MaxPooling2    (None, 19, 19, 256)       0

flatten (Flatten)               (None, 92416)             0

dense (Dense)                   (None, 128)               11829376

dropout_2 (Dropout)             (None, 128)               0

dense_1 (Dense)                 (None, 1)                 129
=================================================================
Total params: 12,200,961
Trainable params: 12,200,065
Non-trainable params: 896
```

Fig. 6. Model 3

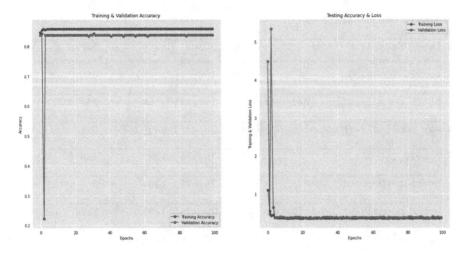

Fig. 7. Accuracy M3

Model	Number of layers	ACC_Val
Model 1	5 layers	8.382
Model 2	4 layers	8.376
Model 3	3 layers	8.376

Fig. 8. Compare the results

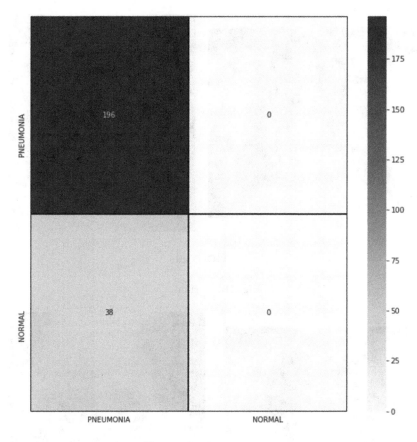

Fig. 9. Confusion matrix

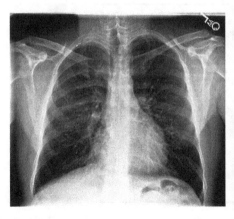 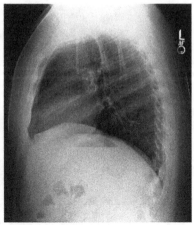

Normal

Fig. 10. Normal

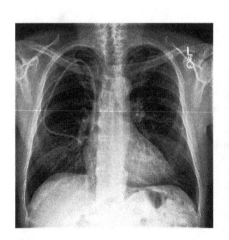 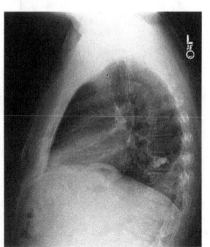

Pneumonia

Fig. 11. Pneumonia

6   Conclusion

Lung image recognition plays an important role in medical imaging. This helps to quickly detect serious illnesses in the lung image. Especially in the current situation of the COVID-19 epidemic, photo identification has proven to be important. The faster the disease is identified, the more effective it will be. Our study is expected to play a part in the early detection of lung x-ray abnormalities. We trained our CNN model with nearly exactly classified pneumonia cases during each validation. However, due to limited resources and time, we have only been researched on the CheXpert dataset. In the future, more in-depth studies on larger datasets are expected to contribute to improving machine learning performance on medical imaging data.

References

1. Xi, X., Chengcheng, Y., Jing, Q., Zhang, L., et al.: Imaging and clinical features of patients with 2019 novel coronavirus SARS-CoV-2. Eur. J. Nucl. Med. Mol. Imaging **47**(5), 1275–1280 (2020). https://doi.org/10.1007/s002-04735-9
2. Jefferson, T., Jefferson, S.K.: Deep learning at chest radiography: automated classification of pulmonary tuberculosis by using convolutional neural networks, April 2017
3. Irvin, J., Rajpurkar, P., Ko, M., Yu, Y., et al.: CheXpert: a large chest radiograph dataset with uncertainty labels and expert comparison, 21 January 2019 (2019, submitted)
4. Bengio, Y., Courville, A., Vincent, P.: Representation learning: a review and new perspectives. IEEE Trans. Pattern Anal. Mach. Intell. **35**, 1798–1828 (2013)
5. Song, Q., Zhao, L., Luo, X., Dou, X.: Using deep learning for classification of lung nodules on computed tomography images (2017). https://doi.org/10.1155/2017/8314740
6. Kingma, D.P., Ba, J.L.: Adam : a method for stochastic optimization (2014). arXiv:1412.6980v9
7. Nguyen, T.H.: Metagenome-based disease classification with deep learning and visualizations based on self-organizing maps. In: Dang, T.K., Küng, J., Takizawa, M., Bui, S.H. (eds.) FDSE 2019. LNCS, vol. 11814, pp. 307–319. Springer, Cham (2019). https://doi.org/10.1007/978-3-030-35653-8_20
8. Hai Nguyen, T., Prifti, E., Sokolovska, N., Zucker, J.: Disease prediction using synthetic image representations of metagenomic data and convolutional neural networks. In: 2019 IEEE-RIVF International Conference on Computing and Communication Technologies (RIVF), Danang, Vietnam, pp. 1–6 (2019). https://doi.org/10.1109/RIVF.2019.8713670
9. Ma, C., Xu, S., Yi, X., Li, L., Yu, C.: Research on image classification method based on DCNN. In: 2020 International Conference on Computer Engineering and Application (ICCEA), Guangzhou, China, pp. 873–876 (2020). https://doi.org/10.1109/ICCEA50009.2020.00192
10. Liu, J., Yang, S., Huang, H., Li, Z., Shi, G.: A deep feature manifold embedding method for hyperspectral image classification. Remote Sens. Lett. **11**(7), 620–629 (2020). https://doi.org/10.1080/2150704X.2020.1746855
11. Zhou, F., Yu, T., Du, R., et al.: Clinical course and risk factors for mortality of adult inpatients with COVID-19 in Wuhan, China: a retrospective cohort study (2020). Lancet **395**(10229), 1054–1062 (2020)
12. Narkhede, S.: Understanding AUC-ROC Curve (2018)
13. Pham, H.H., Le, T.T., Ngo, D.T., Tran, D.Q., Nguyen, H.Q.: Interpreting chest X-rays via CNNs that exploit hierarchical disease dependencies and uncertainty labels (2019). arXiv:1911.06475
14. Litjens, G., et al.: A survey on deep learning in medical image analysis. Med. Image Anal. **42**, 60–88 (2017). https://doi.org/10.1016/j.media.2017.07.005

Counterbalancing Asymmetric Information: A Process Driven Systems Thinking Approach to Information Sharing of Decentralized Databases

Mark Hoksbergen[(✉)], Johnny Chan, Gabrielle Peko, and David Sundaram

University of Auckland, Auckland, New Zealand
m.hoksbergen@auckland.ac.nz

Abstract. This paper explores asymmetric information and how to counterbalance it. It utilizes the case study of a hypothetical company called "Hashable". The purpose of this case study is to exemplify a proposed solution to address the information asymmetry faced by buyers of residential real estate in New Zealand. A procedural response is provided for organizing the information needed to make an informed decision on purchasing a property. A causal loop diagram is introduced to develop an understanding of the various stakeholders involved in the proposed solution and their interaction with the information they provide. This paper highlights the core problems regarding information asymmetry within a transaction. It also provides procedural and technological solutions to counterbalance this information asymmetry while simultaneously reducing information costs and increasing reliability of the information provided.

Keywords: Information asymmetry · Transactions · Decision making · Integrated decentralized databases · Real estate · Disruption · System dynamic models

1 Introduction

The New Zealand (NZ) real estate market is estimated at approximately 1.1 trillion NZ dollars (see Fig. 1). The value of housing stock includes all private sector residential dwellings (detached houses, flats and apartments), lifestyle blocks (with a dwelling), detached houses converted to flats and 'home and income' properties. It does not include vacant land [1].

The number of NZ properties bought and sold in 2018 equates to approximately 200,000 transactions. On average, a person will purchase a property only a few times in their life and it's most likely the largest financial transaction they will ever undertake. These property transactions are often paired with mortgages and will have a lifelong impact on individuals. Thus, information pertaining to a "to be purchased" property is a highly monetarized and becomes a crucial part of buyers due diligence. Yet, the

© ICST Institute for Computer Sciences, Social Informatics and Telecommunications Engineering 2021
Published by Springer Nature Switzerland AG 2021. All Rights Reserved
P. C. Vinh and A. Rakib (Eds.): ICCASA 2020/ICTCC 2020, LNICST 343, pp. 216–230, 2021.
https://doi.org/10.1007/978-3-030-67101-3_18

information presented to buyers can be hard to understand and there are many hidden risks that most are unaware of.

Further, a property purchase transaction comes with a certain amount of stress and logic is often subservient to emotional factors. Most of the information pertaining to a property is given verbally by a real estate agent and primarily consists of subjective criteria for purchasing it. One possible reason for this was established by Allmon and Grant [2] who suggested that the main intermediary, the real estate agent, does not always have the best interest in mind for both the buyer and seller for the sale to proceed.

The value of the NZ housing stock is in the trillion dollar range [3]. Buying and selling residential real estate in NZ is becoming more complex. New rules and regulations are being mandated resulting in more legal responsibilities delegated to real estate agents and buyers. For example, once the initial price negotiations for a property is concluded there is often a deadline to complete the due diligence of the sale by the buyer that, in turn, increases the pressure of the transaction. In the real estate industry many intermediaries are utilized to obtain a satisfactory transaction between a buyer and a seller. For buyers, there is the added complexity of finding all the right documents needed to make an informed decision on a real estate transaction and conduct proper due diligence. For instance, there is a property file that can be requested from the city council (CC). This file contains all the consent notices, forms, code of compliances and reports that the CC holds on file for a particular property. Also, a Land Information Memorandum (LIM) report can be purchased from the CC (NZ$200–NZ $400), which contains information regarding the legal description, lands use, zoning, utilities, consents etc. The property file and LIM report do not always correlate and often have critical information missing. Also, the buyer needs to obtain the property title that gives various caveats, and covenants lodged against it. Then there are a multitude of reports that can be requested, for example, a moisture report, asbestos report, electrician report, builders report, soil test, archeological test, drainage report, geo-tech report and valuation report. These reports are paid for by the buyer and are not reported back to the CC. This can result in the same report being requested multiple times by multiple buyers. When buying a property there are also a lot of other indicators that can assist the sale. These indicators are often verbally transmitted and once the sale is completed, typically, this information is lost.

2   Problems and Solutions

The primary contributor to the problem of information asymmetry faced by buyers of NZ residential real estate is information integration and its visibility. The integration of real estate information among government, CCs, property specialists, and real estate organizations. For example, as mentioned, there may be a discrepancy between the property file held by the CC and the LIM report. Then there are the various building experts, engineers, surveyors and other experts who collect enormous amounts of data relating to a particular property without the obligation to register this information against it. Often specialists are hired by a buyer for their services during the due diligence period. If the sale does not result in an unconditional offer and the property is re-listed this information is lost. Also, this specialist service can sometimes be performed on a particular property multiple times by multiple specialists with different outcomes. This results in a discrepancy between the knowledge base of the average property buyer and the information presented to them, which ultimately contributes to asymmetric information favoring the seller.

In addition, there is also a lot of subjective information communicated on a verbal basis often by real estate agents. For example, the agent may mention that "the house has just been painted." This information could become more valuable if the company name is mentioned, the date and cost of the work and any product and service warranties given. Then there is private information only known to the seller, which they are not legally required to share or submit to the CC for instance. This private information could provide a more accurate account of the property being sold. It is diverse in nature and could range from the date a new hot-water cylinder was installed, a recent repaint of the house including the paint used to the installation of new locks and alarm system.

The most effective solution for solving the aforementioned information asymmetry problems is the creation of a centralized property database supported by blockchain technology and administered by the CC. This property database would collate and synthesize information from multiple stakeholders and redistribute it, tailor-made, upon a customer order. This solution would address the information discrepancy while, simultaneously, increasing the accuracy and security of information presented to the buyer. This would ensure that information on a property is not lost and repeated multiple times and there is a chain of information that is traceable back to the origins of the property. The blockchain technology would provide reliable, verified, information on an asset [4]. Leading to a practical working tool for CCs, real estate agencies and buyers and sellers of real estate. Importantly, it would drastically cut the cost of paperwork involved in the due diligence of buying real estate and significantly enhance the added value of the property file.

The possibility of giving "owners" data set privileges to access the property database could further enhance the reduction of the information asymmetry. The property database would support user accounts for individual property owners. These accounts would allow property owners to upload additional information to the property ledger and administer this information as they see fit. Although this information would not be verified by blockchain it has the potential to improve the code of practice for installers and subsequent warranty claims. The information, for instance, would have a date, installers name, price and possible warranty and would ensure that warranties are transferable to the new owner. It would improve the code of conduct for a large number of trades as a warranty and the trade name is now recorded against the property.

The property database would primarily benefit three customer groups:

- Buyers of real estate: By lower the cost of accessing information to support the due diligence period of a transaction.
- Agents and Specialists: By providing detailed analysis capabilities.
- Government and CCs: By providing richer and more diverse information to support effective governance.

3 A Hypothetical Case Study

The goal of the proposed solution is to "create knowledge from data and information through technology innovation that contributes to the 9th United Nations sustainable development goal[1]." To illustrate this solution, a hypothetical company, called "Hashable" is proposed. The purpose of this case study is to exemplify the current problems discussed as well as providing insights to develop a procedural response for collating and organizing information needed to make an informed decision on purchasing NZ residential real estate. This case study focuses on infomediating by collating information from the various stakeholders and redistributing it through specialized reports to customers. To achieve its goal, Hashable will have to partner with Government and CCs to gain access to the data it needs. This not only means access to public government and CC data but also implies that rules and regulations to encourage data sharing between the various stakeholders will be required. Together with a legal framework to support the reliability of the information provided.

Hashable is a hypothetical company operating in the NZ real estate industry. In 2018 approximately 200,000 properties were sold in NZ [5]. This statistic represents the potential market. In this market consumers require quality information to conduct proper due diligence in their property transaction. These consumers are Hashable's target customers. Hashable also provides analysis services and tools for several government organizations. These products and services include detail statistics on housing markets and associated trends and represents only a small part of the company's business. Hashable has several competitors that also provide a certain level of information to property buyers looking to support their purchase decision. These competitors are:

- REINZ: a nationwide registry that provides basic property facts.
- CCs: provide detailed property information (LIM report).
- Real estate agents: provide detailed property information and history.
- One Roof: nationwide app that synchronizes basic data for buyers.

There are no figures available, but industry specialists believe that information sharing is common among the various competitors in the market.

3.1 Customer, Suppliers and Partners

The company Hashable is reliant on data from a diverse number of sources to create its product and services. The company has identified four main suppliers:

- Government including CCs: provide all real-estate data that is publicly owned.
- Real estate agents: provide commercial data they have acquired. They are rewarded through checking their records with information stored on other databases.
- Specialists: provide specialist reports that are logged with a professional association to be valid. To enable this information sharing and validation, government regulation is required to regulate both the individual specialists and professional associations.
- Homeowners: provide information that meets the expectation of a seller prior to purchasing. Providing this information is market driven and would motivate homeowners to register assets relating to the property, including dates of purchase and valid warranties. This information has been uploaded to the current ledger of the CC personalized database for property owners.

---

[1] Goal 9: Build resilient infrastructure, promote sustainable industrialization and foster innovation.

In addition, the company Hashable has identified three main customers for its product and services:

- Government including CCs: Could access a more detailed report on the residential real estate market in NZ. This would give access to private information over and above the information they already hold on both properties and markets.
- Real estate agents: Could drill down to the individual property level to determine, for example, an accurate price or access information that would enable them to understand a local market in more detail.
- Buyers of real estate: Could access a more comprehensive, verified report on a property, which is reliable and at a lower cost than those available from other sources.

3.2 Industry Analysis

It is important to identify the forces operating in an industry to understand the problems and opportunities that exists that impact a company's competitive advantage. In the case of the company Hashable, and the greater real estate industry in which it resides, the assumption is that the industry is competitive and well established. However, Hashable is focused on occupying a niche within the greater real estate industry where the current rivalry among competitors is low. This lack of competition is due to the relative immaturity of the niche market and the barriers to entry raised by Hashable's ability to develop an extensive database of residential property information.

In an industry where the supplier power is extremely high, Hashable is reliant on data and information provided by third parties. Primarily, government and CCs that hold vast amounts of real estate information. For instance, Land Information New Zealand (LINZ) plays an important role in providing accurate and verified information on every property in NZ. The real estate industry and specialists need to be motivated to share their information. And, private information from individual property owners needs to be made available as it provides the detail and richness of information that sets Hashable apart from its competitors.

The threat of new entrants in the niche market is low, given that the entry barriers are relatively high in terms of time in particular. As mentioned, to make Hashable's product and service attractive, large amounts of information on numerous properties needs to be acquired from the various suppliers and property owners (potential customers/buyers) then verified and collated. In many ways Hashable's core business is similar to that of other infomediaries like Ebay. To entice buyers to its site, Ebay needs a large number of items to be listed and to motivate sufficient items listed it needs a large number of potential buyers. The longer Hashable is established the larger the database becomes, which means new entrants will face higher barriers to entry.

The threat of substitutes is medium. There are several possible substitutes that could disrupt Hashable's business model such as:

- Government regulations could change the way information on properties is shared.
- A change in real estate practices and the parties responsible for verifying the information.

- Law changes regarding which parties are legally required to provide information on a real estate asset.

As long as Hashable can provide accurate, verified, comprehensive, low-cost property information to buyers, the buyer power is low. Buyers purchase information for a one-off fee. Currently Hashable has few competitors that can provide verified, comprehensive information on specific NZ properties. The products and services offered by Hashable are:

- Buyers due-diligence support.
- Real estate market analysis and reporting.
- Government and CC reports that assist in the application of legal and governance compliance.

The Government and CC are both a large supplier and customer. Initially the Government and CC have high buyer power. But once they become established customers of Hashable their power diminishes as switching cost could prove to be too high. Likewise, residential real estate organizations initially have medium bargaining power, which diminishes over time as the amount of information available through Hashable increases.

3.3 Strategy

In 2018 a total of 200,000 properties were sold in NZ [1]. Of those 200,000 property transactions, Hashable estimates that only 60% conducted a proper due diligence. Hence, the company believes that by providing reliable information on properties throughout NZ there is an opportunity to corner the market it operates in by significantly growing its market share. While also growing the number of property buyers who conduct a proper due diligence before purchasing a property.

Using Porter's generic strategy model, Hashable has adopted a narrow focused, cost leadership strategy. The main reason for establishing Hashable is to provide detailed, verified information in the form of easy to understand reports at a low cost to buyers of residential real estate. Currently, the company operates in a niche market and its primary goal is to support buyers in the due diligence period by providing information relating to a specific property. The main product and service offered to buyers are:

- A basic data package: This product delivers all the basic data available on a property from government and CC records in an automatically generated easy to read report.
- A due diligence package: This product adds regional specific statistical data to the location (e.g. economic regional growth, school decile, history, etc.) and checks for missing data. This missing data also highlights the gap in information, which in turn raises a buyer's awareness.

4 Value Chain and Business Processes

Using Porter's value chain model [6], Hashable identified the main support and primary activities of its value chain (see Fig. 1). The support activities are IT infrastructure and human resources. The IT Infrastructure is crucial in order to provide data security and uninterrupted service to Hashable's customers and suppliers. Within the real estate industry transactions are linked to deadlines, so providing on-time, updated information is essential. This is also applicable to information security as the information provided needs to be reliable to make informed decisions such as whether to purchase a property or not. Given that Hashable is an infomediary, it relies on highly skilled IT specialists. It is the responsibility of HR to train, hire and retain these individuals.

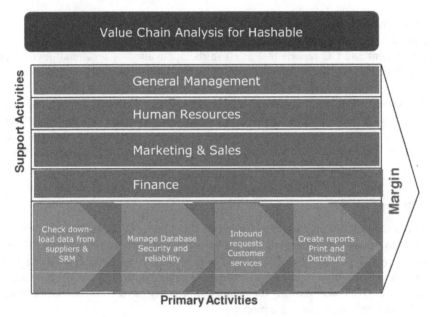

Fig. 1. Hashable's value chain

The company's main primary activities are marketing and sales. Hashable is a new specialized company looking to partner with new suppliers of data and information while maintaining existing suppliers' loyalty. Acquiring new markets and creating new information products for these markets is core to the company's value proposition to both its new and existing customers. Hence, there are five main activities that make up the marketing and sales activities, which are:

- Inbound data deals with aligning all the database information being collected from the data/information suppliers. It also involves the discovery of new information sources and converting it to Hashable's requirements.
- Data management is responsible for information security, structuring data, and looking for new ways to verify and present information.
- Inbound requests handle all standardized requests. This involves checking that the information presented aligns with the requested report and overall quality is maintained.

- Report creation handles all specialized reports and creates new standardized reports. This equates to the research and development activities for the company.

Using Sharp and McDermott [7] definition of business processes, Hashable identified three core business processes (see Fig. 2). Focusing on the primary activities of the company's value chain, the core business processes that follow enable the acquisition and processing of data and production of reports:

- Receiving data and information.
- Data management.
- Creating reports (customer-orders).

These three processes focus on linking suppliers with individual team members at Hashable and, in turn, individual team members with the company's customers. The core processes are designed in such a way that a supplier and a customer have a dedicated contact within the company. This allows Hashable to build strong relationships with its suppliers and customer. For instance, the team member who receives an inquiry from a supplier or customer will be responsible for responding in an appropriate way.

4.1 Receiving Data

Receiving data involves acquiring and verifying data received from suppliers. This determines the quality of Hashable's product and services. The main activates are:

- The inbound data team checks and verifies the data. They determine the supplier and if the data was sent by a verified node.
- The inbound data team is also responsible for supplier relationship management (SRM) and maintains close ties with the company's suppliers.

The primary contribution of the inbound data team is SRM. Hashable is totally reliant on its suppliers for its raw data. The company's most important suppliers are LINZ and CCs. Losing either of these two key suppliers has the potential to put Hashable out of business. Hence, Hashable has long standing contracts with both of these suppliers.

4.2 Data Architecture

Data management involves receipt of the extracted data from the inbound data team after which it is scanned for accuracy and viruses. The data is transformed and loaded into Hashable's database. The data management team is also responsible for locating missing and inaccurate data and communicating this back to the inbound team. This is an important activity because compromised data could result in legal challenges. For example, if a customer purchases a property based on data supplied by Hashable and the data is inaccurate the company could face legal proceedings (Fig. 2).

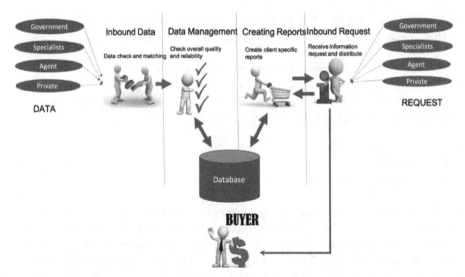

Fig. 2. Hashable's key business processes

Over time these key business processes can evolve into a blockchain based architecture. This would automate the inbound data and data management. The stakeholders can verify the information via different levels of attestation. This would allow a number of applications to be developed and the reports can be generated and presented via multiple apps depending on the users preferences and needs. This blockchain based architecture would increase reliability and significantly decrease the costs associated with creating the reports (Fig. 3). Hashable needs to control the decentralized database and the content. The longer Hashable stays in business the more valuable the database becomes.

4.3 Creating Reports

Creating reports involves receipt of a customer order, the processing of this order, and the collation of the report by the inbound request team. The inbound request team is also responsible for customer relationship management (CRM). They also check whether the funds have been received by the finance department and then send the report to the customer. Again, this process has the potential to result in legal challenges. The team creating the report will probably be the first to notice if the data they are working with is compromised and will raise the issue accordingly.

5 Counterbalancing Information Asymmetry in the Age of Disruption

Hashable relies on providing highly accurate information that customers rely on for large transaction decisions. When inaccuracies occur in reporting, whether they be large or small, it is a disruptive event and the root cause of these inaccuracies need to be ascertained immediately. Discovering the root cause can be difficult and requires a full

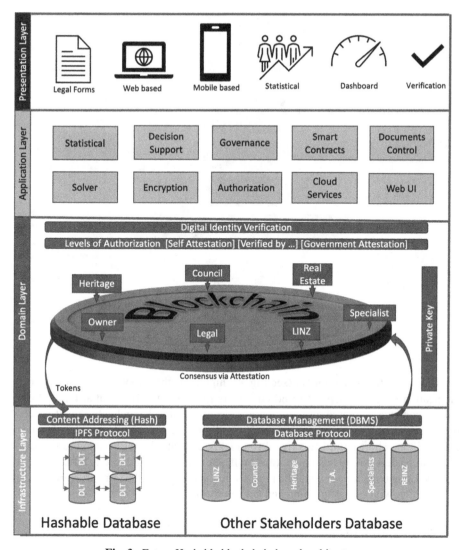

Fig. 3. Future Hashable blockchain based architecture

shutdown. It could be inaccurate supplier data, a virus, mistakes in search algorithms, or human error. These disruptive events negatively impact both Hashable's goal of providing reliable information and the company's reputation. There is a loss of trust that affects the company's relationship with its suppliers and customers. When inaccurate information is detected or provided to customers, regardless of its impact, the team leaders report this to the CEO. In such cases, and others, the Disruptive Event model (see Fig. 4) can be used to guide decision-making and remedy the situation.

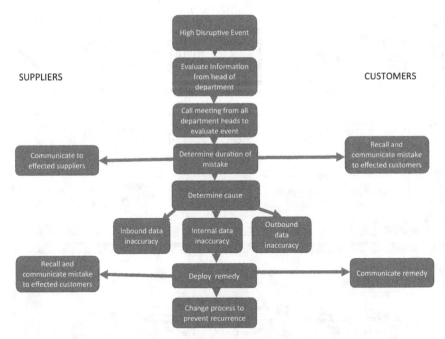

Fig. 4. Disruptive event model

The Disruptive Event model (see Fig. 4), highlights the importance of timely communication with both suppliers and customers to alert them to potential faults. Communication is essential, along with learning from the mistake and subsequent process improvement to prevent future disruptions and ultimately evolve Hashable's business model. In the short term, it is critical to quickly evaluate the information/report from the team leaders before customers (and staff) are informed and there is a full recall of reports. Long term action would be to invest in the company's IT infrastructure to keep it updated as well as staff training and development.

5.1 Procedural Response

As mentioned, a disruptive event is when large financial decisions are made based on inaccurate information. Often a disruptive event is not noticed and can be hard to detect. This is when reports are created with incorrect information, which is subsequently used by Hashable's customers for decision making. Even small errors in information could lead to large legal costs and severely damage the company's reputation [8].

To mitigate and prevent such damage the following procedural response of probe, sense and respond is advocated and explained as follows:

- Probe: information accuracy is a critical aspect of the company's product and service and as such, the system needs to be probed continuously to test its robustness.
- Sense: a close relationship with customers and their continuous feedback is essential.
- Sense: to encourage employees to report even the smallest mistakes.

- Respond: to incorporate a 100% quality and zero fault tolerance culture.
- Respond: to constantly check the quality and accuracy of the generated reports.
- Respond: implement a four eyes system, so that every report is checked by a different person.
- Respond: each report has the creator name on it.
- Respond: Implement an employees' training program to achieve the highest quality work.

5.2 Technological Response

A disruptive event is when reports are created with inaccurate information. This could be caused by a security breach whether it be internal or external [9].

Internal Security Breach: This is the worst kind of security breach especially if it is an internal breach by one of Hashable's own employees. To sense this, enterprise system (SA) HR job satisfaction reports could be used to identify disgruntled employees.

External Security Breach: A close relationship with customers and their continuous feedback is required to sense this type of breach. Using the enterprise system (SAP) SRM and CRM reporting functionality supplier problems and customer dissatisfaction could be identified respectively.

In addition, Hashable could respond by configuring a company specific enterprise system to enable the above mentioned reporting together with the use of Pyramid Analytics and artificial intelligence to identify and analyze disruptive events. Bundling all the high, medium and low disruptive events together for analysis could generate new insights into proactively preventing potential disruptions [10].

Using Stella software, a causal loop diagram (see Fig. 5) was created to understand the effects of a high disruptive event on one of Hashable's intrinsic values, that of 'trust'. In the context of Hashable, the intrinsic value of trust applies to the company's suppliers, customers and employees. The causal loop diagram has been scoped to focus on the core issues for the purpose of clarity rather than drilling down to minor issues. For example, if the company experiences a security breach it negatively effects the level of trust, which impacts the company's brand. Conversely, brand strength can have a positive effect on the level of trust. Trust and brand also influence supplier availability. Both brand strength and supplier availability will increase the profitability of the company.

In addition, a stock and flow (SF diagram) was created. Stella supports the simulation of models (casual loop diagrams) and graphically represent them using four fundamental building blocks. These four blocks are;

- The variable that effects the process.
- The stock or sink represents the cumulative effects the variables have on the process
- The flow, which is the pipe that indicates the changes that can occur over a period time.
- The converter is the regulator of the flow. It can increase or decreases while the value 1 indicates no change.

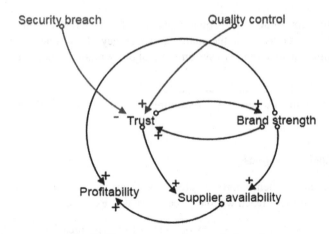

Fig. 5. Consequences of a security breach

In the SF diagram (see Fig. 6), profitability is the measurable activity (sink) and the values were set as follows:

- Security breach at 0.6 stemming the flow.
- Supplier availability at 1.1.
- Brand strength at 1.3.
- Quality control at 1.1.

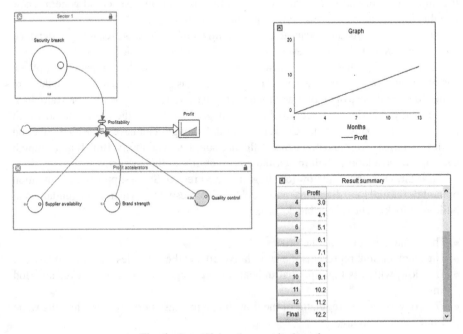

Fig. 6. Quantifying the security breach

The SF diagram will help quantify a security breach and support the decisions by management to increase IT spending to minimize the chance of it happening. It will also allow management to further enhance their quality control program and invest in a quality training program. Only six variables are used in the SF diagram to visualize the disruptive event at one level of abstraction. As mentioned previously, trust is directly associated with the company's brand. Suppliers are only interested in sharing their data with a trusted brand and need to trust the handling of data [11]. The suppliers are also scrutinized by the public when sharing their data. The main control on trust is the ability to perform exceptional quality control. And the greatest disruptive event is when the data is compromised by a security breach.

6 Conclusion

Hashable's core business is providing information from data for potential buyers in the NZ residential real estate market. This will, hopefully, provide knowledge and wisdom to buyers in the due diligence process through the creation of verified reports generated from real estate data gathered from multiple sources.

In essence, the hypothetical company Hashable created a three-tier structure to secure information on a property. First, it links centralized verified data from national and CC records using blockchain technology. Second, reports created by specialists, which have been accredited by the government, are linked to the property giving a historical record of all the reports on the property. Third, it links a personalized database generated by the homeowner to convey all the warranties and maintenance work carried out on the property (see Fig. 7). This three-tier approach enables a verified account of the property that ultimately leads to enhanced decision-making for prospect buyers of residential real estate in NZ.

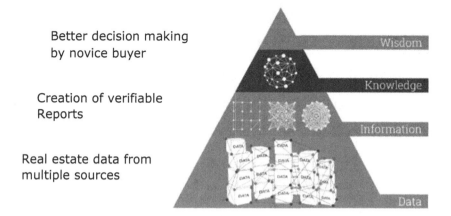

Fig. 7. Data information knowledge wisdom model

References

1. New Zealand General Social Survey 2018: Objectives of the Housing and Physical Environment supplement (2016)
2. Allmon, D.E., Grant, J.: Real estate sales agents and the code of ethics: a voice stress analysis. J. Bus. Ethics **9**, 807–812 (1990). https://doi.org/10.1007/BF00383279
3. Reserve Bank of New Zealand. https://www.rbnz.govt.nz/statistics/key-graphs/key-graph-house-price-values. Accessed 28 July 2020 (2020)
4. Swan, M.: Blockchain: Blueprint for a New Economy. O'Reilly Media Inc, Sebastopol (2015)
5. The Real Estate Institute of New Zealand (REINZ). https://www.reinz.co.nz/
6. Mozota, B.B.: Structuring strategic design management: Michael Porter's value chain. Des. Manag. J. Former Ser. 9, 26–31 (2010). https://doi.org/10.1111/j.1948-7169.1998.tb00201.x
7. Sharp, A., Mcdermoot, P.: Workflow Modeling: Tools for Process Improvement and Applications Development, 2nd edn. Artech House, Norwood (2009)
8. Afzal, W., Roland, D., Al-Squri, M.N.: Information asymmetry and product valuation: an exploratory study. J. Inf. Sci. **35**, 192–203 (2009). https://doi.org/10.1177/0165551508097091
9. Chen, P., Cuzzocrea, A.: Editorial Board Knowledge Management in Organizations (2018)
10. Williamson, O.E.: Transaction cost economics, Chapter 3 (1989)
11. Cyran, M.A.: Blockchain as a foundation for sharing healthcare data (2018)

Nature of Computation
and Communication

Towards Service Co-evolution in SOA Environments: A Survey

Huu Tam Tran[1(✉)], Van Thao Nguyen[1], and Cong Vinh Phan[2]

[1] Distributed Systems Group, Kassel University, Kassel, Germany
{tamth,thaonv}@uni-kassel.de
[2] Nguyen Tat Thanh University, Ho Chi Minh, Vietnam
pcvinh@ntt.edu.vn

Abstract. In a Service-Oriented Architecture (SOA), the need for service evolution comes from service providers and their clients due to changes in requirements and environments. However, enabling controlled service evolution is a critical challenge for the developers since services may be part of different business processes and depend on other services. This paper presents the state of the art of service evolution and in particular, of service co-evolution. The paper also gives an outlook to an emerging trend named microservice and analyzes its advantages and challenges related to service co-evolution. The survey aims to provide a technical overview document to researchers and practitioners who are building industrial-strength adaptive applications related to service co-evolution.

Keywords: Service co-evolution · Service evolution · Service-Oriented Architecture · Software evolution · Service adaptation · SOA

1 Introduction

Service-Oriented Architecture, or SOA, has become a widespread paradigm that provides a flexible IT infrastructure to cope with the increasing pace of business changes and global competition for more than 20 years. As time goes by, our private life and business have been increasingly dependent on SOA applications [1]. Besides, the appearance of Cloud Computing [2] and the Internet of Things [3] or the Web of Things [4] has reinforced this trend even more. The downside of this trend is increasing the complexity of service landscapes. This complexity is due to the sheer size of these systems, the interdependent services, the different levels of service abstractions, the microservice environments and the like. This complexity makes service management as a whole a very substantial challenge for service providers [1].

The fundamental building block of SOA is a service that may play any of the three roles involving service provider, service broker and service consumer. An SOA service is referred to as a discrete entity that can be accessed remotely,

© ICST Institute for Computer Sciences, Social Informatics and Telecommunications Engineering 2021
Published by Springer Nature Switzerland AG 2021. All Rights Reserved
P. C. Vinh and A. Rakib (Eds.): ICCASA 2020/ICTCC 2020, LNICST 343, pp. 233–254, 2021.
https://doi.org/10.1007/978-3-030-67101-3_19

acted on, and updated independently. In the SOA context, the term service evolution is defined as a continuous development of service and expressed by the provisioning and decommissioning of different variants of the service called versions [35]. Another term named service co-evolution refers to a coordinated service evolution [1,10]. Up to date, both of these terms are critical ingredients of the service life-cycle.

A critical question related to SOA services is why we need service evolution and coordinated service evolution (hereby, we denote these terms as (co) evolution). On the one hand, a service (co) evolution is raised in order to satisfying requirements from clients [7]. The requests for adjustments concerning services are usually started from clients for additional functionalities or bug reports. And if the requirements are not satisfied, the clients may switch to another offer. On the other hand, service providers adapt and evolve to the new market trends and attract more clients. Thus, the need for a rapid (co) evolution comes from both service providers and their clients due to the change of requirements and environments [9].

Furthermore, in distributed networks of large-scale environments, every service may depend on other services to avail of certain functionalities. It implies that a change in one service can result in changes in the other service. To prevent outages and failures caused by individual service modifications and updates, coordinated changes are required in such complex systems, i.e., interdependent services must evolve together to maintain compatibility and ties. This phenomenon is called the co-evolution of involved services and contains the meaning of coordination and cooperation of services for co-evolving activities of changes.

Service co-evolution can be seen as a particular case of service evolution [10]. Currently, there is limited support for software service co-evolution since the issue of co-evolution presents intrinsic difficulties. Therefore, this study is intended to systematically review the available literature on service evolution towards service co-evolution.

Our main contributions are as follows: first, we explore and develop a taxonomy for evolutionary changes in SOA environments; second, we review existing approaches for service (co) evolution; third, we discuss and analyze challenging issues related to service (co) evolution.

The rest of the paper is structured as follows: Sect. 2 presents briefly the foundation of service evolution, beginning from software evolution. Section 3 proposes a change taxonomy. Section 4 analyses existing solutions supporting service (co) evolution. Section 5 identifies particular challenges regarding microservice environments. Finally, Sect. 6 concludes the paper.

2   Foundation

In this section, we explore the related contributions in the field of service (co) evolution. We firstly introduce the early contributions to software evolution as the fundamentals of service evolution. In this area, the majority is focused on the laws, the model of software or architectures to facilitate software evolution.

Over time, software evolution has been facing various challenges in order to adapt to new requirements from service providers or service users. In this stage, researchers tried hard to develop the architectures, tools and frameworks to enable the software to be reconfigured at runtime on-the-fly.

2.1 Software Evolution

Software evolution is of great importance in satisfying user requirements under specific changes in the environment [9]. Substantial works have been conducted in related areas promoting software evolution.

In the early days, the term software evolution referred to general software maintenance and configuration. Later, this term has been distinguished as a phase that adapts application software to ever-changing user requirements and operating environments. At the same time, the term maintenance is used to refer to post-delivery activities [11,38].

Nowadays, it is widely accepted that continuous changes are a critical feature of evolution. One of the important research works on software evolution was investigated by Lehman and his colleagues [12], who presented the famous eight laws of software evolution. On the one hand, these laws describe a balance between forces driving new developments. On the other hand, the laws force that slow down progress. In their studies, Lehman et al. [12,13] considered that the changing and adapting requirements from the real-world software systems drive the application to evolve with inevitable and continual feedback. The authors concluded that evolution is an intrinsic and feedback-driven property of software.

Even though Lehman's laws of software evolution have been widely accepted and became basic knowledge of software engineers, there has been no transparency systematic work to fully validate the laws on software quality evolution [14]. Furthermore, most of the rules are just for solving the problems in general static maintenance or software evolution.

In practice, there is a large body of research results available for managing software evolution. These studies fall into the following classifications: (i) analyzing the evolution trend of a software system over a long period of time; (ii) developing effective techniques to support software evolution [38].

At present, researchers have focused on solving two challenging aspects. The first challenge is how to evolve the software. And the second one is how to react with software that has evolved. To the former question, the traditional solution is to improve software development and deployment approaches. With regard to the latter, the users of services have to deal with incompatible interfaces of modified modules and adapt to these changes.

With the advancement of software engineering, the software execution environment has become more dynamic and complex. Traditional methods of maintenance and software evolution face major challenges related to various rapidly changing customer requirements. Therefore, some researchers have proposed new models and tools for evolving the software at runtime. For instance, DYnamic MOdification System (*DYMOS*) by Insup Lee [15] presented general principles for modifying the running software system. Later, *K-Component* by Dowling et al. [16] defined a meta-model for software architecture to provide possibilities for dynamic adaptation. In 2003, *OSGi* (Open Service Gateway initiative) was proposed by researchers at IBM and SUN aiming to improve the practical use of the limited resources in the embedded devices. These architectures are important in the field of software evolution [17].

In general speaking, researchers described these solutions for software evolution as *static software evolution* and *dynamic software evolution*. The static software evolution refers to refactoring the software at the development stage and then install the new version by shutting down the running application. The static software evolution could make the software temporarily unavailable and thus it may cause delays for enterprise business. The dynamic evolution refers to adjusting the behavior of the software at runtime without breaking down the business. Clearly, dynamic evolution improves the software adaptability and can be more competitive in the modern complex and distributed environments. However, the dynamic software evolution also poses more complex challenges as users attempt to apply themselves to the large-scale distributed environment.

Besides, through an extensive survey, Feng-lin et al. [18] discovered that software evolution is closely related to the changing code, module and architecture and its most recent work is on evolution requirements.

In summary, the existing approaches have provided a strong foundation in the development of software evolution. However, these approaches lack aspects of coordinated, distributed evolution where the resolution of service dependencies have to be negotiated with other services.

2.2 Service Evolution

Let us first briefly define the basic terminology used in this paper. This is necessary because there is no general agreement on the terminology in the wider service (co) evolution community.

2.3 Definitions

A service in SOA is defined as a software component that provides certain capabilities over a network to service consumers in a loosely coupled fashion. A service is encapsulated and offers a clearly defined service interface to service consumers. Services may have different owners with different business agendas and they are free to evolve in an independent fashion [5].

According to Papazoglou et al. [5,7], **service evolution** is *"a continuous process of service development through a series of consistent and unambiguous changes"*. It is expressed through a service's different versions and the key challenge is the forward compatibility between different versions. Similarly, a definition of service evolution is given by Wang et al. [19] who stated that service evolution is *"the process of maintaining and evolving services to carter to new requirements and technological changes"*. Both of these definitions have the same views that service evolution involves the deployment of a new service version, which is caused by necessary changes in interface structure, functionality, usage protocol, usage policies, business rules and regulations and more. Service evolution can be viewed on two levels of abstraction, which are linked to the macro and micro perspective. From a macro perspective, services in a network are like individual organisms of a biological population. From a micro perspective, interfaces and interaction protocols up to the service are similar to the physical and behavioral characteristics of an organism. So far, many techniques and tactics have been used to ensure customer compatibility with the service.

In distinguished studies on service evolution [5, 7], Papazoglou et al. provided the fundamentals for service evolution until the present, especially when they distinguished two kinds of changes named **shallow changes** and **deep changes** based on the nature of service evolution.

- **Shallow changes** are "small-scale, incremental changes that are localized to a service and/or are restricted to the consumers of that service", for shallow changes, typically it could lead to mismatches between services at two levels: (i) interface level (i.e., structural), (ii) interaction protocol level (i.e., behavior, such as messaging order mismatches). To solve the shallow changes, the authors proposed a structured approach based on a robust versioning strategy to support multiple versions.
- **Deep changes** are "large-scale, transformational changes cascading beyond the consumers of a service possibly to consumers of an entire end-to-end service chain." Deep changes include operational behaviour changes and policy-induced modifications. Deep changes rely on the assistance of a change-oriented service life cycle methodology to respond appropriately to changes [35]. To date, deep changes are a challenging and open research problem in the context of service engineering.

Furthermore, Papazoglou [5, 7] defines three following concepts:

(i) **Version compatibility** means when we can introduce a new version of either a provider or client of service without changing the other.
(ii) **Backward compatibility** means when a new version of a client is introduced to the providers are unaffected. The client may introduce new features but should still be able to support all the old ones.
(iii) **Forward compatibility** refers to the old version of a client application that could interpret new operation(s) or message(s) introduced by a service.

Some types of changes that are both backward- and forwards-compatible involve the addition of new service operations to an existing service definition, the addition of new schema elements within a service that are not contained within previously existing types [7].

The key problem of service evolution is that the compatibility between the service and its consumers may change when the service evolves. One of the major objectives of the research on service evolution is to reduce the unexpected effects caused by incompatibilities.

We adjust these definitions of service evolution in [5, 7, 19] for service co-evolution by giving a simple notion, i.e., **service co-evolution** stands for a coherent process of evolving and maintaining service and its interdependent services through a series of explicit changes. We further explain this domain by considering the dependency graph shown in Fig. 1 of different service providers offering various services. It shows the service dependency graph S which is a set of different services.

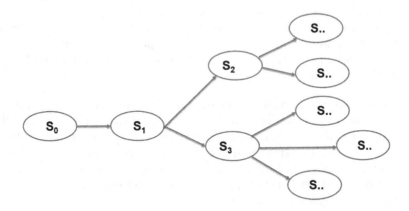

Fig. 1. Dependency graph in service co-evolution scenario

Now, consider node S_0, which is actively connected to all other nodes providing different services without any interruptions in the edges. Similarly, S_1 is connected to the nodes S_2 and S_3 and these nodes are further connected to various other nodes. Considering a scenario, in which S_2 evolves to a new version but S_3 is not affected at all proves a successful service evolution. In this case, the change is confined to the clients of S_2 only. However, in case the evolution of S_2 implies that the nodes S_0, S_1 and S_3 should also evolve in a coordinated fashion, we call this as a co-evolution of service where the evolution is required to update the interdependent services.

On the topic of evolution, we cannot fail to mention adaptation, the counterpart of it. **Adaptation** is a crucial mechanism to keep software and service behaving as expected under certain conditions [5,7]. In service engineering, **adaptation** usually refers to select candidate services when suffering from failure, (re-) composite services for changed business process and distribute new service instances in adapting to emergent workload [7]. The principal difference between adaptation and evolution is that adaptation will not change the service itself, but evolution will [5].

3   Proposed Change Taxonomy

Different change taxonomies for service evolution have been developed over the years. In general, various change taxonomies proposed base on the effects or scope of changes during the interaction process.

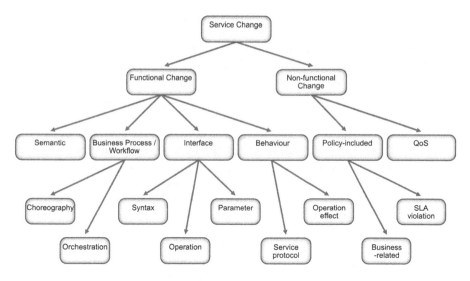

Fig. 2. Proposed change taxonomy

According to Treiber [36], these evolutionary changes involve changes in requirements, changes of the service interface, changes in implementation and QoS [36]. These change activities come from different requirements such as developers, providers, users and service integrators that interact in the interdependent services.

To date, evolutionary changes in existing research works can be defined into various categories such as change of interface, change of semantics protocols, change of requirements and change of business process models.

In this survey, we focus on the solutions of "not compatible and resolvable changes" [1] such as interface, semantic, business process model (workflow) and behavior changes. We distinguished them as follows:

- *Interface changes* refer to modify the signature of the service interface.
- *Semantic changes* refer to modify service properties as declared in interface annotations.
- *Behavior changes* refer to any transformation or modification of service behavior.
- *Business process/workflow changes* reflect a modified business process model of service composition. The demand for changing business processes (internal organizational level) arises due to various reasons, such as new regulations or the emergence of new competitors at the market.

These changes are described in detail in Table 1. We adopt a change taxonomy shown in Fig. 2. The proposed taxonomy is an extension of the classification of evolutionary changes in [23]. Our terminology is consistent with the one used in [21] and shown in Table 1. Some other kinds of changes such as QoS, policy, parameters, optional operations are defined similarly to the previous works in [20,21].

Table 1. Change terminology

Category	Type of change	Characteristic
Non-functional	QoS	– performance of service properties e.g., server load, concurrent users
		– performance of network latency,
		– performance of throughput
	Policy	– change in policy assertions on services, which specify business agreements
Functional	Behavior	– change in the service protocol i.e., prescribed invocation, operational behavior
	Semantic	– cover all changes that are not involved description of services, operations, parameters or return values
	Interface	– change in the interface signature e.g., parameters, operations, message structure
		– addition of new functionality or the update of existing functionality
		– interface changes may affect the implementation, QoS, pre-condition, post-condition, usage of the service
	Business Process/ Workflow	– modify the business process model
		– change in choreography or orchestration model of service composition

4   Positioning Approaches

Existing works for supporting service (co) evolution have mainly focused on the following steps: change detection, change impact analysis and reaction. Their sequences of these processes are depicted in Fig. 3:

(i) Change Detection (CD). Change detection is a critical process in service evolution management. It helps affected services to find out of changes as well as kinds of changes that can be used as the input data for analyzing the impact levels. Researchers classified evolutionary changes into different types of critical changes. However, in many cases, changes in behavioral usually are more complicated and need more effort to adapt by considering the actual values communicated between services and their clients.

These approaches (see Table 2) mainly focused on service interfaces, workflow, semantic and behavior change. These approaches have provided many tools or frameworks such as: *Vtracker* [24], *WSDarwin* [25], WSDLiff [26], *DiCORE* [27]. During the time of this survey, we realized that there are a few works considering behavioral changes.

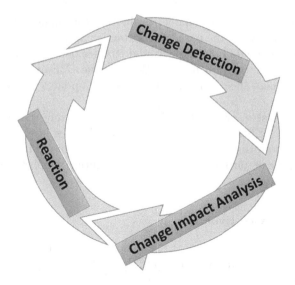

Fig. 3. Service evolution development cycle

(ii) Change Impact Analysis (CIA). The goal of this process is to understand the relationship between the service and the change. The service users should know which parts of the system will be affected by the change and examine them for additional impacts since the modification in one part of service may have subsequent effects on other related services. Significant literature works in this area can be classified into two categories techniques: dependency analysis and trace-ability analysis [28]. Through an impact assessment, it is possible to evaluate the change effects and procedure evolution strategies to reduce risks and maintenance costs.

The output of existing approaches for this phase, usually are models, techniques or design patterns, such as Trust Dependency Graph [29], Versioning Model [30], Dependency Model [31], Change Pattern [19], DiCORE-CIA [27]. Furthermore, we found that there has been special attention paid to the topic of change impact analysis from the research community.

(iii) Change Reaction (CR). This process may involve other steps such as decision-making, propagation of changes and an optional broader changes context to support other affected services (in case of coordinated co-evolve services), eventually giving a set of prioritized actions to adapt new changes. Propagation of changes addresses how the impact of a change can be effectively propagated to other entities with minimal ripple, or what additional changes are required for a service to maintain consistency. As new functionality is added or changed in services, developers must ensure that other system entities are updated and consistent in response.

Existing approaches have mainly focused on changes in business process models (workflow). Some important frameworks are DYCHOR [32] and C3Editor

[33]. The DYCHOR framework enables evaluating the change propagation of a process in choreography on the basis of an extended automated model, while the C3Editor visualizes the different models and enables the definition and application of changes to the private models. Besides, the C3Editor determines and visualizes the partners affected by a change and the updates required for change propagation.

In our view, these approaches could support effectively the coordination of change processes. Additionally, we suppose that changes in a business process model usually require manual intervention by developers. Thus, such changes are out of the scope of automated service (co) evolution support and not further considered in this survey.

4.1 Support Service Evolution

In the scope of evolution services, researchers have spent significant effort on investigating methods and techniques for the management of service changes. These researches can be seen as a precursor and the fundamental for research on service co-evolution since service co-evolution is a special case of service evolution.

Table 2 lists important approaches related to service evolution aspects such as authors, key contributions, available software (denote Yes (Y) or No (N)), and support processes (e.g., change detection (CD), change impact analysis (CIA) or change reaction (CR)). In our view, all of these approaches have high-value results in the field of service (co) evolution in recent years.

These approaches could fall into one of the following categories: (I) Tool/Model-based, (II) Versioning-based, (III) Pattern/Adaptor-based and (IV) Analysis of Change Impact-based. Naturally, some approaches might belong to more than one category, for instance, the work by Khebizi et al. [34] provided a framework, a software tool and patterns to support dynamic change management of business protocols.

(I) Tool/Model-Based
One of the first works handling the problem of service evolution is developed by Treiber et al. [23]. Their work addressed two main problems related to services: (a) what type of information is required for a particular perspective, how all types of information are integrated into a single model, and (b) how these types of information are managed. The first problem concerns the development of an aggregated, flexible and extensible information model for services. The latter is linked to the development of a management framework that can track historical information.

Romano et al. [26] proposed the WSDLDiff tool that can be used to derive the set of delta changes applied to a service. This tool considers the syntax of the WSDL file and the schema file XSD that is used to define the data types of the WSDL interface. Similarly, Li et al. [46], presented critical empirical studies about the most common types of service changes.

Another important framework comes from V. Andrikopoulos et al. [21], who introduced a service specification reference model and introduced the concept of service evolution management. Based on the type and set theory as well as the service specification model, the authors developed an approach to reason and identified the conditions (i.e., a set of changes) under which services can evolve while preserving compatibility. However, their work only focuses on the preventive evolution model and do not pay attention to the impact and adaptation aspects [38].

Fokaefs et al. [24] also published empirical results of evolution scenarios and presented the Vtracker. Specifically, the authors created an intermediate XML representation to reduce the verbosity of the WSDL specification. However, Vtracker does not take into account the syntax of WSDL interfaces. An upgraded Vtracker named WSDarwin [25,40], which can be used to automatically identify changes between different versions of service by comparing interface description documents. WSDarwin tool provided a solution to answer the question of how a client application can be supported in adapting to changed services. However, WSDarwin does not indicate how the Web Service provider could perform the adaptation assistance or how to deal with the dependencies when generating and compiling the client stub.

Latter, Zou et al. [38] proposed a change-centric model in which necessary changes are identified, planned, implemented, tested and then notified to all necessary stakeholders. In the model, the delta is a set of changes from one version to its next version of the service.

Recently, Jahl et al. [27] developed the DiCORE framework that determines the kind of changes, categorizes the changes and shares them with dependent clients. The framework helps the developers to find out the structural changes in workflow. In summary, these tools and models provided practical ways to address the evolutionary challenges, such as detecting changes and analyzing the change impact, eventually supporting related services during an evolution process.

(II) Versioning-Based

Versioning is a traditional and practical way to address the incompatibility issue [18,45]. A robust versioning strategy allows for service upgrades and improvements while continuously supporting previous versions. Leitner et al. [20] presented a comprehensive versioning approach specifically for handling compatibility issues, based on a service version graph and version selection strategies. The proposed framework is used to dynamically and transparently invoke different versions of service through service proxies. In this path, Kaminski et al. [22] outlined various requirements for versioning and demonstrated why common versioning strategies are inappropriate in the context of services. The authors proposed the Chain of Adapters pattern [22] for developing evolving services. However, the adapter does not support the parallel execution of different service implementations. Also, adapter implementations may be faulty and break old clients [45].

In order to fix this faulty and do not break old clients, Weinreich et al. [45] proposed a versioning model for supporting the evolution of service-oriented architectures. The model involves a set of services into a subsystem and assigns them the same version identifier. Even if only one service is changed, all services within the same subsystem will be tagged with a new version number. Consequently, multiple versions of the same subsystem may co-exist. Becker et al. [56] proposed an approach to automatically determine compatibility that could be applied with the compatibility pattern. Similarly, Yamashita et al. [30] introduced a novel feature-based versioning approach for assessing service compatibility and proposed a different versioning strategy, following the W3C standards.

In fact, various versioning approaches are proposed to address the challenges of the service version. At the technical level, these approaches relied heavily on the SOA [18]. In general, they are used together with the design pattern and related tools that will be presented in detail in the next section.

(III) Pattern/Adaptor-Based

Design patterns and adapters have been widely used for software development for structuring solutions. For instance, Wang et al. [19] focused on a common evolution scenario in which a single service is provided by a single provider. In particular, the authors proposed four patterns involving compatibility, transition, split-map and merge-map. These patterns provide generic and reusable strategies for service evolution.

It is worth considering the actual work on service compatibility, which aims to assist services consumers in seamlessly transferring their programs to newer versions [56]. Becker et al. [56] proposed an approach to automatically determine compatibility that could be applied with the compatibility pattern.

In case the change is not compatible, the work of Kaminski et al. [22] introduced an adapter-based approach to maintain multiple versions of service simultaneously. The novel idea of this approach is to use a proxy that enables dynamic binding and invocation for client applications to maintain multiple versions of service on the server-side and [41]. At the same time, Frank et al. [47] distinguished between a service interface (public) and its implementation (private).

To address possible interface mismatches, Dumas et al. [48] suggested an algebra over interfaces and a visual language that allows pairs of provided-required interfaces to be linked through algebraic expressions. Benatallah et al. [49] proposed adapters approach using mismatch patterns, which may capture the possible differences between two interaction protocols.

Similarly, H. R. Motahari Nezhad et al. [57] provided semi-automatic support for adapter generation to resolve interface mismatch and deadlock-free interaction incompatibility. Following previous works of Benatallah et al. [49], Ryu et al. [39] studied the protocol compatibility using path coverage algorithms based on finite state machines (FSM) service model and suggested adapter/ad-hoc protocol as solutions. The reason for using FSM service mmodel is because it is a well-known paradigm based on a formalism that is easy to understand for inexperienced users and is suitable for representing reactive behaviors.

In research work [43], the authors tried to keep client applications being synchronized with evolved services through semi-automatic client updates. In their proposed tool, it first analyzes the delta between different versions of service and exports them into a well-formatted document. After that, drawing on the clients' usage history. Next, they employ a consumer code customized component to highlight the client code fragments that need to be updated. In the same path, Ouederni et al. [44] introduced a framework to resolve interface and behavior mismatches by automatically updating the clients based on compatibility measuring. The update process can be parameterized with some user requirements to prevent the behavior that a designer does not want to appear in the client interface.

(IV) **Analysis of Change Impact-Based**
Basu et al. [37] proposed a technique to extract dependencies from log files. The technique could be adapted to infer the amount of dependent service consumers. Once the dependencies are transfarency, it is also essential to infer the impact of service changes on the applications.

Later, Wang et al. [52] proposed his dependency model in analyzing the impact of service evolution. The authors considered the dependency model to analyze the dependency links among services that work in collaborations. This model extracts the degree of dependency for each link between the elements in one service or between services. It is a foundation for most of the later studies in this field. The dependency model proposes a matrix to describe the dependency relations between services and between elements in one service or more services. However, the disadvantages are also obvious: (a) The model assumes that the dependencies are known at design time, which is invalid in the dynamic environment; (b) The model does not distinguish the change types add, remove and modify. It considers that each type of change results in the same impact. Apart from these disadvantages, the dependency model does not explain how and where to obtain the changes, which is important to service evolution.

Yamashita [30] presented an impact analysis based on usage profiles. This method helps service providers estimate the impact on consumers as well as giving an evolution decision later. In the same fashion, Liao et al. [29] proposed a trust dependency graph that is introduced to analyze the impact on the trust of component services.

Latterly, Jahl et al. [27] also provided framework DiCORE to analyze the impact of changes based on the patterns. This framework allows an intuitive and graphical formulation of patterns while other existing tools completely ignore user-defined change patterns.

Table 2. Existing approaches support service evolution

ID	Author/Reference	Key Contribution	Focus on /Available Software	Process
1	Papazoglou and Andrikopoulos [6,35]	Classify and analyze shallow and deep changes A set of theories and models that unify different aspects of services (description, versioning and compatibility)	All kind of changes/ N	CD, CIA, CR
2	Treibe et al. [36]	SEMF framework to manage the changes on interface, interaction patterns or QoS aspects	Requirement change, Interface change, Implementation change and QoS change/N	CD, CR
3	Romano et al. [26]	A tool to extract changes automatically	WSDL document change/Y	CD
4	Forkaefs et al. [24]	Vtracker tool identifies changes between different version of a service	WSDL Interface change/N	CD
5	Forkaefs et al. [25,40]	WSDarwin tool supports the clients to coevolve with the provider service	WSDL, WADL interface change/Y	CD
6	Wang et al. [19]	A service evolution model A method to analyze service dependencies Proposed four patterns: compatibility, transition, split-map, merge-map	Operation and data type change/N	CIA
7	Basu et al. [37]	A tool can extract dependencies from log files.	Protocol change/Y	CIA
8	Kaminski et al. [22]	A chain of adapters technique approach for deploying multiple service versions	WSDL Interface change/N	CD
9	Zou et al. [38]	A change-centric model and a method for the change impact analysis	WSDL interface change/N	CD, CIA
10	Ryu et al. [39]	A framework supports business protocol	Protocol change/N	CD, CIA
11	Leiner et al. [20]	End-to-end versioning support based on service history	Interface change/N	CD
12	Frank et al. [47]	A service interface proxy for dealing with the incompatibility	WSDL Interface change/N	CD
13	Dumas et al. [48]	An interface adaptation method, in which each interface is represented as an algebra expression that could be transformed and linked accordingly	Interface change/N	
14	Benatallah et al. [49]	Adapters as an approach based on mismatch patterns which captures the possible differences between two interaction protocols	Protocol change/N	CD

(continued)

Table 2. (*continued*)

ID	Author/Reference	Key Contribution	Focus on /Available Software	Process
15	Jahl et al. [27]	Framework DiCORE to determine the kind of changes and the affected components in a business process	Business process change/Y	CD
16	Tran et al. [51,53]	An approach detects and extracts interface changes	WADL file change/N	CD
17	Wang et al. [31,52]	A dependency impact analysis the kind of changes and the affected causes and effects of changes.	Operation and data type change/N	CIA
18	Jahl et al. [55]	An architecture captures and assesses the behavior dimension of services	Behavior changes/N	CD
19	Becker et al. [56]	A versioning framework determines compatibility based on patterns	Interface change/N	CD, CIA
20	Motahari et al. [57]	A semi-automatic method for adapter generation for the mismatches at the interface-level, protocol level	Interface change, Protocol change/N	CD, CIA
21	Yamashita et al. [30]	A change impact analysis approach based on usage profile	Operation and data type change/Y	CIA
22	Li et al. [46]	A method for change impact analysis. Proposed 16 API changed patterns	Operation and API changes/N	CIA
23	Weinreich et al. [45]	A versioning model	Implementation change, Interface change/N	CD
24	Khebizi et al. [34]	A framework with migration patterns	Protocol change/N	CD
25	Liao et al. [29]	A trust analysis model	Interface change, Binding change/N	CIA
26	Ouederni et al. [44]	A framework to resolve the compatibility; An interface model	Internal behavior change. Message parameters change/N	CD
27	Le et al. [43]	A framework for facilitating the service consumer; An interface model	WSDL interface /N	CD
28	Olga et al. [42]	A framework for managing semantic, syntactic and protocol changes	Semantic, syntactic, protocol/N	CD
29	Fang et al. [41]	A version-aware service description model; A version-aware service directory model	Implementation and interface change. Binding change/N	CD
30	Thanos et al. [59]	A framework for semantic drift	Semantic change/Y	CD
31	Juric et al. [58]	A model to support versioning interfaces	WSDL interface, Message parameters change/N	CD

4.2 Support Service Co-evolution

The need for advancements in service co-evolution support is undisputed, just as for all software. One of the most challenging aspects of a service co-evolution is the ability to co-evolve services together in order to retain compatibility and bindings. Obviously, support service co-evolution also means support service evolution since it is a particular case of service evolution. In practice, the processes of a service co-evolution require further co-evolve steps, e.g., coordination among inter-dependency parties. Even though the coordinated distributed service evolution plays an essential part in SOA environments, there is currently a lack of attention being paid to this kind of service evolution.

This section highlights some valuable research works that investigated service co-evolution as the following aspects:

- *Classification of evolutionary changes:* One of the first works handling the problem of service co-evolution is developed by M. Papazoglou [35]. The author proposed a fundamental classification of evolutionary changes in the service-based system. Their work also introduces two types of service changes, one of them called deep-changes. In our thesis, we concentrate on coordinated deep-changes in large-scale service computing scenarios. However, M. Papazoglou did not take into account the special scenario of service evolution, where several services that have to co-evolve together in order to retain compatibility.

- *Requirements for service co-evolution:* It is worth to mention this research work by De Sanctis et al. [1] who first propose eight requirements for service co-evolution. However, the authors mainly focus on general requirements. Even though the authors do not analyze in deep of these requirements, but they bring a small step for the developers towards service co-evolution. Furthermore, the authors presented a solution for service co-evolution based on the Domain Object concept, which supports deep-changes across a service dependency graph, through the decentralized collaboration of evolution agents.

- *A distributed knowledge-based evolution model:* Wang et al. [54] proposed a distributed knowledge-based evolution model named *DKEM* to promote competition and collaboration between services from different vendors. The model regards stability as a key factor in competition and a stability evaluation model is intended to calculate the stability of services, vendors and service-based processes. Based on the evaluation model, two evolution patterns are specified with which new and more stable cooperation among services can be examined automatically by utilizing a runtime self-adaption mechanism. The authors reported that the model *DKEM* is effective for competition and cooperation among services with distributed knowledge and evolved processes have higher stability and reaction efficiency. Nonetheless, the model is designed as a solution to eliminating semantics conflicts between different vendors with different ontologies.

- *Process of co-evolution using meta-models in model-driven engineering:* Cicchetti et al. [60], presented atomic changes and defined the process of co-evolution. The authors also created a differential meta-model with the identified changes. However, in this approach, a number of open questions remain, including issues of systematic validation of the dependency detection, change impact analysis and resolution technique, which necessarily encompasses larger population models and meta-models.

- *A service co-evolution management model and multi-agent architecture for service co-evolution*: Recently, a new research project called PROSECCO[1] [50,51,53,55] provided a general service co-evolution management model and corresponding reference architecture. This architecture involves the different stakeholders, their roles and responsibilities in the service co-evolution as well as the architectural components needed to perform service co-evolution as part of the general service management. The architectural design for service co-evolution equips every service with an agent called Evolution Agent (EVA) that performs the service evolution in collaboration with other agents. The modular EVA architecture makes an EVA easily adaptable for different service environments, such as IoT, web services and microservices.

In summary, during the survey of this work, we found that there are limited results that concentrate on coordinated deep changes in large-scale service computing scenarios. Such evolution support is urgently needed in order to cope with the increasing complexity of SOA environments.

5   Outlook

Recently, a new emerging trend called *microservice* has been one of the fastest-rising trends in the development of enterprise applications and enterprise application landscapes [61]. The term microservice or microservice architecture refers to a new software production model including continuous deployment, continuous delivery and continuous evolving and managing [63].

In a microservice architecture, instead of creating single-layered systems, the development shifted towards a composition of microservices. In that respect, a system is a set of loosely-coupled small services that are isolated in small coherent and autonomous units [62].

Undoubtedly, a microservice architecture is a form of SOA and is considered as the state-of-the-art design concept, which exhibits many advantaged characteristics. One of the greatest advantages of using microservices is the loose coupling, which leads to agile and fast evolution and continuous redeployment [64]. The basic design idea of microservice architectures is to towards a new environment where there are small teams with tight communication between developers and other stakeholders. Each team is responsible for a few small independent services. These teams will work at their own pace deploying new versions of services without considering coordinate services [63]. Consequently, this design is contradictory to service co-evolution requirements that services need coordination of others to achieve their goal.

---

[1] https://www.uni-kassel.de/eecs/fachgebiete/vs/research/prosecco.html.

To date, microservice architecture has been adopted in different forms by many companies such as Netflix, Google, Apple, Microsoft and Amazon. These companies have recognized that by using microservices architecture, their software product delivery cycles will be shorter. Because there is no barrier in timing to releasing new service's version, thus, their customers may update new versions instantly and transparently [63]. However, a speedy producing amount of service versions may need more effort to handle various versions in a short period of time. Subsequently, this leads to another major challenge for service management and service (co) evolution as well.

In summary, applying microservice architectures brings various benefits for service providers. However, it also has made more challenges to managing service (co) evolution due to the service landscape with an enormous variety of independent services. This complexity makes service co-evolution as a real challenge for developers.

6   Conclusions

This paper presents a survey on frequently cited approaches supporting service (co) evolution in SOA environments in the last decades. The paper aims to provide a technical overview of challenges related to service co-evolution. Furthermore, we propose a new taxonomy of changes based on hierarchy and relationships. Additionally, we distinguish three main processes of service evolution that should be handled during service (co) evolution. Finally, we give an outlook to an emerging trend named *microservice* and analyze its advantages and challenges related to service co-evolution.

Acknowledgements. The work described in this paper was conducted by Huu Tam Tran as a part of his Doctoral study under the supervision of Prof. Dr. Kurt Geihs. The first author would like to acknowledge his supervisor, the Distributed Systems Group - University of Kassel and the DFG project named PROSECCO for the support of his research.

References

1. De Sanctis, M., Geihs, K., Bucchiarone, A., Valetto, G., Marconi, A., Pistore, M.: Distributed service co-evolution based on domain objects. In: Norta, A., Gaaloul, W., Gangadharan, G.R., Dam, H.K. (eds.) ICSOC 2015. LNCS, vol. 9586, pp. 48–63. Springer, Heidelberg (2016). https://doi.org/10.1007/978-3-662-50539-7_5
2. Marinescu, D.C.: Cloud Computing: Theory and Practice. Morgan Kaufmann, Burlington (2017)
3. Gubbi, J., Buyya, R., Marusic, S., Palaniswami, M.: Internet of Things (IoT): a vision, architectural elements and future directions. Future Gener. Comput. Syst. **29**(7), 1645–1660 (2013)
4. Pfisterer, D., Römer, K., Bimschas, D., Kleine, O., Mietz, R., Truong, C., et al.: SPITFIRE: toward a semantic web of things. IEEE Commun. Mag. **49**(11), 40–48 (2011)

5. Papazoglou, M.: Web Services and SOA: Principles and Technology, vol. 2. Pearson Education Limited, Harlow, Essex (2012)
6. Andrikopoulos, V., Benbernou, S., Papazoglou, M.P.: On the evolution of services. IEEE Trans. Softw. Eng. **38**(3), 609–628 (2012)
7. Papazoglou, M.P., Andrikopoulos, V., Benbernou, S.: Managing evolving services. IEEE Softw. **28**(3), 49–55 (2011)
8. Ouederni, M., Salaün, G., Pimentel, E.: Client update: a solution for service evolution. In: IEEE International Conference on Services Computing (SCC), pp. 394–401 (2011)
9. Naji, H., Mikki, M.: A Survey of Service Oriented Architecture Systems Maintenance Approaches
10. Tran, H.T., Baraki, H., Geihs, K.: Service Co-evolution in the Internet of Things. EAI Endorsed Trans. Cloud Syst. **1** e5 (2015)
11. Bennett, K.H., Rajlich, V.T.: Software maintenance and evolution: a roadmap. In: Proceedings of the Conference on the Future of Software Engineering ACM, pp. 73–87 (2000)
12. Lehman, M.M., Ramil, J.F.: Software evolution-background, theory, practice. Inf. Process. Lett. **88** 33–44 (2003)
13. Lehman, M.M., Belady, L.A.: Program Evolution: Processes of Software Change. Academic Press Professional Inc., Cambridge (1985)
14. Yu, L., Mishra, A.: An empirical study of Lehman's law on software quality evolution. Int. J. Softw. Inf. **7**, 469–481 (2013)
15. Cook, R.P., Lee, I.: DYMOS: a dynamic modification system. ACM SIGPLAN Notices **18**(8), 201–202 (1983)
16. Dowling, J., Cahill, V.: The K-component architecture meta-model for self-adaptive software. In: Yonezawa, A., Matsuoka, S. (eds.) Reflection 2001. LNCS, vol. 2192, pp. 81–88. Springer, Heidelberg (2001). https://doi.org/10.1007/3-540-45429-2_6
17. Alliance, O.: OSGi Service Platform, Release 3. IOS Press Inc., Amsterdam (2003)
18. Li, F.L., Liu, L., Mylopoulos, J.: Software service evolution: a requirements perspective. In: IEEE 36th Annual Computer Software and Applications Conference Workshops (COMPSACW), pp. 353–358. IEEE (2012)
19. Wang, S., Higashino, W.A., Hayes, M., Capretz, M.A.: Service evolution patterns. In: 2014 IEEE International Conference on Web Services (ICWS), pp. 201–208. IEEE (2014)
20. Leitner, P., Michlmayr, A., Rosenberg, F., Dustdar, S.: End-to-end versioning support for web services. In: IEEE International Conference on Services Computing, SCC 2008, vol. 1, pp. 59–66. IEEE (2008)
21. Andrikopoulos, V., et al.: A theory and model for the evolution of software services. Tilburg University, School of Economics and Management (2010)
22. Kaminski, P., Müller, H., Litoiu, M.: A design for adaptive web service evolution. In: Proceedings of the 2006 International Workshop on Self-Adaptation and Self-Managing Systems, pp. 86–92. ACM (2006)
23. Treiber, M., Truong, H.-L., Dustdar, S.: On analyzing evolutionary changes of web services. In: Feuerlicht, G., Lamersdorf, W. (eds.) ICSOC 2008. LNCS, vol. 5472, pp. 284–297. Springer, Heidelberg (2009). https://doi.org/10.1007/978-3-642-01247-1_29
24. Fokaefs, M., Mikhaiel, R., Tsantalis, N., Stroulia, E., Lau, A.: An empirical study on web service evolution. In: 2011 IEEE International Conference on Web Services (ICWS), pp. 49–56. IEEE (2011)

25. Fokaefs, M., Stroulia, E.: Wsdarwin: studying the evolution of web service systems. In: Bouguettaya, A., Sheng, Q., Daniel, F. (eds.) Advanced Web Services, pp. 199–223. Springer, New York (2014)

26. Romano, D., Pinzger, M.: Analyzing the evolution of web services using fine-grained changes. In: 2012 IEEE 19th International Conference on Web Services (ICWS), pp. 392–399. IEEE (2012)

27. Jahl, A., Baraki, H., Tran, H.T., Kuppili, R., Geihs, K.: Lifting low-level workflow changes through user-defined graph-rule-based patterns. In: Chen, L.Y., Reiser, H.P. (eds.) DAIS 2017. LNCS, vol. 10320, pp. 115–128. Springer, Cham (2017). https://doi.org/10.1007/978-3-319-59665-5_8

28. Dam, H.K., Ghose, A.: Supporting change impact analysis for intelligent agent systems. Sci. Comput. Programm. **78**(9), 1728–1750 (2013)

29. Liao, L., Qi, S., Li, B.: Trust analysis of composite service evolution. In: 2016 IEEE 14th International Conference on Software Engineering Research, Management and Applications (SERA), pp. 15–22. IEEE (2016)

30. Yamashita, M., Vollino, B., Becker, K., Galante, R.: Measuring change impact based on usage profiles. In: 2012 IEEE 19th International Conference on Web Services (ICWS), pp. 226–233. IEEE (2012)

31. Wang, S., Capretz, M.A.: Dependency and entropy based impact analysis for service-oriented system evolution. In: Proceedings of the 2011 IEEE/WIC/ACM International Conferences on Web Intelligence and Intelligent Agent Technology, vol. 01. IEEE Computer Society, pp. 412–417 (2011)

32. Song, W., Zhang, G., Zou, Y., Yang, Q., Ma, X.: Towards dynamic evolution of service choreographies. In: 2012 IEEE Asia-Pacific Services Computing Conference (APSCC), pp. 225–232. IEEE (2012)

33. Fdhila, W., Indiono, C., Rinderle-Ma, S., Reichert, M.: Dealing with change in process choreographies: design and implementation of propagation algorithms. Inf. Syst. **49**, 1–24 (2015)

34. Khebizi, A., Seridi-Bouchelaghem, H., Benatallah, B., Toumani, F.: A declarative language to support dynamic evolution of web service business protocols. Serv. Oriented Comput. Appl. **11**(2), 163–181 (2017)

35. Papazoglou, M.P.: The challenges of service evolution. In: Bellahsène, Z., Léonard, M. (eds.) CAiSE 2008. LNCS, vol. 5074, pp. 1–15. Springer, Heidelberg (2008). https://doi.org/10.1007/978-3-540-69534-9_1

36. Treiber, M., Truong, H.L., Dustdar, S.: Semf-service evolution management framework. In: 34th Euromicro Conference on Software Engineering and Advanced Applications, SEAA 2008, pp. 329–336 (2008)

37. Basu, S., Casati, F., Daniel, F.: Toward web service dependency discovery for SOA management. In: IEEE International Conference on Services Computing, SCC 2008, vol. 2, pp. 422–429. IEEE (2008)

38. Zuo, W., et al.: Managing and modeling web service evolution in SOA architecture. PhD thesis, Université de Lyon (2016)

39. Ryu, S.H., Casati, F., Skogsrud, H., Benatallah, B., Saint-Paul, R.: Supporting the dynamic evolution of web service protocols in service-oriented architectures. ACM Trans. Web (TWEB) **2**(2), 13 (2008)

40. Fokaefs, M., Stroulia, E.: Using WADL specifications to develop and maintain REST client applications. In: 2015 IEEE International Conference on Web Services (ICWS), pp. 81–88. IEEE (2015)

41. Fang, R., et al.: A version-aware approach for web service directory. In: IEEE International Conference on Web Services, ICWS 2007, pp. 406–413. IEEE (2007)

42. Groh, O., Baraki, H., Jahl, A., Geihs, K.: COOP - automatiC validatiOn of evOlving microservice comPositions. In: Seminar on Advanced Techniques Tools for Software Evolution, (Posters, Demos), pp. 1–6 (2019)

43. Le Zou, Z., Fang, R., Liu, L., Wang, Q.B., Wang, H.: On synchronizing with web service evolution. In: 2008 IEEE International Conference on Web Services, pp. 329–336. IEEE (2008)

44. Ouederni, M., Salaün, G., Pimentel, E.: Client update: a solution for service evolution. In: 2011 IEEE International Conference on Services Computing (SCC), pp. 394–401. IEEE (2011)

45. Weinreich, R., Ziebermayr, T., Draheim, D.: A versioning model for enterprise services. In: 21st International Conference on Advanced Information Networking and Applications Workshops, AINAW 2007, vol. 2, pp. 570–575. IEEE (2007)

46. Li, J., Xiong, Y., Liu, X., Zhang, L.: How does web service API evolution affect clients? In: 2013 IEEE 20th International Conference on Web Services (ICWS), pp. 300–307. IEEE (2013)

47. Frank, D., Lam, L., Fong, L., Fang, R., Khangaonkar, M.: Using an interface proxy to host versioned web services. In: 2008 IEEE International Conference on Services Computing, pp. 325–332. IEEE (2008)

48. Dumas, M., Spork, M., Wang, K.: Adapt or perish: algebra and visual notation for service interface adaptation. In: Dustdar, S., Fiadeiro, J.L., Sheth, A.P. (eds.) BPM 2006. LNCS, vol. 4102, pp. 65–80. Springer, Heidelberg (2006). https://doi.org/10.1007/11841760_6

49. Benatallah, B., Casati, F., Grigori, D., Nezhad, H.R.M., Toumani, F.: Developing adapters for web services integration. In: Pastor, O., Falcão e Cunha, J. (eds.) CAiSE 2005. LNCS, vol. 3520, pp. 415–429. Springer, Heidelberg (2005). https://doi.org/10.1007/11431855_29

50. Tran, H.T., Baraki, H., Geihs, K.: An approach towards a service co-evolution in the internet of things. In: Giaffreda, R., Vieriu, R.-L., Pasher, E., Bendersky, G., Jara, A.J., Rodrigues, J.J.P.C., Dekel, E., Mandler, B. (eds.) IoT360 2014. LNICST, vol. 150, pp. 273–280. Springer, Cham (2015). https://doi.org/10.1007/978-3-319-19656-5_39

51. Tran, H.T., Baraki, H., Kuppili, R., Taherkordi, A., Geihs, K.: A Notification management architecture for service co-evolution in the internet of things. In: 2016 IEEE 10th International Symposium on Maintenance and Evolution of Service-Oriented and Cloud-Based Environments (MESOCA), pp. 9–15. IEEE (2016)

52. Wang, S., Capretz, M.A.: A dependency impact analysis model for web services evolution. In: IEEE International Conference on Web Services, ICWS 2009, pp. 359–365. IEEE (2009)

53. Tran, H.T., Jahl, A., Geihs, K., Kuppili, R., Nguyen, X.T., Huynh, T.T.B.: DECOM: a framework to support evolution of IoT services. In: Proceedings of the Ninth International Symposium on Information and Communication Technology, pp. 389–396 (2018)

54. Wang, X., Feng, Z., Chen, S., Huang, K.: DKEM: a distributed knowledge based evolution model for service ecosystem. In: 2018 IEEE International Conference on Web Services (ICWS), pp. 1–8. IEEE (2018)

55. Jahl, A., Tran, H.T., Baraki, H., Geihs, K.: WiP: behavior-based service change detection. In: 2018 IEEE International Conference on Smart Computing (SMART-COMP), pp. 267–269. IEEE (2018)

56. Becker, K., Lopes, A., Milojicic, D.S., Pruyne, J., Singhal, S.: Automatically determining compatibility of evolving services. In: IEEE International Conference on Web Services, ICWS 2008, pp. 161–168. IEEE (2008)

57. Kongdenfha, W., Motahari-Nezhad, H.R., Benatallah, B., Casati, F., Saint-Paul, R.: Mismatch patterns and adaptation aspects: a foundation for rapid development of web service adapters. IEEE Trans. Serv. Comput. **2**(2), 94–107 (2009)

58. Juric, M.B., Sasa, A., Brumen, B., Rozman, I.: WSDL and UDDI extensions for version support in web services. J. Syst. Softw. **82**(8), 1326–1343 (2009)

59. Stavropoulos, T.G., Andreadis, S., Riga, M., Kontopoulos, E., Mitzias, P., Kompatsiaris, I.: A Framework for Measuring Semantic Drift in Ontologies. In: SEMANTiCS (Posters, Demos, SuCCESS) (2016)

60. Cicchetti, A., Di Ruscio, D., Pierantonio, A.: Managing dependent changes in coupled evolution. In: Paige, R.F. (ed.) ICMT 2009. LNCS, vol. 5563, pp. 35–51. Springer, Heidelberg (2009). https://doi.org/10.1007/978-3-642-02408-5_4

61. Ghofrani, J., Lübke, D.: Challenges of microservices architecture: a survey on the state of the practice. In: ZEUS, pp. 1–8 (2018)

62. Wolff, E.: Microservices: Flexible Software Architecture. Addison-Wesley Professional, Boston (2016)

63. El-Sheikh, E., Zimmermann, A., Jain, L.C.: Emerging Trends in the Evolution of Service-Oriented and Enterprise Architectures. Springer, Cham (2016). https://doi.org/10.1007/978-3-319-40564-3

64. Sampaio, A.R., et al.: Supporting microservice evolution. In: IEEE International Conference on Software Maintenance and Evolution (ICSME), pp. 539–543. IEEE (2017)

Analysis of a HIPS Solution Use in Power Systems

Tomas Svoboda[✉], Josef Horalek, and Vladimir Sobeslav

Faculty of Management and Informatics, University of Hradec Kralove, Hradec Kralove, Czech Republic
{tomas.svoboda,josef.horalek,Vladimir.sobesdlav}@uhk.cz

Abstract. The aim of this paper is to conduct a performance comparative analysis of open-source HIPS (Host Intrusion Prevention System) solutions in order to improve security measures in power systems. First, the HIPS technology is introduced with an emphasis on its use for increasing security within power systems. Secondly, selected HIPS solutions are introduced in order to conduct the comparative analysis. Finally, the results of the comparative analysis of the individual solutions are presented with an emphasis on the use of system resources in the deployment of HIPS solutions on Windows workstations.

Keywords: Security · Cybersecurity · Power systems · SCADA · HIPS · Windows

1 Introduction

Currently, the modern society cannot function without the existence of communication connection via computer networks and access to the Internet [1]. The use of this type of communication can be observed throughout the society, be it in systems falling under critical infrastructure of individual countries, in ordinary work activities, or in private home Wi-Fi networks. With the use of these technologies comes the necessity of securing them against unauthorized use, which can, in the field of critical infrastructure and power systems, have a negative impact on the society as a whole.

Significant progress in the field of improving security of power systems was not madeuntil 2010 when Stuxnet was discovered [2]. Considering the cyberattacks on power companies in 2016 and 2017 [3, 4], it is obvious that the area of power systems security is still a current topic. [5] Nowadays, a large number of security solutions are implemented within power systems. These solutions, however, only cover a certain part of security of these systems. [Ponemon] With the increasing number of progressively more sophisticated cyberattacks, which are mostly carried out on the national level and focused on cybernetic espionage, an adequate response to these attacks also requires an increasing degree of sophistication [6]. Currently, the typical defence against cyberattacks targeting power systems is realized by protecting the communication infrastructure by means of

P. C. Vinh and A. Rakib (Eds.): ICCASA 2020/ICTCC 2020, LNICST 343, pp. 255–264, 2021.
https://doi.org/10.1007/978-3-030-67101-3_20

firewalls [7], proxy servers, etc., and critical components of control systems (SCADA server, communication servers, etc.) using anti-malware protection, for instance. [8] However, the use of such security mechanisms does not solve the main security problems of power systems: firstly, the integration of equipment to which standard security policies cannot be applied, and secondly, the existence of internal incidents related to security breaches of power systems [8, 9].

The solution is the implementation of a complex security solution which addresses both of the aforementioned security problems of power systems. The HIPS technology is one of such complex security solutions [10].

The HIPS is one of the intrusion prevention systems which monitors activity on a particular device. The HIPS has defined rules within which it restricts unsolicited access to specific data. The HIPS usually extensively logs data related to the detected situation.

The HIPS technology also monitors suspicious activity on a particular terminal. The monitoring is performed by analyzing network events on the device. The HIPS technology uses a database of monitored objects of the system, which is used to identify a potential intrusion into the computer network by analyzing system calls, application logs and modification of the file system. Simultaneously, a register of trustworthy programs is created [11]. If a program goes beyond its authorization, it is blocked by the HIPS for performing unauthorized actions. Via the HIPS, these mechanisms identify security breaches and violations of a security policy in work with power systems. With the ability to block suspicious activities related to security breaches, an organization can prevent internal incidents in power systems. [12]

The main aim of this paper is to conduct a performance comparative analysis of selected open-source HIPS solutions and their use for protection of power systems. Requirements for processes and operations performed within power systems place heavy demands on them being performed within limited time intervals. These are mainly requirements for data processing speed, data consistency and synchronization. To ensure that operations are performed in the shortest time possible, it is essential to implement a HIPS solution with minimal requirements for system resources. The implementation of a HIPS solution which would lead to consumption of a large amount of system resources would result in extension of time intervals needed for necessary operations within power systems.

2   Methods of the HIPS Solution Analysis

As the methodology of the HIPS tools analysis, the analysis of third-party tools with an emphasis on system resource usage (CPU, RAM and SWAP partition of HDD) was chosen. These tools have the aforementioned HIPS functionalities. The comparative analysis of these tools is based on comparison of system resource usage, i.e. CPU, RAM, and SWAP partition, with the HIPS being deployed on the appropriate Windows testing station.

ReHIPS

The first solution which was part of the comparative analysis of selected HIPS solutions is the ReHIPS product by ReCryptCompany, version 2.4.0. This is an innovative solution. The HIPS agents do not need to be deployed in a special way since they will be registered automatically as soon as the product installation has been completed. The user interface is very simple and intuitive, which contributes to the increased convenience of administration of the solution as a whole.

Figure 1 shows the ReHIPS user interface, where a camera or a microphone can be disabled as a part of AntiSpy protection. The intrusion prevention contains 5 modes, which are the Expert mode, the Standard more, the Permissive mode, the Learning mode and the Disabled mode. It is possible to display a log list in the advanced settings.

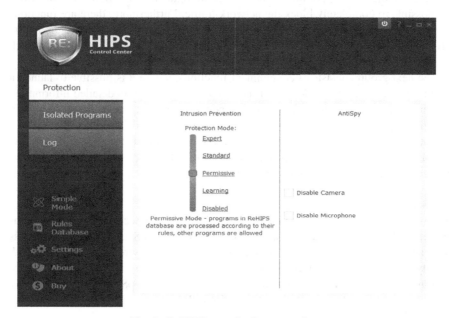

Fig. 1. ReHIPS console. Source: authors

The Expert mode offers maximum protection. Trusted Vendor list is not taken into account in this mode. It displays a large number of notifications. The Standard mode is similar to the Expert mode. The main difference is in the smaller number of displayed notifications. The Permissive mode allows running programs registered in an internal database, based on a set of defined rules. The Learning mode adapts rules to programs registered in the internal database. Programs running within the operating system that are not registered in the internal database can be enabled or disabled in Learning mode. Appropriate actions can be added to the list of registered programs in the internal database. The Disabled mode stops the complex HIPS protection within the device.

Comodo Internet Security

The second tested product with the HIPS functionality is Comodo Internet Security by Comodo. It is a program designed to increase security of the computer network and it has the HIPS technology integrated as one of the offered functionalities.

Functions offered by this product are divided into general functions, firewall functions, containment functions, and advanced functions. General functions include basic functions, which are also displayed in the initial environment. These are the following: the function of launching a scan, searching for updates for the program, protection while shopping online, unblocking applications blocked by security actions, and special online support by Comodo experts.

Firewall functions include, for instance, a function which allows a specific application to connect to the network, or blocks its connection to the network. In firewall functions it is possible to completely block the network traffic. Furthermore, there are functions such as displaying the list of applications which are currently connected to the public network, a function for the network management where it is possible to allow or block connection to an available computer network.

The next group consists of containment functions, where it is possible to launch a function for secured virtual desktop. It is also possible to display detailed information about active processes, launch functions for opening a shared space between classic and virtualized applications, and run applications by virtualization in sandbox.

The last group contains advanced functions which include creation of a rescue disc, displaying records, cleaning terminal points, quarantine, sending files, and task management for specific, currently running tasks.

DeepSecurity

The third solution tested in the comparative analysis is DeepSecurity 9.6. It is a multiplatform solution by Trend Micro. The key assets of DeepSecurity for the business world are security of virtual desktops, security of the cloud environment and, above all, security of physical, virtual and cloud servers. DeepSecurity is optimized for the VMware environment, Amazon Web Services and Microsoft Azure. DeepSecurity offers not only intrusion prevention, but also anti-malware, firewall, log scan and integrity monitoring functionalities.

The following figure depicts the dashboard of the DeepSecurity management server, which is accessible to the user via a web interface. The dashboard shows a status with critical messages and warnings about non-standard activities (Fig. 2).

Fig. 2. DeepSecurity console. Source: authors

The dashboard shows the status of PC in which the solution is deployed. There is also history of specific events, e.g. anti-malware activity events as seen in the figure. It also shows activities of firewall, intrusion prevention system, web reputation, log scan and integrity monitoring.

3 Comparative Analysis of Selected HIPS Solutions

For the purpose of conducting the comparative analysis, a personal computer was used as a single tool for analysing the use of system resources by the tested HIPS solutions. The hardware configuration of the personal computer is the following:

- OS: Windows 10 Pro 64 bit
- CPU: Intel Core 2 Duo E4600 2,4 GHz
- RAM: 2 GB
- GPU: NVIDIA GeForce GT 610 1GB DDR3 SDRAM
- HDD: 1 × HDD 500 GB
- Network adapter: Qualcomm/Atheros L1 Gigabit Ethernet Adapter

System Explorer was used for measuring the system resources. This surveillance tool enables recording information about usage of system resources, especially CPU, RAM, and SWAP partition of HDD. System Explorer includes display and management of tasks and processes along with evaluation of processes based on their security classification using an online database. In order to determine standard usage of system resources, performance of the device was first measured in the initial state without an activated HIPS solution. Subsequently, measurement of performance was conducted on the device with an activated HIPS solution. For this purpose, only the operating system and necessary services were launched: Antivirus program ESET Smart Security and System Explorer.

Figure 3 shows average usage of the device with the time period of 10 minutes in the initial state. Average processor (CPU) usage during the defined time period was 10%. Average usage of RAM during the defined time period was 58%. Average usage of SWAP partition (SWP) was 31%.

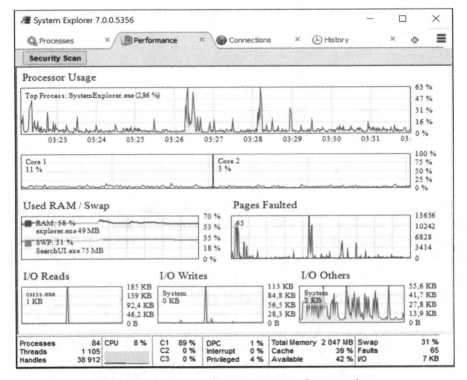

Fig. 3. Standard usage of system resources. Source: authors

ReHIPS

Figure 4 shows average usage of the device during the defined time period of 10 minutes with ReHIPS solution being deployed. Average processor (CPU) usage during the defined time period was 60%. Average usage of RAM during the defined time period was 72%. Average usage of SWAP partition (SWP) was 35%.

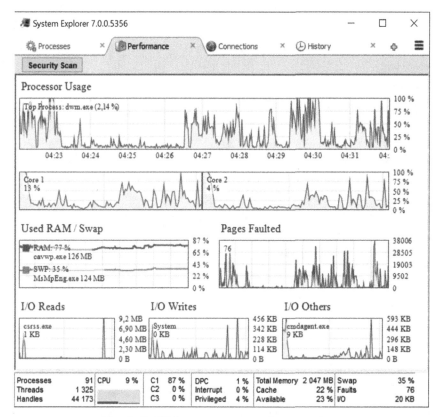

Fig. 4. ReHIPS system resources. Source: authors

Comodo Internet Security

Figure 5 shows average usage of the device during the defined time period of 10 minutes with Comodo Internet Security Pro solution being deployed. Average processor (CPU) usage during the defined time period was 50%. The reason for such usage was fast launch of a device scan. Average usage of RAM during the defined time period was 77%. This means 19% increase of RAM usage in comparison with the initial state. Average usage of SWAP partition (SWP) was 35%.

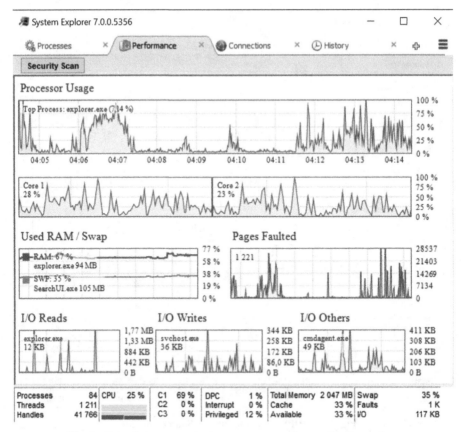

Fig. 5. Comodo internet security pro system resources. Source: authors

DeepSecurity

Figure 6 shows average usage of the device during the defined time period of 10 minutes with DeepSecurity solution being deployed. Average processor (CPU) usage during the defined time period was 75%. This means 65% increase of CPU usage in comparison with the initial state. Average usage of RAM during the defined time period was 81%, which is a significant increase of usage in comparison with the initial state (58%), ReHIPS solution (72%) and Comodo Internet Security Pro solution (77%). Average usage of SWAP partition (SWP) was 44%.

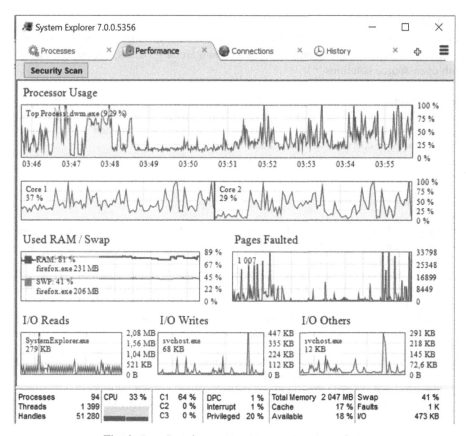

Fig. 6. DeepSecurity system resources. Source: authors

4 Conclusion

The aim of this paper was to conduct a comparative analysis of open-source HIPS solutions with an emphasis on their use within power systems and critical infrastructure protection. For the purpose of the analysis, three open-source HIPS products were selected. These were ReHIPS, Comodo Internet Security and DeepSecurity. The comparative analysis was based on system resources usage comparison, using System Explorer tool.

The results of the analysis clearly demonstrate that DeepSecurity is the most resource-demanding solution. This is partially due to the activated web interface of Deep security solution, which represented the user interface of the application. The fact that DeepSecurity offers a large number of functions and options of their management was identified as one of the main reasons for its high system resource requirements. According to the results of the comparative analysis, ReHIPS product achieved the best results in the testing, or more precisely, it caused the lowest usage of system resources. Other benefits of ReHIPS include automatic agent registration after the product has been installed. The interface used is simple and intuitive, which contributes to the increased convenience of administration of this solution as a whole. In further research, the comparative analysis can be extended to include commercial products and compare them with open-source solutions.

Acknowledgment. This work and the contribution were supported by a Specific Research Project, Faculty of Informatics and Management, University of Hradec Kralove, Czech Republic. We would like to thank Mrs. H. Svecova, a doctoral student, for the practical verification of the proposed solutions and close cooperation in the solution.

References

1. Baykara, M., Das, R.: A novel honeypot based security approach for real-time intrusion detection and prevention systems. J. Inf. Secur. Appl. (2018). https://doi.org/10.1016/j.jisa. 2018.06.004.ISSN22142126
2. Vargas Martinez, C., Vogel-Heuser, B.: A host intrusion detection system architecture for embedded industrial devices. J. Franklin Inst. (2019). https://doi.org/10.1016/j.jfranklin.2019. 03.037.ISSN00160032
3. Lee, R., Assante M. J., Conway, T.: Analysis of the cyber attack on the Ukrainian power Grid. NERC (2016). https://www.nerc.com/pa/ci/esisac/documents/e-isac_sans_ukraine_duc_18m ar2016.pdf
4. Passeri, P.: 2016 Cyber Attacks Statistics. Hackmageddon (2017). https://www.hackmaged don.com/2017/01/19/2016-cyber-attacks-statistics/
5. Ponemon institute: 2016 Cost of Cyber Crime Study & the Risk of Business Innovation. Ponemon Institute LLC (2016). https://go.cyphort.com/Ponemon-SIEM-Report-2017-Page. html
6. Birkinshaw, C, Rouka, E., Vassilakis, V.G.: Implementing an intrusion detection and prevention system using software-defined networking: defending against port-scanning and denial-of-service attacks (2019). https://doi.org/10.1016/j.jnca.2019.03.005, ISBN 1084-8045
7. Cook, A., Janicke, H., Smith, R., Maglaras, L.: The industrial control system cyber defence triage process. Comput. Secur. (2017). https://doi.org/10.1016/j.cose.2017.07.009, ISSN 01674048.
8. Radvanovsky, R., Brodsky, J.: Handbook of SCADA/Control Systems Security, 2nd ed. CRC Press, Taylor & Francis Group, Boca Raton (2016). ISBN 9781498717076.
9. Gregory-Brown, B.: Securing industrial control systems - 2017: A sans survey (2017). https:// www.sans.org/reading-room/whitepapers/ICS/paper/3786.
10. Patel, A., Alhussian, H., Pedersen, J.M., Bounabat, B., Júnior J. C., Katsikas, S.: A nifty collaborative intrusion detection and prevention architecture for Smart Grid ecosystems (2017). https://doi.org/10.1016/j.cose.2016.07.002, ISSN 01674048.
11. Sawant, A.: A comparative study of different intrusion prevention systems. In: Fourth International Conference on Computing Communication Control and Automation (ICCUBEA) (2018). https://doi.org/10.1109/ICCUBEA.2018.8697500, ISBN 978-1-5386-5257-2, Dostupné z: https://ieeexplore.ieee.org/document/8697500/
12. Anilbhai, S. P., Parekh, C.: Intrusion detection and prevention system for IoT. Int. J. Sci. Res. Comput. Sci. Eng. Inf. Technol. **2**(6) (2017)

Behavioral Analysis of SIEM Solutions for Energy Technology Systems

Tomas Svoboda[✉], Josef Horalek, and Vladimir Sobeslav

Faculty of Management and Informatics, University of Hradec Kralove, Hradec Kralove, Czech Republic
{tomas.svoboda,josef.horalek,Vladimir.sobesdlav}@uhk.cz

Abstract. The aim of this article is to analyze SIEM solutions. Emphasizing the use of these systems to ensure data confidentiality, availability, and integrity monitoring energy technology systems. First, the issue of security in the area of energy systems is introduced. In order to maintain the availability, confidentiality and data integrity, the user behavioral analysis modules in SIEM systems are also introduced. The next section presents specific SIEM solutions that can be currently used not only in ICS environments and which will be subject to comparative analysis. This is IBM Security QRadar SIEM and LogRhythm NextGen SIEM. What follows is the introduction and implementation of modules for user behavioral analysis in the mentioned SIEM solutions, including testing own Use Case for testing user behavioral analysis modules. The results of the comparative analysis of user behavioral analysis modules in selected SIEM solutions are presented in the last section.

Keywords: SIEM · Qradar · LogRhythm NextGen SIEM · User and entity behavioral analysis · IBM sense · CloudAI

1 The Issue of Technological Power Systems Safety

Energy technology systems are systems that are used for power system management, or voice communication system; they are also used in management process of power system [1]. These systems are critical in terms of securing power supplies from the producer to the final consumer and have a major economic impact on the functioning of modern society as a whole. In order to ensure reliable electricity supply, the confidentiality, availability and integrity of the data that is crucial to ensuring the correct operation of the power system must be ensured for these systems [1, 2]. Energy technology systems have been vulnerable for decades. Nowadays, the seriousness of potential threats and related cyber-attacks that energy networks and systems can affect become fully understood [3]. The components currently used in energy systems and primarily supporting IT systems are largely dependent on the use of standard PCs and IT technologies. SCADA data servers, SCADA control servers, HMIs, and operator stations utilize standardized operating systems, increasing the risk of potentially exploiting the vulnerabilities of

P. C. Vinh and A. Rakib (Eds.): ICCASA 2020/ICTCC 2020, LNICST 343, pp. 265–276, 2021.
https://doi.org/10.1007/978-3-030-67101-3_21

these systems by intruders and penetrating the power management system [4]. Many of the systems that are currently operating in power systems are out of date. The reason for the obsolescence is the long-term renewal of energy systems, which typically ranges in the decades and the associated cost of this renewal. For the abovementioned reasons, when energy systems are often unable to meet the latest safety recommendations, the likelihood of cyberattacks launched against these kinds of systems is higher [3, 5].

Energy technology systems are systems that are used for power system management, or voice communication system; they are also used in management process of power system. These systems are critical in terms of securing power supplies from the producer to the final consumer and have a major economic impact on the functioning of modern society as a whole. In order to ensure reliable electricity supply, the confidentiality, availability and integrity of the data that is crucial to ensuring the correct operation of the power system must be ensured for these systems [3, 5, 6]. Energy technology systems have been vulnerable for decades. Nowadays, the seriousness of potential threats and related cyber-attacks that energy networks and systems can affect become fully understood. The components currently used in energy systems and primarily supporting IT systems are largely dependent on the use of standard PCs and IT technologies. SCADA data servers, SCADA control servers, HMIs, and operator stations utilize standardized operating systems, increasing the risk of potentially exploiting the vulnerabilities of these systems by intruders and penetrating the power management system [7]. Many of the systems that are currently operating in power systems are out of date. The reason for the obsolescence is the long-term renewal of energy systems, which typically ranges in the decades and the associated cost of this renewal. For the abovementioned reasons, when energy systems are often unable to meet the latest safety recommendations, the likelihood of cyberattacks launched against these kinds of systems is higher (Fig. 1).

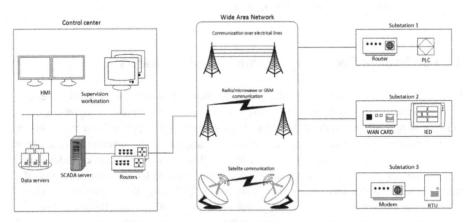

Fig. 1. General energy system architecture. Source: authors

Another potential threat exploitable for technology and energy systems attack, associated with disruption in the availability, confidentiality and data integrity controlling the power system, is at the electric substation level. In particular, the possibility of physical damage to the device type of IED, PLC, RTU, HMI, data ACTIVE servers, communication facilities and supporting infrastructure, including air conditioning units, power equipment, etc. [8] To avoid or mitigate the attack targeting the physical damage to the equipment should be thoroughly monitor and control the access of all people to the technology rooms where they are located. In order to increase the security and unambiguously identify the persons entering the electric station and at the same time protect the external perimeter, a camera surveillance system is typically installed in the electrical substations. In the case of a suspected breach of the physical security of the technological room, it is appropriate to correlate the record from the access card system and the camera system for unambiguous identification of the attacker [7, 8].

As mentioned above, in the event of a misuse of the threats in energy systems, it is necessary to use tools that are capable of monitoring, logging and auditing industrial control systems, communications and security features, IT support systems and access control systems so that, in the event of disruption, they provide as much available information as possible to detect the attacker, or concerning the causes and techniques that led to security breaches. The great variety and the amount of equipment that needs to be monitored in energy systems poses a problem where a vast amount of information from these devices is generated that needs to be recorded. Together with the expansion and modernization of energy systems, it is growing significantly. [9].

The solution ensuring availability, confidentiality and integrity within the energy technology systems is full implementation of the safety requirements of the international standard ISO 27001. Standard ISO 27001, which is also adopted in the framework of the Czech Republic's national legislation under the Cyber Security Act; the Cyber Security Decree, which defines organizational and technical measures for critical information infrastructure elements, including energy systems.

2   User Behavioral Analysis Utilization to Ensure Energy Technology Systems Safety

User Behavioral Analysis (UBA) is a term that includes tracking, collecting and categorizing user data and activities in their communication in the digital environment, respectively in a computer network environment [10]. Historically, the principles of user behavioral analysis have been developed primarily for use in marketing to predict customer buying behavior. At present, the principles of user behavioral analysis are increasingly used in the field of cyber security, because one of the significant risks of cyber security disruption is the attack vector from the internal environment of the organization, i.e. employees or suppliers of the system. UBA is based on threat detection for employees or system vendors. These are threats related to the misuse of users' identities, deliberate, respectively unintentional user errors that can lead to disruption of data availability, confidentiality and integrity [10, 11].

UBA looks for behavior patterns that are then applied to statistical analysis and algorithms to detect anomalies in relation to standard behavior. For this reason, the principles of behavioral analysis are effective because they focus primarily on user interaction and behavior, not on detecting a suspicious event in the vast amount of information that is collected in the SIEM solution [12].

Based on the above principles, Gartner Inc has created a category called user and entity behavior analytics (UEBA). UEBA focuses primarily on preventing data theft or misusing a computer network when user authentication is broken, and a malware or hacker is operating on its network name.

For the purpose of uncovering these cases, UEBA uses three main components [13]:

Data Analytics - UEBA application identifies user behavior and creates a basic user behavior profile with learned parameters. For further analysis, it uses statistical models and rules to compare user behavior with an existing profile. Data analytics implements data confidentiality.

Data Integration - Flexible UEBA applications are able to integrate both structural and non-structural information into an existing security monitoring system. The information also includes SIEM system logs, data flow data and captured data packets. By implementing the data integration, the requirement for the integrity of the transmitted and stored data is ensured.

Data Presentation and Visualization - The UEBA application, or module, presents the results in an efficient way so that it is easy to read and identify behavior patterns that are associated with unauthorized activity and do not conform to a profile that includes standard user behavior. Based on the violation of the user's standard behavior, their risk score is subsequently adjusted. This is an indicator which corresponds to whether or not the user violates the rules. The higher the risk score, the more rules are violated by the user.

UEBA uses machine learning principles to identify future user behavior. In this case Machine learning means that the UEBA module learns to predict future user behavior based on a defined profile.

3   UEBA Implementation in Selected SIEM Solutions

In order to analyze the possibilities of implementation of UBA, a survey of SIEM solutions with respect to Gartner Magic Quadrant 2018 in the field of SIEM solutions. The selection parameter was also the implementation of UBA functionalities within SIEM. Two solutions were selected for this analysis that meet the above-mentioned requirements. These are IBM Security QRadar SIEM and LogRhythm NextGen SIEM. These solutions and implementation UBA functionalities are presented in detail below.

3.1   AlienVault OSSIM

There are currently no manuals concerning UBA implementation in AlienVault OSSIM. There is only a general UBA discussion. As a part of research, a member of the Business Development, AlienVault OSSIM was approached, who confirmed the existence of the UBA module in AlienVault. After installing AlienVault, it was found that AlienVault does not allow UBA principles to be used, but only contains a basic network behavioral analysis (NBA) module. Therefore, it is an inappropriate solution for comparative analysis.

3.2 IBM Security QRadar

UBA module is not a part of the default IBM Security QRadar installation. After performing the basic QRadar installation, the UBA module was installed within the available Extension Management. To install the UBA module, it is necessary to have the IBM Sense log source used to collect UBA information.

The user data collection is shown in the following figure. QRadar is capable of monitoring user behavior based on incoming events from log sources. From these logs, specific events and data are searched using defined rules to serve as input data for the IBM Sense module, which directly matches UBA applications. Based on built-in or created use case and internal UBA algorithm, it further defines a score that is an indicator of potential user risk.

A prerequisite for using IBM Sense and UBA is the existence of a user name, domain, or other identifying attribute in the messages that QRadar collects (logs or events).

The UBA module extracts the "username" and "senseValue" attributes (that is, defining the increment for the score) from the IBM Sense source events, by which it adjusts, in collaboration with Machine Learning, a specific risk score value for that user. The value of the senseValue is defined differently for each of the set rules from the UBA ruleset and corresponds to the "severity" of the event, respectively to a deviation from standard user behavior. The deviation from the standard behavior can be, for example, identification of the device from which the user has logged in, detection of different IP address of the device, incorrectly entered login data, etc. The more a user violates the set rules, the higher his risk score. In the event that a user exceeds a defined score limit, the UBA module creates an event that responds to the creation of an offense representing an alert for suspicious behavior. In addition, the user is also included in a group of very suspicious users.

3.3 LogRhythm NextGen SIEM

Implementation of user behavioral analysis within the product LogRhythm NextGen SIEM (LogRhythm) coincides only partially with implementations in the solution of IBM Security QRadar. UEBA within LogRhythm consists of two modules:

- Scenario Based Analytics (The UEBA AIE Module).

  - Detect known threats with deterministic threat models (i.e., scenario-based analytics).
  - Baseline behavior across weeks.
  - Detect threats in real time with stream-based analytics.

- CloudAI (ML based statistical analytics).

  - Detect hidden threats with AI / ML.
  - Baseline behavior across weeks to months.
  - Achieve near-real-time threat recognition.
  - Provide high-fidelity data to AI Engine.

Same as in the case of IBM Security QRadar, the UEBA modules are not a part of the default LogRhythm installation. Installation of the UEBA AIE module is done through LogRhythm Knowledgebase. Part of the installation is a set of correlation rules for AI Engine, a set of predefined sheets, which include e.g. the lists of privileged accounts, monitored users, banned countries, etc. Picture 2 shows the UEBA AIE correlation rule package in knowledge-based LogRhythm (Fig. 2).

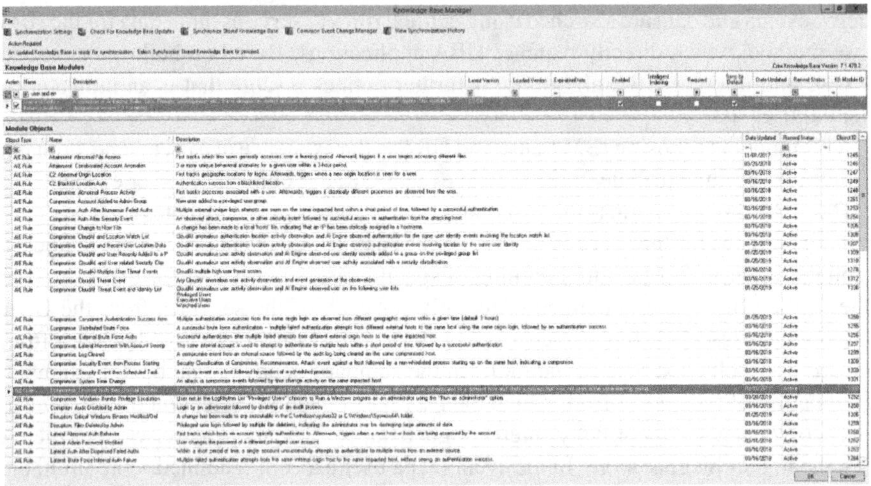

Fig. 2. LogRhythm UEBA AIE module. Source: authors

CloudAI module is not a part of the LogRhythm base license and is subject to separate licensing. Licensing is based on the number of users to which UEBA's rules and principles are applied within the annual subscription. Implementation of UEBA in the LogRhythm solution, compared to QRadar, where the UEBA is part of the basic installation, is financially more demanding.

For LogRhythm solutions AIE and CloudAI there is no need to define any additional log source like in the IBM Sense case at QRadar.

As well as the QRadar, LogRhythm is capable of monitoring user behavior based on incoming events from the source logs. These logs search for specific events and data using defined rules, which are further analyzed by the AI Engine Correlation Rules and CloudAI. To define standard user behavior, thresholds are defined on incoming events. If the threshold is exceeded, the user's risk score is increased.

In particular, the Cloud AI module analyses the following parameters: logon/logoff times, locations, system in use, application used and accesses, time slots that match users' working hours at working days.

The deviation from standard behavior can be the same as in the case of QRadar, e.g. identification of the device from which the user has logged in, detection of different IP address of the device, incorrect login data, etc. The more the user violates the set rules, the higher his risk score.

4   UEBA Modules

This section also demonstrates the usage of its own use case in two of UEBA modules.

4.1   Incorrect Authentication

The first case of use concerns the possibility of UEBA detection of incorrect input of authentication data. The process of incorrectly entering authentication data may not indicate the possibility of attacking the infrastructure if the user mistakenly enters the password. In the case of frequent occurrence of incorrect input of user authentication data, this activity is the reason for this suspected unauthorized access to infrastructure.

QRadar

In the first step, a rule was created to ensure detection. After running the wizard to create an event rule, a rule is generated. The rule is applied when an event specified as QID 28250080 (Failed Login Attempt) is detected. The rule sets attribute values for an event for credibility, relevance, and severity. In addition, a new event will be created. This event modifies the UEBA module score for the user who made the bad login. In addition, a text explaining the use case is displayed. The event falls within the IBM Sense log source and is evaluated by other attribute values for severity, credibility, and relevance (Fig. 3).

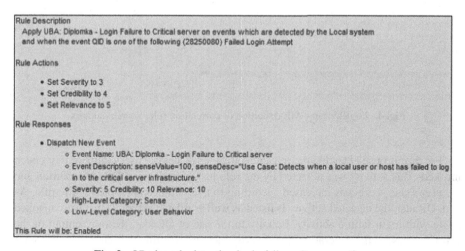

Fig. 3. QRadar rule detecting login failure. Source: authors

An unsuccessful user (username: jne) login event was invoked to test the rule created. This activity was detected by the rule and the risk score was increased by the user according to the parameters defined in the rule.

In the user activity schedule there is apparent an increase in the sense score associated with login failure activity and related activities that were invoked along with the login failure activity. The end result of the entire use case is the generation of a security incident pointing to the very risky behavior of the user.

Logrhythm

The AI Engine module was used to create the correlation rule. Figure 4 shows a preview of the correlation rule definition in the AIE module. The relational rule was set with the same parameters as the QRadar Use case. The rule is applied when an event specified as Authentication Failure is detected.

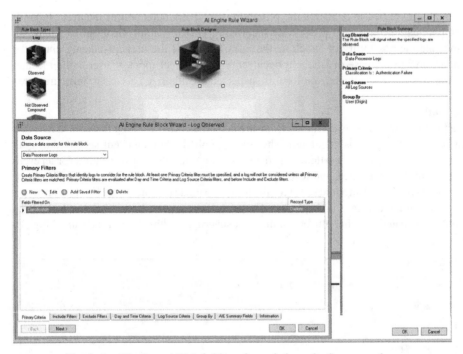

Fig. 4. LogRhythm - AIE definition of correlation rule. Source: authors

For the purpose of testing the rule created, an unsuccessful user login event has been invoked. This activity was detected by the rule just as in the case QRadar solution and the user's risk score was increased according to the parameters defined in the rule. As with QRadar, the detected activity is listed as well as related activities that were invoked along with login failure activity. Equally to the use of QRadar, the only output of the entire use case is the generation of a security incident pointing to highly risky behavior of the user.

4.2 Permission Delegation

The second case of using the UEBA module will be focused primarily on the problem that can be observed from time to time in the network infrastructure. It is an effort to include different users in groups that have a higher range of competences and are not subject to such extensive monitoring of their activities as they are expected to have a certain degree of security risk knowledge. Monitoring is also performed when attempting to delegate permissions to users who do not have access to an administrator account or use an account without administrator privileges.

To detect this activity, a rule has been created that monitors activity on the domain controller. If an activity is detected that records an event of adding or removing a user to a security group, when a user who has performed this activity does not have administrator privileges, a security incident is generated to indicate that. The rule was created as well as in the case of the first Use-Case, via the QRadar installation wizard (Fig. 5).

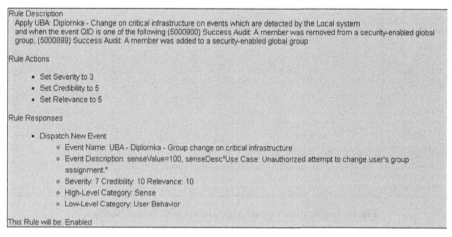

Fig. 5. QRadar - create a rule. Source: authors

After creating the rule, an action was taken to add a normal domain user to a domain administrator group that had been performed by the user. Based on the detected event, the risk score was increased by the user.

LogRhythm

The AI Engine module was used to create the correlation rule. For a relational rule was set with the same parameters as in the case of QRadar Use case. Figure 6 shows a preview of the correlation rule definition in the AIE module. The rule is applied when a received event related to a change of groups is detected in which the user is assigned and this activity is not performed by someone with administrative authority.

After creating a valid rule, an action to add a normal domain user to the domain admin group was made by the user. This activity was detected by the rule created, and the user's risk score was immediately increased, which was immediately visible in application. Same as in the case of the use, QRadar is the only output case of the entire use case of generating a security incident pointing to highly risky behavior of the user.

Fig. 6. LogRhythm - create a correlation rule. Source: authors

5   Conclusion

The aim of this article was to perform a comparative analysis of SIEM solutions empha-sizing modules of user behavioral analysis in SIEM systems and their utility in cyber security energy systems. First, the issue of security in the area of energy systems was introduced with the possibility of using SIEM solutions for monitoring activities. In the following part of the article the general architecture of selected SIEM solutions was introduced, which are currently relevant to deployment in energy systems. Altogether three solutions were chosen for comparative analysis: AlienVault, IBM Security QRadar and LogRhythm NextGen SIEM. At the same time, general principles of user behav-ioral analysis were introduced emphasizing implementation options in selected SIEM solutions.

In the last part of the article, modules of user behavioral analysis were tested on two defined Use-Case emphasizing the possibilities of defining these Use-Case in SIEM solutions and detection of activities that have been invoked in Use Case testing.

In the case of the solution AlienVaultu OSSIM/USM, there was no separate UBA module used for collecting and evaluating information as well as data and monitored users. This functionality was promised to be executed by one of the company's specialists prior to testing Use-Case. Because of the absence of the UBA module, it was not possible to test the defined Use-Case in AlienVault. Utilizing AlienVault in energy systems relative to legislative requirements on auditing logs is problematic because the basic version of the solution includes only the possibility of monitoring the data stream.

At UBA solutions within IBM Security QRadar there was possible to track detailed information about users, which were also applied machine learning models. UBA module QRadaru uses a set of built-in use cases to solve problematic behavior, which can be extended by any custom use case. Defined Use-Case has been successfully deployed to QRadar solutions and their end result has always been manifested by the emergence of a security incident highlighting a potential threat in the infrastructure.

Compared to LogRhythm Solution NextGen SIEM, IBM Security QRadar has the full functionality and licensing of UBA modules already the basic solution. In the case of deployment and use of UBA module in LogRhythm NextGen SIEM solution, as well as QRadar, it was able to track detailed user information, also including machine learning models. The defined Use Case was successfully deployed to LogRhythm by AI Engine and their final outcome was also always the emergence of a security incident highlighting the potential threat of the network infrastructure.

The principal and ultimate added value of the LogRhythm solution is the possibility of creating a so-called Use Case over relevant security incidents, possibly over a user-defined group of events. This includes the ability to add related activities to security incidents that are related to user activity, giving Use Case the ability to compile a detailed overview of the origin of activities and their impact on infrastructure.

Acknowledgment. This work and the contribution were supported by a Specific Research Project, Faculty of Informatics and Management, University of Hradec Kralove, Czech Republic. We would like to thank Mr. J. Nedbal, a graduate of Faculty of management and informatics, University of Hradec Kralove, for the practical verification of the proposed solutions and close cooperation in the solution.

References

1. Keyhani, A.: Design of Smart Power Grid Renewable Energy Systems. John Wiley & Sons, Hoboken (2016)
2. Zakeri, B., Syri, S.: Electrical energy storage systems: a comparative life cycle cost analysis. Renew. Sustain. Energy Rev. **42**, 569–596 (2015). https://doi.org/10.1016/j.rser.2014.10.011. ISSN13640321
3. Jarmakiewicz, J., Parobczak, K., Maślanka, K.: Cybersecurity protection for power grid control infrastructures. Int. J. Crit. Infrastruct. Prot. **18**, 20–33 (2017)
4. Aitel, D.: Cybersecurity essentials for electric operators. Electricity J. **26**(1), 52–58 (2013). https://doi.org/10.1016/j.tej.2012.11.014, ISSN 10406190
5. Peterson, J., Haney, M., Borrelli R.A.: An overview of methodologies for cybersecurity vulnerability assessments conducted in nuclear power plants. Nuclear Eng. Des. **346**, 75–84 (2019). https://doi.org/10.1016/j.nucengdes.2019.02.025, ISSN 00295493
6. LI, L., He W., Li XU, Ash I., Anwar M., Yuan X.: Investigating the impact of cybersecurity policy awareness on employees' cybersecurity behavior. Int. J. Inf. Manag. **45**, 13–24 (2019). https://doi.org/10.1016/j.ijinfomgt.2018.10.017, ISSN 02684012
7. Li, D., Guo, H., Zhou, J., Zhou, L., Wong, J.W.: SCADAWall: a CPI-enabled firewall model for SCADA security. Comput. Secur. **80**, 134–154 (2019). https://doi.org/10.1016/j.cose.2018. 10.002.ISSN01674048
8. Rezai, A., Keshavarzi P., Moravej Z.:. Key management issue in SCADA networks: a review. Eng. Sci. Technol. Int. J. **20**(1), 354–363 (2017). https://doi.org/10.1016/j.jestch.2016.08.011.

9. Nazir, S., Patel, S., Patel, D.: Assessing and augmenting SCADA cyber security: a survey of techniques. Comput. Secur. **70**, 436–454 (2017). https://doi.org/10.1016/j.cose.2017.06.010. ISSN01674048

10. Makkar, A., Kumar, N.: User behavior analysis-based smart energy management for webpage ranking: Learning automata-based solution. Sustain. Comput. Inf. Syst. **20**, 174–191 (2018). https://doi.org/10.1016/j.suscom.2018.02.003.ISSN22105379

11. Yang, L., Wang, Y., Zhou, Y., Wang, J., Fan, Ch., Zhu, Ch.: OA user behavior analysis with the heterogeneous information network model. Phys. A Stat. Mech. Appl. **516**, 552–562 (2019). https://doi.org/10.1016/j.physa.2018.09.116.ISSN03784371

12. Raja, M., Niranjan S., Vasudevan A.R.: Rule generation for TCP SYN flood attack in SIEM Environment. Procedia Comput. Sci. **115**, 580–587 (2017). https://doi.org/10.1016/j.procs. 2017.09.117, ISSN 18770509

13. Maher, D.: Can artificial intelligence help in the war on cybercrime? Comput. Fraud Secur. **2017**(8), 7–9 (2017). https://doi.org/10.1016/S1361-3723(17)30069-6.ISSN13613723

14. Nurmuhumatovich, J.A., Mikusova, M.: Testing trajectory of road trains with program complexes. Arch. Autom. Eng. Archiwum Motoryzacji **83**(1), 103–112 (2019). https://doi.org/ 10.14669/AM.VOL83.ART7

15. Krejcar, O., Frischer, R., Smart intelligent control of current source for high power LED diodes, Microelectron. J. **44**(4), 307–314 (2013). ISSN: 0026–2692, eISSN: 1879–2391

Threads Efficiency Analysis of Selected Operating Systems

Josef Horalek and Vladimir Sobeslav[(✉)]

Faculty of Informatics and Management, University of Hradec Kralove,
Hradec Kralove, Czech Republic
{josef.horalek,vladimir.sobeslav}@uhk.cz

Abstract. The aim of the article is to present results of the testing focused on efficiency of CPU performance and its threads in single-threading and multi-threading modes in various versions of operating systems from the family of Microsoft Windows. The main task was to verify whether the chosen operating system version affects the efficiency of using threads by the operating system, with the emphasis of their upgrade in technological and industrial systems.

Keywords: 7-Zip · WinRAR · Cinebench · AIDA64 · Windows Single-threading · Multithreading

1 Introduction

During development of operating systems from the family of Microsoft Windows, older versions are continuously becoming obsolescent and are being replaced by the newer ones. This life cycle is currently affecting one of the most widespread versions of the operating system, Microsoft Windows 7, whose official support was announced to be terminated on 14 January, 2020. Therefore, this version must be replaced by its successors, Windows 8.1 or Windows 10. In terms of common usage of the operating system, this seems to be rather a trivial concern, however, in the area of technological and industrial use of the systems, this step is quite elaborate as it must be weighed from several viewpoints. The first one is considering the life cycle of operating systems in relation to the applications used, as in the area of industrial and technological use, it is paramount to ensure the maximum functionality of the specialized systems for supervisory control, such as SCADA systems. It is also necessary to take into account possible life expectancy and duration of the official support of the operating system itself, in order to moderate the frequency of operating system upgrades; these can cause various compatibility issues, which often cannot be predicted and can disrupt or even stop the technological systems from functioning. Last but not least, it is necessary to take into account the operating system's performance in relation to the specialized industrial supervisory control systems. With regard to the architecture of such control systems frequently programmed as single-threading applications and still in use in many industrial areas in newer installations, systems with modern multithreading architecture are employed.

P. C. Vinh and A. Rakib (Eds.): ICCASA 2020/ICTCC 2020, LNICST 343, pp. 277–287, 2021.
https://doi.org/10.1007/978-3-030-67101-3_22

With regard to the aforementioned state-of-the-art, a survey was realized, with its results being presented in this article. The survey was comprised of several testing sequences aimed at the efficiency of thread usage across the most used versions of the operating systems from the family of Microsoft Windows.

The aim of the tests realized using two different hardware configurations of the systems was to determine whether newer Microsoft Windows operating systems manage the computations more efficiently in single-threading mode, or multithreading mode. It also aimed to determine which version of the operating system would be more suitable to replace current commonly used Microsoft Windows 7 as the interface between hardware and technological and industrial systems such as SCADA.

In the area of analysis and testing of Microsoft Windows operating systems, many researches and surveys have been conducted and published. The one that is closest to this subject matter are tests focused on the usage of main memory [1] and [2]. The closest to the area we have surveyed is the article "A Survey of Main Memory Acquisition and Analysis Techniques for the Windows Operating System" [3, 4]. However, thread usage research is not getting much attention despite being relevant and affecting efficiency and maintaining the consistency not only in the are of technological systems, but also in regular use of information systems.

1.1 Introduction to Threads Principles

As the aim of the article is to present the results of the testing aimed at the CPU performance efficiency and its thread in single-threading and multithreading modes while employing various versions of the operating systems from the family of Microsoft Windows, it is necessary to briefly introduce the basic features of threads. A thread (often called lightweight process – LWP) is an elementary unit of CPU usage containing program pointer, register, and stack [5, 6]. Data part of the processor and allocated OS resources (together forming a task) are shared by all the threads of a process. Regular or heavyweight process is a task with a single thread.

A task does not do anything if no thread is assigned to it, and any single thread can be assigned only to exactly one task. Therefore, switching between threads leads to lowering the CPU workload as compared to more complicated switching of context in complex processes. Switching between threads represents alignment of a register set, and it is not necessary to make changes in memory [7]. Some systems implement user level of threads in user libraries instead of implementation of threads via system calls. The threads implemented in such a way do not, therefore, require help of the OS and do not cause an interrupt. Switching between user threads is not dependent on the OS and is, therefore, very fast [8, 9]. The use of thread interrupting and switching leads to a relevant solution for the server to efficiently handle multiple queries. User level of thread switching, however, also had its disadvantages. If the OS kernel is a single-thread, every kernel calling by a process results in stopping the whole task until the kernel response. On the other hand, in multithread and multiprocessor system, every process has its program pointer, stack, and address space. This organization method is suitable if the processes ran by individual programs in the system are mutually independent. To state an example, single-processor OS at file server is very often stalled by waiting for drive access. The server's performance would be improved if another process could run while the first one is stalled. However, if other processes want to access the drive or use the same address space (which is not uncommon in file servers), it is impossible to allocate CPU to any processes and the CPU remains unused. If the aforementioned example used multithread architecture or if one task thread was blocked, it would be possible to allocate the CPU to another thread as it is in the same address space. Cooperation of the threads that belong to the same task leads to easier access and higher system performance. As opposed to a process, threads are dependent on each other as all the thread have access to any task address and threads can read or write into any stack of that task's thread. No protection of individual threads is in effect. As opposed to the processes that are ran by different users and can, therefore, behave unfriendly to each other, threads are programmed to help each other, and so any protection of the memory from other threads is unnecessary. In threads, it must be taken into account that if a problem between producer and receiver of the thread requires a shared buffer (as both originate in the same task), to switch between them, not much direction is needed. What is more, in multi-processor systems, every thread can run on a different processor and the performance is thus maximized. All in all, it should be mentioned that threads on user level do not use kernel and switching between them is, therefore, faster than with the threads supported by the kernel. Any kernel calls stall the whole process and as the kernel plans only processes, it has no information about existence of the threads and the waiting process is not eligible for allocation of CPU [10].

2   Testing Methodology

For the practical testing of thread use efficiency in Microsoft Windows, two PC configurations were chosen (Table 1.). These configurations represent standard laboratory equipment in laboratory of operating systems and computer networks at FIM of UHK. Tested operating systems on the hardware configurations were always installed with up-to-date updates available at the time of the testing. Afterwards, testing software was installed. Every measuring was repeated 30 times. For the testing purposes, 64-bit editions of Windows 7 Professional, Windows 8.1 Professional, and Windows 10 Professional were used.

Table 1. Configuration of tested PC

Components	Configuration 1	Configuration 2
CPU	DualCore Intel Core i3-6100, 3,7 GHz (2 cores, 4 treads)	QuadCore Intel Core i7-3770 K, 3,9G (4 cores, 8 treads)
Motherboards	Asus B150I Pro Gaming/Aura	Asus Maximus V Extreme
Chip set	Intel Sunrise Point B150, Intel Skylake-S	Intel Panther Point Z77, Intel Ivy Bridge
RAM	8121 MB (DDR4 SDRAM)	32708 MB (DDR3 SDRAM)
BIOS	AMI (12/22/2017)	AMI (08/19/2013)
Graphics adapter	GeForce GTX 1050 Ti (4 GB)	GeForce GTX 960 (4 GB)
IDE controller	SATA AHCI	SATA AHCI
Disk drive	Kingston SA400S37120G (120 GB, SATA-III)	Intel SSDSC2CW180A3 (180 GB, SATA-III)

2.1   Presentation of Conducted Tests

For the testing of thread usage efficiency in Microsoft Windows operating systems, third party applications that can be used for testing a tasking in single-threading and multithreading modes, were used. Based upon an in-depth analysis of available utilities, the following utilities were chosen and the tests below were executed.

7-Zip 18.05 [11] is a free open-source software. Most of the code is under the GNU LGPL license. Some parts of the code are under the BSD 3-clause License. For the testing, internal Performance benchmark that tests compression and decompression speeds in kB/s, was used. The testing results showcase average value of compression/decompression in MIPS (Million Instructions per Second). Higher MIPS means better results. The tests were run using single (Single-Threading) and all available CPU threads (Multithreading). The testing was repeated thirty times, using 128 MB dictionary size.

WinRAR 5.60 [12] contains a built-in benchmark whose functionality is very similar to those of **7-Zip 18.05**. However, speed is measured in kB/s. The tests were run using single (Single-Threading) and all available CPU threads (Multithreading). The testing was repeated thirty times, using 128 MB dictionary size.

CPU-Z 1.85.0 [13] is a freeware that gathers information on some of the main system devices. For our testing, a benchmark to test single-threading and multi-threading was used. The testing results are measured in points, with more points meaning better results. The testing was repeated thirty times.

Cinebench R15.038_RC184115 [14] uses graphical rendering for testing the CPU in single-threading and multithreading modes. The testing results are measured in points, with more points meaning better results. The testing was repeated thirty times.

AIDA64 CPU Tests [15] use all available threads. Simultaneous multithreading and Hyper-threading were enabled. For the testing, CPU Queen module, which is an integer benchmark specialized in processor prediction and penalties of the CPU, was used. It finds the solutions for the classic "Queens problem" on a 10 by 10 sized chessboard [16]. CPU Zlib measures the performance of processor subsystem and memory combined using the public library Zlib for compression. Furthermore, data encryption speed using CPU AES was tested. The last test was performed using AES CPU Hash, which measured the CPU performance using SHA1 algorithm.

3   Testing Results and Discussion

The gathered data was processed using standard descriptive statistical methods. Arithmetic mean, Variance, and Standard deviation were determined so the gathered data could be relevantly evaluated.

3.1   7-Zip 18.05 Test

The testing results infer that all the tested operating system versions can distribute the workload on individual threads, which is seen while comparing the MIPS results at two QuadCore Intel Core i7-3770K CPUs. Individual measurements have low Variance with maximum deviation of 1.4% from the average, and therefore, the gathered data show high congruity. For the data measured in single-threading, Windows 7 PRO had the best results for both configurations, although deviation among other versions of Microsoft Windows operating system was still below 1.4%, which is negligible for pragmatic evaluation. In multithreading mode, for Configuration 1, the best results were achieved by Windows 10 PRO operating system, and for Configuration 2, Windows 7 PRO. Respective deviations were below 1.2%, which is negligible. Full results are showcased in Table 2.

Table 2. Overall performance (MIPS) for 7-Zip 18.05

Single-threading			
Configuration 1	Arithmetic mean (MIPS)	Variance σ^2	Standard deviation σ
Windows 7 PRO	5463,5	162,6	12,8
Windows 8.1 PRO	5407,2	228,4	15,1
Windows 10 PRO	4740,7	820,5	28,6
Configuration 2	Arithmetic mean (MIPS)	Variance σ	Standard deviation σ
Windows 7 PRO	5386,4	76,6	8,8
Windows 8.1 PRO	5369,7	451,2	21,2
Windows 10 PRO	5327,0	102,8	10,1
Multithreading			
Configuration 1	Arithmetic mean (MIPS)	Variance σ^2	Standard deviation σ
Windows 7 PRO	14552,3	1510,6	38,9
Windows 8.1 PRO	14422,6	732,2	27,1
Windows 10 PRO	14648,9	369,0	19,2
Configuration 2	Arithmetic mean (MIPS)	Variance σ^2	Standard deviation σ
Windows 7 PRO	25896,6	4585,0	67,7
Windows 8.1 PRO	25661,6	8299,0	91,1
Windows 10 PRO	25669,2	3395,8	184,3

3.2 Test WinRAR 5.60

The results of this test are similar to the first one, except for that while using multi-threading in Configuration 1, Windows 8.1 had the best results. Maximum deviation of individual operating system versions was 7%, which was measured in Configuration 1 multithreading. The data alone is the measured with minimum variance, which is below 1%, therefore is considered as measurement error. Full results are showcased in Table 3.

Table 3. Overall performance (kB/s) for WinRAR 5.60

Single-threading

Configuration 1	Arithmetic mean (kB/s)	Variance σ^2	Standard deviation σ
Windows 7 PRO	1523,1	2,1	1,5
Windows 8.1 PRO	1517,4	1,3	1,2
Windows 10 PRO	1515,4	1,8	1,4
Configuration 2	Arithmetic mean (kB/s)	Variance σ^2	Standard deviation σ
Windows 7 PRO	1557,8	5,5	2,3
Windows 8.1 PRO	1556,0	11,5	3,4
Windows 10 PRO	1515,0	23,0	4,8

Multithreading

Configuration 1	Arithmetic mean (kB/s)	Variance σ^2	Standard deviation σ
Windows 7 PRO	4585,8	454,0	21,3
Windows 8.1 PRO	4971,4	33,0	5,7
Windows 10 PRO	4943,8	42,5	6,5
Configuration 2	Arithmetic mean (kB/s)	Variance σ^2	Standard deviation σ
Windows 7 PRO	9548,0	76,4	8,7
Windows 8.1 PRO	9524,3	28,3	5,3
Windows 10 PRO	9428,0	68,6	8,3

3.3 Test CPU-Z 1.85.0 64-Bit

The results while using CPU-Z are different from the others, especially considering their accuracy while using Configuration 1 while measuring in single-threading mode, where the deviations reached value of up to 6%. However, with Configuration 2, the value was below 1% in both single-threading and multithreading. Therefore, it can be inferred that the performance of DualCore Intel Core i3-6100 in single-threading mode is greatly dependent on the type of the calculations used in the given test. Overall, the best values were achieved by Windows 7 and Windows 8.1. Full results are showcased in Table 4.

3.4 Test Cinebench R15.038_RC184115

The results of the tests while using Cinebench R15.038_RC184115 show generally the most stable results not only among individual operating system versions, but also in both single-threading and multithreading modes. For both configurations and modes, the best results were achieved by Windows 7, although compared to the other versions of the operating system, results were below 1%, which is a negligible deviation and can be considered as a measurement error. Full results are showcased in Table 5.

Table 4. CPU-Z 1.85.0 64-bit

Single-threading			
Configuration 1	Arithmetic mean (points)	Variance σ^2	Standard deviation σ
Windows 7 PRO	355,4	141,8	11,9
Windows 8.1 PRO	386,1	194,6	14,0
Windows 10 PRO	357,4	99,0	9,9
Configuration 2	Arithmetic mean (points)	Variance σ^2	Standard deviation σ
Windows 7 PRO	403,0	0,2	0,5
Windows 8.1 PRO	402,9	0,4	0,6
Windows 10 PRO	383,8	3,3	1,8
Multithreading			
Configuration 1	Arithmetic mean (points)	Variance σ^2	Standard deviation σ
Windows 7 PRO	1104,8	0,4	0,6
Windows 8.1 PRO	1102,5	2,3	1,5
Windows 10 PRO	1049,4	0,9	1,0
Configuration 2	Arithmetic mean (points)	Variance σ^2	Standard deviation σ
Windows 7 PRO	1968,8	127,9	11,3
Windows 8.1 PRO	1974,9	0,2	0,4
Windows 10 PRO	1814,3	73,1	8,6

Table 5. Cinebench R15.038_RC184115

Single-Threading			
Configuration 1	Arithmetic mean (points)	Variance σ^2	Standard deviation σ
Windows 7 PRO	160,0	0,0	0,0
Windows 8.1 PRO	158,6	0,2	0,5
Windows 10 PRO	157,3	3,3	1,8
Configuration 2	Arithmetic mean (points)	Variance σ^2	Standard deviation σ
Windows 7 PRO	145,0	0,0	0,0
Windows 8.1 PRO	144,4	0,2	0,5
Windows 10 PRO	143,5	0,3	0,5
Multithreading			
Configuration 1	Arithmetic mean (points)	Variance σ^2	Standard deviation σ
Windows 7 PRO	407,2	1,5	1,2
Windows 8.1 PRO	405,4	0,4	0,7
Windows 10 PRO	394,2	5,1	2,2
Configuration 2	Arithmetic mean (points)	Variance σ^2	Standard deviation σ
Windows 7 PRO	719,6	2,4	1,6
Windows 8.1 PRO	718,9	2,3	1,5
Windows 10 PRO	711,6	9,4	3,1

3.5   Test AIDA64 CPU Tests

The last performed tests were aimed at comparison of the CPUs working in multi-threading mode. To perform these tests, AIDA64 CPU Tests utility was used along with CPU Queen module, which is a benchmark specialized in processor prediction and penalties of the CPU. It finds the solutions for the classic "Queens problem" on a 10 by 10 sized chessboard [16]. CPU Zlib measures the performance of processor subsystem and memory combined using the public library Zlib for compression. Furthermore, data encryption speed using CPU AES was tested. The last test was performed using AES CPU Hash, which measured the CPU performance using SHA1 algorithm.

The results showcased in Tables 6 and 7 show that performance and work efficiency are almost unaffected by the chosen operating system and that the individual results vary by 1% at maximum. Throughout their iterations, the individual tests show minimum variance and standard deviation and point at the performance of individual computing system configurations being stable and not showing any significant deviations.

Table 6. AIDA64 CPU tests multithreading – configuration 1

Configuration 1	Test	Arithmetic mean	Variance σ^2	Standard deviation σ
Windows 7 PRO	CPU Queen (points)	25 258,9	225,73	15,02
	CPU Zlib (MB/s)	166,0	0,37	0,60
	CPU AES (MB/s)	8 420,1	0,45	0,67
	CPU Hash (MB/s)	2 128,0	45,25	6,73
Windows 8.1 PRO	CPU Queen (points)	25 218,4	133,43	11,55
	CPU Zlib (MB/s)	167,8	0,35	0,59
	CPU AES (MB/s)	8 419,7	0,23	0,48
	CPU Hash (MB/s)	2 117,2	1,16	1,08
Windows 10 PRO	CPU Queen (points)	25 163,5	295,65	54,32
	CPU Zlib (MB/s)	167,8	0,28	0,53
	CPU AES (MB/s)	8 414,9	0,83	0,91
	CPU Hash (MB/s)	2 116,6	0,25	0,50

Table 7. AIDA64 CPU tests multithreading – configuration 2

Configuration 2	Test	Arithmetic mean	Variance σ^2	Standard deviation σ
Windows 7 PRO	CPU Queen (points)	49 461,5	75,75	8,70
	CPU Zlib (MB/s)	331,9	4,03	2,01
	CPU AES (MB/s)	15 283,7	5,51	2,35
	CPU Hash (MB/s)	3 167,9	10,83	3,29
Windows 8.1 PRO	CPU Queen (points)	49 469,7	95,43	9,77
	CPU Zlib (MB/s)	332,5	0,98	0,99
	CPU AES (MB/s)	15 279,2	6,06	2,46
	CPU Hash (MB/s)	3 163,0	0,50	0,71
Windows 10 PRO	CPU Queen (points)	49 393,2	63,33	25,25
	CPU Zlib (MB/s)	335,4	2,89	1,70
	CPU AES (MB/s)	15 245,4	65,34	8,08
	CPU Hash (MB/s)	3 157,6	0,25	0,50

4   Conclusion

The aim of the article was to find the answer as to which version of Microsoft Windows operating system would be the most suitable to replace the obsolescent, yet widespread, Windows 7. The analysis and the testing were aimed at performance of Windows 8.1 and Windows 10 in processing and using CPU threads from the viewpoint of the used operating system version. For the purposes of the analysis, five different utilities were used. The utilities served to survey the operation execution in single-threading and multithreading modes. Individual tests were evaluated using chosen descriptive statistics methods in order to eliminate random and systematic measurement errors. From the gathered data it is unequivocally clear that all the three Microsoft Windows versions had shown minimum deviations, and it can be, therefore, stated that thread usage efficiency in both single-threading and multithreading modes is same in all the tested systems, with maximum deviation being below 3% with the exception of the CPU-Z test, where deviation reaching up to 6% was measured while using Configuration 1 in single-threading mode.

It can be, therefore, ascertained that currently used Windows 7 systems can be substituted by Windows 8.1 or Windows 10 as their efficiency of thread usage by the CPU remains unchanged. As for the employment of the operating systems in technological and industrial systems, taking into account the aforementioned long-term life cycle of system replacement, it is more suitable to employ Windows 10 Pro as its life cycle is fully open and without any announced terms of the official support termination.

Acknowledgment. This work and the contribution were supported by a Specic Research Project, Faculty of Informatics and Management, University of Hradec Kralove, Czech Republic. We would like to thank Mr. J. Spacek, a graduate of Faculty of management and informatics, University of Hradec Kralove, for the practical verification of the proposed solutions and close cooperation in the solution.

References

1. Okolica, J., Peterson, G.L.: Windows operating systems agnostic memory analysis. Digit. Invest. **7**, S48–S56 (2010). https://doi.org/10.1016/j.diin.2010.05.007. ISSN 17422876. Accessed 27 Feb 2019

2. Stüttgen, J., Cohen, M.: Anti-forensic resilient memory acquisition. Digit. Invest. **10**, S105–S115 (2013). https://doi.org/10.1016/j.diin.2013.06.012. ISSN 17422876. Accessed 27 Feb 2019

3. Vömel, S., Freiling, F.C.: A survey of main memory acquisition and analysis techniques for the windows operating system. Digital Investigation **8**(1), 3–22 (2011). https://doi.org/10.1016/j.diin.2011.06.002. ISSN 17422876. Accessed 27 Feb 2019

4. Skaletsky, A., et al.: Dynamic program analysis of Microsoft Windows applications. In: 2010 IEEE International Symposium on Performance Analysis of Systems and Software (ISPASS), White Plains, NY, pp. 2–12 (2010). https://doi.org/10.1109/ISPASS.2010.5452079

5. Eich, M., Vögele, T.,: Design and control of a lightweight magnetic climbing robot for vessel inspection. In: 2011 19th Mediterranean Conference on Control and Automation (MED), Corfu, pp. 1200–1205 (2011). https://doi.org/10.1109/med.2011.5983075

6. Kwon, H., Kim, T., Yu, S.J., Kim, H.K.: Self-similarity based lightweight intrusion detection method for cloud computing. In: Nguyen, N.T., Kim, C.-G., Janiak, A. (eds.) ACIIDS 2011. LNCS (LNAI), vol. 6592, pp. 353–362. Springer, Heidelberg (2011). https://doi.org/10.1007/978-3-642-20042-7_36

7. Anders Larsson; AliView: a fast and lightweight alignment viewer and editor for large datasets. Bioinformatics **30**(22), 3276–3278 (2014). https://doi.org/10.1093/bioinformatics/btu531

8. Tanchaisawat, T., Bergado, D.T., Voottipruex, P.: Numerical simulation and sensitivity analyses of full-scale test embankment with reinforced lightweight geomaterials on soft Bangkok clay. Geotext. Geomembr. **26**(6), 498–511 (2008). https://doi.org/10.1016/j.geotexmem. ISSN 0266-1144

9. Ambrogio, G., Filice, L., Gagliardi, F.: Formability of lightweight alloys by hot incremental sheet forming. Mater. Des. **34**, 501–508 (2012). https://doi.org/10.1016/j.matdes.2011.08.024. ISSN 0261-3069

10. Cheng, Y., Fu, X., Du, X., Luo, B., Guizani, M.: A lightweight live memory forensic approach based on hardware virtualization. Inf. Sci. **379**, 23–41 (2017). https://doi.org/10.1016/j.ins.2016.07.019. ISSN 0020-0255

11. 7-Zip. 7-Zip (2018). Dostupné z. https://www.7-zip.org/. Accessed 25 Feb 2019

12. RARLAB. RARLAB products (2019). Dostupné z. https://www.rarlab.com/. Accessed 25 Feb 2019
13. CPU-Z: System information software. cpuid (2019). Dostupné z. https://www.cpuid.com/softwares/cpu-z.html. Accessed 25 Feb 2019
14. CINEBENCH [online]. MAXON Compute (2019). Dostupné z. https://www.maxon.net/en/products/cinebench/. Accessed 25 Feb 2019
15. AIDA64 User manual. ABSEIRA (2019). Dostupné z. https://www.aida64.co.uk/user-manual/aida64-user-manual. Accessed 25 Feb 2019
16. Queens Problem: Wolfram Math World. Wolfram Research (2019). Dostupné z. http://mathworld.wolfram.com/QueensProblem.html. Accessed 25 Feb 2019
17. Nurmuhumatovich, J.A., Mikusova, M.: Testing trajectory of road trains with program complexes. Arch. Automot. Eng. – Arch. Motoryzacji **83**(1), 103–112 (2019). https://doi.org/10.14669/AM.VOL83.ART7

An Architecture for Intelligent e-Learning Platform for Student's Lab Deployment

Peter Mikulecky, Vladimir Sobeslav[✉], Matej Drdla, and Hana Svecova

Faculty of Informatics and Management, University of Hradec Kralove,
Rokitanskeho 62, 50003 Hradec Kralove, Czech Republic
{peter.mikulecky,vladimir.sobeslav,matej.drdla,hana.svecova}@uhk.cz

Abstract. For better understanding and better learning of new technologies, there is welcome to have some hands-on experiences with these subjects. This helps with knowledge adoption and also increases learning efficiency. In this article, there is analyzed inputs for a proposal of this system and requirements, which should be meet for such system, and also there is identified learning subjects and areas, which could use this tools. This article deals with and describes an architecture, which can help with automation and deployment labs, which can students use for learning and their research. There is described the architecture for a system, which is able to deploy these environment into more cloud type providers and also is open and able to handle more types run-time technologies, especially virtualization (e.g. OpenStack, Kubernetes and more). The architecture describes platform, which consists an portal or a learning web-based tool, which can be used for learning and also for interface of student labs, which can be automatically deployed based on input conditions with automation tools to some public or private cloud services.

Keywords: Learning · Lab deployment · Automation · Private cloud · Public cloud

1 Introduction

The learning of new technologies should not include only theoretical knowledge and learning without touching it. There should be also included some hands-on experience, which increase learning speed and the depth of knowledge. Thanks of this, students are faster in learning and the learning process is faster and more efficient.

The hands-on experience can be delivered via giving students an environment that matches the real environment and students can play with it and try to understand these technologies and contexts.

There are a few challenges, which should be met. For example, how to students will access course resources (theory and practise, thus hands-on environment).

P. C. Vinh and A. Rakib (Eds.): ICCASA 2020/ICTCC 2020, LNICST 343, pp. 288–299, 2021.
https://doi.org/10.1007/978-3-030-67101-3_23

The deployed lab has to run on some platform and there are basically three option [8] - use some private cloud solution (based on requirements use Infrastructure as a Service on demand solution, e.g. OpenStack [29], VMware [39], Hyper-V [27] or Kubernetes [21,25]), use some public cloud solution (e.g. Microsoft Azure [27], Amazon Web Services [2], Google Cloud Engine [15]) or use some hybrid cloud solution or more solutions together.

2   Problem Definition

The learning process of any learning subject basically includes two phases:

1. Learning the theoretical aspects,
2. Learning the practical aspects and exercises.

Students first learn the basic knowledge they should subsequently demonstrate and deepen within exercises that should help them with the application of acquired knowledge.

To be able to do these exercises, students should have resources, where they can do some basic tasks and get hands-on experiences and also can play with technology if this is possible.

There are a lot of opportunities for hands-on learning and getting resources for these students lab. In general, there can be used any cloud resources environments, which can provide run-time platform for this area. There can be used public provider clouds or there can be used private cloud solutions.

Thanks of virtualization and thanks of abstraction between application and hardware resources, there are possibilities for not taking care about where services will be running and thanks of this, these labs with good architecture layer can be used on more cloud solutions.

Lab environments should meet requests in many areas, which can be required for some specific environment and deployment. It can depend on usage, but generally speaking, areas are:

- availability, which means how will be defined service level agreement of these services,
- accessibility, which means how many students will share the same resources (lab and physical resources)
- performance, which means how much resource will be available for each lab and how many labs will be able to run in each time,
- price, which requests the highest cost effectiveness for such environments and whole implementation,
- and others.

Each from these areas can be different for specific setup, for example the environment for students in school area will be different for students in business area. This research is defining architecture for real deployment of solution for lab deployment, but there should be analysed specific environment setup and its requirements.

2.1 Subjects and Areas

The school and education subject, for which should be able to use this solution are mainly Information Technologies subjects, where for students could be helpful to have hands-on experiences. Between these subjects and technologies belong:

- Desktop and Server Operating Systems (e.g. Linux-based Operating Systems, Windows Server and Client and platforms run on top of these technologies),
- Virtualization Platforms like virtual machines and container virtualization (e.g. VMware virtualization, Hyper-V, Docker and Kubernetes),
- Applications, where is not easily to run and deploy it on standalone machines (e.g. databases, application based on backend and frontend layers, large enterprise systems and platforms),
- and many others.

2.2 Cloud Computing Solution

The designed environment could be able to run on Private and also Public Cloud Computing solutions [8]. Each Cloud Computing solution brings specific advantages and disadvantages, so there is needed to choose this one, which will meet requirements and run will be the most suitable.

On Fig. 1, there are shown basic Cloud Computing solution types, which can be used for implantation of this system.

This figure also shows a third type, hybrid cloud solution, which can be used and it means that solution is using both, private and public cloud solutions, and thanks for that can optimize benefits of both solutions.

The background of such a solution should be virtualization - mainly Infrastructure as a Service (IaaS) solution, but there could be possible to use also another Cloud Computing solutions, such Platform as a Service (PaaS) and Software as a Service (SaaS), but this paper is mainly concerned with the Infrastructure as a Service solution.

2.3 Cloud Based Educational Companies and Institutions

On the market, there is a lot of companies and institutions, which are delivering some e-Learning services, which also includes providing student's labs, where they can learn.

But on the other hand, these solutions are not publicly available and therefore there is no generic architecture that describes the possibilities and uses and the best practises.

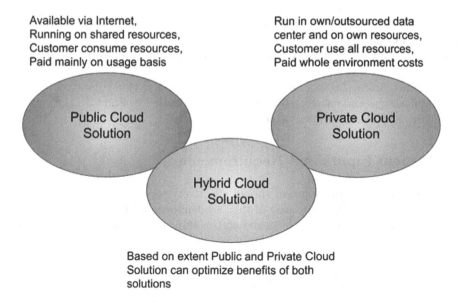

Available via Internet,
Running on shared resources,
Customer consume resources,
Paid mainly on usage basis

Run in own/outsourced data
center and on own resources,
Customer use all resources,
Paid whole environment costs

Public Cloud
Solution

Private Cloud
Solution

Hybrid Cloud
Solution

Based on extent Public and Private Cloud
Solution can optimize benefits of both
solutions

Fig. 1. Basic Cloud Computing solution and their main benefits.

3   Related Works

A lot of research works is based on some learning platform usage, which can be used in learning or analysed cloud computing usage in learning areas.

Alabbadi [1] analyses the usage of cloud computing services in learning and defines the Complete Cloud Computing Formation Model for cloud computing usage analysis. The similar analysis are Babu [4] and Sanchez [32] with Agent Based Cloud Computing Architecture.

Dahdouh [9] examines how to interconnect more e-learning and cloud computing platforms and also describes architecture of e-learning system based on Spark and Hadoop [10].

Thomas [37] analyses a potential of cloud computing usage in learning and his advantages and disadvantages.

Between another similar studies, which are considers to cloud computing usage in e-learning and education, but on regular basis, belong also An [3], Dong [12], Fernandez [13], Gonzalez-Martinez [16], Horalek [17], Juan [20], Mikulecky [28], Siddiqui [34], Sommerville [35].

Barak [5] and Stantchev [36] examine this area more in behaviour aspects and Boja [7] and Maresova [24] examines economics aspects of cloud computing usage in learning and education.

Another studies are focused to another cloud computing usage in school or scientific area. For example Horalek [18] describes model for cloud computing usage in scientific calculations. Also Tuncay [38] analyses an effective usage of cloud computing in educational institutions. Xu [40] defines an architecture of virtual laboratory for network security education.

Some studies helps with cloud computing usage optimization. Kumar [22] analyses workload prediction with using the neural networks. Komarek [23], Pavlik [31] and also Sebastio [33] study availability and performance of cloud services.

Ghobaei-Arani [14] examines how to effectively use cloud data centers for virtual machines and resource efficiency is also addressed by Zhu [41]. Bartuskova [6] describes a framework for resource management.

4   System Inputs and Requirements

The architecture of the solution should effectively serve the purpose, which is mainly student learning. Because of this, students should be able to use it any time and also should be able to rebuild and/or skip the environment to any state of course.

Some of main requirements has been introduced in Problem Definition section (availability, accessibility, performance and price), but anyway, based on specific requirement, some of these can be changed, modified or omitted entirely.

From the requirement, there are implicated system inputs for particular usage of this architecture. There should be included and considered above all:

- how many user will be active (have deployed lab), inactive (be able to deploy lab) or how many labs can each user deploy,
- how will be setup time to live of deployed labs and if will be deleted after some period,
- how user accounts will be handled, if there will be some local user management solution or some integration to another user management solution,
- how user will connect to the environment, if there is needed some VPN, another external portal or is public Internet available,
- if there will be used private or public cloud solution and if public, which provider will be chosen for deployment,
- which virtualization platform will be used for control plane (this means learning application) and if virtual machines or containers,
- which virtualization platform will be used for data plane (virtual user environments) and if virtual machines or containers,
- how much will be used automation for deployment and which configuration will be on user side,
- for which education subject will be the lab environment and his possibilities used and how,
- if there will be used only one type of deployment and used for whole subject topic or will be possible switching between e.g. lessons,
- and possibly much more other, based on implementation and specific requirements.

5   System Architecture

The architecture of entire system is based on some components, which are inter-connected and mainly there are used open-source tools and software.

Figure 2 shows basic architecture concept, which consists parts of a system for deployment of student environments and these components are important for successful implementation and working setup of this architecture.

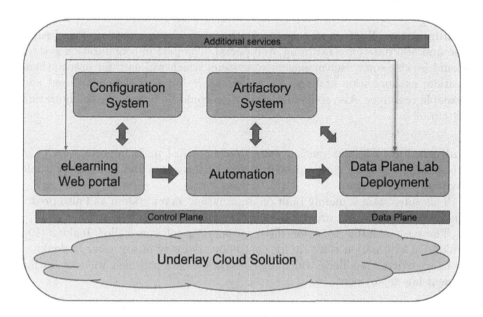

Fig. 2. Basic lab deployment system architecture.

5.1   Components

The whole system consists a few components, which each act like subsystem of this solution and have its own meaning.

These components are split to 2 parts:

1. Control plane, which takes care of the whole platform,
2. Data plane, where run student deployed labs.

The both part are running on top of some cloud solution. Both part can share the same cloud solution but also cannot and for example control plane can run on public cloud solution and data plan on private cloud solution. Also there is possible to run data plane on public and private cloud solution and there can be implemented some logic for choosing, where each lab will run

e-Learning Web Portal. The main component of the solution for students is e-Learning Web portal, where courses are available for student and students use it for learning process. This is mainly web page, where are located learning materials and resources, exam and practical exercises, which student should complete via their deployed labs.

This portal can be used also some existing e-Learning solution, where can be implemented some trigger for building lab or labs can be deployed separately without connection to e-Learning system.

Configuration System. The configuration system consists store of configuration and also data for e-Learning Web portal. The part of configuration system should be also some user management system, which will used for user authentication, authorization and also for quotas store for management of used and available resources. Also some billing solution could be part of the configuration system.

Automation. The automation subsystem is one of main important parts of this solution. It helps with automatizing of deployments and routines in whole environment.

This subsystem is mainly built on automation server system and also predefined procedures, which are done during deployment.

The most suitable tools for these purposes is software called Jenkins [19]. Jenkins is automation software for continuous delivery of software. In Jenkins, there are written pipelines, which are consists procedures which are done during student lab deployment.

Data Plane Lab Deployment. This part of solution means all deployed student labs. These labs may consist virtual machines with installed application and/or with specific configuration, containers, which run specific application.

In some specific situation, there can be run virtual machines with nested virtualization, where can run another virtual machines or containers.

Additional Services. The part of solution can be external or internal services, which can help with management and run of the environment. Between these services, there can belong:

- Monitoring solution,
- external e-Learning System,
- external user management solution,
- external accounting and billing system,
- supporting web services non-directly related to e-Learning,
- and a lot of others.

Between additional services can belong also integration parts with another external systems.

5.2   User Deployment Workflow

When user is starting learning and requesting any new lab deployment, there should be a few steps, which should be done before and after lab will be successfully deployed. The workflow of this action should be:

1. Student logins to e-Learning system with provided credentials,
2. e-Learning system validate user credential, system authorization, permissions and current deployed resources,
3. Student is using e-Learning system, if there is needed some lab, student will start request for resources,
4. System is validating available resources and user resource quota, current state and predefined Cloud Computing solutions and rules and after this, lab deployment will start,
5. System start deployment, build pipeline run for this based on request and current state of system,
6. System run pipeline for user lab deployment via predefined deployment workflow,
7. After lab is successfully deployed, inform user via predefined notification and also provide credential and information how to login to deployed lab.

This is basic workflow for student lab deployment, but there can be differences and also another steps, which can come with local requirements and implementation.

5.3   Another Workflows and Functions

There is also needed to have some another workflows for management whole cluster to be able to manage whole environment successfully. This system is not only about student lab deployment, but also management current deployed labs and also their life cycle.

Between these workflows and functions should belong:

- Regular check for current usage of labs and comparing student resource validity,
- Based on requirements, upgrade current labs to the newest versions (optionally with current student state),
- Process and pipeline for destroying deployed labs with expired time to live or deactivated users and resource cleanup and optimization,
- Resource validation and possibility for migration to another Cloud Computing solution, if enabled,
- Upgrading artifact stored contents based on upstream updates (e.g. new packages, new operating system images, docker images),
- Automatically triggered test deployments, which will ensure, that there will be possible to deploy labs in each time and for preventing non-working state,
- Regular monitoring of the whole environment and all interconnected components,

- Data synchronization of with another e-Learning systems or management systems if needed (e.g. users, classes),
- and some specific others.

Thanks to automation, there should be prepared pipelines, which will be trigger by scheduled triggers and will start based on configuration. But this is not only about system implementation, but also about processes for specific implementation.

6   Proof of Concept Lab Deployment System

To be sure, this infrastructure is working and is possible to implement it, there were implemented and tested proof of concept setup with basic and small configuration.

For testing purposes, there were created basic web portal and with basic form for creation of student lab. This lab has two alternatives: 3 and 6 virtual machines based on Ubuntu 18.04.2 LTS (Bionic Beaver) with installed and configured basic Kubernetes cluster.

Th configuration system stored some service, like basic user management subsystem and also store of available lab configurations.

Artifact system stored Ubuntu images and also some repositories in Gerrit code software, where has been store pipeline configuration for Jenkins automation server. For Linux repositories has been used upstream repositories, but also could be used some package management server like a part of artifact system.

Jenkins has been used like automation system with a written pipeline, which received trigger from e-Learning Web portal with configuration, start pipeline run, which deployed student lab.

Deployed labs has been installed to OpenStack based cloud, where also has been running virtual machines with rest of infrastructure (control plane).

After this first phase, there were second phase, which consists verification on some public cloud solution. There were chosen Amazon Web Services cloud, which provides Amazon Elastic Compute Cloud (EC2) solution for virtual machines. Because there has been needed some changes in written deploy pipeline, this pipeline has been extended with additional parameters, which are related for deployment to AWS cloud.

7   Conclusion

This paper describes architecture of system, which can be used like support for the learning of technical subjects mainly. This architecture contains web interface, which is for user interaction, automation subsystem, which serves for lab deployment automation, core subsystem, which is managing user and system requests and also opened virtualization subsystem, which can be used like private or public cloud solution.

This architecture concept can be used in large usage variants and thanks of this, can be modified on specific environment requirements and possibilities, because there are a lot of variants for usage and also technical and non-technical requirements for learning and possibilities of the particular institution, school or university.

The whole architecture is possible to built on open source technologies so this can be possible for next development and the architecture in opened for another extensions and specifics.

The main benefit of this architecture is in the openness for future development and there are possibilities to change and/or modify it for needs of the specific organisation, which can be some educational institution or also some software company, which wants to deliver labs for their employees. And between another benefits belong the openness for underlay virtualization platforms, which can be on premise cloud solution or some public cloud solutions.

The architecture also provides and recommends the usage of highest layers of virtualization (e.g. container virtualization), but there is possible to use more traditional type of virtualization (virtual machines based virtualization).

Acknowledgment. This work and the contribution were supported by a Specific Research Project, Faculty of Informatics and Management, University of Hradec Kralove, Czech Republic. We would like to thank Mr. Lubos Mercl, a graduate of Faculty of management and informatics, University of Hradec Kralove, for the practical verification of the pro-posed solutions and close cooperation in the solution.

References

1. Alabbadi, M.M.: Cloud computing for education and learning: education and Learning as a Service (ELaaS). In: 14th International Conference on Interactive Collaborative Learning, ICL 2011–11th International Conference Virtual University, pp. 589–594 (2011)
2. Amazon Web Services offers reliable, scalable, and inexpensive cloud computing services. https://aws.amazon.com/. Accessed 30 Jan 2019
3. An, W., Huang, L.: E-learning exploration based on cloud computing. In: Measurement Technology and Engineering Researches in Industry, PTS 1–3, Applied Mechanics and Materials, vol. 333–335, pp. 2226–2230 (2013)
4. Babu, S.R., Kulkarni, K.G., Sekaran, K.C.: A generic agent based cloud computing architecture for e-learning. Adv. Intell. Syst. Comput. **248**, 523–533 (2014). https://doi.org/10.1007/978-3-319-03107-1_58
5. Barak, M.: Science teacher education in the twenty-first century: a pedagogical framework for technology-integrated social constructivism. Res. Sci. Educ. **47**(2), 283–303 (2017). https://doi.org/10.1007/s11165-015-9501-y
6. Bartuskova, A., Krejcar, O., Selamat, A., Kuca, K.: Framework for managing of learning resources for specific knowledge areas. In: 13th International Conference on Intelligent Software Methodologies, Tools, and Techniques (SoMeT 2014), Frontiers in Artificial Intelligence and Applications, vol. 265, pp. 565–576 (2014)
7. Boja, C., Pocatilu, P., Toma, C.: The economics of cloud computing on educational services. In: 3rd World Conference on Learning, Teaching and Educational Leadership (WCLTA 2012), Procedia Social and Behavioral Sciences, vol. 93, pp. 1050–1054 (2013)

8. Buyya, R., Vecchiola, C., Selvi, S.T.: Mastering Cloud Computing, 3rd edn. McGraw Hill, New York (2013)
9. Dahdouh, K., Dakak, A., Oughdir, L.: Integration of the cloud environment in e-learning systems. Trans. Mach. Learn. Artif. Intell. **5**(4) (2017)
10. Dahdouh, K., Dakkak, A., Oughdir, L., Ibriz, A.: Large-scale e-learning recommender system based on Spark and Hadoop. J. Big Data **6**(1), 2 (2019). https://doi.org/10.1186/s40537-019-0169-4
11. Doelitzscher, F., Sulistio, A., Reich, C., Kuijs, H., Wolf, D.: Private cloud for collaboration and e-Learning services: from IaaS to SaaS. Computing (Vienna/New York), **91**(1), 23–42 (2011). https://doi.org/10.1007/s00607-010-0106-z
12. Dong, B., Zheng, Q., Yang, J., Li, H., Qiao, M.: An e-learning ecosystem based on cloud computing infrastructure. In: 9th IEEE International Conference on Advanced Learning Technologies (ICALT 2009), pp. 125–127 (2009)
13. Fernandez, A., Peralta, D., Herrera, F., Benítez, J.M.: An overview of e-learning in cloud computing. In: Uden, L., Corchado Rodríguez, E., De Paz Santana, J., De la Prieta, F. (eds.) Workshop on Learning Technology for Education in Cloud (LTEC 2012). Advances in Intelligent Systems and Computing, vol. 173, pp. 35–46. Springer, Heidelberg. https://doi.org/10.1007/978-3-642-30859-8_4 (2012)
14. Ghobaei-Arani, M., Rahmanian, A.A., Shamsi, M., Rasouli-Kenari, A.: A learning-based approach for virtual machine placement in cloud data centers. Int. J. Commun. Syst. **31**(8), e3537 (2018)
15. Google Cloud Engine. https://cloud.google.com/compute/. Accessed 30 Jan 2019
16. Gonzalez-Martinez, J.A., Bote-Lorenzo, M.L., Gómez-Sánchez, E., Cano-Parra, R.: Cloud computing and education: a state-of-the-art survey. Comput. Educ. **80**, 132–151 (2015)
17. Horalek, J., Cimler, R., Sobeslav, V.: Virtualization solutions for higher education purposes. In: 25th International Conference RADIOELEKTRONIKA 2015, pp. 383–388. IEEE (2015)
18. Horalek, J., Soběslav, V.: Analysis and solution model of distributed computing in scientific calculations. In: Younas, M., Awan, I., Holubova, I. (eds.) MobiWIS 2017. LNCS, vol. 10486, pp. 314–324. Springer, Cham (2017). https://doi.org/10.1007/978-3-319-65515-4_26
19. Jenkins. https://jenkins.io/. Accessed 30 Jan 2019
20. Juan, Y., Yi-xiang, S.: The initial idea of new learning society which based on cloud computing. Mod. Educ. Technol. **20**(1), 14–17 (2010)
21. Kubernetes - Production-Grade Container Orchestration. https://www.kubernetes.io/. Accessed 30 Jan 2019
22. Kumar, J., Singh, A.K.: Workload prediction in cloud using artificial neural network and adaptive differential evolution. Future Gener. Comput. Syst. **81**, 41–52 (2018)
23. Komarek, A., Pavlik, J., Soběslav, V.: high level models for IaaS cloud architectures. In: Barbucha, D., Nguyen, N.T., Batubara, J. (eds.) New Trends in Intelligent Information and Database Systems. SCI, vol. 598, pp. 209–218. Springer, Cham (2015). https://doi.org/10.1007/978-3-319-16211-9_22
24. Maresova, P., Sobeslav, V.: Effective evaluation of cloud computing investment - application of cost benefit method analysis. E M Ekonomie Manage. **2**(20), 134–145 (2017)
25. Mercl, L., Pavlik, J.: The comparison of container orchestrators. In: Yang, X.-S., Sherratt, S., Dey, N., Joshi, A. (eds.) Third International Congress on Information and Communication Technology. AISC, vol. 797, pp. 677–685. Springer, Singapore (2019). https://doi.org/10.1007/978-981-13-1165-9_62

26. El Mhouti, A., Erradi, M., Nasseh, A.: Using cloud computing services in e-learning process: benefits and challenges. Educ. Inf. Technol. **23**(2), 893–909 (2018). https://doi.org/10.1007/s10639-017-9642-x
27. Microsoft - official website. https://microsoft.com. Accessed 30 Jan 2019
28. Mikulecky, P., Mercl, L.: Clouds for smart learning environments. In: 12th International Scientific Conference on Distance Learning in Applied Informatics Conference Proceedings (DIVAI 2018), pp. 473–480 (2019)
29. OpenStack. https://www.openstack.org/. Accessed 30 Jan 2019
30. Komarek, A., Pavlik, J., Sobeslav, V.: Performance analysis of cloud computing infrastructure. In: Younas, M., Awan, I., Holubova, I. (eds.) MobiWIS 2017. LNCS, vol. 10486, pp. 303–313. Springer, Cham (2017). https://doi.org/10.1007/978-3-319-65515-4_25
31. Pavlik, J., Sobeslav, V., Komarek, A.: Measurement of cloud computing services availability. In: Vinh, P.C., Vassev, E., Hinchey, M. (eds.) ICTCC 2014. LNICST, vol. 144, pp. 191–201. Springer, Cham (2015). https://doi.org/10.1007/978-3-319-15392-6_19
32. Sánchez, M., Aguilar, J., Cordero, J., Valdiviezo-Díaz, P., Barba-Guamán, L., Chamba-Eras, L.: Cloud computing in smart educational environments: application in learning analytics as service. New Advances in Information Systems and Technologies. AISC, vol. 444, pp. 993–1002. Springer, Cham (2016). https://doi.org/10.1007/978-3-319-31232-3_94
33. Sebastio, S., Ghosh, R., Mukherjee, T.: An availability analysis approach for deployment configurations of containers. IEEE Trans. Serv. Comput. **PP**, 1 (2018)
34. Siddiqui, S.T., Alam, S., Khan, Z.A., Gupta, A.: Cloud-based e-learning: using cloud computing platform for an effective e-learning. In: Tiwari, S., Trivedi, M.C., Mishra, K.K., Misra, A.K., Kumar, K.K. (eds.) Smart Innovations in Communication and Computational Sciences. AISC, vol. 851, pp. 335–346. Springer, Singapore (2019). https://doi.org/10.1007/978-981-13-2414-7_31
35. Sommerville, I.: Teaching cloud computing: a software engineering perspective. J. Syst. Softw. **9**(86), 2330–2332 (2013)
36. Stantchev, V., Colomo-Palacios, R., Soto-Acosta, P., Misra, S.: Learning management systems and cloud file hosting services: a study on students' acceptance. Comput. Hum. Behav. **31**(1), 612–619 (2014)
37. Thomas, P.Y.: Cloud computing a potential paradigm for practicing the scholarship of teaching and learning. Electron. Libr. **29**(2), 214–224 (2011)
38. Tuncay, E.: Effective use of cloud computing in educational institutions. Procedia Soc. Behav. Sci. **2**, 938–942 (2010)
39. VMware - official site. https://www.vmware.com/. Accessed 30 Jan 2019
40. Xu, L., Huang, D., Tsai, W.-T.: Cloud-based virtual laboratory for network security education. IEEE Trans. Educ. **57**(3), 145–150 (2014)
41. Zhu, Q., Agrawal, G.: Resource provisioning with budget constraints for adaptive applications in cloud environments. IEEE Trans. Serv. Comput. **5**(4), 497–511 (2012)
42. Zurita, G., Baloian, N., Frez, J.: Using the cloud to develop applications supporting geo-collaborative situated learning. Future Gener. Comput. Syst. - Int. J. Grid Comput. Sci. **34**, 124–137 (2014)

Improved Packet Delivery for Wireless Sensor Networks Using Local Automate Based Autonomic Network Architecture in a ZigBee Environment

K. N. Sanjay[1,2]([✉]), K. Shaila[2], and K. R. Venugopal[3]

[1] Department of Electronics and Communication Engineering, VTU-RC, Vivekananda Institute of Technology, Bengaluru, Karnataka, India
sanjaykenkare@gmail.com
[2] Vivekananda Institute of Technology, Bengaluru, Karnataka, India
[3] Bangalore University, Bengaluru, Karnataka, India

Abstract. A low cost, low power personal area network is formalized by IEEE 802.15.4 standard ZigBee Wireless Sensor Network. The most common way to construct a WSN using ZigBee is to use tree type network topology. This leads to large amount of energy consumption because of congestion in network. The node failures in a network topology, results in reconstructing the route of existing structure. Thus, a Local automate based autonomic network architecture is deployed at the MAC layer of ZigBee protocol. The architecture considers previous occurrences of probabilities of nodes and learns their behavior during transmission. This record an active state of each node, that inturn reduces congestion when neighboring node failure occurs. Simulation results provide 20% increase in unicast and multicast delivery rate. Finally, throughput of an entire network in a larger density dynamic environment increases.

Keywords: Autonomic network architecture (ANA) · LACAS · Local automate (LA) · Wireless Sensor Network · ZigBee

1 Introduction

With the expanding modernity of remote correspondences and detecting advances, different sensor-based applications, like industrial robots and electro-mechanical mechanization, creates enormous monetary and social implications. The potential for much more prominent effect has broad investigations on WSNs with ZigBee standards. This determines the industrial system and application layers for detecting information delivery rate [1–3].

The process requires backbone network with static environment and related nodes that are mobile. These nodes rely on the available power supply. Normally, traffic information is overheard to the cluster of a tree and its responsibilities in considering larger

P. C. Vinh and A. Rakib (Eds.): ICCASA 2020/ICTCC 2020, LNICST 343, pp. 300–309, 2021.
https://doi.org/10.1007/978-3-030-67101-3_24

density nodes. The information retrieved by each and every node in network leads to a main cluster node, which simultaneously receives supervisory message leading to congestion in a tree structure [4–6].

The Autonomic network Architecture is as shown in Fig. 1. It comprises of four dependent parameters while designing a MAC layer with ANA architecture.

Sensor Network Application: Disturbances occurred while changing MAC structure with WSNs that should not affect the built-in applications of WSNs.

Self-Configuring, Self-Healing: While introducing ANA, there exists adaptive nature when intermediate nodes fails and re-routes through the shortest path with existing neighboring nodes.

Self-Optimization, Self-Productive: Self-configuration leads to optimization of distance and the network becomes more productive.

Stochastic P2P Overlay: The occurrence of node at each successful transmission leads to consideration of probability in larger density nodes. This, provides basis for stochastic point to point overlay [7–10].

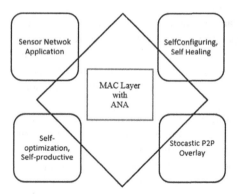

Fig. 1. Autonomic network architecture in MAC layer of WSNs.

Motivation: The vast application of ZigBee in real-time dynamic environment scenario requires design complexity for congestion with unicast and multicast deliveries. These involve designing of active and sleep modes of specific nodes at top layer of a network layer. Thus, designing MAC protocols is a primary concern that involves reliability, fault tolerance and throughput of network in a dynamic environment supporting unicast and multicast deliveries.

Reliability is appreciable during lesser congestion. Fault tolerance can be achieved by providing multi-rate transmission with effective unicast and multicast deliveries. Due to congestion if delivery of packets is unfair, it results in lower throughput. Thus, while designing ZigBee based application the designer has to address end user concern at lower data rates.

Contribution: The integration of complex dynamic environment designed for ZigBee can be achieved using Learning Automate based Autonomic Network Architecture (LA-ANA). The packet delivery ratio is to be optimized in a dynamic environment at smaller space with larger density sensor nodes that involves unicast and multicast delivery rates during low data rate operations. The designed architecture is figured at lower part of network layer of TCP/IP protocol called MAC layer. This provides a feasible solution in handling large sensor nodes by managing its rate of transmission with variable delivery rates. The Master/Slave combination is used with respective nodes based on their probability of occurrence in a routed path within dynamic environment and its range of communication.

Organization: Related work and Problem definition is discussed in Sect. 2 and 3 respectively. System and Mathematical model is discussed in Sect. 4. Implementation of the work using ZigBee with LA-ANA architecture is described in Sect. 5. Simulation and its performance evaluation are discussed in Sect. 6.

2 Related Work

Due to advances in technology for communication in various static and dynamic environments requires multi-rate selection in particular with industrial applications as discussed in [1]. Thus, while operating with lower data rate requires more attention of user and its capability in providing the solution for a desired application. Li et al. [2] utilizes the entire network covering larger density nodes in a dynamic environment that could handle with coexistence networks beyond an available Wi-Fi gains frequency for multiple propagation.

Denial of service attack in autonomicity [3] has to be handled in a better way combining Hilbert transformation along with trust evaluation of sensor node activity. Thus, at transmitting and receiving sections a low cost digital solution can be calculated in handling the congestion along with multicast and unicast packet deliveries. This application can be utilized in real-time health monitoring systems and in railway monitoring that are self-powered and has higher throughput as discussed in [4–7].

In designing, application oriented protocol disturbing MAC layer of the network using autonomicity is considered. It includes interference aware with layer decomposition [8]. This involves threading channels and their dependencies on neighboring network cast. Thus, leading to multi-packet reception and can be efficiently used in an indoor dynamic environments [9, 10].

The module based approach as discussed in [11] provides a feature selection that discriminates multiple analysis for device omission and fewer electrical applications. This brings in an enhancement in IoT and the concept of coexistence [12]. The module leads to two layered design in a ZigBee environment, increasing implementation cost but provides low powered network. This requires fast error recovery techniques as robustness in WSNs is different [13, 14].

3   Problem Definition

Problem Statement: The dynamic environment design using ZigBee with transmission of large number of packets at comparable low data rate can cause congestion. This can be avoided by limiting unicast and multicast delivery.

The objective of our work is to.

i.   Implement unicast and multicast at lower rate of transmission.
ii. Increasing throughput by considering the active and sleep nodes accordingly in unicast and multicast delivery rate.

Assumptions: Few of our assumption in building the network model are -

i.   Combined process of Local automate and Autonomic Network Architecture.
ii. Active and Sleep node selection based on their probability of occurrence in a selected shortest path.

4   System and Mathematical Model

The trouble-free network at larger density with low data rate is implemented using LA based ANA architecture. This leads to increased packet delivery ratio and fault tolerance level in a dynamic environment. The architecture involves back pressure mechanism while calculating probability of occurrence of each node and at an initial stage local automate process addresses at lower layer of Network Layer (MAC Layer). This is followed by Autonomic Network Architecture that involves an intermediate node and sink node with data flow rate regulation. This improves the overall packet delivery rate and supports unicast and multicast deliveries during low data rates. Thus, network throughput is substantially increased with lowered fault occurrence.

4.1   Mathematical Model

Let us consider n number of nodes in a ZigBee dynamic environment with specific time t at $n + 1$ scenario is given by,

$$P_{(n+1)} = \left[P_{(1)}, P_{(2)}, \ldots, P_{(i)}, \ldots, P_{(n+1)} \right] \tag{1}$$

where, $P_{(n+1)}$ is the probability of occurrence of each node.

The prediction of an error node and its neighboring data acquired is $e(n + 1)$ and is computed as,

$$e(n + 1) = \left| P_{(n)}(i + 1) - P_{(n)}(j + 1) \right| \tag{2}$$

The probability of the ith and j^{th} node with active/sleep mode is considered.

This process, finds actual probability of occurrence of each node in an active path chosen between source and destination.

The ANA based environment can be modeled as $P_{ANA(n)}$ and is given by,

$$P_{(n)} = \left[P_{(i)}, P_{(j)}, P_{(n+1)}\right] \tag{3}$$

The selected probability rely on neighboring nodes if an active node fails ($P_{(n)}$). Thus, involving a complete LA-ANA based architecture while routing larger packets in a larger density dynamic environment.

5 Implementation

The LA-ANA based architecture is implemented in two phases for a ZigBee environment. Figure 2 illustrates the random placement of nodes in a dynamic environment. At few places, nodes are nearby and a large gap can be found at center. This kind of randomness is considered and the propagation of unicast and multicast is explained using Fig. 3.

Fig. 2. Sensor nodes are varyed from 20–50.

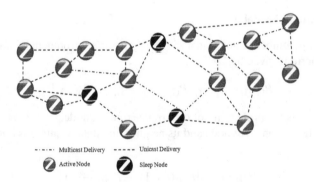

Fig. 3. ZigBee network environment

Multicast delivery is provided for a larger distance and unicast is handled at shorter distance as shown in Fig. 3. The inactive nodes represented, is due to lower battery levels, multiple requests from neighboring nodes and many more such conditions. In such a situation, unicast and multicast delivery rate is switched between nodes based on probability of occurrence in the shortest path. The process is so called *Local automate with Autonomic Network Architecture*. This architecture provides greater adaptability and increased throughput. The process is explained using flowchart as shown in Fig. 4.

In first phase, the network is configured in an AODV environment. Now, source and destinations nodes are located with initial probabilities. The probability of each node is considered based on the occurrence as an intermediate nodes from source to destination.

With shortest path chosen from a source to destination and distance number is provided for the entire selected path. Once, selection is chosen, packets are sent at normal data rate in unicast delivery. The second phase commences as LA-ANA chooses generic path defined primarily in an initial phase.

Now, the algorithm chooses earlier probabilities of nodes and then estimates new distance in case of node failure. Then, second phase returns the determined new probabilities of path that are updated. Next, find error nodes and making the process recursive and adaptive. While considering these nodes that are not pre-defined can be located and can be assigned with functionality as a new originator based on the probability. If the probability of occurrence is too low then sensor functionality can be enhanced based on neighboring activities leading to multicast delivery with forwarding packets at much higher transmission rate. This supports normal delivery rate in multi-hop transmission. Hence, unicast and multicast delivery can be achieved at much simpler process using the LA-ANA based architecture at the MAC layer of the protocol stack.

The timing diagram shown in Fig. 5 is for ZigBee environment. The packet sent from the source is with host controller wherein intermediate nodes I_i and I_j are involved. The retransmission, successful transmission and acknowledgement availability is provided in timing diagram. The dotted lines in nodes I_i and I_j represents presence of nodes in case of node failure with either I_1 or I_2. This complete setup provides an autonomic network based architecture for a ZigBee environment.

6 Simulation and Performance Evaluation

6.1 Simulation Environment

The ZigBee operating rage is at 2.4 GHz with 100 m range is selected. The power density of propagation limit is doubled due to increase in reception level at multi-range transmission to support multicast delivery. The value of 5 is chosen as a random number for phase 2 of path loss. The NS2 simulation environment is selected to build simulation environment with time of 50msecs. Protocol disturbed are MAC protocol with SNR bound reception and 20 dBm of total transmitted power.

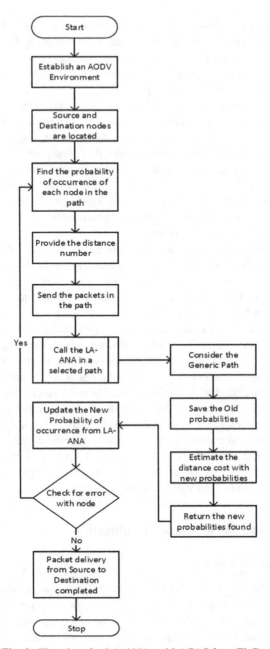

Fig. 4. Flowchart for LA-ANA and LACAS for a ZigBee

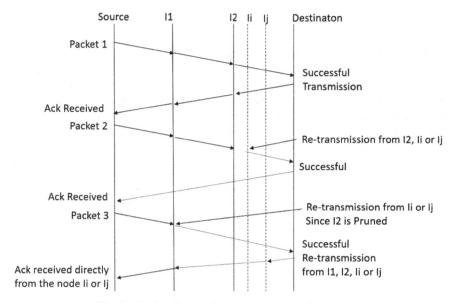

Fig. 5. Timing diagram between active and sleep nodes

6.2 Performance Analysis

The packet delivery and rate of change in probabilities of occurrence of nodes in shortest path chosen play a vital role in increasing throughput. Figure 6 shows the throughput of LA-ANA based network compared with LACAS network. There is substantial increase in throughput and is around 25% at larger density nodes. The throughput has reduced not less than 50% while involving 1000 nodes in a larger density dynamic environment.

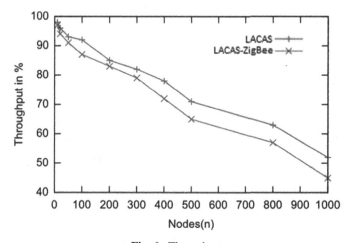

Fig. 6. Throughput

Hence, provides the users with LACAS-ZigBee algorithm capability in handling larger density nodes.

Figure 7 and Fig. 8 shows unicast and multicast delivery in LACAS-ZigBee and is better than the LACAS environment. This is due to congestion control at MAC layer and large density nodes that is considered in our scenario. There is 20% improvement in unicast delivery and around 15% in multicast delivery ratio. This substantial increase with delivery ratios is due to local automate that considers probability of occurrence of each node with its active and sleep nodes in a routed path. Thus, providing a stable design for designing ZigBee environment.

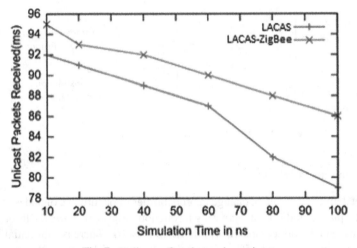

Fig. 7. Delivery of packets using unicast.

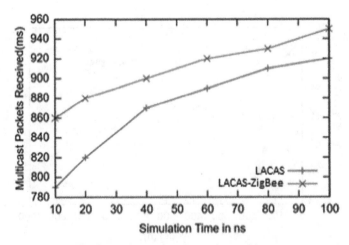

Fig. 8. Delivery of packets using multicast.

7   Conclusions

The cascode architecture is deployed for a ZigBee based dynamic environment. The process involves adaptability in choosing active nodes in presence of failing neighboring nodes mainly grounded on probability of occurrence. It provides a controlled congestion mechanism with increased throughput leading to improved unicast and multicast delivery ratio between source and destination. Thus, applying for a larger denser network in a dynamic environment provides greater adaptability during transmission.

References

1. Kong, L., Cao, Y., He, L., Chen, G., Wu, M., He, T.: Multi-rate selection in ZigBee. IEEE/ACM Trans. Netw. **27**(3), 1055–1068 (2019)
2. Li, P., Yan, Y., Yang, P., Li, X., Lin, Q.: Correction to "coexist Wi-Fi for ZigBee networks With fine-grained frequency approach". IEEE Access **7**, 170474–170484 (2019)
3. Chen, H., Meng, C., Shan, Z., Fu, Z., Bhargava, B.: A Novel low-rate denial of service attack detection approach in ZigBee wireless sensor network by combining hilbert-huang transformation and trust evaluation. IEEE Access **7**, 32853–32866 (2019)
4. Vayssade, T., Azais, F., Latorre, L., Lefevre, F.: Low-cost digital test solution for symbol error detection of RF ZigBee transmitters. IEEE Trans. Device Mater. Reliab. **19**(1), 16–24 (2019)
5. Alwan, O., Rao, K.P.: Dedicated real-time monitoring system for health care using ZigBee. Healthc. Technol. Lett. **4**(4), 142–144 (2017)
6. Gao, M., Wang, P., Wang, Y., Yao, L.: Self-powered ZigBee wireless sensor nodes for railway condition monitoring. IEEE Trans. Intell. Transp. Syst. **19**(3), 900–909 (2018)
7. Ding, F., Song, A., Zhang, D., Tong, E., Pan, Z., You, X.: Interference-aware wireless networks for home monitoring and performance evaluation. IEEE Trans. Autom. Sci. Eng. **15**(3), 1286–1297 (2018)
8. Shao, C., Park, H., Roh, H., Lee, W.: DOTA: physical-layer decomposing and threading for ZigBee/Wi-Fi Co-transmission. IEEE Wirel. Commun. Lett. **8**(1), 133–136 (2019)
9. Wang, Z., Kong, L., Xu, K., Chen, G., He, L.: PPM: preamble and postamble-based multi-packet reception for green ZigBee communication. IEEE Trans. Green Commun. Netw. **3**(3), 817–827 (2019)
10. Alvarez, Y., Heras, F.L.: ZigBee-based sensor network for indoor location and tracking applications. IEEE Lat. Am. Trans. **14**(7), 3208–3214 (2016)
11. Hebbar, S., Pattar, P., Golla, V.: A mobile ZigBee module in a traffic control system. IEEE Potentials **35**(1), 19–23 (2016)
12. Bihl, T., Bauer, K., Temple, M.: Feature selection for RF fingerprinting with multiple discriminant analysis and using ZigBee device emissions. IEEE Trans. Inf. Forensics Secur. **11**(8), 1862–1874 (2016)
13. Guardarrama, J., Freire, R., Areu, O.: A proposed wireless system to real time monitoring in power transformer. IEEE Lat. Am. Trans. **14**(4), 1570–1574 (2016)
14. Ndih, E.M., Cherkaoui, S.: On enhancing technology coexistence in the IoT era: ZigBee and 802.11 case. IEEE Access **4**, 1835–1844 (2016)

Hybrid Domain Steganography for Embedding DES Encrypted QR Code Using Random Bit Binary Search

B. S. Shashikiran[1(✉)], K. Shaila[2], and K. R. Venugopal[3]

[1] VTU-RC, Department of Electronics and Communication Engineering,
Vivekananda Institute of Technology, Bengaluru, Karnataka, India
shashikiran.bisileri@gmail.com
[2] Department of Electronics and Communication Engineering,
Vivekananda Institute of Technology, Bengaluru, Karnataka, India
[3] Bangalore University, Bengaluru, Karnataka, India

Abstract. Steganography is a technology used for hiding the digital information into an electronic document so that it can be used only by the authorized entity and not available to trespassers. In the recent era, QR code is used versatile in all the applications. The data capacity of QR code is more as the information is codified in the form of image. Image Steganography can be achieved in spatial, transformation or hybrid domain. In this paper, a novel hybrid domain Steganography is employed for embedding encrypted QR code image in Source Image to get stego Image using Discrete Wavelet Transforms and Random Bit Binary Search (DWT - RBBS) technique. The information is encrypted using DES encryption algorithm and is codified to QR code image. This QR code image is then embedded into the source image using DWT-RBBS technique resulting in multiple level of security.

Keywords: DES · DWT · QR code · RBBS · Stego image · Steganography · Source image

1 Introduction

With the rapid growth in technology and business, QR code [1] is gaining a lot of importance in day to day technical and business activities. Initially QR code was using in the automotive industries just to track the vehicles during manufacturing. Presently, QR codes have become very common outside the automotive industry due its Storage capacity, fast readability and can be easily scanned. The application of QR code [2] is extended to item identification, product tracking, document management and so on. In near future, QR code [3] can be used massively in most of the fields to make it easy for tracking the information. Just by scanning the QR code by mobile devices or the scanning devices, information can be read and used further, making things simple for getting the information. Most of the application or organization needs to protect the information from the unauthorized persons. Since the information can be easily accessible just by

P. C. Vinh and A. Rakib (Eds.): ICCASA 2020/ICTCC 2020, LNICST 343, pp. 310–322, 2021.
https://doi.org/10.1007/978-3-030-67101-3_25

scanning QR code leads to information security issues. Whenever the secured information is stored in QR code, it needs to be protected from the unauthorized person. This can be achieved by providing security to the information. The cryptography techniques can provide a security to the information and steganography techniques can hide the QR code [4]. Combining cryptography and steganography, information is strongly secured and safe.

Cryptography [5] is an art and practice of techniques used for secure communication between the authorized entities in the presence of unauthorized entity. Cryptography [6] falls into two basic types namely symmetric key cryptography where same key is used and is called private key, asymmetric key cryptography uses different keys. To encrypt the message in asymmetric key cryptography, anyone can use the key called public key to encrypt a data or message so that only authorized person can decrypt using a key called private key. Digital data is represented as a binary digit of strings. The cryptosystem needs to process these strings in to another string. Generally, a cipher is a secret code created using some mathematical functions. In block ciphers, binary plain text is processed for encryption in group of bits at a time. There are Enormous block cipher algorithms which are in use, few of them are DES (Digital Encryption standard), Triple DES [7], AES (Advanced Encryption standards) and so on. This work is focused towards DES encryption algorithm.

Steganography [8, 9] is also a technique for securing information by concealing secret information in other information. The intention of steganography is to hide information from unauthorized person. The information can be a text, audio or image/video represented in digital form. Based on the type of information steganography is classified [10] as text steganography, audio steganography and image steganography nevertheless combination of these can be used. The most interesting and trending type of steganography is image based because of the enormous features of digital image. In image steganography, the secret information can be either a text message or other image, this secret information bits are hidden in cover image. Image steganography is mainly classified into three major types. Spatial domain, transformation domain and hybrid domain-based [11] steganography.

Commonly it is considered that cryptography and steganography are the two faces of the same coin serving the same purpose with different approaches. Cryptography does employ altering the structure of the information whereas steganography does not alter the structure of the information. The usage of steganography combined with an encryption results in high security of an information. The purpose of this work is to provide information security at multilevel by hiding DES encrypted message QR code in cover image.

1.1 Motivation

With the widespread development in digital technology the information plays a vital role and got tremendous usage. This information needs to be secured and many algorithms have been developed. Cryptography is used for encrypting the information and steganography used to hide the information. With the development of QR code, it is rapidly used in many applications as it can store more information than previously existing bar code. The QR code is easily accessible by any QR code scanner to get the information and is easily available everywhere as it is not secured for access by unauthorized persons. The main idea is to secure or embed this QR code and its information from the intruders and to make it available for authorized persons by employing cryptography and steganography together.

1.2 Contribution

The QR code is used for storing the data efficiently and the information stored in the QR code is available to public straightforwardly by scanning it. When the information stored in the QR code need to be available for limited users and need to be protected from the intruders, it should be protected. In this work information is encrypted using DES encryption and then stored in QR code to protect the information at first level. To increase the security feature for the QR code, it is embedded into source image using steganography technique. Steganography is performed in hybrid domain using DWT technique. Random bit binary search is used for replacement of bits to embed the QR code in sub bands of source image in the proposed work.

1.3 Organization

Related work and Problem definition is discussed in Sect. 2 and 3 respectively. Implementation of the work using proposed method is described in Sect. 4. Performance evaluation is discussed in Sect. 5.

2 Related Work

Cryptography and steganography are practiced for providing security to electronic information. With development of electronic information, the entire world is adapting to the changes of digital technology era such that every information is accessible at finger tips. Development of QR code made every information availability much easier raising difficulty in providing security to electronic information. Cryptography and steganography algorithms are developed and employed at different level in providing security and embedding information respectively. The encrypted information is codified to QR code and embedded in source image increases the robustness to information security.

Iuliia et al. [12] provided the information of the QR code features and structure for encoding the information in it and also developed two level QR code which has public and private storage level. Public level is a common QR storage level and private level is designed by modifying the black region by specific pattern. This QR code is used for document authentication. Baharav and Ramakrishna et al. [13] proposed a blending of image into QR code which alters the source pixel in QR code so that they are transformed to any RGB values using statistical analysis to increase the storage capacity. Gonzalo et al. [14] developed a concept of embedding QR code in images with bounded PDE (Probability of detection error) where the embedded information is visibly available in the resulted image and it adds a constraint on the resolution of the image.

High capacity QR code for fast decoding is proposed in [15] for decoding the color QR code at the faster rate. Algorithm is designed based on cross module interference and quadratic discriminate analysis, mainly to avoid the distortion during decoding message from QR code. ASA_QR algorithm [16] provided security to the information at two stages. In the first stage, message is encrypted using symmetric key cryptography and codified to QR code image. In the later stage, QR code image is embedded into cover image in random manner using steganography technique making it difficult to extract the information for the unauthorized persons. Simple bit replacement steganography technique is employed for embedding QR code.

Linjieet et al. [17] developed an algorithm for efficient steganography using UED -Uniform Embedding Distortion function by incorporating STC and the embedding modification is spread uniformly to quantize the DCT coefficients. Vahid et al. [18] proposed a steganography algorithm by minimizing the statistical detectability on the content of image by estimating the multivariant gaussian function.

Vladimír et al. [19] proposed an algorithm to embed encoded secret information using QR code into an image. QR code is embedded into an image using DWT – Discrete wavelet transform. Secret information encoded into a QR code image is protected with encryption algorithm to provide high level of security to information. DWT is applied on a cover image to get its sub bands. HH sub band is used for embedding QR code just by using LSB replacement technique.

Daphney and Girish [20] developed an algorithm to hide data using image steganography and QR code. Information to be hidden is encoded in QR code and this QR code is embedded in to cover media. Cover media can be an audio, image or a video. Based on the cover media selected the QR code is embedded using LSB technique. Ramesh et al. [21] proposed hybrid steganography algorithm for embedding QR coded secret information into an image using DWT technique. The embedding and extraction of QR code is performed in frequency domain and the text message is codified to QR image. The text information is not encrypted before converting into QR code image.

3 Problem Definition

3.1 Problem Statement

It is noticed that QR code is widely used with the development of electronic media. QR code stores the data efficiently and is easily accessible. Securing information embedded in QR code is important when it is a private data and it is a challenging task. The proposed work is to develop an algorithm to encrypt the information using DES encryption and codify it to QR code to provide first level of security. Embedding QR code in source image is achieved by steganography using DWT and RBBS to provide security at high level.

3.2 Objectives

The objective of our work is to

i.   To provide data security using DES encryption.
ii. To integrate the encrypted message in QR code.
iii. To Embed QR code in an image.

3.3 Assumptions

Few of our assumption in building the Algorithm are:

i.   Size of the cover image is M × M i.e., square image.
ii. Size of the QR code image is less than M/2 × M/2 of cover image.
iii. DES encrypted information should be within the limit of QR code capacity.

4 Implementation

In the proposed method an algorithm is developed to provide security at multiple levels. In this work, secret information is encrypted using DES algorithm and converted to QR code image. The QR code is then hidden in an image using steganography technique. The prerequisite for the work is the DES encrypted information capacity should be based on the version and Error-correction level of QR code used and the QR code image size should be less than the half of the cover image used for steganography. The cover image is decomposed into its R, G and B planes. Each decomposed plane are transformed to frequency domain using DWT technique resulting in four sub-bands LL, LH, HL and HH. In the frequency domain the QR code image containing DES encrypted information is embedded in HH band of each plane using random binary search technique. IDWT is applied on all the bands to generate the stego image in spatial domain.

To retrieve the information embedded in stego image, DWT is applied to decomposed R, G and B planes of stego image and random binary search technique is applied to HH bands of each plane to get the QR code image. This QR code image is then scanned to get the DES encrypted information which is then decrypted to get original information. The block diagram for the embedding and retrieving secret information using QR code is as shown in Fig. 1.

4.1 Embedding Process

The process of embedding secret information is done at multiple levels. The information is first considered as plain text and this plain text is encrypted using DES encryption standards. Block diagrams in Fig. 2 shows the DES encryption and decryption method. A QR code is generated on the DES encrypted information to get QR code image. This QR code image is resized as per the assumption made.

This QR code image is embedded in cover image or source image. DWT is applied on source image R, G and B planes to get four sub bands. The sub-band LL contains the maximum information of the image and attributes of images are present in other three sub-bands which are redundant for the information of source image and hence these sub bands are used for embedding QR code image.

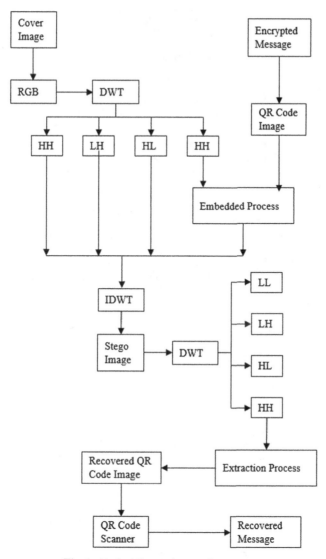

Fig. 1. Embedding and extraction process

The source image is represented by,

$$S(i,j) = \begin{bmatrix} S(0,0) & S(0,1) & \cdots\cdots & S(0,N-1) \\ S(1,0) & S(1.1) & \cdots\cdots & S(1,N-1) \\ \vdots & \vdots & & \vdots \\ S(M,0) & S(M,1) & \cdots\cdots & S(M-1,N-1) \end{bmatrix}$$

Here, M = N

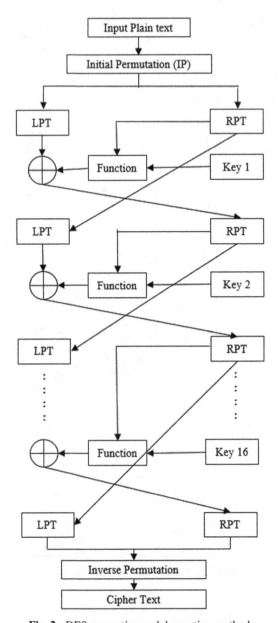

Fig. 2. DES encryption and decryption methods

The QR code image is represented by

$$Q(m,n) = \begin{bmatrix} Q(0,0) & Q(0,1) & \cdots\cdots & Q(0,K-1) \\ Q(1,0) & Q(1.1) & \cdots\cdots & Q(1,K-1) \\ \vdots & \vdots & & \vdots \\ Q(L,0) & Q(L,1) & \cdots\cdots & Q(L-1,K-1) \end{bmatrix}$$

Here, $K = L$

DWT is applied to source image resulting in sub-bands LL, LH, HL and HH. The last three bands are used for embedding QR code image and hence they are converted to UNM of 1 byte between 0 to 255. The sub-band HH is considered and divided into upper and lower nibbles. 7,6,5,4 are the upper nibble bit planes and 3,2,1,0 are the lower nibble bit planes. The random binary search is done in the topmost bit plane of the upper nibble and number of 0's and 1's are counted, whichever is highest in the considered plane. Then, pixels of lower nibble are replaced with QR code image pixels. Similar steps are carried on HL and LH.

Sub-bands coefficients of a source image after applying DWT are represented by

$$\hat{S}(i,j) = \begin{cases} \widehat{S_1}(m,n)\cdots LL \text{ band} \\ \widehat{S_2}(m,n)\cdots LH \text{ band} \\ \widehat{S_3}(m,n)\cdots HL \text{ band} \\ \widehat{S_4}(m,n)\cdots HH \text{ band} \end{cases}$$

Embedding of QR code image into HH, HL and LH sub bands are done using the bit replacement in lower nibble based on the position of binary number selected at one of the bit plane at upper nibble. For all the bands same operation is performed.

Pictorial representation of embedding process is shown in Fig. 3.

Sub-band coefficients after hiding data in transformation domain can be represented by,

$$\left.\begin{array}{l} \widehat{S_1}(m,n)\cdots LL \text{ band} \\ \widehat{D_2}(m,n)\cdots LH \text{ band} \\ \widehat{D_3}(m,n)\cdots HL \text{ band} \\ \widehat{D_4}(m,n)\cdots HH \text{ band} \end{array}\right\} = \hat{D}(i,j)$$

Applying IDWT to get the image in spatial domain is the stego image represented by,

$$D(i,j) = \begin{bmatrix} D(0,0) & D(0,1) & \cdots\cdots & D(0,N-1) \\ D(1,0) & D(1.1) & \cdots\cdots & D(1,N-1) \\ \vdots & \vdots & & \vdots \\ D(M,0) & D(M,1) & \cdots\cdots & D(M-1,N-1) \end{bmatrix}$$

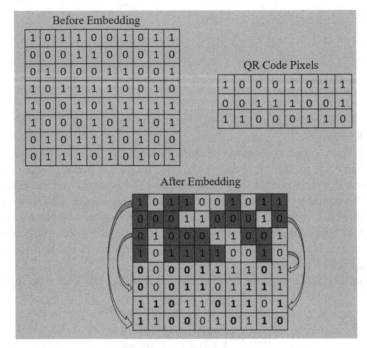

Fig. 3. Random bit replacement

4.2 Decryption Process

For recovering or decrypting secret information from QR code image embedded in stego image reverse operation need to be performed. DWT is applied on stego image to get the sub-bands. HH, HL and LL sub-bands are upgraded to UNM represented by a byte i.e., between 0 to 255. Upper nibble of all sub-bands contains the information of source image and lower nibble contains part of the source image and embedded QR code image. Binary search is done on the topmost bit plane of the upper nibble and based on the maximum count of binary number either 0's or 1's, corresponding bits at the lower nibble are retrieved and arranged properly to get the QR code image. This QR code is scanned and DES encrypted information is obtained. The obtained encrypted information is decrypted to recover the hidden information.

The sub-bands coefficients are obtained by applying DWT on the stego-image represented by

$$\hat{D}(i,j) = \begin{cases} \widehat{D_1}(m,n) \cdots LL \text{ band} \\ \widehat{D_2}(m,n) \cdots LH \text{ band} \\ \widehat{D_3}(m,n) \cdots HL \text{ band} \\ \widehat{D_4}(m,n) \cdots HH \text{ band} \end{cases}$$

Decrypting QR code images from sub-bands HH, HL and LH involves reverse process of finding the bits in lower nibble based on the position of binary number selected at one of the bit plane at upper nibble. For all the sub bands same operation is performed. Pictorial representation of embedding process is shown in Fig. 4.

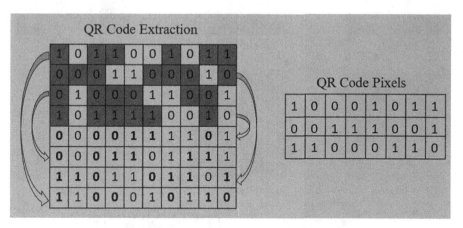

Fig. 4. QR code extraction using random bits

5 Performance Analysis

To understand the performance analysis, algorithm is tested on more than 100 images and few of them are shown in Fig. 5. The encryption process is performed by embedding DES encrypted QR code image in source image. the MSE and PSNR are considered as performance parameters with a regular source image of size 512×512 (8 bit pixel) and a QR code image is of size 256×256 (8-bit pixel) provides the hiding capacity much greater than 0.375, 0.468, 0.5625 bpp (the analysis is based on the number of QR code image bits and number of bits representing secret information used to embed in source image).

Different source images are used for embedding QR code images and its PSNR is tabulated in the results. Higher the hiding capacity, the PSNR value decreases. PSNR is maintained around 54 dB in the proposed algorithm.

Fig. 5. (a) – (f) cover image, (g) QR code image, (h) Encrypted QR code, (i) QR code Extracted, (j) Extracted DES encrypted QR code

For Different source images, the QR code without encryption and with DES encryption images are embedded to get stego image. The PSNR, NAE and BER obtained is as shown in Table (1).

Table 1. Performance values obtained for embedding QR code with and without encryption

Source Images	PSNR in dB without DES	PSNR in dB with DES
Image1	54.7310	54.7759
Image2	53.8156	53.8692
Image3	50.3404	50.3763
Image4	51.8876	51.9408
Image5	54.4728	55.5316
Image6	53.7281	53.7622

Proposed algorithm is compared with existing methods and it is observed that existing algorithms are performing well with steganography process but not involved in embedding QR code. The proposed algorithm results in good PSNR with an added security using encryption to QR code. The comparison of PSNR with existing algorithm is tabulated in Table 2.

Table 2. Comparison of proposed algorithm with other methods

	Reversible data hiding method	DWT-LSB method	QR code steganography method	Proposed method
Encryption	No	No	Yes	Yes
PSNR	46.21	52.43	50.24	54.67

6 Conclusions

Providing security to an information is utmost important in the digital era. Steganography is beneficial for embedding message or information. The embedding encrypted information QR code image in source image is proposed in the algorithm. The multiple level of security is provided to ensure the information cannot be hacked easily. The first level of security is provided using DES encryption and security is extended by converting the information to QR code and the next level of security is provided by embedding using steganography technique. The existing DES algorithm is used for encrypting secret information and steganography is performed in hybrid domain by applying DWT and random bit binary search employed to replace the bits for embedding QR code. The proposed algorithm resulted in good PSNR with multiple levels of security.

References

1. Chang, J.H.: An introduction to QR code using scholarly journals. Sci. Ed. J. **1**(2), 113–117 (2014)
2. Yuan, T., Wang, Y., Xu, K.: Two-layer QR codes. IEEE Trans. Image Process. **28**(9), 4413–4428 (2019)
3. Liu, Z., Zeng, Q., Wang, C., Lu, Q.: Application research of QR code barcode in validation of express delivery. In: Shen, G., Huang, X. (eds.) ECWAC 2011. CCIS, vol. 143, pp. 346–351. Springer, Heidelberg (2011). https://doi.org/10.1007/978-3-642-20367-1_56
4. Yanti, N., Surya, W.A., Akhyar, A., Frica A.A.: Implementation of Advanced Encryption Standard (AES) and QR code algorithm on digital legalization system. In: International Conference on Energy, Environment, Epidemiology and Information System (ICENIS), pp 1–7 (2018)
5. Alexandre, B., Richard, D., Nuno, A., Nuno, L., Marco, V.: Understanding how to use static analysis tool for detecting cryptography misuse in software. IEEE Trans. Relaibility **68**(4), 1384–1403 (2019)
6. Suguna, S., Dhanakoti, V., Manjupriya, R.: A study on symmetric and asymmetric key encryption algorithms. Int. Res. J. Eng. Technol. (IRJET) **3**(4), 27–31 (2016)
7. Kaur, N., Sodhi, S.: Data Encryption Standard Algorithm (DES) for secure data transmission. Int. J. Comput. Appl. **8**, 31–37 (2016)
8. Hang, Z., Kejiang, C., Weiming, Z., Nenghai, Y.: Comments on steganography using reversible texture synthesis. IEEE Trans. Image Process. **26**(4), 1623–1625 (2017)
9. Jie, W., Xiaoqing, J., et al.: A cover selection HEVC video steganography based on intra prediction mode. IEEE Access **7**, 119393–119402 (2019)
10. Sharma, R., Sharma, N.: A more private & secure E-mail system using image steganography (EPS) and data mining. In: International Conference on Advances in Information Communication Technology and Computing, Article no 104, pp 1–5 (2016)
11. Lokesswara Reddy, V.: Improved secure data transfer using video steganographic technique. Int. J. Rough Sets Data Anal. **4**(3), 16 (2017)
12. Iuliia, T., William, P.: Two-level QR code for private message sharing and document authentication. IEEE Trans. Inf. Forensics Secur. **11**(3), 571–583 (2016)
13. Baharav, Z., Kakarala, R.: Visually significant QR codes: image blending and statistical analysis. In: International Conference on Multimedia and Expo (ICME), pp 1–6 (2013)
14. Arce, G.R., Lau, D.L., Villarreal, O.P.: QR images: optimized image embedding in QR codes. IEEE Trans. Image Process. **23**(7), 2842–2853 (2014)
15. Lin, Pei-Yu., Chen, Y.-H.: High payload secret hiding technology for QR codes. EURASIP J. Image and Video Process. **2017**(1), 1–8 (2017). https://doi.org/10.1186/s13640-016-0155-0. Springer Open Access
16. Dev, S., Mondal, K., et al.: Advanced steganography algorithm using randomized intermediate QR host embedded within any encrypted secret message. Int. J. Mod. Educ. Comput. Sci. **6**, 59–67 (2012)
17. Guo, L., Ni, J., Shi, Y.: Uniform embedding for efficient JPEG steganography. IEEE Trans. Inf. Forensics Secur. **9**(5), 814–825 (2014)
18. Sedighi, V., Cogranne, R., Fridrich, J.: Content-adaptive steganography by minimizing statistical detectability. IEEE Trans. Inf. Forensics Secur. **11**(2), 221–234 (2016)
19. Vladimír, H., Martin, B., et al.: Image steganography with using QR code and cryptography. In: Conference on Radio Elektronika, Slovak republic, pp 1–4 (2016)
20. Daphney, J., Girish, S.: A method of data hiding in QR code using image steganography. Int. J. Adv. Res. Ideas Innov. Technol. **4**(3), 1111–1113 (2018)
21. Ramesh, M., Prabakaran, G., Bhavani, R.: QR-DWT code image steganography. Int. J. Comput. Intell. Inf. **3**(1), 9–13 (2013)

Design and Testing a Single-Passenger Eco-Vehicle

Tri Nhut Do[(⊠)], Quang Minh Pham, Hoa Binh Le-Nguyen,
Cao Tri Nguyen, and Hai Minh Nguyen-Tran

Van Lang University, Ho Chi Minh City 700000, Vietnam
trinhutdo@gmail.com, minh.minhphamquang@gmail.com,
binh.lnh@vlu.edu.vn, nguyencaotriktcn@gmail.com,
nthminh79@gmail.com

Abstract. Protection of the living environment for sustainable development is a concern of mankind. In particular, reducing CO_2 emissions is the top criteria. A number of technologies that include a method of improving fossil fuel consumption effectiveness have been introduced into new automobiles in order to limit the negative effects caused by CO_2. In this paper, new technological solutions will be proposed. They are combined in a novel method in order to improve vehicle engine performance, to improve ignition and air return systems and to reduce friction between vehicle and environment when it is moving. The propsed method is applied into a new implemented vehicle for Eco Mileage Challenge (EMC) 2019 which is organized annually by Honda Vietnam Compapy. All tests and tournament results of 240 km per liter of RON98 gasoline in average prove that the propsed method is feasible and effective in fuel savings.

Keywords: Fuel savings · CO_2 emissions · Sustainable development · Green life

1 Introduction

Fossil fuels are increasingly exhausted. The use of fossil fuels as the main source of energy for people to convert to other forms of energy for essential human life such as electricity, mechanical energy has been increasing CO_2 emissions. Since its invention in the 20th century to the present, cars and vehicles have helped people move faster and more conveniently. This makes people dependent on them and this growing demand is the main reason for the increase in toxic gases such as CO and CO_2. With the goal of slowing down emissions or reducing them in the near future, a lot of new technologies in automobile manufacturing have been developed. Technologies aimed at reducing fuel consumption and exhaust emissions take time to be adopted by all manufacturers, thus their impact and payback time to the consumer will be close to a decade [1]. The fuel that vehicles consume depends on many factors, such as the vehicle mass, the efficiency of the powertrain, and the duty cycles imposed on the vehicle or powertrain [2]. In order to address the factor of vehicle mass, many significant efforts that can be found in [3, 4] have been made to reduce the weight. For the second factor, hybridization and electrification make the powertrain system more efficient [5–7].

P. C. Vinh and A. Rakib (Eds.): ICCASA 2020/ICTCC 2020, LNICST 343, pp. 323–329, 2021.
https://doi.org/10.1007/978-3-030-67101-3_26

Recent progress in automatic driving technologies that include GPS-based or non-GPS-based [8] affects the third factor, duty cycles. Applied technologies in hybrid electric vehicles make it be are more fuel efficient compared to conventional vehicles due to the optimization of the engine operation and recovery of kinetic energy during braking. Therefore, they are represent a good and feasible solution to reduce fuel consumption and related emissions [9]. Moreover, focus on driver behaviour improvement for fuel consumption benefits is also taken into account in [10].

In this paper, all above factors and issues of vehicles and cars will be addressed. They are analyzed then solutions on vehicle engine, technology and vehicle electricity system will be proposed. They are detailed as follows: Sect. 2 decribes several solutions on engine, technology and electricity system with the aim of proposing a design method for fuel consumption reduction; testing results by the proposed method and discussion are in the Sect. 3 and conclusion will be given in Sect. 4.

2 Solutions and Design Method

2.1 Solution on Engine

Basically, the engine core is the cylinder with the piston inside moving up and down the cylinder. Single cylinder engines are typical of most lawn mowers, motobike. Cars have more than one cylinder such as four, six and eight cylinders in common. In a multi-cylinder engine, the cylinders usually are arranged in one of three ways: inline, V or flat (also known as horizontally opposed or boxer).

The engine going to be enhanced in this project is the single cylinder engine from Honda Vietnam Company. It consists of several parts such as Spark plug, Valves, Piston, Piston Rings, Connecting rod, Crankshaft and Sump.

The spark plug supplies the spark that ignites the air/fuel mixture so that combustion can occur. The intake and exhaust valves open at the proper time to let in air and fuel and to let out exhaust. Note that both valves are closed during compression and combustion so that the combustion chamber is sealed. A piston is a cylindrical piece of metal that moves up and down inside the cylinder. Piston rings provide a sliding seal between the outer edge of the piston and the inner edge of the cylinder. The rings serve two purposes: they prevent the fuel/air mixture and exhaust in the combustion chamber from leaking into the sump during compression and combustion and keep oil in the sump from leaking into the combustion area, where it would be burned and lost. The connecting rod connects the piston to the crankshaft. It can rotate at both ends so that its angle can change as the piston moves and the crankshaft rotates. The crankshaft turns the piston's up-and-down motion into circular motion just like a crank on a jack-in-the-box does.

The origin engine has been enhanced aims to reduce fuel consumption. It is shrunk and its weight dropped by half by cutting off unnecessary parts and components. The ignition steering wheel is also replaced in order to increase early ignition angle. The camshaft level is ground in order to reduce the force of the spring. The crankshaft is replaced by other higher level one on order to reduce the size of the combustion chamber. The pot is replaced to increase engine torque. The concave piston is replaced by a convex one in order to reduce combustion chamber size.

The carburetor has been improved as well by several method which include utilizing a 35 cc electronic carburetor, using moderation to optimize the fuel line, reducing the size of the float chamber, using activated carbon for the return air option, increasing the fuel-wind ratio from 18:1 to 26:1.

For ignition, the direct method is employed and the Iridium multi-point spark plug is utilized in order to improve ignition system to create a strong spark.

For return air, the method of refluxing exhaust air by pump is used. The return hot air is taken from the hottest point in the engine.

All improved solutions have been proposed aiming to reduce fuel consumption when the vehicle moves on street.

2.2 Solution on Technology

Firstly, several new technology are applied. A digital electronic temperature sensor is utilized in order to monitor the temperature of the return hot air stream. In the other hand, the engine rotation speed, the vehicle speed are monitored by digital electronic multimeter devices. In order to determine fuel consumption, a liquid sensor is ultilized and a program is coded by employing the following algorithm:

$$\begin{cases} ignore \quad if \quad new\_level \geq last\_level \\ save \quad new\_level \quad if \quad new\_level \geq last\_level \end{cases} \tag{1}$$

A software uses GPS system in order to monitor the position and to display speed, gravity, distance and position of the driver when vehicle moving during the test is developed as well.

Secondly, several methods are employed in order to improve the friction coefficient which include using low-coefficient viscosity; viscosity by forced method to reduce friction in the gearbox; changing crankshaft ball bearing, camshaft ball bearing and ball bearings at the wheels and using the smooth/non-spiny wheels as well.

2.3 Solution on Electricity System

The vehicle's electricity system is designed, calculated by re-selecting parts that are no longer in accordance with the original design of the manufacturer, in order to optimize the vehicle's performance. The more powerful and accurate integrated circuit (IC) is used in order to achieve the best optimal fuel efficiency.

2.4 Design Method

Our proposed method is a scientific combination of solutions that affect on the vehicle engine, apply new technology into monitoring and controlling the vehicle electricity system in order to optimize its performance and to reduce fuel consumption.

Design of Chassis. The chassis is built enough for one driver to drive. In order to save fuel, the chassis mass is reduced and its surface is covered by a kind of low wind coefficient paint in order to reduce friction as much as possible. Metal types such as Iron, Stainless Steel and Aluminum are utilized to make the chasis in dimesion of 2400 mm in length by 500 mm in wideth by 800 mm in height and in weight of 32 kilograms. The chasis level from ground is 100 mm. Figure 1 shows the chassis details.

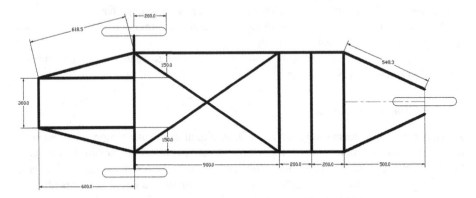

Fig. 1. Chassis drawing.

Design of Steering Mechanism and Clutch Separation Mechanism. It is made to fit the chassis. Specially, the wheel rotation angle is optimized in order to ensure the convenience in control.

Design and Implement of Vehicle Body. The vehicle body is designed based on the principles of aerodynamics to minimize friction that can cause and hinder the speed of the vehicle. Therefore, composite material is selected due to the lightweight but its firm and aesthetically.

In details, the composite material as following advantages:

- *Small specific weight.*
- *Good rigidity.*
- *Easy to work on any surface.*
- *Simple fabrication.*
- *High durability.*
- *Especially low processing costs.*

The vehicle body is made by utilizing following materials:

- *The no 2117 unsaturated Polyester resin type which is made in Singapore.*
- *The Mat 300 g/m2 glass fiber which is made by China.*
- *Curing catalyst of methyl ethyl keton peroxide (MEKP).*
- *Mold release agent, NaOH (10%), HCl (10%), seawater and distilled water.*

The vehicle body is made by following steps:

- *The mold is created. After processing the mold, its surface is cleaned and coated with a mold release agent.*
- *Clay, fiberglass and composite are applied on the mold later. Fiberglass is cut into shape and dried in minutes. The weight ratio of resin and fiberglass is 60 and 40, respectively.*
- *Conduct a retreading one by one layer of fiberglass.*
- *Roll the resin thoroughly into each layer so that the resin wet the yarn evenly and avoid the formation of air bubbles.*
- *After rolling is completed, allow to cure for 8 h at room temperature. However, drying should be better.*

Figure 2 shows the implmented vehicle body after casting.

Fig. 2. Vehicle body.

Design of Whole Vehicle. Other parameters and specifications of designed vehicle are listed in Table 1.

Table 1. Vehicle specifications.

Parameters	Specifications
Transmission ratio	6
Distance between 2 motor Shafts	460 mm
Driving posture	Sit down to drive
Steering angle Turning radius	8500 mm
Steering mechanism	Trapezoidal scales, rotating shafts, grippers
Winning structure	Disc brakes
Clutch separation mechanism	Directly from the engine

3   Testing Results and Discussion

3.1   Test at University

The implemented vehicle was tested on a distance of 9.5 km which is equal to the distance that it will have to perform at Honda EMC 2019. The driver is tasked to drive the implemented vehicle smoothly over several laps of school yard in order to complete a round test of 9.5 km distance. The elapsed time for each round test is around 30 min. The fuel comsuption in milliliter for each round test was recorded carefully by high precision electronic fuel meter and shown as in Table 2.

Table 2. Testing records.

Round no	Fuel consumption [milliliters]
#1	53
#2	54
#3	52
#4	51
#5	49
#6	52
#7	46
#8	47
#9	48
#10	50

According to Table 2, the mean and standard deviation is 50.2 ± 2.66 [ml] per round test which means that the implemented vehicle could travel an average distance of 189.24 km with only 1 L of RON95 gasoline.

3.2 Performance at the EMC 2019

The Eco-fuel-saving Honda contest was first organized by Honda Vietnam Company in 2010. After 9 years of successful organization in Vietnam, the contest has attracted an increasing number of participating teams with achievements that are enhanced year by year. With the main challenge of "How many kilometers can you travel with 1 L of gasoline?", The Honda Eco Mileage Challenge (Honda EMC) contest is a playground where participants have the opportunity to apply their novel innovative ideas and unique technology into Honda's 4-stroke engine to create competitive vehicles in terms of fuel efficiency, travel the farthest distance with only 1 L of gasoline.

At Honda EMC 2019, each team performed 8 laps on a total distance of 9.5 km with an average speed of at least 25 km/h and an average time of 22 min 24 s. Fuel consumption efficiency (km per liter) is calculated based on actual fuel consumption and the team with the highest performance is the winner.

As a result, a team with implemented vehicle performed an average of 220 km per liter of RON98 gasoline and ranked in top 50 over 158 participating teams.

4 Conclusion

A desgin method of a single-passenger eco-vehicle has been proposed with solutions for innovation of vehicle body, improvement of engine and enhance of driving aiming to save fuel consumption. Many tests at university proved that ability in fuel consumption is low at 189.24 km per liter of RON95 gasoline. The standard deviation of 5.29% prove the stability of desgined vehicle in traveling path. The more detailed and scientific designs will be researched and implemented to optimize the ability of eco-vehicle fuel consumption in the future.

Acknowledgement. Thanks to TDMU students for implementing and testing the vehicle.

References

1. Alson, J., Ellies, B., Ganss, D.: Interim Report: New Powertrain Technologies and Their Projected Costs. U.S. Environmental Protection Agency EPA420-R-05-012 (2005)
2. Alvarez, M., et al.: Reducing road vehicle fuel consumption by exploiting connectivity and automation: a literature survey. In: Proceedings of International Symposium on Advanced Vehicle Control, Beijing, China, pp. 1–6, July 2018
3. Galos, J., Sutcliffe, M., Cebon, D., Piecyk, M., Greening, P.: Reducing the energy consumption of heavy goods vehicles through the application of lightweight trailers: Fleet case studies. Transp. Res. D, Transp. Environ. **41**, 40–49 (2015)
4. Hardwick, A.P., Outteridge, T.: Vehicle lightweighting through the use of molybdenum-bearing advanced high-strength steels (AHSS). Int. J. Life Cycle Assess. **21**(11), 1616–1623 (2015). https://doi.org/10.1007/s11367-015-0967-7
5. Liu, J., Peng, H.: Modeling and control of a power-split hybrid vehicle. IEEE Trans. Control Syst. Technol. **16**(6), 1242–1251 (2008)
6. Kim, N., Cha, S., Peng, H.: Optimal control of hybrid electric vehicles based on Pontryagin's minimum principle. IEEE Trans. Control Syst. Technol. **19**(5), 1279–1287 (2011)
7. Kum, D., Peng, H., Bucknor, N.K.: Supervisory control of parallel hybrid electric vehicles for fuel and emission reduction. J. Dyn. Syst. Meas. Control **133**(6), 061010 (2011)
8. Do, T.N., Tan, U-X.: Novel velocity update applied for IMU-based wearable device to estimate the vertical distance. In: IEEE 2019 1st International Conference on Electrical, Control and Instrumentation Engineering (ICECIE), Kuala Lumpur, Malaysia, pp. 1–4 (2019)
9. Tang, L., Rizzoni, G., Onori, S.: Energy management strategy for HEVs including battery life optimization. IEEE Trans. Transp. Electrification **1**(3), 211–222 (2015)
10. Hari, D., Brace, C.J., Vagg, C., Poxon, J., Ash, L.: Analysis of a driver behaviour improvement tool to reduce fuel consumption. In: 2012 International Conference on Connected Vehicles and Expo (ICCVE), Beijing, China, pp. 208–213 (2012)

A Study on the Methology of Increasing Safety for Cometto MSPE System

Hai Minh Nguyen Tran$^{(\boxtimes)}$, Quang Minh Pham,
Hoa Binh Le Nguyen, Cao Tri Nguyen, and Tri Nhut Do

Van Lang University, Ho Chi Minh City 700000, Vietnam
nthminh79@gmail.com, minh.minhphamquang@gmail.com,
binh.lnh@vlu.edu.vn, nguyencaotriktcn@gmail.com,
trinhutdo@gmail.com

Abstract. In recent years, the heavy transport industry has been developing strongly, the transportation of super long and overweight packages is more advantageous due to modern transportation systems applying the achievements and development of technology. The leading trailer manufactors in the world such as: Cometto, Nicolas, Kamag, and Goldhofer… increasingly research and manufacture for this heavy transport industry. In Vietnam, leading transport companies have invested in self-propelled tractors from Cometto (Italy) to transport these goods. However, during operation, safety has been revealed. Therefore, in order to further enhance the safety of the entire system when transporting large economic parcels to the required location, a method is proposed that the throttle valve have been attached to appropriate position in the hydraulic pump system. The efficiency of throttle assembly is verified in practice when applying this improved trailer system for transporting the drilling rigs up to 3,200 tons in Vietnam.

Keywords: MSPE · Heavy transport · Self-propelled trailers · Hydraulic system

1 Introduction

Recently, the transport of oversized and overweight packages with high safety requirements for people and the cargo is extremely important to businesses in the heavy transport industry. The road surface is the most common object to be damaged during the transportation of these special packages. Therefore, many methods proposed as solutions to solve this road surface problem in [1, 2]. The oversized and overweight packages such as: 1) Oil rig components need to be transported from the installation location to the Barge and then pulled to the sea for completion; 2) Transformers from several dozen tons to nearly 300 tons need to be transported to power stations; 3) Concrete beam girders that need to be transported into a common site are transported using large-capacity tractors to push or pull cargo trailers, which is called the towing method and illustrated in Fig. 1.

P. C. Vinh and A. Rakib (Eds.): ICCASA 2020/ICTCC 2020, LNICST 343, pp. 330–338, 2021.
https://doi.org/10.1007/978-3-030-67101-3_27

Fig. 1. The use of high-powered tractors to push or pull convoys of cargo trailers

In order to overcome the disadvantages caused by the towing method such as: 1) The tractor speed is asynchronous; 2) The tractor steering centers are different, making it difficult to control; modern self-propelled trailer with many special functions is used instead of tractors as illustrated in Fig. 2.

Fig. 2. A modern self-propelled trailers transporting oil-shore

When the system is utilized, the obtained advantages are as follows:

- Because the system requires only one operator to operate via remote control, the trailer speed is highly synchronous.
- The trailer steering center is unique.

The navigation for the system normally employs GPS algorithm, IMU algorithm [3], vision algorithm [4] and combination techniques of the above algorithms [5].

Transporting oversized and overweight packages by self-propelled trailer has been very popular around the world. However, very few companies in Vietnam use this method due to high investment costs. Even so, Vietranstimex put money into an Italian

self-propelled trailer system named Cometto [6] in a Modular Self-Propelled Electric
(MSPE) type. The Cometto system outstanding features can be listed such as:

- The vertical and horizontal couplings connect the modules together according to the
  size and load of the package. This is a flexible feature of the system.
- The ability to rotate the package in place 360° of the steering system.
- The system's steering center can be changed easily to respond to difficult off-road
  situations.

During the operation of the Cometto MSPE, the most common problem is that the
electronic load cell (ELS) valve is often damaged or faulty. In order to overcome the
problem, a novel solution that a throttle valve N is inserted between tap J and ELS
valve was proposed. After the throttle valve N was installed, the MSPE system worked
very stably. The proposed MSPE system was utilized in order to safely transport and
launch a lot of oversized and overweight packages.

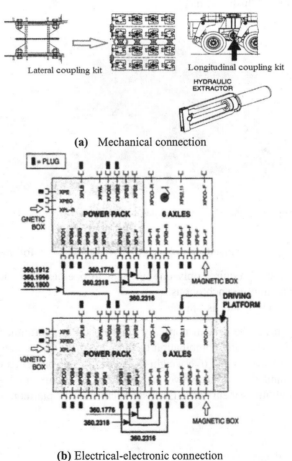

(b) Electrical-electronic connection

Fig. 3. Main system components of Cometto MSPE.

The remainder of this paper is structured as follows: the basic Cometto MSPE is described and the proposed method is in Sect. 2; Sect. 3 shows results via projects that apply the proposed method and the paper is concluded in Sect. 4.

2   The Proposed Method for the Cometto MSPE

2.1   The Basic Cometto MSPE

The main system components (as illustrated in Fig. 3) consist of Power Pack Unit (PPU); The 4/4/3 MSPE and The 6/4/3 MSPE. The PPUs and modules are utilized according to the package weight and size.

2.1.1   The Power Pack Unit

The PPU (as depicted in Fig. 4) is considered to be a key component of a MSPE. It consists of an electronic control system [8] and a hydraulic system.

Fig. 4. Cometto power pack unit

Pumps are used in the hydraulic system has parameters as listed in Table 1.

Table 1. The pumps in the hydraulic system

Variable displacement pumps	
Lifting and steering pump	A11VLO190
2 motorization pumps	A4VG180 + A4VG125

2.1.2   Modules

The parameters of modules such as 6-axis type (6/4/3) and 4-axis type (4/4/3) with a maximum load for one axle of 34 tons are listed as in Table 2. Modules are connected by 3 connection types of mechanic, hydraulic and electronic. The connections are configured in back to back coupling (serial configuration) and side by side coupling (parallel configuration) as depicted in Fig. 5.

Table 2. Module parameters

Weights	MSPE 4/4/3 (4 axles)	MSPE 6/4/3 (6 axles)
Speed (km/h)	0.5 5 10	0.5 5 10
Axle load (2 suspensions), ton	34 34 31	34 34 31
Total gross weight, ton	136 136 124	204 204 186
Dead weight, ton	1.77	26
Payload, ton	186.3 186.3 106.3	178 178 160
AXLES		
Axle lines quantity	4 (8 suspensions)	6 (12 suspensions)
Driven axles quantity	2	4
Braked axles with A.S.R. quantity	2	2

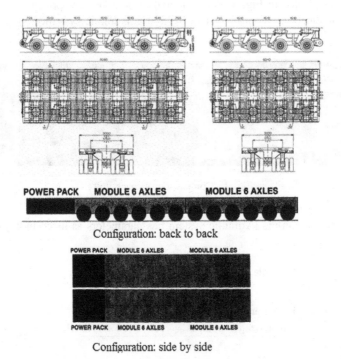

Configuration: back to back

Configuration: side by side

Fig. 5. Module configurartion

2.2 The Proposed Method

The functions of hydraulic steering and lifting/lowering which are described in [9] are supplied by the pump A11VO. This type of pump is used due to the hydraulic oil flow automatically changes when the load changes. The function working pressure is adjusted by the proportional valve ELS.

In this section, we propose method of putting a new throttle valve N [7] (as in Fig. 6-a) at position between valve ELS and tap J. The valve N is used to temporarily replace the valve ELS when it is suddenly damaged or failed as illustrated in Fig. 6-b.

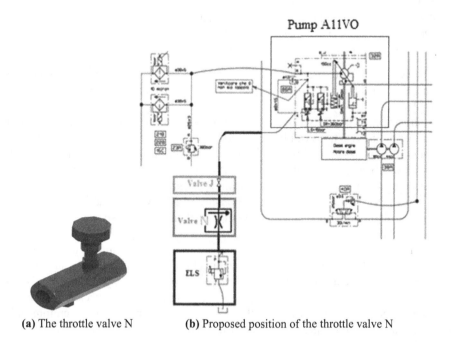

(a) The throttle valve N   (b) Proposed position of the throttle valve N

Fig. 6. The proposed hydraulic pump system

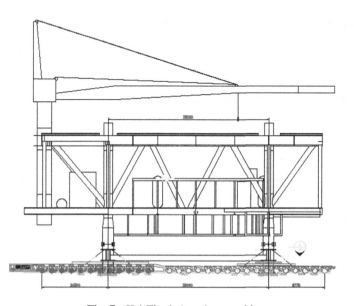

Fig. 7. Hai Thach 1 project topside

The valve ELS is controlled by the electronic system as follows:

- When the diesel engine is started, the pressure reaches 15 bar immediately. The engine speeds up to 900 rpm after 5 s. At this moment, the pressure will reach 220 bar.
- When the steering and lifting/lowering are adjusted, the pressure fluctuates around 220 bar and peaks at 300 bar.
- Brake pressure maintain from 170 bar to 220 bar.

The system pressure drops down when the ELS valve are damaged or failure. At this moment, tap J must be closed in order to forcefully increase the system pressure up to 360 bar.

Malfunction of the ELS valve is very dangerous for the whole system because it determines all the functions of lifting, lowering, steering and braking when operating a Cometto MSPE. However, closing tap J jeopardizes the A11VO pump as it must work at full power to push the piping system pressure up to 360 bar. Therefore, the tap J cannot be closed for a long time. Practical experience shows that ELS valves often catch fire when working because the suction coil of ELS valves is always electrically soaked and the temperature in Vietnam is hotter than Europe; especially in Cometto factory in Italy.

In the case if the tap J and the ELS valve are damaged or failure at the same time (case called as valve leak), all functions including lifting/lowering, steering and braking will stop working and uncontrollable. This causes the packages flipped because it is off-center. This damaged case is very dangerous; especially, when the package is located both on the jetty and the barge and the tides are fast rising/falling. Therefore, this damaged case cannot happen. However, if this damaged case happens, an immediate corrective action is required.

The proposed action method is to add throttle valve N between tap J and valve ELS and this is the fastest solution. By turning only the throttle valve N when the ELS valve is damaged or failure, the system pressure (shown on the steering pressure gauge) will reach to 200 bar or to 220 bar. The system works stably because of those pressures. The throttle valve N continues to be adjusted if higher pressure is needed.

3   The Evaluation of Proposed Method

The MSPE system works very stable and safe after putting the throttle valve N at the connection between tap J and valve ELS. Therefore, a lot of petroleum packages are relocated safely and effectively. The key project named as Bien Dong 1 – Hai Thach 1 had been applied the proposed method is desribed in details as following (Fig. 8):

Topside Project (as shown in Fig. 6):

- Topside: 3,200 Ton
- Wide of topside : 35 m
- Long of Topside : 45 m
- High of Topside: 40 met
- Client: PTSC/Bien Dong POC

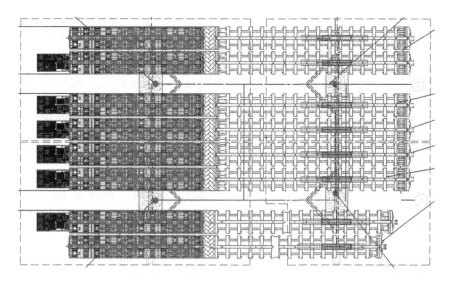

Fig. 8. Configuration of trailers for Hai Thach 1 project

- Location: PTSC Port, Vung tau, S.R.Viet Nam.
- Duration: 2012.

Each trailer is configured as follows: 6 PPU and 227 axles (as shown in Fig. 7).

In this project, the proposed MPSE system is tasked to relocate the 3,200-ton upper block of Hai Thach 1 a distance of 500 m and then to launch it to barges.

During operation, the ELS valve failure occurs when the trailer is relocating packages across the bridge between the jetty and the barge. The working pressure drops to almost 0 bar immediately and the system stops working. All functions of steering, lifting and braking are totally uncontrollable. At this moment, the throttle M is installed at the proposed position and the technician adjusts the throttle valve N so that the steering pressure and the lift/lower pressure rise again, up to 220 bar. It takes less than 1 min to install the throttle valve N compared with 30 min spending when acting to replace the faulty ELS valve by the good one.

In addition to the aforementioned typical project, other projects (as listed in [10]) applied the proposed method. Therefore, our Vietranstimex Company has become the leading company in Southeast Asia and the 34th rank in the world in the oversized and overweight transportation.

4   Conclusion

Because the valve ELS very often happens failures during the actual operation of the trailer system. Furthermore, in the inevitable damage caused by a faulty valve, safety comes first. Thanks to the proposal of installing throttle valve N at the connection between valve J and valve ELS, it increases the safety of the operator and the trailer system; at the same time, increasing the mobility of the transport equipment and significantly reducing trailers troubleshooting time in cargo as well. This alternative proposed method has been applied in practice to many projects of transporting over-sized and overweight packages in Vietnam from 2012 to 2020. The great results obtained by the proposed method are the best evidence for the efficiency.

However, because throttle valve N only operates manually and the ELS valve opens and closes automatically through electronic card control in the PPU, it is not possible to completely replace the ELS valve by the throttle valve N. Therefore, the replacement of the faulty ELS valve by the throttle valve N is only temporary and the faulty ELS valve needs to be replaced by a good one as soon as the unloading of packages is completed.

In addition to Cometto, each company that produces MSPE system such as Goldhofer, Nicolas and Kamag has different strengths, but all of them are for absolute safety for operators and goods by applying technology to enhance advanced performance.

Acknowledgment. This project is supported by Van Lang University (VLU) Electronics and Electrical Engineering Division, Ho Chi Minh City 700000, Vietnam.

Conflict of Interest. The authors declare no conflict of interest.

References

1. Černá, L., Zitrický*, V., Daniš, J.: The Methodology of Selecting the Transport Mode for Companies on the Slovak Transport Market. Research Article, Open Access (2006)
2. Hameed, P.K.S., Prathap, R.C.: Study on impact of vehicle overloading on national highways in varying terrains. Int. J. Eng. Res. Technol. (IJERT) 7(1) (2018). ISSN:2278-0181
3. Do, T.N., Liu, R., Yuen, C., Zhang, M., Tan, U-X.: Personal dead reckoning using IMU mounted on upper torso and inverted pendulum model. IEEE Sens. J. 16(21), 7600–7608 (2016). ISSN:1558-1748
4. Do, T.N., Soo, S.Y.: Foot motion tracking using Vision. In: IEEE 54th International Midwest Symposium on Circuits and Systems (MWSCAS), pp. 1–4, August 2011. ISSN:1558-3899
5. Do, T.N., Soo, S.Y.: Gait analysis using floor markers and inertial sensors. Int. J. Sens. 12 (2), 1594–1611 (2012). ISSN:1424-8220
6. Cometto: Self- Propelled Module Trailer - Use and Maintenance (2018)
7. Cometto: Self- Propelled Module Trailer - Electronic Manual (2018)
8. Cometto: Self- Propelled Module Trailer - Electric Electronic Diagrams (2018)
9. Cometto: Self- Propelled Module Trailer - Hydraulic Diagrams (2018)
10. Nguyen-Tran, H.M., Pham, Q.M., Le-Nguyen, H.B., Nguyen, C.T., Do, T.N.: A study on methodology of improvement the hydraulic system for Cometto self-propelled trailer system. Adv. Sci. Technol. Eng. Syst. J. (ASTESJ) 5(5), 799–807 (2020). ISSN:2415-6698

Author Index

Akhtar, Salwa Muhammad 16
Anh, Duong Tuan 65

Bagula, Antoine 44
Bui, Phuong Ha Dang 192

Chan, Johnny 123, 216

Dang, Son Hai 203
Dinh, Bao Ngoc 131
Do, Tri Nhut 323, 330
Drdla, Matej 288

Geihs, Kurt 3

Hasan, Mahmudul 123
Hieu, Duong Ngoc 65
Hoang, Chu Duc 113
Hoksbergen, Mark 216
Horalek, Josef 255, 265, 277
Huynh, Hiep Xuan 31, 203

Kinh, Bui Tan 65

Le Nguyen, Hoa Binh 330
Le, Hong Anh 103, 131
Le, Tan-Long 55
Le-Nguyen, Hoa Binh 323

Machaka, Pheeha 44
Mikulecky, Peter 288

Nguyen, Cao Tri 323, 330
Nguyen, Hai Thanh 31, 192, 203

Nguyen, Hang Bich Thi 31
Nguyen, Dung 131
Nguyen, Van Thao 233
Nguyen-Tran, Hai Minh 323

Peko, Gabrielle 216
Pham, Quang Minh 323, 330
Pham-Quoc, Cuong 55
Phan, Cang Anh 31, 203
Phan, Cong Vinh 233

Saleem, Kiran 169
Sanjay, K. N. 300
Shaila, K. 300, 310
Shashikiran, B. S. 310
Siricharoen, Waralak Vongdoiwang 182
Sobeslav, Vladimir 255, 265, 277, 288
Sundaram, David 216
Svecova, Hana 288
Svoboda, Tomas 255, 265

Thanh Tung, Nguyen 113, 141
Thuy, Pham Thu 113
Tran, Hai Minh Nguyen 330
Tran, Huu Tam 233
Tran, Toan Bao 192

Ul Haque, Hafiz Mahfooz 16, 169

Van Pham, Dang 82, 148
Van, Thao Nguyen 3
Venugopal, K. R. 300, 310
Vu, Phan Hien 55

Author Index

Printed in the United States
By Bookmasters